AF689779

# MAINTENANCE AND CHILD SUPPORT IN PRIVATE INTERNATIONAL LAW

No one would dispute that the duty to provide for those that you have a legal and moral obligation to support is very important. With the movement and migration of people both within Europe and globally, there are more and more families and relations who live in different States. Therefore it is imperative that suitable and workable methods exist to create maintenance obligations and then secure the transfer of funds, particularly from abroad. In the book the provisions in EU Maintenance Regulation no 4/2009 and the Hague Maintenance Convention of 2007 are analysed in order to discover what developments and therefore potential improvements have been made in relation to the recovery of maintenance from abroad. The book also includes an empirical study on the first year of operation of the Maintenance Regulation. Data collected has been analysed in order to supplement the critique of the instruments. The information and analysis is used to suggest suitable solutions for the future which include, amendments to the Regulation and recommendations for best practice.

**Volume 17 in the series Studies in Private International Law**

**Studies in Private International Law**

Recent titles in the series

Volume 4: Cases and Materials on EU Private International Law
Stefania Bariatti

Volume 5: International Commercial Disputes: Commercial Conflict of Laws in English Courts
Jonathan Hill and Adeline Chong

Volume 6: International Child Abduction: The Inadequacies of the Law
Thalia Kruger

Volume 7: Mediating International Child Abduction Cases
Sarah Vigers

Volume 8: International Antitrust Litigation: Conflict of Laws and Coordination
Edited by Jürgen Basedow, Stéphanie Francq and Laurence Idot

Volume 9: The Governing Law of Companies in EU Law
Justin Borg-Barthet

Volume 10: Intellectual Property and Private International Law: Comparative Perspectives
Edited by Toshiyuki Kono

Volume 11: Child Abduction within the European Union
Katarina Trimmings

Volume 12: International Surrogacy Arrangements: Legal Regulation at the International Level
Edited by Katarina Trimmings and Paul Beaumont

Volume 13: The Hague Child Abduction Convention: A Critical Analysis
Rhona Schuz

Volume 14: Interregional Recognition and Enforcement of Civil and Commercial Judgments: Lessons for China from the US and EU Law
Jie Huang

Volume 15: The Recovery of Maintenance in the EU and Worldwide
Edited by Paul Beaumont, Burkhard Hess, Lara Walker and Stefanie Spancken

Volume 16: Australian Private International Law for the 21st Century: Facing Outwards
Edited by Andrew Dickinson, Thomas John and Mary Keyes

# Maintenance and Child Support in Private International Law

Lara Walker

•HART•
PUBLISHING
OXFORD AND PORTLAND, OREGON
2017

**Hart Publishing**
An imprint of Bloomsbury Publishing Plc

Hart Publishing Ltd
Kemp House
Chawley Park
Cumnor Hill
Oxford OX2 9PH
UK

Bloomsbury Publishing Plc
50 Bedford Square
London
WC1B 3DP
UK

**www.hartpub.co.uk**
**www.bloomsbury.com**

Published in North America (US and Canada) by
Hart Publishing
c/o International Specialized Book Services
920 NE 58th Avenue, Suite 300
Portland, OR 97213-3786
USA

**www.isbs.com**

**HART PUBLISHING, the Hart/Stag logo, BLOOMSBURY and the Diana logo are trademarks of Bloomsbury Publishing Plc**

First published in hardback, 2015
Paperback edition, 2017

© Lara Walker 2015

Lara Walker has asserted her right under the Copyright, Designs and Patents Act 1988 to be identified as the Author of this work.

All rights reserved. No part of this publication may be reproduced or transmitted in any form or by any means, electronic or mechanical, including photocopying, recording, or any information storage or retrieval system, without prior permission in writing from the publishers.

While every care has been taken to ensure the accuracy of this work, no responsibility for loss or damage occasioned to any person acting or refraining from action as a result of any statement in it can be accepted by the authors, editors or publishers.

All UK Government legislation and other public sector information used in the work is Crown Copyright ©. All House of Lords and House of Commons information used in the work is Parliamentary Copyright ©. This information is reused under the terms of the Open Government Licence v3.0 (http://www.nationalarchives. gov.uk/doc/open-government-licence/version/3) except where otherwise stated.

All Eur-lex material used in the work is © European Union, http://eur-lex.europa.eu/, 1998–2017.

**British Library Cataloguing-in-Publication Data**
A catalogue record for this book is available from the British Library.

ISBN: PB: 978-1-50991-550-7
HB: 978-1-84946-717-9

Typeset by Compuscript Ltd, Shannon
Printed and bound in Great Britain by
Lightning Source UK Ltd

To find out more about our authors and books visit www.hartpublishing.co.uk. Here you will find extracts, author information, details of forthcoming events and the option to sign up for our newsletters.

# SERIES EDITORS' PREFACE

Paul Beaumont has to declare an interest in this book given that he was Lara Walker's PhD supervisor and the book is an updated and adapted version of her PhD thesis.

This is the first book-length analysis in English of the EU Maintenance Regulation 2009 and of the Hague Maintenance Convention and Protocol 2007. It is largely analytical but it also contains some empirical research on the first year of operation of the EU Maintenance Regulation. Maintenance is undoubtedly the area of international family law that affects the most people. When the EU Regulation and Hague Convention are fully operational (ie people in the EU are making full use of the former and many more States have adopted the latter) many thousands of cases will be processed every year. For child support cases this will contribute a high volume of work for Central Authorities but probably very little judicial business. For spousal support and other forms of family maintenance the volume will be less but the potential for contested litigation is significantly higher.

This book falls squarely into the pragmatic school of private international law scholarship. Dr Walker offers a balanced approach to the debate between 'automatic' enforcement of foreign judgments on the basis of 'mutual trust' in the EU and the concern to safeguard the human rights of individuals. She argues that this can best be achieved through having a 'public policy' defence at the recognition and enforcement stage and favours its reintroduction into EU law in that area. She defends conflicts justice being sacrificed to substantive justice in the limited category of cases where a strong rights-based analysis requires this. Public policy is the tool to achieve this. She makes a very coherent argument that public policy is a sufficient tool (alongside non-enforcement based on an irreconcilable judgment) and therefore the exceptions to enforcement of certain default judgments (Regulation & Convention) and for procedural fraud (Convention) could be subsumed within public policy in future instruments.

Dr Walker also makes a convincing case for the development of minimum standards in relation to Central Authorities. These would include staffing levels, professional training, specialist training in the instruments handled by them, and bespoke IT systems (like i-support). She also argues that further work should be done by or on behalf of the EU Commission to develop a guide to good practice on the Maintenance Regulation.

We welcome this significant monograph alongside the already-published edited volume in this series: P Beaumont, B Hess, L Walker and S Spancken (eds), *Recovery of Maintenance in the EU and Worldwide* (Hart, 2014). The two books complement each other with very little overlap and as a package make an excellent resource for anyone involved or interested in cross-border maintenance issues.

Paul Beaumont (University of Aberdeen)
Jonathan Harris (King's College, London)

# PREFACE

This book is based on the author's doctoral thesis, which was presented for the degree of PhD at the University of Aberdeen in September 2013. The thesis was entitled 'The Latest Private International Law Maintenance Regime, Internationally and in Europe: Slowly Paving the Road to Success but the Road is Long and Further Developments are Required', and was researched between September 2010 and June 2013. For the purposes of this book the thesis was updated to include developments up until June 2014. The author's PhD was funded by the College of Arts and Social Sciences at the University of Aberdeen. Without this funding the PhD would not have been possible. During the second two years of her PhD the author worked as a research assistant on a project on the 'Recovery of Maintenance in the EU and Worldwide' generously funded by the European Commission.

This book includes empirical research from a study which was carried out by the author as part of her work as a research assistant, and also for the purpose of the PhD. The data was initially presented at an international conference, held in Heidelberg in 2013, which was part of the Commission funded project. The collection of this data would not have been possible without the assistance of the Central Authorities operating under the Regulation. The author is indebted to all the personnel who took the time to respond to the questionnaire and to those who provided further information over the course of the research.

The author is particularly grateful to her supervisor, Professor Paul Beaumont, who provided excellent support and advice throughout the course of her PhD, and before that during her LLM (by research) and her LLB. The author would also like to thank her examiners for an interesting and thought provoking viva. The author is very grateful to her colleagues at Sussex who have taken the time to comment on later drafts of this book, and to those who have provided support and advice during her first year as a Lecturer. Finally, the author would like to thank her family and friends who have supported her during the course of her studies.

# CONTENTS

# TABLE OF CASES

## European Court of Justice

## European Court of Human Rights

## UK



## Other Jurisdictions

# TABLE OF LEGISLATION

## EU Legislation

*Primary Legislation*



*Secondary Legislation*

## Conventions of the Hague Conference on Private International Law

## Human Rights Conventions



## UK Legislation



## Other National Legislation

# 1

# Introduction

## I. Introduction

This book focuses on the latest private international law maintenance and child support regime, internationally and in Europe. Notably, Council Regulation (EC) 4/2009 of 18 December 2008 on jurisdiction, applicable law, recognition and enforcement of decisions and cooperation in matters relating to maintenance obligations (Maintenance Regulation),[1] and the Hague Convention of 23 November 2007 on the International Recovery of Child Support and other Forms of Family Maintenance (the 2007 Hague Convention or Maintenance Convention). These two instruments were negotiated in order to improve the recovery of maintenance in cross border situations. The Regulation entered into force on 18 June 2011 and applies in each Member State.[2] The Convention entered into force on 1 January 2013. The first two States to ratify the Convention were Albania and Norway. The Convention has applied in Bosnia and Herzegovina from 1 February 2013, Ukraine from 1 November 2013,[3] and the EU ratified the Convention as a regional organisation on 9 April 2014.[4] The main purpose of this book is to highlight the positive changes introduced by the new regimes, but to then identify some particular areas where further developments are required. Therefore there is room for more work in this area, in order to strengthen the current regimes and even develop a further regime at the European level, in order to address the issues that were not dealt with adequately this time round.

The two new instruments are a notable step forward from the previous regime which was somewhat confusing. At the international level there was the 1956

[1] [2009] OJ L7/1.

[2] Denmark is not a party to the Regulation but has agreed to implement the Regulation to the extent that it amends Brussels I (Council Regulation (EC) 44/2001 of 22 December 2000 on jurisdiction and the recognition and enforcement of judgments in civil and commercial matters [2001] OJ L012/1 (Brussels I)). See Agreement OJ L149/80, 12.6.2009.

[3] See the status table, available at www.hcch.net/index_en.php?act=conventions.status&cid=131, accessed 10 June 2014. The United States has also signed the Convention. Barack Obama has now signed the US implementing legislation for the Convention, which will allow the US to ratify the Convention in due course. See, www.hcch.net/index_en.php?act=events.details&year=2014&varevent=381, accessed 31 October 2014.

[4] www.hcch.net/index_en.php?act=status.comment&csid=1109&disp=resdn, accessed 10 June 2014. The Convention applies in all Member States except Denmark from 1 August 2014.

New York Convention and four different Hague Conventions, all of which only applied between the relevant Contracting States.[5] The Hague 2007 Convention was designed with the aim of building 'upon the best features of existing Hague Conventions and other international instruments, in particular the United Nations *Convention on the Recovery Abroad of Maintenance* of 20 June 1956'.[6] Instead of having a number of instruments which dealt with the different aspects of the recovery of maintenance separately, the new Convention addresses each element within one instrument, except applicable law which is dealt with by the Hague Protocol.[7] This alone has to be a step towards success. In Europe the previous regime for the collection of maintenance was dealt with by Brussels I,[8] a Regulation that is primarily concerned with commercial matters. The fact that there is now a Regulation designed specifically for maintenance claims is another step forward. The specific aim of the Maintenance Regulation was to: 'eliminate all obstacles which still today prevent the recovery of maintenance in the European Union.'[9]

Negotiations for the Convention and the Regulation were ongoing at similar times, with the Convention completed first, resulting in harmony between the two instruments in the areas where this could be achieved. Progress made in the long negotiations in The Hague resulted in some of the provisions of the Convention being used in the Regulation.[10] However, this was not possible across all areas. Aspects where the Regulation benefited significantly from the negotiations in The Hague are: the provision of free legal aid in all child support cases, extensive duties for Central Authorities and the adoption of a separate Protocol on applicable law.

## II. Aim and Structure

This book critically assesses the latest private international law regime internationally and in Europe. Therefore the focus is on the Maintenance Regulation and the 2007 Hague Convention. The book does not consider other regional instruments on the recovery of maintenance and child support from abroad, or internal rules on the private international law of maintenance and child support.

[5] These instruments will be discussed in more detail in ch 2 s IV. For information on which States are party to these Conventions, see www.hcch.net/index_en.php?act=text.display&tid=25, and http://treaties.un.org/pages/ViewDetailsIII.aspx?&src=TREATY&mtdsg_no=XX~1&chapter=20&Temp=mtdsg3&lang=en, accessed 10 June 2014.

[6] 2007 Hague Convention.

[7] Protocol of 23 November 2007 on the Law Applicable to Maintenance Obligations (Protocol). The Protocol applies in all the EU Member States apart from the UK and Denmark. See Council Decision of 30 November 2009 on the conclusion by the European Community of the Hague Protocol of 23 November 2007 on the Law Applicable to Maintenance Obligations [2009] OJ L 331/17.

[8] Brussels I (n 2).

[9] SEC (2005) 1629, s 1.2, available at http://eur-lex.europa.eu/LexUriServ/LexUriServ.do?uri=COM:2005:0649:FIN:EN:PDF, accessed 10 June 2014.

[10] See, P Beaumont, 'International Family Law in Europe—the Maintenance Project, the Hague Conference and the EC: A Triumph of Reverse Subsidiarity' (2009) 73 *Rabels Zeitschrift* 509.

This book will first look at the history of the recovery of maintenance from abroad by giving an overview of the earlier instruments and explaining what changes have been made in the new regime. In this chapter the aims and objectives of the new instruments will be set out. It will begin to be questioned how achievable these aims and objectives really are, and whether they can be accomplished simply by addressing the areas chosen. At the end of the chapter, overall data on the first year of operation of the Regulation will be presented. This is to discover how many applications there have been and what the spread of these applications is. Have there been as many applications as expected? Do some States receive more applications than others? Which States send these applications? Are there any links between the number of applications received and size of population?

The book will then focus on specific topics in order to see what achievements or errors have been made in these areas, and highlight where further progress is still needed. This will be done by first addressing the scope of the instruments, then looking specifically at jurisdiction, applicable law, recognition and enforcement, actual enforcement and administrative cooperation. Chapters three and four address the scope of each of the instruments. These chapters explore to whom and what relationships the instruments apply. Chapter three also considers characterisation and questions whether the lack of a clear definition of 'maintenance' may be problematic. These considerations are supplemented by the discussion below on maintenance as a concept. Chapter five addresses jurisdiction under the Maintenance Regulation. This chapter focuses on the lack of coherence within the EU across the family law instruments. This might be problematic as it could impact directly on any difficulties with characterisation, if different courts are dealing with different aspects of related proceedings. This can then influence whether a judgment can be recognised and enforced. Chapter six analyses the applicable law regime under the Hague Protocol. The book determines how this regime will apply when combined with the rules on direct jurisdiction in the Maintenance Regulation. The aim is to discover in what circumstances the rules in the Protocol are likely to result in the application of a law other than the law of the forum. This is important as the use of the Protocol determines the procedure for recognition and enforcement under the Regulation. The two procedures for recognition and enforcement are evaluated in chapter seven. The benefits and drawbacks of each procedure is scrutinised and these are compared with the other procedures that apply in the EU in the other instruments under Title V. The chapter examines the role of fundamental human rights in this area, explores to what extent the application of an applicable law regime really justifies the abolition of *exequatur* and questions the viability of having two different procedures operating under the one instrument. Chapter eight then examines the recognition and enforcement procedure under the Convention. This also has two separate procedures resulting in four procedures in total. Given that within the EU the same Central Authorities will be applying the Maintenance Regulation and the Hague 2007 Convention, the viability of this will be assessed.

Once these technical areas have been analysed, chapter nine then looks at the provisions on actual enforcement. In contrast to the Convention the Regulation does very little in the area of enforcement and the provisions on actual enforcement are virtually non-existent. It is questioned whether this is the correct approach and how effective other mechanisms in the EU legal order might be to secure actual enforcement. The chapter also considers the role of the European Court of Human Rights (ECtHR) in this area. Any solutions provided in this area need to be effective, because if enforcement is not realised the steps taken in other areas will not make any real difference to the overall picture of the recovery of maintenance from abroad. Finally chapter 10 examines the new provisions on administrative cooperation and the role of Central Authorities under the two instruments. Analysis of data collected is an important aspect of both these chapters, which focus on the practical impact of the Regulation in order to examine how the instrument is being applied.

The areas that this book will not address are: legal aid,[11] public bodies,[12] and competent authorities (other than Central Authorities).[13] An in-depth analysis of whether data protection laws and the rights of privacy of debtors are adequately protected in each State is also excluded. This would require a comparative analysis of the national laws in each State which goes beyond the aim of this book. Finally, the relationship between the new instruments and the old multilateral and bilateral instruments on maintenance will not be addressed.[14] None of these areas were considered by the Commission, in their impact assessment, as points to be reviewed in order for the new instrument to achieve its objective.[15]

[11] The Convention requires the provision of free legal aid in all child support cases, unless the application is manifestly unfounded (Article 15). This provision was then incorporated into the Regulation (Article 46). For a description and analysis of the provisions see: Beaumont (n 10) 509; I Curry-Sumner, 'Administrative Co-operation and Free Legal Aid in International Child Maintenance Recovery: What is the Added Value of the Regulation?' (2010) 3 *Nederlands Internationaal Privaatrecht*, s 4; and L Walker and P Beaumont, 'Empirical Study on the Early Operation of the EU Maintenance Regulation' in Beaumont et al (eds), *The Recovery of Maintenance in the EU and Worldwide* (Oxford, Hart Publishing, 2014).

[12] The Convention follows the Hague Convention of 2 October 1973 Convention on the Recognition and Enforcement of Decisions Relating to Maintenance Obligations (Enforcement Convention) by incorporating public bodies as applicants, and the Regulation gives effect to the case law of the Court of Justice of the European Union (CJEU) under the Brussels Convention by incorporating a provision on public bodies. See D Martiny, 'Jurisdiction, Recognition and Enforcement in Cases of Reimbursement Claims by Public Bodies', in Beaumont et al (eds) (n 11) 485.

[13] In this case it is expected that the majority of applicants will use the Central Authority system, because free legal aid will only be provided under this route. However, the use of other competent or accredited bodies should not be too problematic in this area, which only involves the transfer of money. For information on competent bodies and the importance of accreditation in the area of intercountry adoption see the Guide to Good Practice no 2, available at www.hcch.net/index_en.php?act=text.display&tid=45, accessed 10 June 2014.

[14] For some information on this see, A Borrás, 'The Necessary Flexibility in Applying the New Instruments on Maintenance' in K Boele-Woelki, T Einhorn, D Girsberger, S Symeonides (eds), *Convergence and Divergence in Private International Law, Liber Amicorum Kurt Siehr* (The Hague, Eleven International Publishing & Schulthess, 2010) 173, 173–92.

[15] SEC (2005) (n 9).

## III. Methodology

The book includes information gained from an empirical study on the first year of operation of the Regulation,[16] and uses these data to analyse the application of specific provisions of the Regulation. The gathering of these data is very important for the advancement of knowledge in the area, because they are the first data to exist on the recovery of maintenance in the European Union.[17] The dates chosen were 1 October 2011 to 30 September 2012. However, many of the questionnaires were returned late so in some cases the information may cover applications sent in a different time period.[18] The questionnaire covered incoming and outgoing applications. The objective was to discover how many applications there had been and whether new provisions, such as legal aid and the inclusion of requests for specific measures are working well under the Regulation. The questionnaires were completed to a different level by each Central Authority and therefore there are more data on some States than others. The Central Authorities that completed the questionnaire are: Belgium, Czech Republic, Estonia, France, Finland, Greece, Hungary, Ireland, Italy, Latvia, Lithuania, Malta, Poland, Portugal, Romania, Slovenia, Sweden, England and Wales and Northern Ireland. Some Central Authorities provided some overall data. These are: Austria, Cyprus, Germany, Luxembourg, Netherlands, Slovakia, Spain and Scotland. No information at all was collected from Bulgaria. Gibraltar reported that there had been no applications in the relevant period.[19]

The main problem faced by Central Authority personnel when they completed the questionnaire was data available to them on their databases. Where databases do exist they are generally different.[20] The feedback also highlighted that databases were not always reliable. The information gained will be displayed throughout this book in order to provide some insight into how the Regulation is working in practice, the number of applications that are circulating under it, and initial findings on how long it is taking to process applications under the new system. The difficulties highlighted above are taken account of and it is recognised that these data may not always be accurate. However, data provided will be

[16] The questionnaire is available at Annex I.

[17] When the European Commission carried out its impact assessment on the need for a new instrument on maintenance it had no data on the number of applications in this area and instead based the arguments on ancillary information that could give some indication on the scale of the problem, such as migration data and intra community marriage and divorce statistics. Green Paper on Maintenance (presented by the Commission) Obligations COM (2004) 254 Final. Therefore, even data on the total number of applications circulated (see ch 2 s VI) has been very useful and important for international organisations and practitioners working in this area.

[18] For example the information provided by the Central Authority for England and Wales only covers the period from January 2012 to 30 September 2012.

[19] As Gibraltar received or sent no applications at all then this Central Authority is not included in the graphs, tables and databases relating to the statistical research.

[20] Spain reported that as of 1 February 2013 it still did not have an electronic database. Electronic databases will be discussed in detail at ch 9 s VI below.

presented and given the high volume of applications there is enough information to give an overview of the operation of the Regulation. The information collected through the empirical research is supplemented by an in-depth analysis of the Maintenance Regulation, the Hague 2007 Convention and the documents produced in relation to these that are in the public domain.

## IV. Approach: Pragmatism

This book takes a pragmatic approach.[21] Whilst this approach is essentially part of private international law theory, pragmatism cannot strictly be considered a theory as it is a theory which rejects a theoretical approach. 'Pragmatists are sceptical about an overarching theory that satisfactorily explains why states apply the rules of foreign legal systems'.[22] In this respect Rabel has recognised that theoretical views can create artificial barriers and can therefore be a hindrance rather than a help in this area of law.[23]

Pragmatism is the approach favoured by the majority of British private international law scholars.[24] However, it was founded by the German scholar Rabel and is recognised by scholars in other States.[25] The approach is also recognised and utilised by international organisations such as the European Group for Private International Law and the Hague Conference on Private International Law.[26]

Pragmatists seek to find real solutions to deal with specific legal problems.[27] This is in line with the purpose of this book which seeks to suggest suitable solutions to particular difficulties with the instruments on maintenance, such as jurisdiction and recognition and enforcement. However it is recognised that when applying and developing law to find these real solutions, the proper administration of justice should be ensured. Pragmatists consider that the concept of justice

[21] This approach is supported in *Anton* and also by Hartley in his review of *Anton* (P Beaumont and P McEleavy, *Anton's Private International Law*, 3rd edn (Edinburgh, SULI/W Green, 2011) and T Hartley, 'Review: Private International Law by AE Anton' (2012) 8 *Journal of Private International Law* 407).

[22] Beaumont and McEleavy (n 21) 2.92.

[23] E Rabel, 'An Interim account on Comparative Conflicts Law' (1947–1948) 46 *Michigan Law Review* 625, 635.

[24] Beaumont and McEleavy (n 21) 2.96.

[25] See G Kegel, 'Fundamental Approaches' in *International Encyclopaedia of Comparative Law Volume III, Private International Law* (Tübingen, Mohr Siebeck, 1986) 12–16.

[26] Beaumont and McEleavy (n 21) 2.97–2.99.

[27] This is seen to be the approach of British lawyers generally. 'The instinct of the English lawyer is to test a proposed rule by its practical bearing on normal human activities and expectations. It is a method that in his opinion the purpose of the law, which is at bottom to promote justice and convenience, can best be furthered. He is nothing if not an empiricist and pragmatist.' (J Fawcett and J Carruthers, *Cheshire, North and Fawcett: Private International Law*, 14th edn (Oxford, Oxford University Press, 2008) 37.

is of primary importance.[28] This book seeks to find solutions that assist with the free circulation and enforcement of cross border judgments, whilst ensuring that the rights and legitimate expectations of individuals are protected. Previously theorists have considered that this means systems of substantive private international law should be coordinated in order to create an international society that has regard to the interests of individuals.[29] However, Kegel (a pragmatist) also seeks to protect the interests of individuals but takes a different approach to this. He distinguishes between conflicts justice and substantive justice, suggesting that the former should normally prevail over the latter.[30] However, he recognises that because 'justice is based on an evaluation of interests, very strong interests representing substantive justice may justify a preference for substantive justice.'[31] Therefore the proper administration of justice would be best achieved by a strict interpretation of the law, which should be constructed in a way that ensures that justice is achieved by the effective enforcement of cross border judgments. However, this law should not be so restrictive as to undermine the interests, rights and legitimate expectations of individuals.

Substantive justice or substantive law includes fundamental human rights. Therefore this book takes a slightly different angle to the pragmatic approach by including an analysis of fundamental human rights. Even though the evaluation of human rights could be considered as a more theoretical approach, rather than a strictly practical approach, it can still be reconciled with pragmatism. This is because justice is based on an 'evaluation of interests'.[32] Therefore fundamental human rights, which are an example of substantive justice, should prevail over the outcomes of conflicts justice in some exceptional situations in order to promote justice. Given that fundamental human rights are principles of law in the UK,[33] the EU,[34] and in many countries internationally,[35] it would be inappropriate to take an approach that ignores these rights completely. In particular this book asserts that within the EU there is a European notion of public policy which includes fundamental human rights.[36] As such public policy plays an important role in the analysis as it is used as a formula to encapsulate human rights and advance justice by evaluating the interests and expectations of individuals. Therefore, building on

[28] Beaumont and McEleavy (n 21) 2.95, and Kegel (n 25) 13.

[29] For example Battiffol, see Kegel (n 25) 14.

[30] Kegel (n 25) 15.

[31] Ibid.

[32] Ibid.

[33] The UK is party to the European Convention on Human Rights (ECHR) which is implemented in UK law by the Human Rights Act 1998.

[34] EU law states that human rights are principles of EU law and refers specifically to the rights included in the European Charter and the ECHR (Art 6 TEU). However Title V of the TEU promotes the concept of mutual recognition as well as human rights, two concepts that are difficult to reconcile (see ch 7 s V for an analysis).

[35] For information on the core international human rights treaties, including ratifications, reservations and declarations see, www.ohchr.org/EN/HRBodies/Pages/TreatyBodies.aspx, accessed 10 June 2014.

[36] This derives from Art 6 TEU. See ch 7 ss IV–V.

the earlier formulation of Kegel this book asserts that substantive interests, which include fundamental rights, should prevail over conflicts justice and mutual recognition in exceptional situations.

Not only does the pragmatic approach seek to achieve the proper administration of justice in terms of the private international law rules and how they are constructed, the approach also considers how the law actually works in practice through scrutiny and critical evaluation of court practice,[37] and administrative bodies. This is primarily because pragmatists have a 'desire to discover the living law.'[38] As a result pragmatists are also known for their ability to 'analyse innovative, international developments in private international law, for example by encouraging states to solve problems through international administrative and judicial co-operation.'[39] This book adheres to this element of pragmatism by including data gathered through empirical research on the first year of operation of the Regulation (as described in the methodology). Therefore, this book follows the school of pragmatism, which evaluates law primarily on the concept of the proper administration of justice and further considers how the law actually works in practice.

## V. 'Maintenance' as a Concept

Maintenance can come in a variety of forms and 'no clear-cut concept of maintenance exists'.[40] Some forms of maintenance are generally accepted and other forms vary depending on the laws and rules in a particular State. The right of the child to be maintained by his or her parents should be considered as a general rule accepted globally. Article 27 of the United Nations Convention on the Rights of the Child (UNCRC) requires that both parents provide maintenance for their child, and encourages State parties to sign up to international agreements on maintenance.[41] However, although these rules are in place, even in States where

[37] Kegel (n 25) 12.

[38] Ibid.

[39] Beaumont and McEleavy (n 21) 2.93.

[40] D Martiny, 'Maintenance Obligations in the Conflict of Laws' (1994) 247 *Recueil des Cours* 131, 150.

[41] Every State in the world is a party to the UNCRC except for the USA and Somalia. See the status table at http://treaties.un.org/Pages/ViewDetails.aspx?src=TREATY&mtdsg_no=IV-11&chapter=4&lang=en, accessed 10 June 2014. However, we know that the United States accepts that parents should provide maintenance for their children, and in fact was the country which pushed for legal aid in all child support cases in the negotiations at The Hague. The UNCRC includes this provision for a variety of reasons, but one of the main ones is to help to ensure that children have an adequate standard of living. This book does not include an analysis of this concept or the social factors that may hinder this. However, it is important to note the importance of the payment of child support in this context. See, European Union Agency for Fundamental Rights, 'Developing Indicators for the Protection, Respect and Promotion of the Rights of the Child in the European Union' (2010)

there is legal provision for maintenance the law is not always followed and where obligations do exist there are often delays at the enforcement stage.[42] Where there are delays with States' national systems, the possibility of recovering maintenance from abroad would appear to be a major leap. Despite this the Convention on the Rights of the Child encourages State parties to sign up to multilateral and bilateral Conventions on this topic, of which there are many, specifically the New York Convention of 1956.[43] Therefore, international documents recognise that parents have a responsibility to provide for their children by paying maintenance in order to support them. These documents also encourage the enforcement of such obligations. It is very important that the new provisions on maintenance are successful in achieving the fulfilment of these obligations.

Traditionally, the obligation arises as a moral obligation for parents to support their biological children. This moral requirement underpins the responsibility highlighted in Article 27 of the UNCRC. However, parents should also support adopted children, and in some cases parents will also be obliged to support their step children.[44] In respect of adopted children this duty would appear sensible and clear. If you take steps to adopt a child as a couple then both parents should support that child if the relationship between the adults does not continue. One could even argue that the requirement is higher for adoptive parents as they would have taken significant steps to adopt a child. The introduction of the child into the environment in the case of adoption is a highly planned and detailed process, something that cannot always be said for natural parents.[45] A child cannot be adopted by accident and there would always be a clear intention by the parents who should be aware of the responsibility they were taking on.

The position of adoptive parents can be distinguished from the position of children after the break-down of an adult relationship. Family units are subject to change and changes in the adult relationship may affect who cares for the child and whom pays child support. Some legal systems recognise the responsibility of a step parent to provide for a step child that is in an adult's care. However, sometimes this position is difficult to reconcile with obligations to provide for that person's biological children from an earlier marriage or relationship that

s 4.3 and M Groff, 'The Potential of the 2007 Child Support Convention: Addressing Global Poverty and Supporting Economic Rights' in Beaumont et al (eds) (n 11).

[42] See R Hodgkin and P Newell, *Implementation Handbook for the Convention on the Rights of the Child*, 3rd edn UNICEF, 2007) 401–02 for a description of some of the problems with the recovery of maintenance in selected countries.

[43] United Nations Convention on the Recovery Abroad of Maintenance. This will be discussed at ch 2 s III below.

[44] Some States also require step parents to support the child of their spouse. See Martiny (n 40) 150. For a general discussion on legal parentage see, Council of Europe, *Legal Problems Relating to Parentage: proceedings XXVIIth Colloquy on European Law Foundation for International Studies*, Valletta (Malta) 15–17 September 1997.

[45] See also, T Callus, 'A New Parenthood Paradigm for Twenty-First Century Family Law in England and Wales?' (2012) 32 *Legal Studies* 347, 360.

has since broken down.[46] This could be particularly problematic if the debtor is on a low income. The judiciary will be left in a difficult position of determining how the money should be allocated by a method that is fair and also in a way that means that the support given is not minimal. If the money allocated per month is so small that it really makes no difference, then the costs involved of transferring money at an international level may render the obligation pointless. In such situations there would be little point in establishing or enforcing such an obligation, until the debtor's situation improved. Another issue with obligations concerning step parents to their step children is the question of whether the step parent should still support the child after divorce. This again would be a question for the law of a particular State.

In addition to the situations described above there are now a variety of methods by which children can be conceived, through assisted reproductive technology (ART)[47] such as IVF and surrogacy.[48] Questions as to who is the parent and from whom child support obligations flow therefore get more and more complicated. The child may be biologically related to one, both or neither member of the couple who will be their intended parents. A child conceived by ART could have up to six legal parents in a variety of combinations.[49] As reproductive technologies increase the situation will become more complicated. A child with a two parent embryo can potentially have six parents and researchers are currently seeking permission to begin experiments to create three parent embryos.[50] If this happens a child could potentially have up to seven parents, and with continuing advances in this area who knows what the position will be in the future. Potential policy questions in relation to ART cases are:

— How many individuals may serve a recognised parenting role for a given child? In multiple parent situations, how should the different aspects of the parenting roles be distributed?[51]

[46] In order to determine if maintenance was payable in such cases, States party to the Hague Protocol would apply the law designated by the Protocol, and other States would apply the *lex fori* or their own private international law rules. This is because in these cases it is presumed that 'parentage' exists. Therefore the Protocol can be used to determine which law will apply to establish whether a maintenance obligation exists. See ch 6 for more details.

[47] For a general analysis of ART see, M Abdul-Kareem and A Killian (eds), 'Assisted Reproductive Technologies' (2010) 11 *Georgetown Journal of Gender and the Law* 411, in particular 411–13.

[48] For an in-depth discussion on surrogacy see K Trimmings and P Beaumont, 'General Report on Surrogacy' in K Trimmings and P Beaumont (eds), *International Surrogacy Arrangements: Legal Regulation at the International Level* (Oxford, Hart Publishing, 2013) 439, in particular 439–64 and fn 1, and K Boele Woelki, '(Cross-Border) Surrogate Motherhood: We Need to Take Action Now!' in Permanent Bureau (eds), *A Commitment to Private International Law* (The Hague, Intersentia 2013) 47.

[49] These are: sperm donor, egg donor, gestational mother, gestational mother's husband, intended mother and intended father. See www.heidelberg-conference2013.de/tl_files/downloads-abstracts/abstracts-ab-3-3-2013/Presentation_Reynolds_Paikin_Parentage.pdf, accessed 10 June 2014.

[50] 'Consent to Create 3-parent Embryos' The Sunday Times, 17/03/2013, p 9; however this is still a matter of debate.

[51] See Abdul-Kareem and Killian (n 47) 414–25. See also *ML, AR v RW, SW* [2011] EWHC 2455 (Fam) where the children had two biological parents who were both known to them, three legal parents and another 'parent'. They lived with their 'two' mothers but had regular contact with the

— Which should be more determinative of parental responsibilities and parental status—the bio-genetic connection or the intention to become a parent?[52]

This book does not set out to solve any of these problems, as that would be beyond the scope of this book. States are only just starting to solve these problems when faced with the task of determining who the parent is, and therefore who has child support obligations that flow from this status. In respect of relationships arising out of ART, the rules under the maintenance instruments have no role to play in the difficult task of determining 'parentage'. The instruments specifically do not include this responsibility.[53] Once a relationship of 'parentage' is established the instruments can then be applied to determine if a maintenance obligation exists. The court applying the instruments or recognising an obligation should not then consider the preliminary question of 'parentage' which has already been addressed, by the appropriate national law.[54] These matters are drawn to the reader's attention to highlight the many problems and questions that exist when determining parentage and then maintenance.

Maintenance payable to adults is very different to child support. This is because unlike child support, where it is argued that internationally it is accepted that there is a moral obligation for a parent to support their child, there is no international moral obligation for adults to support or maintain each other. Rather

biological father and his partner as part of the arrangement entered into before the conception. See also *Schneider v Germany* (App no 17080/07) ECHR 15 September 2011, where the biological father wanted to have access to his child, who had a different legal father. The Court held that ultimately this was a decision for the national authorities, however in reaching its decision the domestic courts should not follow general legal assumptions but assess the situation on the basis of the best interests of the particular child. In these situations the issue of maintenance becomes more difficult because how many 'parents' does a child actually need? Would they all have an obligation to pay maintenance and why? These are questions that this book does not answer but aims to highlight cause for concern in the future.

[52] See, Callus (n 45) 347. Callus considers that in these situations parentage and parenthood should be distinguished. Parentage is determined by the biological link and parenthood is used to determine the factual situation. 'Placing intention at the heart of parenthood has as its justification the actual parental function' (367). The 'purpose of the law must surely be to give effect to the daily life and experience of children and to legally recognise those who are most implicated in their day to day welfare' (368).

[53] See Recital 21 of the Regulation, Art 1 of the Protocol and A Bonomi, 'Explanatory Report on the Protocol of 23 November 2007 on the Law Applicable to Maintenance Obligations' paras 29–32 (Bonomi Report), available at www.hcch.net/upload/expl39e.pdf, accessed 10 June 2014. These provisions are discussed in further detail at ch 3 s II below. See also A Bonomi, 'The Hague Protocol of 23 November 2007 on the Law Applicable to Maintenance Obligations' (2008) 10 *Yearbook of Private International Law* 333, 337–40.

[54] See Recital 25 which states that recognition of a maintenance obligation 'does not imply the recognition by that Member State of the family relationship, parentage, marriage or affinity underlying the maintenance obligations which gave rise to the decision.' In particular see ch 6 on applicable law. See also ch 7 s VI, B where possible get outs for Member States are discussed, in terms of public policy, if they do not wish to recognise an obligation arising from a 'parentage' that is against their public policy. However, this is extremely difficult under the Regulation due to the abolition of *exequatur*, but may be more likely under the Convention.

obligations to pay maintenance to other adults (whether it be spouses, ex-spouses or elderly family members) and the expectations of parties to do so are shaped by national laws and standards. Therefore maintenance payable to adults is complicated and the law varies significantly in each State.[55]

In most States spouses are expected to maintain each other,[56] but this is not always the case on or after divorce.[57] Not all laws necessarily grant maintenance, whether as a one off payment or periodical payments between former spouses on divorce. In some States there is usually provision for maintenance; such as the UK and Denmark. However, even in States where it is generally accepted that there is an obligation to pay maintenance after divorce, this will not be absolute. When establishing a maintenance obligation courts may take a variety of factors into account, such as the needs and resources of the parties, as well as the ability to pay.[58] Fundamentally the main difference between child support and other forms of maintenance, in these type of States, is that with child support the 'need' element is assumed, resulting in the moral duty to provide support.[59]

In other States maintenance is only payable in certain circumstances such as if one of the parties was at fault and in that case only the innocent party will receive payment, for example Austria and Belgium. In other States such as the Czech Republic it is very unusual that maintenance will be granted on divorce.[60] In addition to spouses that are traditionally 'married', there are now a number of other *de facto* relationships akin to marriage that may be protected under the law of a specific State and thereby result in a maintenance obligation, both during the relationship and after the relationship has ended.[61] Since the laws vary, the

[55] See K Boele-Woelki, B Braat and I Sumner (eds), *European Family Law in Action, Volume II* (Antwerp, Intersentia, 2003) 41–95; and J Miles, 'Financial Relief Between Cohabitants on Separation: Options for European Jurisdictions' in K Boele-Woelki and T Sverdrup (eds), *European Challenges in Contemporary Family Law* (Antwerp, Intersentia, 2008) 269–87.

[56] See, Martiny (n 40) 147–48.

[57] Ibid, 148–49. For more information on maintenance laws in relation to divorce in Europe, including countries outside the EU, see Boele-Woelki, Braat and Sumner (n 55) 41–95.

[58] Section 25(2)(a)–(h) of the Matrimonial Causes Act 1973 lists a variety of factors that a court should take into account.

[59] Child maintenance is a children's rights issue that is 'concerned with upholding and protecting children's welfare insofar as its aim is to address the child's ongoing material needs in the event of parental divorce or separation with a view to avoiding and alleviating child poverty.' (H Stalford, *Children and the European Union Rights, Welfare and Accountability* (Oxford, Hart Publishing, 2012) 119–20.)

[60] Boele-Woelki, Braat and Sumner (n 55) 41–54.

[61] See, JM Carruthers, 'De Facto Cohabitation: The International Private Law Dimension' (2008) 12 *Edinburgh Law Review* 51 where a list of various forms of partnerships are given at pages 52–53. These are: regulated (*de iure*) partnerships that are registered or formalised according to the law of a particular State, regulated (*de iure*) partnerships like the first category but some statutory consequences may be excluded by the parties, *de facto* unions established not by formal regulation but under which statutory obligations may still arise, *de facto* cohabitation where some or all of the statutory consequences may be excluded by agreement of the parties and *de facto* cohabitation unregulated by law. These various relationships that can be regulated or unregulated, can apply to heterosexual or same sex couples depending on the laws in each State. The obligations that arise will vary in each State depending to what extent these relationships are regulated.

requirements and resulting obligations to pay maintenance in such cases depends on the location or the nationality of the parties and the grounds of jurisdiction and/ or applicable law that are selected. Therefore, the role of party autonomy is important in this area if parties' preconceived expectations of their duties to provide or not to provide maintenance after divorce are to be met. This is particularly true where jurisdiction falls in the court of an EU Member State other than the UK or Denmark (where forum law applies). In all other EU States the law applicable to the maintenance dispute is determined by the Hague Protocol, which may not be applied uniformly.[62]

The other big difference in the law of Member States in relation to maintenance on divorce is the distinction between maintenance and matrimonial property or the characterisation of 'maintenance'. The Court of Justice of the European Union (CJEU) ruled in *Van den Boogaard* that lump sum payments can be regarded as maintenance in certain situations.[63] However, a lump sum payment will not always be maintenance,[64] and in cases where it is considered as a division of matrimonial property then the Regulation will not apply. When determining if an order is for maintenance or matrimonial property judges are meant to look at the 'purpose' of the order and why the sum is being allocated. However, since the distinction between matrimonial property and maintenance is not necessarily clear, this may result in conflicting judgments if different issues are being dealt with by separate courts.[65]

In addition to spousal and child maintenance there are also a variety of other forms of family maintenance that may be recoverable in certain States. Examples of this are payments from older children to maintain their parents, and payments between siblings.[66] Expectations in relation to who has a moral obligation or duty to provide for whom in these situations arise from beliefs and understandings that might be shaped by national law or wider socio-cultural patterns.[67] Therefore, maintenance covers a wide range of obligations. The extent to which these arise depends on the laws and traditions of particular States, with the exception of child support which should generally be available. The Convention and the Regulation vary in scope and cover different types of maintenance obligations. The scope of the instruments will be discussed in greater detail below.

[62] See chs 3 and 6.

[63] *Van den Boogaard v Laumen* [1997] ECR I-1176. This case will be fully analysed at ch 3 s III below.

[64] For an example see the Scottish case *C v C* [2007] CSOH 191. (See ch 3 s III for further analysis.)

[65] This area will be analysed fully at ch 5 ss II–IV and ch 7 s III below.

[66] See, Martiny (n 40) 149–50 and see the declarations made by Ukraine in relation to the Hague 2007 Convention www.hcch.net/index_en.php?act=status.comment&csid=1068&disp=resdn, accessed 10 June 2014, discussed at ch 4 below.

[67] For example see M Maclean and J Eekelaar, 'The Obligations and Expectations of Couples within Families: Three Modes of Interaction' (2004) 26 *Journal of Social Welfare and Family Law* 117.

## VI. Conclusion

The duty to provide for those that you have a legal and moral obligation to support is extremely important. With the movement and migration of people both within Europe and globally there are more and more families and relations who live in different States.[68] Therefore it is imperative that suitable and workable methods exist to create maintenance obligations and then secure the transfer of funds, particularly from abroad. The provisions in the Regulation and the Convention will be analysed in order to discover what positive developments have been made in relation to the recovery of maintenance from abroad. When analysing the developments and then suggesting improvements to the Regulation and mechanisms for good practice, the book seeks to suggest solutions and improvements that assist in ensuring the effective enforcement of cross border maintenance obligations whilst protecting the rights and legitimate expectations of the parties involved. This is in line with the pragmatic approach or theory, which is the approach taken by the majority of British private international law scholars,[69] and the Hague Conference on Private International Law.[70]

[68] Within Europe alone, each year between 2004 and 2008 there were over 3 million migrants. (See, Eurostat, 'Migrants in Europe: A Statistical Portrait of the First and Second Generation' (2011) p 16). Data gathered by the UN suggests that in 2005, 191 million people lived in a country other than the one in which they were born. For more information and a breakdown of this figure see the Factsheet at www.un.org/esa/population/migration/hld/Text/Migration_factsheet.pdf, and the press release at www.un.org/migration/presskit/pressrelease12sept.pdf, accessed 10 June 2014. See also A Laquer Estin, 'Migration, Remittances and Child Support' in Beaumont et al (eds) (n 11) particularly s III.

[69] See, Beaumont and McEleavy (n 21) 2.87–2.99.

[70] Ibid, 2.97–2.99.

# 2

# History of the Recovery of Maintenance from Abroad

## I. Introduction

The need to be able to recover maintenance and child support from abroad has been clear for many years and the search to find a successful method for achieving this has been a matter of longstanding debate and frustration. Since the First World War there has been a great deal of movement of persons between States for a number of reasons. Effective measures are needed in this area not only to support wives and children but to reduce the impact on State welfare bills. This is because if the debtor is not maintaining those that he or she has a duty to maintain, in many cases the State will have to support the parties instead.

## II. First Steps—A Regime for the UK and His Majesty's Dominions

The UK Government took the first steps to remedy this in the Maintenance Orders (Facilities for Enforcement) Act 1920. The Act was designed in order to allow deserted wives, from England, Wales and Northern Ireland, to acquire maintenance from their husbands who had returned to or moved to other colonies. For the purposes of the Act, 'maintenance' was defined as: 'an order other than an order of affiliation for the periodical payment of sums of money towards the maintenance of the wife or other dependants of the person against whom the order is made'.[1] The Act worked by means of a dual court enforcement system and applied to wives and 'legitimate' children. In its first year of application it saved around two million pounds of tax payer's money.[2] The fact that millions of pounds were involved as long ago as the 1920s gives an indication of the scale of the problem even then.

[1] s 10.
[2] HC Deb 8 December 1967 vol 755 cc1837–95, 1850.

The Act required the other State to also create reciprocal legislation. This was done by New Zealand, Australia, South Africa and Southern Rhodesia.[3] The Act did not apply in Canada until 1948,[4] and even then it only applied in certain provinces.[5] However, there were many problems with the 1920 Act, in particular, the geographical scope. The Act did not apply in Scotland and it could not apply to the USA since it was not one of His Majesty's Dominions. Another hurdle that became more apparent as time passed was the fact that the Act only protected 'legitimate' children.[6] There were also several problems with the methods and sanctions in relation to the 'actual enforcement of the orders'.[7] The Act was updated in 1972.[8] This extended the provisions to Scotland, and was also the somewhat belated legislation to enable the UK to accede to the 1956 New York Convention.

## III. The First International Regime

The first attempt to create an international document in this area occurred just after the dual court enforcement system was created in the UK. In 1929 The International Institute for the Unification of Law (UNIDROIT) on the initiative of the League of Nations began to work on Maintenance. A draft Convention was produced in 1938.[9] The work was interrupted by the Second World War and following this, the United Nations (UN) assumed responsibility for the work. The next draft was completed in 1949, and was reviewed in 1951.[10] This draft covered traditional private international law rules. It provided that judicial decisions

[3] HC Deb 27 June 1927 vol 208 cc15–16, 16.

[4] This created problems for deserted wives. An example is 'this morning I had a letter from one of my own constituents, a woman who was betrayed by a man in the Royal Canadian Air Force. She actually obtained an affiliation order against him in the courts for 15s. a week. He has returned to America—he is an American citizen who was serving in the Canadian Air Force—and the affiliation order is now some £50 in arrears. This unfortunate woman is in great difficulties and has a baby. She is owed £50 by this man who is living with his parents in Los Angeles, and nothing can be done about it, either with the American authorities or, as things are at present, apparently, with the Canadian authorities.' HC Deb 19 December 1945 vol 417 cc1448–64, 1452–53.

[5] Alberta, British Columbia, Manitoba and Saskatchewan, see HC Deb 02 February 1948 vol 446 cc229–31W, 230W.

[6] Art 10. The number of 'illegitimate' births in the UK had been growing and between 1955 and 1965 the figure had doubled from 31,455 to 66,780, see HC Deb 8 December 1967 vol 755 cc1837–95, 1849.

[7] See below at ch 9, particularly n 18.

[8] Maintenance Orders (Reciprocal Enforcement) Act 1972. This Act had three parts: the first part updated the earlier Act, the second part allowed the UK to accede to the 1956 New York Convention and the third part was designed to allow the UK to create obligations with States that neither of the first two parts applied to, such as the USA.

[9] K Lipstein, 'A Draft Convention on the Recovery Abroad of Claims for Maintenance' (1954) 3 *International and Comparative Law Quarterly* 125, 126.

[10] Ibid.

were to be enforceable in the courts of other countries if the original court had jurisdiction and the decision was not subject to appeal. However, a decision could not be enforced if it conflicted with the public policy of the State or was inconsistent with another decision which concerned the same matter. There was also an exception which suggested that the 'judgment to be enforced was not to be contrary to the law of the enforcing court, if this was the law applicable according to its own rules of Private International Law.'[11] In 1952 the Legal Secretariat produced an alternative draft which was inspired by the Maintenance Orders (Facilities for Enforcement) Act 1920.[12] This draft sought to eliminate the problems with the traditional private international law regime, which did not appear to be workable at that time due to disagreements between civil and common law States.[13]

The final result of the negotiations and discussions was the UN Convention on the Recovery Abroad of Maintenance of June 1956 (New York Convention).[14] This Convention created a system of international assistance, because no agreement could be reached on the recognition of foreign maintenance orders at this stage. The Convention included no provisions on jurisdiction. It simply provided for agencies to be established that could transmit applications between each other, thus trying to facilitate the payment of maintenance claims. 'The purpose of this Convention is to facilitate the recovery of maintenance to which a person … who is in the territory of one of the Contracting Parties, claims to be entitled from another person … who is subject to the jurisdiction of another Contracting Party.'[15]

The New York Convention gave no indication of its scope, it simply used the term 'claims to be entitled'.[16] There was no attempt to define what 'maintenance' was, nor was there an attempt to define or limit the relationships which would determine 'entitlement'. Therefore, the New York Convention must have been capable of applying to both 'legitimate' and 'illegitimate' children and possibly many other relationships such as child to parent or siblings. It is presumed it would be for the discretion of State bodies to determine whether the claimant was actually entitled to maintenance in a certain case, and how they made this decision would be up to the courts and depend on the law that was applied in a particular case. Consequently, this first international Convention was very basic in terms of traditional private international law rules. It only provided for a means of transmitting applications, rather than dealing with difficult legal issues by

[11] Ibid, 127.

[12] Ibid, 128.

[13] Ibid, 127–28.

[14] Available at www.hcch.net/index_en.php?act=publications.details&pid=4161&dtid=45, accessed 21 May 2014. For a full list of signatures, ratification and accessions see http://treaties.un.org/Pages/ViewDetailsIII.aspx?&src=TREATY&mtdsg_no=XX~1&chapter=20&Temp=mtdsg3&lang=en, accessed 21 May 2014.

[15] Ibid, Art 1.

[16] Ibid.

stipulating rules in the areas of scope, jurisdiction, applicable law and recognition and enforcement.

However, the New York Convention did start paving the road to where the law is now. It established a basic form of the Central Authority in the context of transmitting and receiving agencies, and it mentioned legal aid. 'The Transmitting Agency may transmit to the Receiving Agency an opinion as to the merits of the case and may recommend that free legal aid and exemption from costs be given to the claimant.'[17] It is interesting that the agencies were allowed to encourage the provision of legal aid, especially since the two new instruments were the first to establish free legal aid in all child support cases.[18]

## IV. The Regime Established by the Hague Conference

A second Convention on maintenance for children was produced by the Hague Conference, also in 1956.[19] This could supplement the limited provisions in the New York Convention as it covered applicable law. The Convention covers children up to the age of 21 years and the general rule is that the law of the child's habitual residence should apply. If this changes then the law of the child's new habitual residence will be applicable.[20] Contracting States determine whether the Convention applies to 'illegitimate' children on the basis of the applicable law.

The next international Convention relating to maintenance was concluded by the Hague Conference in 1958.[21] This again concerned maintenance obligations to children up to the age of 21, but covered recognition and enforcement of decisions in this area. The Convention provided that decisions given in one Contracting State should be recognised and enforced in another Contracting State without a revision of the decision to create the obligation.[22] However, the Convention laid down indirect grounds of jurisdiction as a prerequisite for recognition and enforcement. These are: that either the maintenance creditor or debtor had their habitual residence in the State where the decision was rendered at the

[17] Ibid, Art 4(3).

[18] Arts 15 and 16 of the Convention and Art 46 of the Regulation.

[19] Convention on the Law Applicable to Maintenance Obligations towards Children, 1956 (French only). 14 States are party to the Convention (13 Member States and 1 non-member) and two other Member States signed the Convention, but did not ratify it. See, www.hcch.net/index_en.php?act=conventions.status&cid=37, accessed 21 May 2014.

[20] Ibid, Art 1.

[21] Convention Concerning the Recognition and Enforcement of Decisions Relating to Maintenance Obligations towards Children 1958 (French only). Twenty States are a party to this Convention (19 Member States and one non-member State) and two other Member States signed but did not ratify it. See, www.hcch.net/index_en.php?act=conventions.status&cid=38, accessed 21 May 2014.

[22] Ibid, Art 2.

time when the proceedings were instituted,[23] or that the defender submitted to the jurisdiction of the authority, either expressly or by defending on the merits of the case without objecting to the jurisdiction.[24] There are also grounds on which recognition and enforcement can be refused. In the 1958 Convention, these are: if the decision was given in default but this only applies where the executing authority considers that this was not the defendant's fault,[25] if the decision was subject to *lis pendens*,[26] or the decision was manifestly incompatible with the public policy of the State.[27]

For States that had signed up to the three Conventions there was a comprehensive regime for recovering maintenance from abroad for children. The transmitting and receiving agencies established under the New York Convention could ensure that decisions and applications were passed to the relevant authorities. The 1956 Convention introduced rules on applicable law and the 1958 Convention completed the picture with rules on recognition and enforcement and indirect grounds of jurisdiction. However, the picture was not ideal as States were party to a different combination of the instruments, the references to actual enforcement were minimal,[28] and there was no mechanism for adults to recover maintenance outside the basic regime created by the New York Convention.

The next work on maintenance was not completed until 1973. Two Conventions were adopted by the Hague Conference at this time. They covered applicable law and enforcement of maintenance obligations in respect of any maintenance creditor.[29] Although both the Conventions apply to adults, they both aim to co-ordinate the provisions of their equivalent Conventions that relate to children.[30] The Conventions also apply to obligations in relation to children who are 'not legitimate'.[31] Both Conventions apply to 'maintenance obligations arising from a family relationship, parentage, marriage or affinity, including a maintenance obligation in respect of a child who is not legitimate.'[32] Although the Conventions determine what relationships they can apply to they still give no definition of the term 'maintenance'.[33] It is presumed that the term 'maintenance' will be defined by the relevant applicable law.

[23] Ibid, Arts 3(1) and (2).
[24] Ibid, Art 3(3).
[25] Ibid, Art 2(2).
[26] Ibid, Art 2(4).
[27] Ibid, Art 2(5).
[28] See Ibid, Arts 7, 10 and 11.
[29] Hague Convention of 2 October 1973 on the Law Applicable to Maintenance Obligations (Applicable Law Convention), which 15 States are party to, www.hcch.net/index_en.php?act=conventions.status&cid=86, accessed 21 May 2014 and Hague Convention of 2 October 1973 Convention on the Recognition and Enforcement of Decisions Relating to Maintenance Obligations (Enforcement Convention), which 24 States are party to (23 Member States and one non-member State) /www.hcch.net/index_en.php?act=conventions.status&cid=85, accessed 21 May 2014.
[30] See the preambles of both these Conventions.
[31] See Art 1 of both Conventions.
[32] Ibid.
[33] See Ch 1 of both Conventions.

In the applicable law Convention the overriding rule is that the law applicable should be that of the habitual residence of the creditor.[34] This can be set aside if there is no obligation under that law, but an obligation would exist under the law of the common nationality of the creditor and the debtor.[35] If the creditor is still unable to obtain maintenance under the law of the common nationality then there is a provision which appears to let the creditor have a free choice because it simply states 'the internal law of the authority seised shall apply',[36] and the Convention does not regulate jurisdiction. However whatever the applicable law is it can be set aside by Article 7 where the parties are related 'collaterally or by affinity' if the debtor can show that there is no such obligation under the law of their common nationality, or if there is not one the law of the habitual residence of the debtor. In the case of ex spouses, the law that applied to the divorce will also apply to maintenance obligations.[37] The law designated under the Convention should be used to determine, from whom the creditor can claim maintenance, who is allowed to institute the proceedings and the extent of the obligation of the debtor where a public authority seeks reimbursement.[38] The application of the law designated by the Convention can only be refused if it is contrary to the public policy of the forum.[39] The Convention also permitted Contracting States to make some reservations so that the Convention need not apply to all the relationships listed in Article 1.[40]

The 1973 Enforcement Convention can apply to the same relationships that are listed in the Applicable Law Convention.[41] The Convention provides that a decision given in one Contracting State should be recognised in another Contracting State, as long as it complies with the jurisdictional requirements in Articles 7 or 8, and the decision is final in the State of origin.[42] For the purposes of the Convention, jurisdiction must be founded on; the habitual residence of either the debtor or the creditor.[43] Since the creditor is seen as the weaker party in maintenance obligations, the debtor is generally not permitted to sue in his own forum. However, there is no differentiation in the text between these two bases of jurisdiction and it would appear that they are both equal, in the sense that either the creditor or the debtor could sue in either forum. Therefore the debtor could sue in his own forum under the Enforcement Convention. The Verwilghen Report states that: '[n]o comment is needed on the first principle: it is simply a matter of applying the rule "*actor sequiter forum rei*".'[44] This suggests that it is for the plaintiff to

[34] Applicable Law Convention (n 29) Art 4.
[35] Ibid, Art 5.
[36] Ibid, Art 6.
[37] Ibid, Art 8. In countries where the divorce was granted or recognised.
[38] Ibid, Art 10.
[39] Ibid, Art 11.
[40] Ibid, see Arts 13, 14, 15 and 24.
[41] Enforcement Convention (n 29) Art 1.
[42] Ibid, Art 4.
[43] Ibid, Art 7.
[44] M Verwilghen, 'Explanatory Report on the 1973 Hague Maintenance Conventions (1975) para 50, available at www.hcch.net/index_en.php?act=publications.details&pid=2946&dtid=3, accessed 21 May 2014 (Verwilghen Report).

sue in the forum of the defendant's residence, rather than the debtor suing in his own State. However this is not clear from the wording of the Convention, because the term debtor is used rather than defendant.[45] The Verwilghen Report does not elaborate further than this.[46] This could suggest that Verwilghen considered that the Convention or earlier practice was clear on this matter when drafting the Report.

Alternatively, jurisdiction can be founded on the nationality of both the parties if it is the same,[47] or a jurisdiction that the debtor has either expressly agreed to or not contested.[48] If the parties are divorced the State of the divorce court will also have jurisdiction in the maintenance claim (but only if no other court has jurisdiction under Article 7).[49] Recognition and enforcement can be refused on various grounds, such as: if the decision is manifestly contrary to the public policy of the State addressed; if the decision was obtained by fraud in connection with a matter of procedure; if proceedings having the same purpose are pending in the State addressed; and if the decision is incompatible with another decision between the same parties for the same purpose.[50] Recognition and enforcement can also be refused if the decision was rendered by default, in certain circumstances.[51]

At this stage the position was rather complicated, with the possibility that five different Conventions on Maintenance could be applicable in one State; four Hague Conventions, two that relate only to children, and one UN Convention. Work began in 1995 to look into the viability of these Conventions, and the current system, by the Hague Conference.[52] A document on the Conventions

[45] Unlike Art 4 of the Maintenance Regulation (Council Regulation (EC) 4/2009 of 18 December 2008 on jurisdiction, applicable law, recognition and enforcement of decisions and cooperation in matters relating to maintenance obligations [2009] OJ L7/1), where jurisdiction is based on the habitual residence of the creditor or the 'defendant'. Meaning that the creditor can sue in their State or the debtor's State, but the debtor can only sue in the creditor's State. This is similar to the indirect rules of jurisdiction in the new Convention where you can sue in either the creditor or the respondent's State, again meaning that the debtor cannot sue in their own State.

[46] In fact the Report instead gives a detailed description of the ground that favours the creditor, Verwilghen Report (n 44) para 50.

[47] This was an additional ground that is not found in the 1958 Convention. See Preliminary Document no 1, M Pelichet, 'Note on the Operation of the Hague Conventions Relating to Maintenance Obligations and of the New York Convention on the Recovery Abroad of Maintenance' para 70, available at www.hcch.net/index_en.php?act=publications.details&pid=4098&dtid=35, accessed 21 May 2014 (Pelichet Note).

[48] Enforcement Convention (n 29) Art 7.

[49] Ibid, Art 8, and see the Verwilghen Report (n 44) at para 53. The rule was included because some of the Commission 'wished to take account of the fact that the Hague Convention of June 1 1970, *on the recognition of divorces and legal separations* already existed.' (Verwilghen Report, ibid, para 53). The inclusion of this ground was particularly controversial because it includes a *perpetuatio juris* in that the divorce court will continue to have jurisdiction in the case of revision of a maintenance decision at a later date (see Preliminary Document no 1, Pelichet Note (n 47) paras 30–33).

[50] Ibid, Art 5.

[51] Ibid, Art 6.

[52] See Preliminary Document no 1, Pelichet Note (n 47). The document also lists further instruments that cover maintenance: Montevideo Convention of 15 July 1989 on Support Obligations, Rome Convention of 6 November 1990 between the Member States of the European Communities on the Simplification of Procedures for the Recovery of Maintenance Payments, and Brussels-Lugano

and any potential issues arising from their operation was drawn up by Michel Pelichet. The document highlighted several points that it was considered should be examined further. These were: party autonomy in the choice of applicable law; Article 8 of the 1973 Convention—the question of *perpetuatio juris* in respect to the continuing jurisdiction of the divorce court under Article 8 of the 1973 Convention, the incidental question, the problem of a review of the merits and the practice followed in the United Kingdom, scope *ratione personae* of the New York Convention of 1956, the costs of translation and free legal assistance and the co-ordination between the application of the Hague Conventions and the New York Convention of 1956.[53]

A Special Commission was held by the Hague Conference in November 1995, to discuss the operation of the Hague Maintenance Conventions and the New York Convention. The points listed above were addressed during the Commission. However, the Commission concluded that no revision of the treaties should be proposed:

> The four Hague Conventions on maintenance obligations and the New York Convention of 1956 are sound treaties. The difficulties in applying the Hague Conventions on recognition and enforcement of decisions and the New York Convention are to a much greater extent due to differences in the standard of living between the countries Parties to those Conventions, as well as to frequently incompatible religious or philosophical convictions and, above all, to the systematic bad faith of maintenance debtors. Hence the Special Commission considers that in the present state of affairs, it seems pointless to propose a revision of any of those Treaties.[54]

Legal assistance was 'discussed at length during the Special Commission'.[55] However it was considered that it would be very difficult to reach agreement on legal assistance because States 'have such different practices'.[56] Despite this, agreement on legal assistance was reached just over 10 years later in the 2007 Convention.[57] The 1995 Special Commission recommended that: a meeting on the five maintenance Conventions be held every four to five years, the Secretary General keep an up to date list of the authorities designated under the New York Convention, and

and San Sebastian Conventions on jurisdiction and the enforcement of judgments in civil and commercial matters.

[53] Preliminary Document no 1, Pelichet Note (n 47) para 139.

[54] General Conclusions of the Special Commission of November 1995 on the operation of the Hague Conventions relating to maintenance obligations and of the New York Convention of 20 June 1956 on the Recovery Abroad of Maintenance, para C6.

[55] Ibid, para D7.

[56] Ibid, para 8.

[57] It is great that agreement was reached in this area meaning that free legal aid/assistance will now be provided in all child support cases. Agreement at the international level meant that this provision was also incorporated into the Regulation. This provision was considered to be important because '[a]pplicants for maintenance generally have limited resources and even financial barriers may inhibit use by them of opportunities otherwise provided by the new Convention.' (Preliminary Document no 10 of May 2004, W Duncan and C Harnois, 'Administrative and Legal Costs and Expenses under the new Convention on the International Recovery of Child Support and other Forms of Family Maintenance, including Legal Aid and Assistance', para 39).

distribute this to the authorities of the Member States of the Hague Conference at least once a year, and to convene an informal working group to draft model forms to accompany files sent under the New York Convention, and ensure receipt of them.[58]

The decision to start work on revising the current position was taken in 1999. William Duncan drew up a note on the desirability of revising the Hague Conventions on maintenance obligations and to include rules on judicial and administrative cooperation.[59] A questionnaire on maintenance obligations was sent out to State parties in 1998.[60] The note, questionnaire and responses received were available for consideration at the following Special Commission meeting on maintenance obligations in April 1999. The Special Commission concluded that it would be desirable to produce a new Convention on Maintenance. It was recommended that 'the Hague Conference should commence work on the elaboration of a new worldwide instrument'.[61] That instrument should:

- contain as an essential element provisions relating to administrative cooperation,
- Be comprehensive in nature, building upon the best features of the existing Conventions, including in particular those concerning the recognition and enforcement of maintenance obligations,
- Take account of future needs, the developments occurring in national and international systems of maintenance recovery and the opportunities provided by advances in information technology,
- Be structured to combine the maximum efficiency with the flexibility necessary to achieve widespread ratification.[62]

It is interesting to note that the French expert considered that the new Convention had to address two main areas. These were administrative cooperation and recognition and enforcement of decisions.[63] However, the responses to the questionnaire relating to recognition and enforcement 'suggested that the regime established by the Hague Conventions of 1958 and 1973 on recognition and enforcement were working reasonably well with no practical operational difficulties'.[64] The responses to the questionnaire did not create the full picture though because; the reasons given for non-ratification of the Conventions 'included

[58] General Conclusions of the Special Commission of November 1995 on the operation of the Hague Conventions relating to maintenance obligations and of the New York Convention of 20 June 1956 on the Recovery Abroad of Maintenance, para 54.

[59] See Preliminary Document no 2 of January 1999, W Duncan, 'Note on the desirability of revising the Hague Conventions on maintenance Obligations and including in a new instrument rules on judicial and administrative cooperation'.

[60] Available at, www.hcch.net/upload/wop/maint1999pd1.pdf, accessed 21 May 2014.

[61] Report on and the Conclusions of the Special Commission on Maintenance Obligations of April 1999 (December 2009) p 22.

[62] Ibid.

[63] Conclusions and Recommendations, para 44. See chs 7, 8 and 10 below for a discussion on these provisions.

[64] Ibid, para 23.

constitutional problems concerning the bases of indirect jurisdiction'.[65] In response to this recommendation, the Special Commission on General Affairs of May 2000 concluded that 'the drawing up of a new comprehensive convention on maintenance obligations, which would improve the existing Hague Conventions on this matter and include rules on judicial and administrative cooperation',[66] should be a priority. The final Convention was concluded in 2007, eight years after the negotiations began.

## V. Recovery of Maintenance in Europe

In the European Union, maintenance was dealt with under the Brussels Convention[67] and then under Brussels I.[68] Brussels I covered jurisdiction and recognition and enforcement in relation to maintenance obligations. The specific provisions and how they differ from the current regime will be discussed in more detail in the relevant chapters. There is no definition of the term maintenance in the Brussels Convention, the Brussels Regulation or the EU Maintenance Regulation. There are some decisions of the Court of Justice of the European Union (CJEU) that give some guidance on scope and other aspects of maintenance, but these decisions only apply in specific circumstances.

*De Cavel v de Cavel* (no 2) was heard by the CJEU under the 1971 Protocol to the Brussels Convention.[69] The case concerned interim measures to pay maintenance in respect of divorce proceedings before a French court. The German authorities refused to enforce the decision under the Brussels Convention because they considered that the decision fell outside the scope of the Convention. The German authorities made a reference to the CJEU to discover whether the Convention could apply. In particular they asked whether the Brussels Convention applied to the enforcement of an interlocutory order made in divorce proceedings where one party was awarded maintenance, and whether the Convention applied to payments of interim compensation, also awarded in a judgment relating to the dissolution of the marriage.[70] The CJEU considered that the 'compensatory payments' provided for 'are concerned with any financial obligations between former spouses after divorce which are fixed on the basis of their respective needs and

[65] Ibid, and see ch 8 s III for more details.

[66] Conclusions of the Special Commission of May 2000 on General Affairs and Policy of the Hague Conference, Preliminary Document no 10 of June 2000, para 9.

[67] Convention of 27 September 1968 on jurisdiction and the enforcement of judgments in civil and commercial matters (Brussels Convention).

[68] Council Regulation (EC) 44/2001 of 22 December 2000 on jurisdiction and the recognition and enforcement of judgments in civil and commercial matters [2001] OJ L012/1 (Brussels I).

[69] C-120/79 *Louise de Cavel v Jaques de Cavel* [1980] ECR I-00731.

[70] Ibid, 734.

resources and are equally in the nature of maintenance.'[71] This meant that the payments could be considered as civil matters for the purpose of the Convention. After confirming that the payments could fall under the scope of the Convention the CJEU considered whether the fact that the primary claim did not come under the scope of the Convention precluded the Convention being applied to the whole matter. The CJEU decided that this was not the case and there was nothing to prevent the enforcing court treating the separate parts of the judgment as individual claims. The Court referred to Article 42 of the Convention, which provides that:

> where a foreign judgment has been given in respect of several matters and enforcement cannot be authorized for all of them, the Court shall authorize enforcement for one or more of them, and with Article 24, which provides that application for such provisional, including protective, measures—which are, by definition, ancillary measures as may be available under the law of a contracting State may be made to the courts of that State 'even if, under this Convention, the courts of another contracting State have jurisdiction as to the substance of the matter'.[72]

It is important that judgments are enforced in foreign States as far as possible, however the fact that this could apply where another court had jurisdiction to deal with the substance of the matter could result in conflicting or irreconcilable judgments.[73] If this does happen the ability of different courts to deal with different aspects of a related matter may cause more harm than good if this precludes recognition of one of the decisions.[74] Even though the Brussels Convention aimed to fix this problem through the provisions on *lis pendens* and related actions, these provisions did not necessarily solve all the problems that could arise in this area in the context of maintenance. These provisions and potential difficulties that may arise are discussed in detail in the chapter on jurisdiction.[75]

The Court held that the Brussels Convention applied to both the 'enforcement of an interlocutory order made by a French court in divorce proceedings whereby one of the parties to the proceedings is awarded a monthly allowance and … to an *interim* compensation payment, payable monthly'.[76] It is clear that the Convention applied to financial provision arising out of divorce if this was for maintenance, and was not just limited to the enforcement of maintenance obligations that are not related to decisions on personal status. However, what was not clear was whether the French compensation payment '*prestation compensatoire*' was generically considered as a 'maintenance obligation' within the EU, or whether it only was in this particular case because it was an 'interim' payment/ provisional or protective measure. Martiny believed that the decision meant that 'ancillary orders can be considered to be "maintenance" in the terms of the Convention but, it did

[71] Ibid, 740.
[72] Ibid.
[73] See ch 7 s III.
[74] Ibid and see ch 5 s IV.
[75] See ch 5.
[76] *De Cavel* (n 69) 741–42 (emphasis added).

not yet mean that a French "*prestation compensatoire*" is necessarily covered.'[77] On the other hand McEleavy stated that in *de Cavel*, a *prestation compensatoire* fell within the scope of maintenance obligations. He then suggested that the Court 'confirmed for the purposes of the Convention such obligations could be interim only or payable after divorce.'[78] Actually, the text of the judgment is very unclear on this matter. The Court simply clarified that enforcement cannot be rejected purely on the basis that the payment is an interim payment, rather than making any concrete statements about the nature of a '*prestation compensatoire*'.[79] The main decision seemed to centre on the fact that the ancillary proceedings can be split from the principal claim. The CJEU did not make definitive statements other than including 'interim' payments within the scope of Article 24.

The other decision of the CJEU which relates to scope is *Van den Boogaard*.[80] This case concerned the distinction between maintenance and matrimonial property, but did not clarify the issues addressed above that arose in *de Cavel*. The particular concern was whether a lump sum payment could be considered as maintenance or if the term only related to periodical payments. The CJEU held that an award for maintenance should be designed to 'enable one spouse to provide for himself or herself'[81] or it should take into account the 'needs and resources of each of the spouses.'[82] The case focused on the concept of needs but it is open to interpretation. The outcome in the case highlights problems with the characterisation of maintenance. The decision in *Van den Boogard* will be discussed in greater detail below along with difficulties faced by national courts in determining the scope of the new Maintenance Regulation, in light of this decision.[83] The CJEU has also ruled on irreconcilable judgments in the context of maintenance. In *Hoffmann*[84] the CJEU considered that the judgments were in fact irreconcilable, where an earlier decision on maintenance conflicted with a later decision on divorce.

The majority of the case law of the CJEU in the area of maintenance relates to the enforcement of the payment. This can be seen in cases like: *Offermanns*,[85] *Gemeente Steenbergen*,[86] *Romana Slanina*,[87] and *Theodores Kallianos*.[88] Other case law of the CJEU has not been directly on the recovery of maintenance but instead in relation to external matters that affect the maintenance payment. For example

[77] D Martiny, 'Maintenance Obligations in the Conflict of Laws' 247 (1994) *Recueil des Cours* 131, 216.

[78] P Beaumont and P McEleavy, *Anton's Private International Law*, 3rd edn (Edinburgh, SULI/W Green, 2011) 887.

[79] See, *de Cavel* (n 69) particularly 741, paras 10–11.

[80] C-220/95 *Van den Boogaard v Laumen* [1997] ECR I-1176.

[81] Ibid, para 22.

[82] Ibid.

[83] See ch 3.

[84] C-145/86 *Hoffmann v Krieg* [1988] ECR 645, see ch 7 s III.

[85] C-85/99 *Vincent Offermanns and Esther Offermanns* [2001] ECR I-2285.

[86] C-271/00 *Gemeente Steenbergen and Luc Baten* [2002] ECR I-10508.

[87] C-363/06 *Romana Slanina v Unabhängiger Finanzsenat, Außenstelle Wien* [2009] ECR I-11111.

[88] C-323/06 P *Theodores Kallianos v Commission of the European Communities*, 31 January 2012.

the payment of maintenance by the public body when the debtor could not pay because he was in prison[89] and the recovery of tax on the amount paid as maintenance.[90] These latter cases did not focus directly on the maintenance provisions, but rather those on citizenship. Although there are a number of applications for the recovery of maintenance from abroad, as evidenced by the empirical study, there is limited case law on this topic before the European Court.[91]

In addition to the provisions in Brussels I, the European Enforcement Order Regulation (EEO)[92] assists applicants with the enforcement of uncontested claims. The EEO allows judgments, court settlements and authentic instruments in respect of uncontested claims to be automatically recognised and enforced in another Member State. No intermediate proceedings are required, allowing uncontested claims to be processed and enforced immediately. The EEO can still be used to enforce claims under the new regime and will be discussed in detail in chapter nine on enforcement.

The question of developing a new Regulation which dealt solely with maintenance was first addressed in November 2000. At this point it was considered that although the quick and effective recovery of maintenance claims is essential, 'this does not necessarily imply that a separate legal instrument has to be drawn up. Maintenance creditors are already covered by provisions of the Brussels Convention and of the future Brussels I Regulation.'[93] However in November 2003 a first meeting of experts took place, with the purpose of producing a Green Paper on maintenance obligations.[94] The Green Paper was launched in April 2004 and was first debated at a public meeting organised by the Commission in June 2004.[95] The Green Paper took into account work at both the international level and within the Community. It included a list of questions that should be considered when designing instruments on maintenance. Some particular issues raised were: should the concept of maintenance be defined, are there areas that may make it difficult to abolish *exequatur* (such as public policy), could salary attachment orders be automatically enforceable throughout the EU, should specific

[89] C-302/02 *Nils Laurin Effing*, [2005] ECR I-00553.

[90] C-403/03 *Egon Schempp v Finanzamt Munchen V* (Grand Chamber) [2005] ECR I-06421.

[91] It is noted that there are currently three cases pending before the CJEU on the Maintenance Regulation. These are C-442/13 *Nagy v Nagy* (concerning Article 12 *lis pendens*), C-408/13 *Huber v Huber* and C-400/13 *Sanders v Verhaegen* (both on whether internal German rules conflict with the Maintenance Regulation).

[92] Regulation (EC) 805/2004 of 21 April 2004 of the European Parliament and of the Council creating a European enforcement order for uncontested claims [2004] OJ L143/15 (EEO).

[93] Draft programme of measures for the implementation of the principle of mutual recognition of decisions in civil and commercial matters (the Action Programme) adopted by the JHA Council on 30 November 2000, OJ C 12, 15 January 2001, 4. See also M Hellner, 'The Maintenance Regulation: A Critical Assessment of the Commission's Proposal' in K Boele-Woelki and T Sverdrup (eds), *European Challenges in Contemporary Family Law* (Antwerp, Intersentia, 2009) 343, 344–46.

[94] Staff Working Document, Annex to the Proposal for a Council Regulation on Jurisdiction, Applicable Law, Recognition and Enforcement of Decisions and Cooperation in Matters Relating to Maintenance Obligations—Impact Assessment, SEC/2005/1629, s 1.4.

[95] Ibid, ss 1.2 and 1.3. See also the Green Paper on Maintenance Obligations (presented by the Commission) COM (2004) 245 final (Green Paper).

conflict-of-law rules be adopted on enforcement actions, what mechanisms can be set up for the transmission of cases, what should Central Authorities be responsible for, in what areas could more detailed rules on administrative cooperation be envisaged in the Community (that would not be successful in The Hague), should time limits be set and is it possible to envisage electronic transmission of files at both the Community and Hague level?[96] The points raised on jurisdiction mainly considered the indirect rules to be adopted in The Hague and little consideration was given to suitable direct rules of jurisdiction at the Community level.[97]

Following this, as part of the 2004 Hague Programme, the European Council requested the Commission prepare a 'draft instrument on the recognition and enforcement of decisions on maintenance, including precautionary measures and provisional enforcement.'[98] The experts who prepared the Green Paper met again in May 2005. This meeting was held to discuss three draft proposals that the Commission had prepared on maintenance obligations.[99] The three proposals were: a draft Regulation on applicable law, a draft Regulation on the recovery of maintenance claims that would modify Brussels I and a draft Directive to improve the recovery of maintenance by establishing minimum common rules relating to access to information decision making and enforcement of decisions.[100] The Commission considered that the main objective of the proposal was to 'accelerate and simplify enforcement of decisions, in order to guarantee the effective recovery of maintenance.'[101] This encompassed five specific objectives.[102] These were:

1. Re-establish harmony within the EU.[103]
2. Remove intermediate measures—eg the *exequatur* procedure.[104]
3. Improve and simplify enforcement procedures.[105]

[96] Green Paper (n 95) 44–49.

[97] Ibid, 13–16. This is somewhat disappointing given the problems that may arise in this area which result from issues relating to the characterisation of maintenance in divorce proceedings (see chs 3 and 5 below).

[98] Annex I to the Presidency Conclusions of the Brussels European Council, November 2005, 41.

[99] Staff Working Document (n 94) s 1.4.

[100] Ibid, s 1.4.

[101] Ibid, s 3.

[102] Ibid, s 3.

[103] This is because previously Brussels I applied as well as the Hague Conventions and the 1956 New York Convention. It is believed that this objective has more or less been achieved at both the Community level and the international level, at least in the context of Maintenance. However, more could be done to achieve harmony across the EU private international law family law instruments more generally (see below at ch 5 at n 42 in particular).

[104] This was achieved across the majority of EU States, however, because it was not achieved across the board this creates a somewhat complicated system where Central Authorities have to deal with two different procedures. It is also questionable whether such a step was necessary (see ch 7 below). Further in their assessment the Commission hinted that the removal of these measures may not actually have any impact on the overall objective because: 'intermediate measures do not significantly contribute to time delays in maintenance claims [so] their enactment would do little to accelerate enforcement.' (Staff Working Document (n 94) s 4.1).

[105] The Commission recognised that the abolition of *exequatur* would not be sufficient to achieve enforcement of maintenance orders. However, the final text of the Maintenance Regulation achieved little in relation to actual enforcement; in fact the Convention signifies greater improvement in this area (see ch 9).

4. Enhance cooperation.[106]
5. Clarify what is the applicable law.[107]

This book begins to explore what achievements were made in relation to points 2, 3, 4 and 5 in the relevant chapters. It also considers other areas, not listed, where it is believed there are problems and issues that were not addressed.

In January 2006 the Commission sent a proposal to the Council for a Regulation on: jurisdiction, applicable law, recognition and enforcement of decisions and cooperation in matters relating to maintenance obligations.[108] The stated ambition of this proposal was to 'eliminate *all* obstacles which still today prevent the recovery of maintenance in the European Union.'[109] This is extremely ambitious and this book questions whether it is possible to remove all these obstacles without regulating every aspect of the process. It was considered that the stated objective could not be achieved by the fine tuning of other instruments and therefore a new instrument would be required to find solutions.[110] The Commission identified three requirements that should be used to guide the development of the new instrument. These were: simplifying the citizens' life, strengthening legal certainty and ensuring effectiveness and continuity of recovery.[111]

The final text of the Regulation was adopted in December 2008 and covers all of the aspects in the Commission's 2006 proposal, apart from applicable law. When the final text was decided it benefited from the fact that agreement had already been reached at The Hague since the Convention was finalised in 2007.[112] This means that applicable law is governed by the Hague Protocol. The development of the Protocol by the Hague Conference meant that the UK could opt in to the Regulation, but not apply rules on applicable law, since the UK applies forum law in this context. A separate Protocol in this area allowed agreement on all other areas of the instruments at the regional and international level, whilst maintaining rules on applicable law for the States that wanted these. The provisions on legal aid and administrative cooperation in the Convention were incorporated in the Regulation.[113]

[106] The main text on administrative cooperation was achieved at the international level in The Hague. The text in the final version of the Regulation has slight nuances and there are some additional provisions but in reality these differences do little to fulfil the objective of enhancing cooperation further in the Community. (See ch 10 below and the questions raised in the Green Paper (n 95)). It has been argued that a repeat of the provisions was a mistake and they should have been incorporated in a different way. See Hellner (n 93) and I Curry-Sumner, 'Administrative Co-operation and Free Legal Aid in International Child Maintenance Recovery: What is the Added Value of the Regulation?' (2010) 3 *Nederlands Internationaal Privaatrecht* 611.

[107] See ch 6 below and Hellner (n 93) s 2.4.3.

[108] SEC (2005) 649 final, 2005/0259 (CNS), available at http://eur-lex.europa.eu/LexUriServ/LexUriServ.do?uri=COM:2005:0649:FIN:EN:PDF, accessed 21 May 2014.

[109] Ibid, s 1.2 (emphasis added).

[110] Ibid.

[111] All these objectives are very practical and therefore support the pragmatic approach taken by this book when analysing the new instruments (see ch 1).

[112] See, P Beaumont, 'International Family Law in Europe—the Maintenance Project, the Hague Conference and the EC: A Triumph of Reverse Subsidiarity' (2009) 73 *Rabels Zeitschrift* 509.

[113] See ch 10 for a full analysis.

## VI. The Initial Impact of the Regulation

In the Regulation's first year of operation there were over 4162 applications. The figures provided by England and Wales only accounted for nine months (January—September 2012) rather than 12 so the figure was higher. Having said that the months missing are from the beginning stages of the Regulation and Ireland reported that they received no applications in the first six months. This highlights that the uptake of the Regulation was slow. At the Heidelberg Conference it was suggested that the figures were lower than expected, which could suggest a lack of knowledge and awareness of the new system.[114] For example, some States provided information on the number of each application by type. In this case there were only 193 applications reported for establishment of a new decision under Articles 56(1)(c) and (d).[115] Given the improvements in the new system, which allows applicants to apply through the Central Authorities,[116] and provides free legal aid in all child support cases, it was expected that there would be an increase in applications because of the benefits for applicants. This would suggest that there is a lack of public awareness of the Regulation in general; and a lack of knowledge of the process and how simple it is to make an application under the new system. International institutions and national governments should consider creating a short handbook for potential applicants to raise awareness of the system. This handbook should explain the ease of making an application under the new system, which should encourage potential applicants to proceed with an application.

Out of the total number of applications received, the Central Authority for England and Wales received the highest number of incoming applications (862) and Malta and Gibraltar received the least, zero. Several States such as: Belgium, Czech Republic, Estonia, Finland and Greece received around 130 applications. The first graph below shows the distribution of all incoming cases between the Member States. The second graph is designed to display information on the population of the Member States that participated in the study.[117]

[114] However, it is difficult to reach concrete solutions on this as this is the first set of data collected on the recovery of maintenance within the EU. The earlier documents of the European Commission (Staff Working Document (n 94) s 2.3 and Green Paper (n 95) 6) state that there are no European statistics on the number of maintenance claims requiring cross border recovery. It was concluded that there was a need for a new instrument on the basis of migration data and statistics on intra EU marriage and divorce.

[115] For further information on applications by type see L Walker and P Beaumont, 'Empirical Study on the Early Operation of the EU Maintenance Regulation' in Beaumont et al (eds), *The Recovery of Maintenance in the EU and Worldwide* (Oxford, Hart Publishing, 2014) 337, 344–46.

[116] See ch 10.

[117] The Figures were taken from the CIA World Factbook at www.cia.gov/library/publications/the-world-factbook/wfbExt/region_eur.html, accessed 21 May 2014.

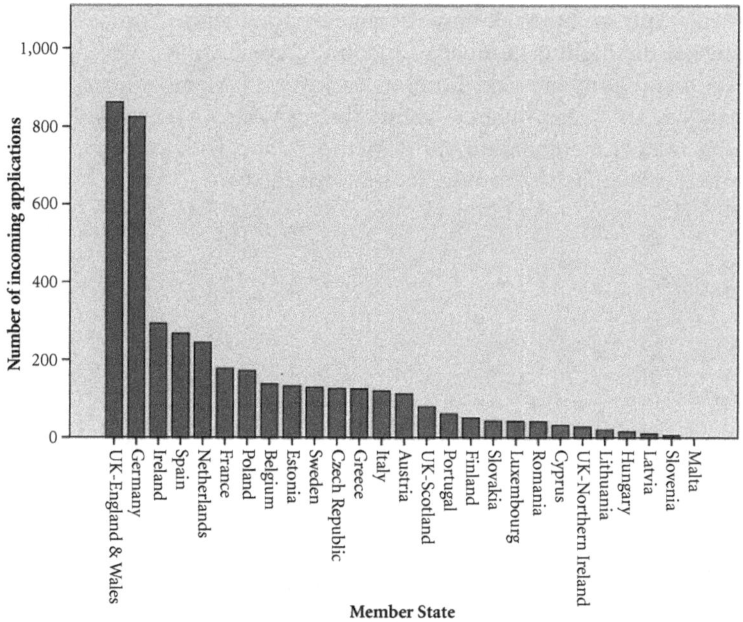


**Figure 2.1: Total number of incoming applications per Member State**

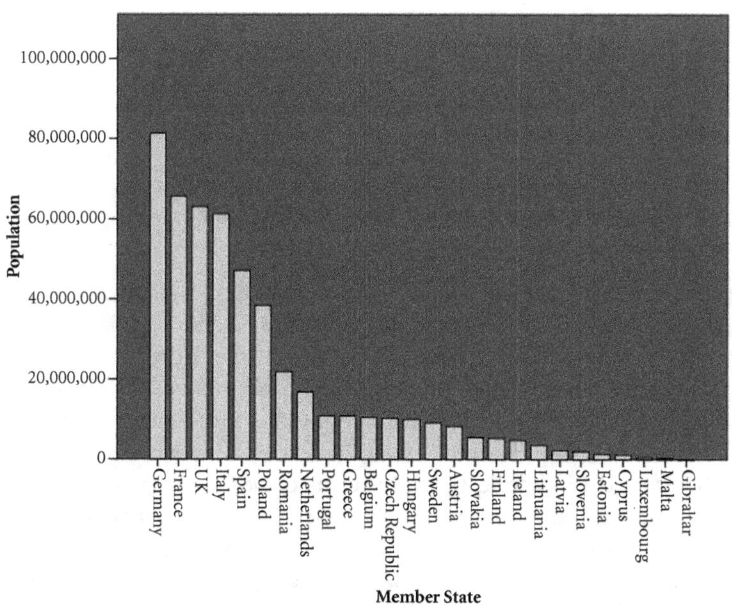


**Figure 2.2: Population per Member State**

Germany, France and the UK have the highest populations but Germany and the UK received the highest number of incoming applications. The distribution of population and number of applications between the Member States is not necessarily related. The diagram below shows the relationship between the number of incoming cases and population of the Member State, with a best fit line, to determine whether there is any correlation between the two.

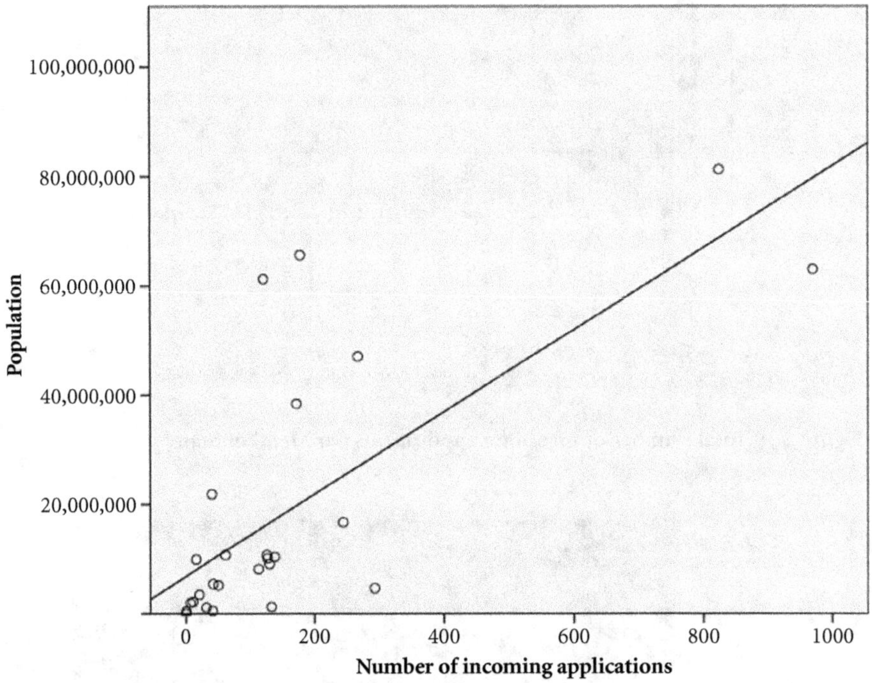


**Figure 2.3: Population and number of incoming applications**

In the diagram, each Member State is represented by a circle. France, Italy and Ireland do not fit with the general pattern. France has the second highest population, but only received 178 applications. Italy has the fourth highest population but only received 121 applications, whereas Ireland received 293 applications but has a lower population than the majority of Member States. Germany has the highest population but received less incoming applications than the UK (as a whole) by around 150 applications. In terms of percentage, 14.8 per cent of the total EU population lives in the UK, but the UK had 21.9 per cent of the total incoming applications. The best fit line indicates that there is not necessarily a direct correlation between the number of incoming applications and the size of the population. The following graph indicates clearly the pattern.

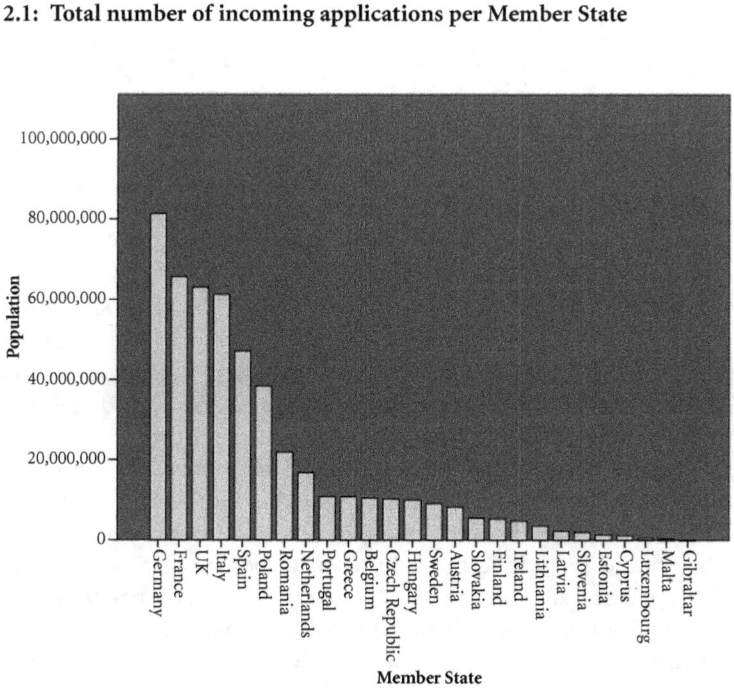

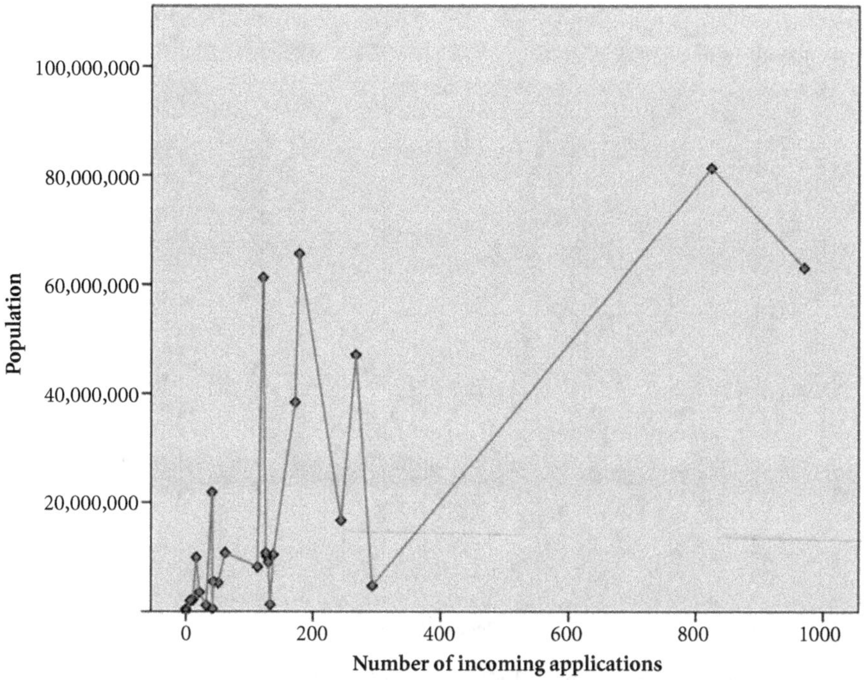


**Figure 2.4: Pattern of incoming applications against population**

The above diagrams give an indication of the spread of incoming applications across Member States in the first year of operation of the Regulation. They also show that there is no direct link between size of population and number of applications received. The other key question to be addressed in this overall picture is which State sent these applications. The majority of applications received (according to the information provided) were sent by Poland (indicated in diagonal stripes). This is the case for England and Wales, Germany, Italy, The Netherlands, Greece, Sweden and Ireland. In respect of other Member States most applications received by Finland came from Estonia and vice versa. An overall picture can be seen in the graph below which displays information on applications received by Member States which is split into the sending State by pattern.[118]

[118] A table of this information is available at Annex II. Unfortunately, there is no data on which States sent applications to Austria, France or Spain.

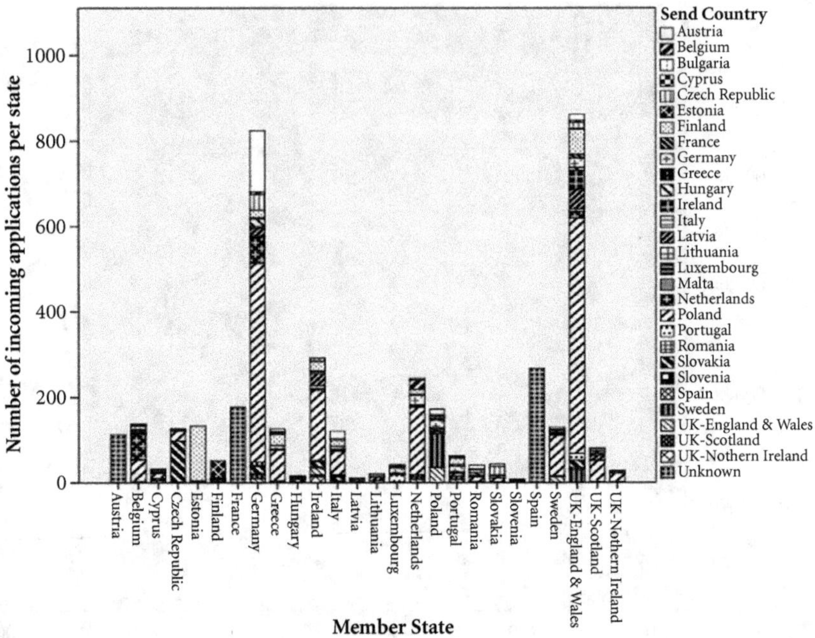


**Figure 2.5: Applications received, divided by sending State**

This gives an overall picture of the incoming applications received in the first year, which States received these applications, and which State the applications originated in. Given that there is no direct correlation between number of applications and population size does this indicate general trends in migration across the EU? If so is this affected by the free movement provisions or does it just indicate general trends in migration?

It was unsurprising that Finland and Estonia transmitted applications between each other because they are geographically very close and also the language is similar.[119] In relation to Polish citizens they originally emigrated in order to find better work prospects.[120] When Poland first joined the EU in 2004, the only three States that opened their labour markets to Polish citizens were the UK, Ireland and Sweden.[121] This was before the economic crisis, so both the UK and Ireland had thriving economies at this time. Prior to this Germany had been a popular State, for Poles to emigrate to, but since the labour market did not open until

[119] See www.migrationinformation.org/Feature/display.cfm?ID=825, at 'The Difficult Return of Ethnic Finns', accessed 21 May 2014.

[120] http://migrationinformation.org/Profiles/display.cfm?ID=800, accessed 21 May 2014.

[121] Ibid, and see www.euractiv.com/socialeurope/free-movement-labour-eu-27-linksdossier-188290, accessed 21 May 2014.

much later, Poles began to move to the UK and Ireland instead.[122] Then when the Netherlands opened its borders in 2007, this also became a popular destination country. However, as a result of the global crisis it was reported in 2008 that around half of the EU citizens who had moved to the UK since 2004 had returned to their State of origin.[123] These trends in migration begin to explain why there are so many applications from Poland, particularly to Germany, the UK, Ireland, Sweden and the Netherlands. Italy opened its labour market to Poles in 2006, indicating why they also have a number of applications from Poland. Greece also received a number of applications from Poland. Portugal is a Member State which did not receive many applications from Poland. However, it is unclear why there are not many applications between Poland and Portugal because Portugal opened its labour market in 2006 without restrictions.[124] One possible explanation could be language restrictions but this is not decisive because it is presumed that such problems would be similar in both Portugal and Greece.

In relation to Ireland there appear to be two reasons why it received so many applications: high immigration followed by high emigration. On the one hand it opened its labour market in 2004 when its economy was thriving, encouraging mass immigration. However, Ireland has faced many problems since the global crisis which has meant many people have since left the country. In fact in 2011 Ireland had the highest rate of emigration, per size of population, in Europe.[125] This indicates that the Irish population is changing constantly, which will result in families living in separate States. Further, not only do Germany and the UK have two of the highest populations, in 2011 they had the highest rate of immigration within the EU.[126] These two factors combined indicate why they received such a high number of incoming applications.

# VII. Conclusion

This chapter explores how much has been achieved since work first began on the recovery of maintenance and child support from abroad in the 1920s. Significant progress has been made since the first bilateral enforcement Act, which applied to the UK and its overseas dominions, and the first international Convention which focused solely on cooperation and made no attempt to regulate traditional aspects of private international law. What followed was a rather complicated scenario

[122] http://migrationinformation.org/Profiles/display.cfm?ID=800, accessed 21 May 2014.
[123] Ibid.
[124] www.euractiv.com/socialeurope/free-movement-labour-eu-27-linksdossier-188290, accessed 21 May 2014.
[125] http://epp.eurostat.ec.europa.eu/statistics_explained/index.php/Migration_and_migrant_population_statistics, accessed 21 May 2014.
[126] Ibid.

where the future work of the Hague Conference designed Conventions to complement the 1956 New York Convention, which resulted in five different international Conventions being applicable in this area. In contrast to this abundance of Conventions at the international level, in the European Union maintenance was governed by a Regulation primarily designed for commercial matters.

The current position is a significant step forward in this area. The two new instruments regulate the traditional aspects of private international law (including applicable law, through the Hague Protocol) in addition to judicial and administrative cooperation and free legal aid in child support cases. The Regulation is already in full operation as indicated above. However, it is suggested that applications are not as high as they should be. This is unfortunate as State welfare systems will generally have to support children where the absent parent does not. The data on incoming applications also indicates general trends in migration across the EU, which could be explored further when applications increase. It is hoped that the Hague Convention will be widely ratified in the future so that the new system can replace the earlier system. This book will now look at specific areas of the new instruments: scope, jurisdiction, applicable law, recognition and enforcement, and administrative cooperation, in order to determine what has really been achieved and indicate where further development and more clarification is required.

# 3

# Scope: Maintenance Regulation

## I. Introduction

No definition of the term 'maintenance' is included in the Maintenance Regulation and instead the Regulation requires that the term maintenance obligation should be 'interpreted autonomously'.[1] The lack of a definition of the term may lead to problems with characterisation, when a maintenance order is related to other claims. The Regulation applies to relationships that arise from a family relationship, parentage, marriage or affinity.[2]

The scope of the Regulation is very different to the core scope of the Convention which only covers child support and spousal support (with some qualifications). The core scope of the Convention can be extended to cover other types of family relationship but this is optional.[3] Although the scope of the Regulation appears much broader at a first glance, the full range of scope may not be applicable in all cases. This is because the applicable law may have a narrower scope and it is the law that applies in each case that determines which obligations are available and can be enforced. The applicable law is determined by the Hague Protocol on applicable law in most EU Member States.[4]

## II. Relationships the Regulation Applies to

The Regulation applies to claims relating to 'child support'. There appears to be no cap on the age that children are covered up to under the Regulation, however legal aid must only be provided in respect of parent child relationships until the

[1] Council Regulation (EC) 4/2009 of 18 December 2008 on jurisdiction, applicable law, recognition and enforcement of decisions and cooperation in matters relating to maintenance obligations (Maintenance Regulation) [2009] OJ L7/1, Recital 11.

[2] Ibid, Art 1(1), see also Recital 11.

[3] See ch 4.

[4] Protocol of 23 November 2007 on the law applicable to Maintenance obligations (Protocol). The Protocol applies to all Member States except for the UK and Denmark. In the UK it is always the *lex fori* that applies.

child reaches 21.[5] This may create difficulties because some States only consider citizens as children until they reach 18. For example, the Latvian law on the minimum amount a child's parent should provide only covers children until they reach 18 years old.[6] The Regulation should apply to maintenance obligations between parents and their children as required by the United Nations Convention on the Rights of the Child (UNCRC). However, it is unclear to what extent step parents, or other forms of 'extended parents' will be required to provide for 'their' children under the Regulation.[7] The relevant applicable law will be used to determine whether a maintenance obligation exists under the Regulation. However, the term 'parentage' cannot be determined by the Protocol. The Regulation and the Protocol do not give an autonomous definition of 'parentage', and one will not be developed by the Court of Justice of the European Union (CJEU) at a later date in this context as it is clear from the text that the instruments are not designed to cover these matters. Recital 21 states:

> It needs to be made clear in this Regulation that these rules on conflict of laws determine only the law applicable to maintenance obligations and do not determine the law applicable to the establishment of family relationships on which the maintenance obligations are based. The establishment of family relationships are to be covered by the national law of the Member States, including their rules of private international law.[8]

This is confirmed by the Hague Protocol which states that the Protocol 'shall determine the law applicable to maintenance obligations'[9] and then gives an illustrative list of relationships, including parentage. The only requirement is that it should always apply to children regardless of the marital status of their parents.[10] This is clarified further in the Bonomi Report which states the Protocol 'is not intended to determine the law applicable to the family relationships from which the maintenance obligation arises.'[11] Therefore, 'the law applicable to the family relationships to which Article 1(1) refers needs to be determined in each Contracting State on the basis of the rules of conflicts of laws in force and generally applicable in that State.'[12] Therefore, the Protocol determines the law that applies to specify from which relationships a maintenance obligation arises but does not determine the law applicable to parentage.

The general rule under the Protocol is that maintenance obligations shall be governed by the law of the habitual residence of the creditor.[13] However there

[5] Maintenance Regulation Art 46.

[6] Regulation No 348, 1 July 2003, available at www.likumi.lv/doc.php?id=76937, accessed 21 May 2014.

[7] See ch 1 s V for a brief consideration of some of these relationships and difficulties that may arise.

[8] Maintenance Regulation Recital 21.

[9] Art 1(2) of the Protocol (n 4).

[10] Ibid.

[11] A Bonomi, 'Explanatory Report on the Protocol of 23 November 2007 on the Law Applicable to Maintenance Obligations' (HCCH, 2009) (Bonomi Report) para 23.

[12] Ibid, para 24, see ch 6 for more details.

[13] See Protocol (n 4), Art 3.

are many alternatives to this.[14] In a specific case the Regulation cannot be used to establish a maintenance obligation in another Member State if no obligation to pay maintenance arises from that type of family relationship under the applicable law. The applicable law determines 'whether, to what extent and from whom the creditor may claim maintenance'.[15] Therefore the conclusion is that the Regulation should almost always cover obligations between parents and their children and between married couples as most European countries protect these relationships under their national law.[16] Although spouses generally have a duty to maintain each other during marriage, this is not always the case on divorce.[17] Again, as with parentage, there is no indication of what exactly is meant by the term 'spouse' such as whether this should apply to civil partnerships.[18] It is a question for the State to determine whether this is a relationship between 'spouses', some other form of family relationship or no relationship at all. The answer to this incidental question will determine which Article of the Protocol should apply or indeed whether the Protocol should apply at all.[19]

Relationships arising out of family relationships or affinity will not always be covered, because there is a special rule in Article 6 of the Protocol that prevents this in certain situations. Where the obligation does not arise from a parent-child relationship towards a child,

> the debtor may contest a claim from the creditor on the ground that there is no such obligation under both the law of the State of the habitual residence of the debtor and the law of the State of the common nationality of the parties, if there is one.[20]

If the obligation does not arise under the relevant applicable law, and the applicable law is applied correctly, then no maintenance obligation can arise in that context even though it is within the overall scope of the Regulation. However, if the applicable law is applied incorrectly and an obligation is created then it will be recognised and enforced like any other decision, under the Regulation, as it is technically not possible to refuse enforcement on the wrong application of the applicable law.[21] It is not clear whether the enforcing authority can refuse to

[14] Ibid, Arts 4–8, these are discussed in detail in ch 6.

[15] Protocol on applicable law (n 4), Art 11a.

[16] However, in this context if the marriage was carried out abroad and is not in fact recognised under the law of the State, this does not mean that a maintenance obligation should not arise out of the 'marriage'. 'Recognition in a Member State of a decision relating to maintenance obligations has as its only object to allow the recovery of the maintenance claim determined in the decision. It does not imply recognition by that Member State of the family relationship, parentage, marriage or affinity underlying the maintenance obligations which gave rise to the decision.' (Recital 25).

[17] In some States maintenance is only provided in certain types of divorce, ie fault based or where there is already an agreement. In other States some provision of maintenance is generally always provided between former spouses and in other States maintenance on divorce is very unusual. For a description of some of the State laws in 2003, see K Boele-Wolki, B Braat and I Sumner (eds), *European Family Law in Action Volume II* (Antwerp, Intersentia, 2003) 41–54.

[18] See ch 6 for more details.

[19] Ibid.

[20] Art 6 of the Protocol (n 4).

[21] See ch 7 s VI.

enforce a maintenance obligation if it was outside the scope of the Regulation.[22] Therefore, although the Regulation can cover all the relationships listed in Article 1, this does not mean that in every case all such obligations will be upheld.

## III. Characterisation

Another issue in relation to the scope of the Regulation in the context of spousal maintenance is the characterisation of maintenance; in particular the distinction between maintenance and matrimonial property. There is no definition of the term 'maintenance' in the Regulation, which simply requires that maintenance obligations should be 'interpreted autonomously'.[23] The characterisation of these claims has been a problem in the past because in some States, such as England and Wales, Northern Ireland and Ireland, there is no conceptual distinction between the two concepts as 'both are used to satisfy the goals of "fairness" or "proper provision"'.[24] As there was some confusion in this area due to different perceptions across the EU, the CJEU has provided guidance on this.[25] *Van den Boogaard* concerned the enforcement of an English 'maintenance' decision in the Netherlands. The English Court had dealt with the dissolution of the marriage and maintenance in its decision. Ms Laumen sought a clean break, accordingly the High Court awarded her a lump sum payment so that periodical maintenance was unnecessary. The money awarded included money from the sale of moveable property and the transfer of a painting and immoveable property.[26]

Ms Laumen had sought to enforce the judgment in the Netherlands under the Hague Enforcement Convention. The Amsterdam Court considered that the High Court's decision also concerned property rights and therefore could not be regarded as a decision in respect of maintenance obligations within the meaning of Article 1 of the Enforcement Convention. The Amsterdam Court then tried to find bases to enforce the decisions under the Brussels Convention. The Court then referred the question to the CJEU, asking in substance whether a decision ordering

> payment of a lump sum and transfer of ownership in certain property by one party to his or her former spouse is excluded from the scope of the Brussels Convention by virtue of point 1 of the second paragraph of Article 1 thereof on the ground that it relates to property arising out of a matrimonial relationship, or whether it may be covered by the Convention on the ground that it relates to maintenance.[27]

[22] Contrast this with the position under the Convention, see ch 8 s II.

[23] Maintenance Regulation Recital 11.

[24] M Harding, 'The Harmonisation of Private International Law in Europe: Taking the Character out of Family Law?' (2011) 7 *Journal of Private International Law* 203, 208.

[25] C-220/95 *Van den Boogaard v Laumen* [1997] ECR I-1176.

[26] Ibid, paras 3–4.

[27] Ibid, para 15.

The Advocate General pointed out that the English courts can rule on maintenance and matrimonial property in one decision. The CJEU also took account of this and considered that

> the court from which leave to enforce is sought must distinguish between those aspects of the decision which relate to rights in property arising out of a matrimonial relationship and those which relate to maintenance, having regard in each particular case to the specific aim of the decision rendered.[28]

In order to do this the enforcing court should look at the aim behind the decision. If the award is to be considered maintenance then the award should be 'designed to enable one spouse to provide for himself or herself'[29] or it should take into account 'the needs and the resources of each of the spouses'.[30] If on the other hand the award is 'solely concerned with dividing property between the spouses, the decision will be concerned with rights in property'.[31] Whether or not the payment is made in a lump sum should make no difference to the purpose of the award.[32]

The Court concluded that a decision

> ordering payment of a lump sum and transfer or ownership in certain property by one party to his or her former spouse must be regarded as relating to maintenance and therefore as falling within the scope of the Brussels Convention if its purpose is to ensure the former spouse's maintenance.[33]

Therefore, the Court has not looked to provide a common interpretation or definition of maintenance in order to take account of the wide range of laws and systems for separating matrimonial property and maintenance across the EU. Rather than having regard for State practice the enforcing court is encouraged to look at the purpose of the award in order to determine whether it is in fact maintenance. The Member States all have different laws and systems in this area and it

[28] Ibid, para 21.

[29] Ibid, para 22.

[30] Ibid, para 22.

[31] Ibid, para 22.

[32] Ibid, paras 23–24.

[33] Ibid, para 27. Lord Justice Thorpe considers that several propositions can be derived from the decision in *Van den Boogaard*. Firstly, 'whether a claim is for maintenance depends upon an autonomous interpretation of the term, and the label given to the claim by national law is not decisive: second, payment of a lump sum or transfer of property may be in the nature of maintenance if it is intended to ensure the support of a spouse; third, payment of a lump sum or transfer of property which serves only the purpose of a division of property or compensation for non-material damage is not in the nature of maintenance; fourth, a payment or transfer of property intended as a division of assets will concern "rights in property arising out of a matrimonial relationship"; fifth, whether a claim relates to maintenance will depend on its purpose, and in particular whether it is designed to enable one spouse to provide for himself or herself or if the needs and resources of each of the spouses are taken into consideration in the determination of its amount, or where the capital sum set is designed to ensure a predetermined level of income; sixth, where the provision is solely concerned with dividing property between the spouses, the decision will be concerned with rights in property arising out of a matrimonial relationship and will not therefore be enforceable under Brussels I' (Council Regulation (EC) 44/2001 of 22 December 2000 on jurisdiction and the recognition and enforcement of judgments in civil and commercial matters [2001] OJ L012/1 (Brussels I)). (*Moore v Moore* [2007] EWCA Civ 361, para 80.)

is questionable whether an investigation into the purpose of the award will always reach the same result, because the distinction between 'need' and 'fair division of the assets' may not always be clear.

The Scottish decision in *AB v CD*[34] concerned the enforcement of a capital sum under Brussels I. The action was undefended and Lord Brodie had to decide whether the award of a capital sum of £1,000,000 could be considered as maintenance and thereby capable of being enforced under Brussels I. The pursuer prepared evidence of her salary and outgoings for the purpose of the trial. This showed that her monthly net income was less than her outgoings.[35] The judge considered that the lump sum award was appropriate.[36] Following this he determined to what extent that sum could be defined as maintenance by making reference to the decision in *Van den Boogaard*.[37] Lord Brodie then considered the relevant provisions of the Family Law (Scotland) Act 1985[38] and decided that he could award half the sum, £500,000, as a lump sum maintenance payment with the aim of 'making an award of financial provision and that is to provide the pursuer with the means to provide for herself'.[39] The fact that the pursuer provided evidence that her income could not meet her expenditure showed that there was 'need' in the case and this may have persuaded Lord Brodie to reach the decision he did. If Lord Brodie had not classified part of the claim as 'maintenance' the pursuer would not have had an effective method of getting her decision enforced in France because there was no EU Regulation covering matrimonial property. This could be seen as an example of Lord Brodie taking a pragmatic approach in order to ensure the enforcement of the decision. However, this will not necessarily provide legal certainty or an autonomous interpretation throughout the European Union. McEleavy argued that; 'whatever the benefits for the pursuer and the desire to secure a just outcome, this instrumental classification does not bear up to detailed scrutiny, and certainly not from a comparative perspective.'[40] It is unclear what McEleavy's main objections are here, but he seems to imply that Lord Brodie did not apply the relevant Scottish legislation correctly when interpreting the case.[41] This highlights that it may be difficult to interpret national legislation in light of *Van den Boogaard* where the wording is different. Lord Brodie took a pragmatic approach to try and achieve consistency, and he did not allow

[34] *AB v CD* 2007 Fam LR 53; [2006] CSOH 200.

[35] *AB v CD* 2007 Fam LR 53, 56.

[36] Ibid, 59.

[37] Ibid, 59–60.

[38] Ibid, 60.

[39] Ibid, 60.

[40] P Beaumont and P McEleavy, *Anton's Private International Law*, 3rd edn (Edinburgh, SULI/W Green, 2011) 889.

[41] The relevant Scottish legislation is s 9 of the Family Law (Scotland) Act 1985. S 9(a) does refer specifically to 'matrimonial property', which is the provision that McEleavy considers the case was decided under (ibid). However, s 9(b) allows the judge to make an assessment on the basis of fairness and economic disadvantage and ss 9(d) and (e) allowed the judge to make a decision on the basis of 'needs' whether this is in relation to dependence or the possibility of suffering severe financial hardship.

the wording of section 9 to hinder this. However just because he took this approach, it does not mean that judges in other Member States will be convinced by the reasoning and actually enforce the judgment,[42] or that other judges will take this approach. It is clear that the process of characterisation is not precise or exact and therefore it will be difficult to achieve an autonomous interpretation of *Van den Boogaard* across the EU where a variety of different legislation is applicable.[43]

An alternative outcome was reached in *C v C*,[44] another undefended action. Lord Malcolm refused to take the same approach and distinguished the case from *AB v CD* on the basis that Mrs Scott had not provided information about her income so he could not calculate a payment in this case.[45] As there was no evidence of income it is difficult to determine whether there was any 'need' in the case, or, as Lord Malcolm assumed, the award was simply a fair division of the assets, thus matrimonial property. Lord Malcolm also distinguished the case from *Van den Boogaard* because in that case the wife had no earning capacity, and this was not an issue in the present case.[46] It is not clear whether the cases of *AB* and *C* were really that different nor whether the outcome would have been altered if Mrs Scott had provided information on her income, which showed she was living on low means. It is also unclear whether the outcomes would have altered had the actions been defended. What is clear is that the 'purpose' of an award could easily be interpreted differently across the 28 Member States and the outcome will often be far from certain for applicants.[47]

The approach taken by Lord Brodie, of specifically classifying something as maintenance, was also taken by the English Court in *Kremen*.[48] A sum of £12.5 million was awarded to W, which included child maintenance and school fees. This was to be made as a lump sum payment. Of this award £8.3 million was to be 'certified as "constituting maintenance"'.[49] It was stated that this had been certified as maintenance so that any enforcement action could take place under the Maintenance Regulation as per *Van den Boogaard*.[50] It is unclear from the judgment what the remaining £4.2 million is to be classified as, why that amount is not

42 McEleavy certainly was not convinced, and he is more familiar with Scots law and policy than a judge from a civilian legal system.

43 For example see the discussion on C-120/79 *Louise de Cavel v Jaques de Cavel* [1980] ECR I-00731, 37–38 in ch 2.

44 *C v C* [2007] CSOH 191.

45 Ibid, para 9.

46 Ibid, para 9.

47 See the opinion of Lord Hope when discussing the previous position in Scots law under the Divorce (Scotland) Act 1976. He considers that although the Act allowed for a great deal of flexibility when giving financial awards on divorce, the flexibility was not a problem because jurisdiction in all divorce proceedings remained with the Court of Session. However, when jurisdiction was extended to the sheriff courts the Act had to be changed and this flexibility reduced to ensure legal certainty (*Miller v Miller* and *McFarlane v McFarlane* [2006] 2 AC 618, 649–51). Therefore, a flexible approach in the EU that gives discretion to judges is unlikely to be successful due to the broad range of jurisdictions across the Member States and internally.

48 *Kremen v Agrest* [2012] EWHC 45 (Fam).

49 Ibid, para 91.

50 Ibid, paras 76–80.

maintenance, or indeed how W should seek enforcement of this amount. Further, in respect of the £8.3m it is unclear to what extent this obligation can actually be enforced under the Maintenance Regulation as H appears to have assets dispersed throughout a number of States,[51] and it is unclear where he is residing. According to the judgment, he left the UK in September 2010 and since then it would appear as though he had been either in Russia or in Israel. This case is illustrative of the difficulties a claimant may face, in a high money case, when trying to get their maintenance order and other claims enforced in cross border cases.

In addition to the often blurred distinction between maintenance and matrimonial property, certain courts also sometimes consider part of these payments to be 'compensation'.[52] In *McFarlane*,[53] the wife was awarded yearly payments that exceeded her needs. On appeal the amount awarded was lowered to an amount that met her needs. Mrs McFarlane raised the point before the House of Lords and further appeal was allowed. The yearly payments granted at first instance were to cover maintenance and compensation but no distinction (of the amount) was made, and only a total amount was ordered. Mr McFarlane's earnings far outweighed the needs of either party so a high award could not be considered unfair or excessive. Baroness Hale considered that Mrs MacFarlane was

> entitled to a share in the very large surplus, on the principles both of sharing the fruits of the matrimonial partnership and of *compensation* for the comparable position which she might have been in had she not compromised her own career for the sake of them all.[54]

The problem here is, if this were an international case how would Mrs McFarlane, or someone in another jurisdiction, be able to enforce such an order. Would the applicant have to do so under two different instruments (or one instrument and then through the private international law rules of a particular State)[55] and if so, which court would decide what amount of money was enforceable under each?[56] Lord Nicholls considered that there is nothing to suggest that 'periodical payment orders be limited to payments needed for maintenance.'[57] Therefore if the order is not purely for maintenance it would follow that the other part of the order would be categorised as something else. The distinction becomes clearer when

[51] Ibid, paras 30–59.

[52] *McFarlane* (n 47) 674.

[53] Ibid.

[54] Ibid, 665.

[55] In relation to the payment for compensation it is questionable whether this is maintenance, matrimonial property or compensation for loss in terms of a compensatory payment that may arise in a delictual claim (dealt with under Brussels I). In the case of matrimonial property no document has been concluded at this time, but the Commission's proposal is available at http://ec.europa.eu/justice/policies/civil/docs/com_2011_126_en.pdf, accessed 21 May 2014. The UK and Ireland have not opted in to this instrument. In this respect, Rabel has recognised that, 'factual situations are regulated differently by the individual systems of private law.' (G Kegel, 'Fundamental Approaches' in *International Encyclopaedia of Comparative Law Volume III, Private International Law* (Tübingen, Mohr Siebeck, 1986) 14.)

[56] In this respect see *Kremen* (n 48) where the Court determined the amount of money that should be enforceable as 'maintenance'.

[57] *McFarlane* (n 47) 635.

Lord Nicholls considered what should happen if the order is reviewed at a later date. The point to be considered is whether the Court can review Mrs McFarlane's expenditure in order to determine whether she has invested the excess money wisely. Lord Nicholls put forward the view that although the Court can review how she spent the money for her needs (maintenance), the money received for compensation had to be treated differently because this was loss related and therefore 'not directly affected by the use she makes of her resources.'[58] Since each element of the claim was to be treated differently at the review stage this would suggest that the compensation claim is distinct from 'maintenance', and would be enforceable in Europe under Brussels I rather than the Maintenance Regulation.[59]

## IV. Conclusion

The term 'maintenance' is somewhat ambiguous. Therefore the decision in *Van den Boogaard* is still relevant today as the Maintenance Regulation does not in fact give us a clear idea of what 'maintenance' is. The Regulation only clarifies the relationships which the Regulation should apply to,[60] and then provides that 'the term "maintenance obligation" should be interpreted autonomously'.[61] As there has been no attempt to define maintenance in the Regulation,[62] one has to assume that if there was ever an issue of whether a claim was for matrimonial property or maintenance the CJEU would refer back to the ruling in *Van den Boogaard*. Therefore the autonomous interpretation, in relation to spousal support, referred to in Recital 11, must be that an award that is designed to take into account the needs and the resources of the parties or enable one spouse to live by themselves is maintenance.[63] However, dividing the assets and providing for the other spouse on divorce is complicated and transfers of money can be regarded as maintenance, matrimonial property or even compensation.

Different jurisdictions have varying views on how payments can be categorised, what provision can actually be made, whether there should be clean breaks, and to what extent. Therefore if there really is to be an autonomous interpretation of 'maintenance' within the European Union then the Regulation should have

[58] Ibid, 648.

[59] However, see, D Martiny, 'Maintenance Obligations in the Conflict of Laws' (1994) 247 *Recueil des Cours* 131, 216 for a discussion of the French term '*prestation compensatoire*'. A view expressed here is that compensatory payments are a question of matrimonial property so would therefore be excluded from the Brussels I Regulation and the Maintenance Regulation, and see above at ch 2 s V.

[60] Maintenance Regulation Art 1 and Recital 11.

[61] Ibid, Recital 11.

[62] 'It has been remarked, however, that "a maintenance payment is perhaps easier to recognize than define".' (Martiny (n 59) 215.)

[63] It could be considered that this would also apply to relationships of affinity, ie there has to be an element of need in order for an award to be considered as maintenance.

contained a clearer definition. The concepts of need, fairness and compensation are not always clearly differentiated in this area and may be open to interpretation. In this respect Martiny states:

> It has to be accepted that, in domestic family law, there is often no clear distinction between maintenance and other forms of financial relief. The legislator often creates hybrid claims: their nature is intended or at least accepted. So it is difficult even in domestic law to characterize them in an unequivocal way. All these systems have their peculiarities and follow on their own logic. Thus the main problem for private international law is not only to decide which legal system or concept is to be decisive in the characterization process but also to find an appropriate solution for the single measure or claim itself.[64]

If it is impossible to give a definition of 'maintenance' then measures should be taken in other areas, such as jurisdiction, to minimise potential problems that could be created by alternative views on 'maintenance' by different courts.[65] If this is not done conflicts of characterisation could result in irreconcilable judgments if separate proceedings are ongoing in different jurisdictions on aspects of divorce, maintenance or matrimonial property.[66] This is a great concern for applicants living in the UK, because the UK will not be opting in to the matrimonial property regime.[67] Therefore these applicants may only get certain aspects of a monetary claim arising from divorce enforced in another Member State if elements of the claim are characterised as matrimonial property. Further, where part of a claim is considered as something other than maintenance, such as compensation, and the amount is either defined or not defined,[68] it is unclear what will happen to the payment. It is uncertain whether the whole order could be circulated as a maintenance obligation or if part of the claim would be circulated as something else under another instrument.

It is highly problematic as the English judgments are not always specific and vary, never mind judgments from other Member States. For example in *Macfarlane*, some of the claim is described as compensation but the amount is undefined,[69] whereas in *Kremen* a particular amount of money is established as maintenance, whilst the rest of the claim is 'not maintenance' but we do not know what that payment actually is.[70] These cases highlight the difficulties that could be faced by applicants when trying to get a monetary claim enforced abroad, when the amount of the payment is undefined or unclearly 'characterised'.

[64] Martiny (n 59) 216–17.

[65] See ch 5 s IV.

[66] The possibility of having different courts dealing with these aspects is discussed in ch 5 ss II and IV. See also ch 7 s III.

[67] No document on matrimonial property has been concluded yet (see ch 5 n 8). The UK and Ireland have not opted in to this instrument. There is also a proposal relating to the property consequences of Civil partnerships, available at http://ec.europa.eu/justice/policies/civil/docs/com_2011_127_en.pdf, accessed 5 June 2013. For further information on the matrimonial property proposal see B Campuzano Diaz, 'The Coordination of the EU Regulations on Divorce and Legal Separation with the Proposal on Matrimonial Property Regimes' (2011) 13 *Yearbook of Private International Law* 233.

[68] *McFarlane* (n 47) and *Kremen* (n 48).

[69] *McFarlane* (n 47) 618.

[70] *Kremen* (n 48) para 91.

# 4

# Scope: The 2007 Hague Convention

## I. Introduction

Unsurprisingly, the Hague Convention also fails to contain any definition of the term 'maintenance'.[1] However, the Convention is distinct from the Maintenance Regulation[2] in the sense that it does not just refer to maintenance in general terms, but distinguishes in the title between 'child support' and other 'forms of family maintenance'. This distinction could have been made to emphasise that obligations of 'child support' are necessary, in keeping with the United Nations Convention on the Rights of the Child (UNCRC).[3] Whereas the term 'other forms of family maintenance' is very vague, leaving it open to Contracting States to determine what, if any, obligations 'other forms of family maintenance' may lead to.

The scope of the Convention is determined by Article 2 and States can refuse to recognise and enforce a maintenance decision, if the decision does not fall within the scope of the Convention. With the exception of applications for child support the scope of the Convention is rather complicated. This is because, in order for the Convention to be attractive to as many States as possible, there are several options in relation to overall scope. Contracting States can make reservations and declarations on the areas of maintenance they want covered under the Convention.[4] These preferences or extensions will only apply when the other State has also made the same declaration. Therefore this can result in a complicated system whereby individual States can recognise different relationships as being within the scope of the Convention, depending on what State the application originated in.

[1] Hague Convention of 23 November 2007 on the International Recovery of Child Support and other forms of Family Maintenance (the 2007 Hague Convention) See the definitions in Art 3.

[2] Council Regulation (EC) 4/2009 of 18 December 2008 on jurisdiction, applicable law, recognition and enforcement of decisions and cooperation in matters relating to maintenance obligations [2009] OJ L7/1.

[3] See ch 1 s V.

[4] See, A Borrás, 'The Necessary Flexibility in Applying the New Instruments on Maintenance' in K Boele-Woelki et al (eds), *Convergence and Divergence in Private International Law, Liber Amicorum Kurt Siehr* (Eleven International Publishing & Schulthess, 2010) 173, 183–88 for an explanation of the areas where either a reservation or declaration is permitted.

## II. Child Support

The first paragraph defining scope applies to child support and is relatively straightforward. This paragraph requires that the Convention applies to maintenance obligations arising from a parent-child relationship, up until the child is 21 years old.[5] This sets out a general rule that all States must adhere to at least until the 'child' reaches 21. However, Contracting States can make a reservation to lower the age of application to children under 18 years old.[6] Borrás describes this as a reservation *ratione personae*.[7] If a State makes this reservation then the Articles on child support cannot apply to 'children' between 18 and 20 in any case or situation. Contracting States can also make a declaration to raise the age of application of the Convention in certain cases.[8]

The first two States that ratified the Convention, therefore bringing it into force, declared[9] the right to enforce certain child support applications in favour of children up to the age of 25.[10] This means that in relation to incoming applications they can decide whether to enforce these applications in respect of older children. However, in the case of outgoing applications the enforcing State only has to recognise and enforce child support applications for children up to the age of 21, unless they have also made a similar declaration. Otherwise they can simply decide that such applications are outside the scope of the Convention. Ukraine on the other hand has made a reservation to lower the age of application to 18.[11] The EU and Bosnia and Herzegovina have made no reservations or declarations in this respect, so the Convention will apply to children up until they reach 21. The Convention expressly states that these provisions must apply regardless of the marital status of the parents.[12]

[5] 2007 Hague Convention Art 2(1)(a).

[6] Ibid, Arts 2(2) and 62. 'Each of the reservations permitted by the 2007 Convention is the consequence of a problem that has been impossible to resolve during the negotiations and for which the only solution has been to allow the disagreeing States to make a reservation.' (Borrás (n 4) 184.)

[7] Borrás (n 4) 184.

[8] 2007 Hague Convention Arts 2(3) and 63.

[9] The Convention includes declarations in addition to reservations. Some legal writers 'are of the opinion that it is possible to accept certain "declarations" or "faculties" (*facultés*) as a mechanism "less brutal" than reservations, which allows the Convention to be fine-tuned to the needs of Contracting States.' (Borrás (n 4) 186.

[10] See, www.hcch.net/index_en.php?act=conventions.status&cid=131, accessed 21 May 2014, to view reservations, declarations or notifications of Contracting States. Norway declares it will 'enforce maintenance decisions in favour of children beyond 21 years, however not beyond 25 years. Norway reserves the right not to stipulate maintenance for children beyond 21 years'. Albania declares 'the right to enforce maintenance obligations even for adult children up to age of twenty-five years, provided that they attend the high school or university, according to Article 197 of the Family Code.'

[11] However they have made a declaration under Art 63 to apply the Convention to adult children in certain circumstances. These are incapacitated adult children and adult children in education up to the age of 23.

[12] 2007 Hague Convention Art 2(4). No reservations can be made in this respect. This has to be correct because parents have rights and responsibilities towards their children and these must exist no matter whether or not the parents are married. Article 2 of the UNCRC states that the provisions

## III. Spousal Support

There are two different categories of spousal support under the Convention. Where the application for spousal support is linked to and made at the same time as an application for child support then 'such a claim should fall within the compulsory scope of the whole Convention',[13] when the application is for recognition and enforcement or enforcement of a decision. All other claims for spousal support fall into the separate category in Article 2(1)c). This Article removes the need to apply the provisions on administrative cooperation, in Chapters II and III, to applications purely for spousal support. However, Contracting States can make a declaration extending the whole Convention to applications for spousal support.[14]

Norway, Albania and the EU have opted to make the provisions on administrative cooperation applicable to applications for spousal support.[15] The Borrás and Degeling Report states that these provisions 'will only apply where two States concerned have made a declaration extending those Chapters to spousal support in accordance with Article 63.'[16] Suggesting that if Norway was dealing with an application from Albania or an EU Member State then these provisions would apply, but in the case of an application from a Contracting State that has not made the declaration then the provisions on administrative cooperation need not apply. This appears straightforward. However Norway has also made a declaration in accordance with Article 30(7).[17] Norway declares that 'it will only recognize and enforce maintenance arrangements when the application is made

should apply to children without discrimination, while Art 18 requests that States 'use their best efforts to ensure recognition of the principle that both parents have common responsibilities for the upbringing and development of the child.' It seems inevitable that these 'common responsibilities' should include the provision of money in order to feed and care for the child. This should be for a suitable amount depending on the circumstances and assets of both parties. Article 27 requires that both parents pay maintenance and that State parties sign up to suitable international agreements. 'States Parties shall take all appropriate measures to secure the recovery of maintenance for the child from the parents or other persons having financial responsibility for the child, both within the State Party and from abroad. In particular, where the person having financial responsibility for the child lives in a State different from that of the child, States Parties shall promote the accession to international agreements or the conclusion of such agreements, as well as the making of other appropriate arrangements.'

[13] 2007 Hague Convention Art 2(1)(b) and see A Borrás and J Degeling, 'Explanatory Report on the Convention on the International Recovery of Child Support and other Forms of Family Maintenance (HCCH, 2009) (Borrás and Degeling Report) para 47.

[14] By making a declaration under the 2007 Hague Convention Art 63.

[15] See www.hcch.net/index_en.php?act=conventions.status&cid=131, accessed 5 June 2014.

[16] Borrás and Degeling Report (n 13) para 48.

[17] A State may declare, in accordance with Art 63, that applications for recognition and enforcement of a maintenance arrangement shall only be made through Central Authorities. Borrás considers that the 'effect of such a declaration is that all applications would have to be processed through Central Authorities. The States that make such a declaration do not reject the application of the Convention to maintenance arrangements, but they consider this filtering process as a necessary additional safeguard in the case of maintenance arrangements.' (Borrás (n 4) 188).

through Central Authorities.'[18] Therefore Norway will only accept applications that are made through Central Authorities even where that State has not made a declaration, and has chosen not to apply the provisions on Central Authorities for spousal support. As such because Ukraine and Bosnia and Herzegovina have not made a declaration in this respect, so the applications will not necessarily go through Central Authorities, the implication is Norway would not recognise and enforce spousal support applications from these States where the application is not made through the Central Authority. This would imply that the question of scope in this respect is more complicated than the Borrás and Degeling Report suggests. This is important when recognition and enforcement can be refused on this basis.

## IV. Other Forms of Maintenance

Contracting States can also make a declaration to extend the scope of the Convention to cover other kinds of family maintenance.[19] This allows States to choose to extend the application to any maintenance obligation 'arising from a family relationship, parentage, marriage or affinity, including in particular obligations in respect of vulnerable persons.'[20] If a State does choose to extend the scope of the Convention beyond child support and spousal maintenance, then the declarations will only have effect when an application is made by another State that has also made a declaration regarding the specific relationship in the application. Ukraine has made several declarations in this area. For children under 18 this includes obligations from grandparents, stepparents and adult siblings. Obligations also arise in relation to incapacitated adults from their adult children, adult grandchildren, adult siblings and adult stepchildren. However because these declarations only apply bilaterally and no other extensions have been made at this time, it is unclear what effect these declarations will have, if any. The EU declares that within seven years, in light of the experience acquired and other declarations made, it will 'examine the possibility of extending the application of the Convention as a whole to all maintenance obligations arising from a family relationship, parentage, marriage or affinity.'[21] Norway, Albania and Bosnia and Herzegovina have not extended the scope of the Convention beyond child and spousal support.

[18] www.hcch.net/index_en.php?act=status.comment&csid=1067&disp=resdn, accessed 21 May 2014.
[19] 2007 Hague Convention Art 2(3).
[20] Ibid.
[21] www.hcch.net/index_en.php?act=status.comment&csid=1109&disp=resdn, accessed 21 May 2014.

# V. Conclusion

At first reading the provisions on scope in the Convention seem relatively straightforward. However when taking into account the fact that all Contracting States have a variety of means by which they can alter the scope, the final result could be complicated. This is even more so when declarations to alter the scope can only apply between Contracting States that have made the same declarations. Therefore, the scope covered by the Convention could alternate substantially even within a Contracting State, depending on what other Contracting State is involved in that application.[22] The true extent of these variations will only become apparent once the Convention is more widely ratified. If the application is outside the scope of the Convention, as given in that State's declarations and reservations, then the decision may not need to be recognised and enforced.

[22] 'The outcome of this is a complicated network of diverse relations between States which are bound by the new instruments. Clearly, it would be preferable, in the interests of the unification of the rules, both on a general and on a Community-wide basis, to bring about a real streamlining of rules without exceptions. However, diversification and fragmentation are the price which has to be paid for having wider coverage and acceptance of certain instruments.' (Borrás (n 4) 192.)

# 5

# Jurisdiction

## I. Introduction

The Maintenance Regulation and the Hague 2007 Convention differ greatly in this area because the Regulation has direct rules of jurisdiction,[1] whereas the Convention has indirect rules.[2] The significant difference between the instruments is that at the recognition and/or enforcement stage the jurisdictional basis chosen under the Regulation cannot be reviewed by the enforcing courts, but jurisdiction under the Convention can. However, although the procedure is very different some of the grounds of jurisdiction are similar. This chapter will analyse the various grounds of jurisdiction available under the Maintenance Regulation.[3] In doing so it will highlight similarities with and differences from the previous grounds under Brussels I.[4] It will also identify any divergence from the indirect grounds of jurisdiction under the Maintenance Convention in order to draw attention to situations where EU based creditors may have problems getting their orders recognised in a non EU State.

In particular, the chapter will look at the relationship between the Maintenance Regulation and Brussels IIbis[5] in terms of jurisdiction. It will briefly describe the

[1] Council Regulation (EC) 4/2009 of 18 December 2008 on jurisdiction, applicable law, recognition and enforcement of decisions and cooperation in matters relating to maintenance obligations (Maintenance Regulation) [2009] OJ L7/1; M Hellner, 'The Maintenance Regulation: A critical assessment of the Commission's Proposal' in K Boele-Woelki and T Sverdrup, *European Challenges in Contemporary Family Law* (Antwerp, Intersentia, 2009) 343, 350.

[2] (Hague Convention of 23 November 2007 on the International Recovery of Child Support and other forms of Family Maintenance (the 2007 Hague Convention.) The main reason for this is that it is not possible to agree on direct rules at the international level yet. See, W Duncan, 'Jurisdiction to Make and Modify Maintenance Decisions—The Quest for Uniformity' in T Einhorn and K Siehr (eds), *Intercontinental Cooperation through Private International Law Essays in Memory of Peter E. Nygh* (TCM Asser Press, 2004) 89, at 98–105.

[3] A shorter version of this chapter is available at L Walker, 'From Brussels I and the Maintenance Convention to the Maintenance Regulation: Is the Resulting Maintenance Regulation Consistent with the other EU PIL Instruments?' (2013) 6 *Nederlands Internationaal Privaatrecht* 167. The indirect rules of jurisdiction contained in the Convention will be discussed further in ch 8 of this book.

[4] Council Regulation (EC) 44/2001 of 22 December 2000 on jurisdiction and the recognition and enforcement of judgments in civil and commercial matters [2001] OJ L012/1 (Brussels I).

[5] Council Regulation (EC) 2201/2003 of 27 November 2003 on jurisdiction, recognition and enforcement of judgments in matrimonial matters and matters of parental responsibility, repealing Regulation (EC) No 1347/2000 [2003] OJ L 338/1 (Brussels IIbis).

bases of jurisdiction contained in Brussels IIbis to highlight that the jurisdictional grounds are different. This means that two courts, or possibly even three courts, could be determining the different elements of a divorce.[6] The difficulties that may arise for applicants as a result of this, such as exorbitant proceedings, rush to court and the possibility of irreconcilable judgments will be discussed. It will be argued that some form of hierarchy of jurisdiction should have been considered where there are related causes of action, in order to minimise problems for applicants in these cases.

Finally, this chapter will consider the negative provisions on the limitation of the jurisdiction of debtors in modification proceedings. These provisions were discussed in the negotiations to the Convention and are almost identical in both instruments. They are designed to prevent debtors from modifying earlier judgments in a different State to the State where the proceedings were heard first, when the creditor is still habitually resident in that State. However, there are some exceptions to this general rule and these will be discussed.

## II. Jurisdiction in EU Family Law

Jurisdiction in the area of private international law of family law within the EU is rather complicated. This is because the two current family law instruments; the Maintenance Regulation and Brussels IIbis have different grounds of jurisdiction. This could be a problem because sometimes maintenance is related to divorce proceedings (personal status),[7] or parental responsibility proceedings. Therefore, is it really suitable to have varying jurisdictional grounds in the two instruments, where the first court seised is considered to have jurisdiction when any of the grounds are satisfied?[8] As such in divorce there could be up to three different courts dealing with the different aspects of the case, since the EU has separated divorce, maintenance and matrimonial property into different instruments.[9] This

[6] '[I]n many, if not most instances, issues pertaining to maintenance will arise as an ancillary matter in divorce, matrimonial property or parental proceedings, each of which is subject to distinct jurisdictional regimes, and in the case of matrimonial property, a regime not yet the subject of European Harmonisation.' (P Beaumont and P McEleavy, *Anton's Private International Law*, 3rd edn (Edinburgh, SULI/W Green, 2011) 900).

[7] Although many expect that the majority of cross border maintenance cases will be for child support there are likely to be a number of cases for spousal support. A recent study suggests that there are approximately 1 million divorces in the EU each year, and 140,000 of these have an international element. (See http://conflictoflaws.net/2013/new-french-book-on-european-divorce-law/, accessed 23 May 2014.)

[8] Under the Maintenance Regulation if two courts are seised for the same proceedings then the court second seised must stay proceedings until the first court has decided whether it has jurisdiction to hear the case or not (Art 12). In the context of related proceedings the court second seised may stay proceedings but this is not a requirement (Art 13). These rules on *lis pendens* were taken directly from Brussels I (Arts 27 and 28).

[9] No Regulation on matrimonial property has been concluded at this time, but the Commission's proposals are available at http://ec.europa.eu/justice/policies/civil/docs/com_2011_126_en.pdf, and

position is not ideal because a lack of coherence may lead to separate proceedings in different States in relation to divorce and monetary claims arising out of the divorce such as maintenance and matrimonial property claims. The system may encourage longer proceedings in different States at a greater cost, and could also result in irreconcilable judgments, if there is a disagreement on the characterisation of 'maintenance' by two courts hearing different aspects of the case.[10]

The Maintenance Regulation does not clearly address the relationship between itself and Brussels IIbis in terms of these kinds of applications. Due to problems with the characterisation of maintenance in certain situations, it would be better if the Regulation did address its relationship with Brussels IIbis in order to encourage coherence where necessary. The previous relationship between Brussels IIbis and Brussels I was described as this:

> Maintenance obligations are excluded from this Regulation as these are already covered by Council Regulation No 44/2001. The courts having jurisdiction under this Regulation will generally have jurisdiction to rule on maintenance obligations by application of Article 5(2) of Council Regulation No 4/2001.[11]

The new Maintenance Regulation describes potential problems with the earlier jurisdictional bases in Brussels I. It indicates that these should be improved but does not explicitly mention the relationship, in terms of jurisdiction, between Brussels IIbis and itself.[12]

## III. General Grounds of Jurisdiction

There are several grounds of jurisdiction available for maintenance applications, made under the Regulation. Article 3 lays down the general provisions, which are similar to those laid out in Article 5(2) of Brussels I. These are: the court of

http://ec.europa.eu/justice/policies/civil/docs/com_2011_127_en.pdf, accessed 24 May 2014. The UK and Ireland have not opted in to these proposals. See for example *Moore v Moore* [2007] EWCA Civ 361, where the Spanish Court could deal with the divorce and the English Court matrimonial property.

[10] The Regulation gives no definition of the term 'maintenance', but this is addressed to some extent in the decision in C-220/95 *Van den Boogaard v Laumen* [1997] ECR I-1176 (see ch 3). For a discussion of some of the issues in relation to maintenance as a consequence of personal status see D Martiny, 'Maintenance Obligations in the Conflict of Laws' (1994) 247 *Recueil des Cours* 142, 151–52. Bonomi recognises a similar problem in respect of the proposed Regulations on Matrimonial Property and Succession. A Bonomi, 'The Interaction Among the Future EU Instruments on Matrimonial Property, Registered Partnerships and Successions' (2011) 13 *Yearbook of Private International Law* 217, 226–27.

[11] Brussels IIbis Recital 11. Art 5(2) of Brussels I states: 'in the courts for the place where the maintenance creditor is domiciled or habitually resident or, if the matter is ancillary to proceedings concerning the status of a person, in the court which, according to its own law, has jurisdiction to entertain those proceedings, unless that jurisdiction is based solely on the nationality of one of the parties.'

[12] See Maintenance Regulation Recitals 15–19.

the place where either the defendant or creditor is habitually resident.[13] (Under Brussels I, jurisdiction could be based on domicile or habitual residence.[14]) The court which has jurisdiction to entertain proceedings concerning the status of the person if the matter relating to maintenance is ancillary to those proceedings, and that jurisdiction is not based solely on the nationality of one of the parties,[15] or the court which has jurisdiction to entertain proceedings concerning parental responsibility if the matter relating to maintenance is ancillary to those proceedings and that jurisdiction is not based solely on the nationality of one of the parties.[16] This final ground is new and could be useful in consolidating the position between the Maintenance Regulation and Brussels IIbis. These grounds can also be seen in the Hague Convention.[17] However, in the case of the Convention, jurisdiction based on the habitual residence of the creditor, or on the court that can hear a case on status or parental responsibility, are not acceptable grounds of indirect jurisdiction for all States as Contracting States can make reservations in respect of these grounds of jurisdiction.[18] The Regulation does not allow reservations and therefore all Member States accept these grounds of jurisdiction. There

[13] Ibid, Art 3(a) and (b). Here the provision for domicile has been removed and the only basis is the habitual residence of one party. This benefits the creditor as she can sue in her own jurisdiction or the defenders (who would normally be the debtor, unless the debtor is looking for a modification order, meaning that the debtor cannot sue in his own jurisdiction). This is because the creditor is generally seen to be the weaker party in maintenance proceedings. However, given the changes in other parts of the Regulation the bias in favour of the creditor may be going too far. Is it fair that the creditor can sue in her own jurisdiction when in the majority of cases that decision will be automatically enforced in the state of enforcement (debtor's State) without the possibility of challenging the decision? There is no space for the public policy safety valve, and if the debtor considers his rights of defence have been breached he can only challenge this in the State of origin (Art 19, see ch 7 s VI). Further legal aid is available for all creditors in child support cases but not for debtors (Art 46 of the Maintenance Regulation). Therefore, although this ground of jurisdiction is normal in instruments on maintenance (unlike commercial instruments where the rule is the debtor should be sued in his own State) the other developments in the Maintenance Regulation may now mean that this ground of jurisdiction is unfair, and the system taken as a whole may not necessarily ensure the proper administration of justice in relation to debtors. However, it would be preferable to change the recognition and enforcement procedures rather than the jurisdictional grounds in order to resolve this bias (see ch 7 s VIII).

[14] Brussels I Art 5(2) see n 11.

[15] Maintenance Regulation Art 3(c). This is identical to the previous position.

[16] Ibid Art 3(d).

[17] 2007 Hague Convention Arts 20(a)(c) and (f).

[18] In relation to jurisdiction based solely on the habitual residence of the creditor, the US authorities cannot accept this because of the due process clause in the Fourteenth amendment. This 'operates as a limitation on the jurisdiction of state courts to enter judgments affecting rights or interests of non-resident defendants.' (*Kulko v Superior Court of California* 436 U.S. 84 (1978) 91). In order for the US to be able to ratify the Convention it had to be possible to make an exception in this respect because in order for jurisdiction based on the habitual residence of the creditor to be acceptable there has to be some link between the debtor and the forum (see the interesting rules in Art 20 of the Convention and pp 88–93 of A Borrás and J Degeling, 'Explanatory Report on the Convention on the International Recovery of Child Support and other Forms of Family Maintenance (HCCH, 2009) (Borrás and Degeling Report)). Therefore, if a decision made in Europe based solely on the habitual residence of the creditor is to be enforced in the US under the Maintenance Convention, it is possible that the US court may refuse to recognise and declare enforceable the decision. (See ch 8 s III for a full analysis of this reservation). See also, A Borrás, 'The Necessary Flexibility in Applying the New Instruments on Maintenance' in K Boele-Woelki, T Einhorn, D Girsberger, S Symeonides (eds), *Convergence and*

is also no way, under the Regulation, for the enforcing court to review the grounds of jurisdiction used by the court of origin.

The general grounds of jurisdiction under Brussels IIbis are slightly different to the grounds under the Maintenance Regulation. Rather than allowing the applicant (usually equivalent to the creditor) to make an application in either the State in which they or their partner is habitually resident, the grounds are focused firstly on common habitual residence or joint applications.[19] It also allows jurisdiction based on the respondents' habitual residence (which would presumably be the debtor in the majority of maintenance applications).[20] In addition, Brussels IIbis allows jurisdiction based on the applicant's habitual residence, but this is limited as it requires that the applicant has been resident in a particular State for a certain period of time, before being able to use this connecting factor.[21] The main reason behind this is to restrict the jurisdiction of the applicant. This is not the case under the Maintenance Regulation, where the creditor can seise a court in a Member State where either party is habitually resident and there are no qualifications to this, because in maintenance the creditor is seen as the weaker party. Therefore, technically divorce proceedings could be started in one State and maintenance proceedings in another, because the general grounds are different.[22]

## IV. Lack of Coherence and Possible Solutions

Article 3(c) of the Maintenance Regulation does allow for jurisdiction in the same courts that are determining status, but this is an alternative, and it is not required that this ground is used.[23] Divorce and spousal maintenance proceedings can have the same objective,[24] in the sense that you cannot have divorce without a decision on spousal maintenance as it is essentially an outcome of the divorce whether some form of maintenance will be provided or not.[25] Since the petitioner would generally want a judgment that not only clarifies his status but also gives an order for maintenance (and probably matrimonial property), it is questionable whether

*Divergence in Private International Law, Liber Amicorum Kurt Siehr* (The Hague, Eleven International Publishing & Schulthess 2010) 173, 184.

[19] See Brussels IIbis Art 3(a) points i, ii and iv.

[20] Ibid, Art 3(a) point iii.

[21] Ibid, Art 3(a) points v and vi.

[22] Tebbens considers that 'legal practitioners dealing with international divorce litigation in Europe are confronted with a startling multiple fragmentation'. (H Tebbens, 'Divorce—A Fundamental Right?' in Permanent Bureau (eds), *A Commitment to Private International Law* (The Hague, Intersentia, 2013) 123, 133.

[23] See Maintenance Regulation Art 13 on related actions which only suggests that the court seised second 'may' stay proceedings.

[24] See, C-406/92 *The owners of the cargo lately laden on board the ship 'Tatry' v The owners of the ship 'Maciej Rataj'* [1994] ECR I-5460, paras 38–41.

[25] See ch 1 s V.

it is correct to always treat divorce and maintenance as distinct claims. There are two different approaches to this. The first is that they are always treated as distinct claims with different jurisdictional bases.[26] The alternative is that the related claims are dealt with by the same court.

> However, in divorce proceedings especially jurisdiction under domestic law was extended for *practical reasons* to ancillary claims for maintenance. As part of divorce proceedings an order for payment of maintenance can be made in favour of the spouse and the children of the union. These are regarded as 'consequential matters' (*Folgesachen*). This is the practice in France, Germany (*Verbundzuständigkeit*), and Sweden.
>
> The position that both proceedings emerge from the same complex and all matters should be adjudicated together has gained ground. Where there is jurisdiction in matters of family status, the court is also competent to deal with an ancillary order for maintenance. This is also the approach of English law. Divorce is seen as a complex of several issues; the financial consequences constitute only one of them.[27]

There is a trend towards dealing with ancillary claims for maintenance in the same jurisdiction as the divorce case. This is more practical than dealing with the claims separately in different jurisdictions, where the claims are related, and helps ensure certainty for applicants.

Although there is a trend towards dealing with these claims together and they are seen as related proceedings in the sense that they have the same objective, the dissolution of the marriage, the claims can be dealt with by different courts under the European Union system. Under the rules on *lis pendens* and related actions, taken directly from Brussels I, the court first seised must hear the case if it has jurisdiction under one of the heads of jurisdiction. The court first seised has no discretion to decline jurisdiction, if it has jurisdiction, whether on *forum non conveniens* or any other grounds.[28]

Despite the fact that these claims should be dealt with together and are seen as related proceedings in the sense that they have the same 'objective',[29] the *lis pendens* provision would not necessarily apply. This is because although the two sets of proceedings could be considered to have the same objective, it is unlikely that the court second seised of these connected proceedings would pronounce the two proceedings as having the 'same cause of action' as referred to in the *lis pendens* provision. In the *Tatry* case the Court of Justice of the European Union (CJEU) distinguished between the English language version of the Brussels Convention and the other language versions.[30] This is because the other language versions of the Brussels Convention distinguish between 'objective' and 'cause of action'.

[26] See, Martiny (n 10) 255.

[27] Ibid, 255 (emphasis added).

[28] U Magnus and P Mankowski, *Brussels I Regulation*, 2nd edn (Munich, Sellier, 2012) 566–68. But cf Art 15 Brussels IIbis, which allows transfer of jurisdiction to a court better placed to hear the case in relation to children. Unfortunately, there is no equivalent in the Maintenance Regulation and the court first seised must hear the case.

[29] See, *The 'Tatry'* (n 24) where the CJEU discusses the object of the action at paras 41–43.

[30] Ibid, para 38.

The CJEU considered that even though the English language version does not distinguish between cause of action and objective, that 'language version must be construed in the same manner as the majority of the other language versions in which the distinction is made'.[31]

The distinction between 'same objective' and 'same cause of action' may be regarded as minimal and in other situations would not make too much difference. However, in the context of maintenance and divorce proceedings the 'same objective' in the sense of 'dissolution of the marriage' and clean break on divorce, is very different to considering that the proceedings have the 'same cause of action' as required by the English language version of the Maintenance Regulation. It is unclear whether the reasoning in the *Tatry*,[32] which refers to the same objective, would apply to claims which do not have the same cause of action. This seems very unlikely as the Article refers to action and not objective, and the French and Spanish versions of the text refer to the same objective 'and' the same cause of action, rather than the same objective 'or' the same cause of action.[33] Therefore, for practical reasons Article 12 would have been more flexible if it had referred to 'objective' rather than 'action'. This would have meant that the court second seised in maintenance as an ancillary proceeding should have stayed proceedings, which would have created more certainty for parties. This is particularly important because irreconcilable judgments which pose a risk of

> non-enforcement should be avoided at the earliest stage possible in order to save the parties and the judicial systems involved time and money—not only economic values but also, in respect to the parties, important components of the right to effective access to justice as guaranteed by and to be optimised under Article 6(1) ECHR as well as under Community law itself.[34]

This is critical in maintenance disputes because of problems relating to the characterisation of maintenance claims which could vary from jurisdiction to jurisdiction.[35]

[31] Ibid.

[32] Ibid, para 43.

[33] The French language version of the Maintenance Regulation refers to both the object and the cause of the action ('Lorsque des demandes ayant le même objet *et* la meme cause'). The Spanish text makes the same distinction ('Si se formulasen demandas con el mismo objeto *y* la misma causa'). However, although these language versions list both the words as distinct terms, it is required that both the object and the cause of action are the same. Therefore, this should not make any difference because even though the object might be the same the cause of action is not.

[34] Weller in B Hess, T Pfeiffer and P Schlosser, *The Brussels I Regulation 44/2001. The Heidelberg Report on the Application of Regulation Brussels I in 25 Member States* (Study JLS/C4/2005/03), Munich: Verlag CH Beck 2008 (Heidelberg Report) 174. See also below on recognition and enforcement at ch 7 s III.

[35] See above at ch 3 s III. A further problem with the rules on *lis pendens* and related actions, is that they only apply to proceedings in another Member State and not proceedings in a third State. Therefore, spousal maintenance proceedings could be ongoing in the UK and America at the same time. There would be no obligation to stay either of the proceedings so ultimately you could end up with two orders. In fact, the courts in EU Member States would not be able to decline jurisdiction in favour of a non-EU court even where the two pending applications have the same cause of action. If

Since it is not possible to classify divorce and maintenance proceedings as the 'same cause of action'; it is Article 13 that applies rather than Article 12. Article 13 requires that the action is related, and where it is it gives some form of discretion to the court second seised to decide whether to stay proceedings or not. The Article is designed to apply where actions 'are so closely connected that it is expedient to hear and determine them together to avoid the risk of irreconcilable judgments resulting from separate proceedings.'[36] According to the CJEU (when ruling on the same provision in the Brussels Convention) Article 13 should be given a broad interpretation.[37] Its purpose is 'to improve the coordination in the exercise of judicial functions within the Community and to avoid conflicting and contradictory decisions, even where the separate enforcement of each is not precluded'.[38] Maintenance and divorce proceedings can result in separately enforceable judgments, but they are related. However they will not necessarily result in conflicting judgments, but may do if the divorce court gives some allocation of maintenance as an interim payment.[39] Therefore, the question of whether Article 13 can actually be used and how often it will be used is not clear at this point. Where, the claims are generally combined under the national law of the court second seised, then that court should decline jurisdiction under Article 13. If Article 13 is not used by the court second seised then this may create difficulties and uncertainty for the parties.

There are a broad variety of grounds of general jurisdiction under the Maintenance Regulation, with not only the grounds under the Maintenance Regulation being suitable but also those under Brussels IIbis if the claim for maintenance is related to divorce proceedings. The availability of numerous alternative grounds of jurisdiction has been criticised in the past as this can encourage a rush to court.[40] This is a problem which tends to benefit the stronger party as they are more likely to be in a position to seek legal advice. The lawyer can then direct them to the court where they would be likely to get the most advantageous result. This

the two subsequent judgments conflict with each other, they would be irreconcilable and therefore could be refused recognition under Art 24(d) or Art 21(2). The Brussels I recast includes discretionary provisions on *lis pendens* and related actions that apply to third States (Regulation (EU) 1215/2012 of the European Parliament and of the Council of 12 December 2012 on jurisdiction and the recognition and enforcement of judgments in civil and commercial matters (recast) [2012] OJ L351/1(Brussels I recast) Art 33 and see Recital 23).

[36] Maintenance Regulation Art 13(3).

[37] See, *The 'Tatry'* (n 24) para 53.

[38] Ibid, para 55.

[39] See also *Hoffmann v Krieg* [1988] ECR 645 at paras 21–25 where a maintenance decision was considered irreconcilable with a divorce decision. This was because the maintenance agreement in the case presupposed the existence of a matrimonial relationship, which no longer existed because of the divorce.

[40] For an analysis of the problems resulting from alternative grounds of jurisdiction see M Ni Shuilleabhain, 'Ten Years of European Family Law: Retrospective Reflections from a Common Law Perspective' (2010) 59 *International and Comparative Law Quarterly* 1021; B Campuzano Diaz, 'The Coordination of the EU Regulations on Divorce and Matrimonial Property' (2011) 13 *Yearbook of Private International Law* 233 and D Hodson, 'Quo Vadis? The Family Lawyer Goes Forum Shopping' (2012) *Private Client Business* 158.

problem is increased by the *lis pendens* rule which gives advantage to the court first seised. The *lis pendens* rule is important in order to ensure legal certainty, but it will not help in situations where one court is seised for divorce proceedings and another court is seised for maintenance. Unfortunately the rule on related actions that may apply does not necessarily guarantee legal certainty because it is at the discretion of the court second seised whether the proceedings will be stayed. This is problematic because the rules are designed to ensure the 'proper administration of justice'.[41] Further, related judgments are then sometimes dealt with badly at the recognition and enforcement stage if they are deemed to be 'mutually exclusive' when in actual fact they are not.[42] These factors highlight the benefits of a more coherent approach to cross border family law. Campuzano Diaz considers that:

> [the] EU Private International Law system is quite complex and forces us to apply several Regulations for solving a matrimonial dispute and the issues arising from it. In addition the Regulations differ in their substantive and territorial scope and have to be supplemented in some cases by uniform conflict of law rules elaborated outside the EU, notably by The Hague Conference on Private International Law. A great effort to explain this system will be required if we want it to be correctly understood and applied by legal practitioners. In the future when the negotiation of all the pieces of this fragmentary system is concluded, EU institutions should consider the possible compilation of this system into a single text.[43]

It is doubtful that matrimonial disputes will be able to be resolved under one Regulation anytime soon. However, a way of avoiding this problem but maintaining a variety of grounds of jurisdiction would be to create a hierarchy of jurisdictional grounds.[44] This would improve legal certainty and help protect the weaker party. This could be particularly beneficial in relation to spousal maintenance obligations where the court determining status can have jurisdiction under Article 3(c). This ground for jurisdiction could be placed first in order to ensure that the court that has jurisdiction in divorce also has jurisdiction for spousal maintenance. This would be the court that was seised for divorce and it would have to be established under one of the grounds provided in Brussels IIbis. That court would then deal with the divorce and all the related financial matters,[45] but this

[41] Weller, 'Heidelberg Report' (n 34) 175. This also highlights the benefits of a more coherent approach to cross border family law within the EU.

[42] *Macualay v Macaulay* [1991] 1 WLR 179, discussed at ch 7 s III.

[43] Campuzano Diaz (n 40) 252–53. Although we are still probably a long way away from a single text, the EU institutions should try to coordinate the system and make it as coherent as possible so that the texts complement each other as much as possible. Further, the more coherent the system is, the easier it will be to ultimately create a single text as the instruments will already be linked.

[44] See, EPEC, Study to inform a subsequent Impact Assessment on the Commission proposal on Jurisdiction and Applicable Law in Divorce Matters, available at http://edz.bib.uni-mannheim.de/daten/edz-k/gdj/05/study.pdf, accessed 23 May 2014. It is argued that Brussels IIbis could be improved by introducing a hierarchy of grounds in order to increase legal certainty and protect the weaker party (p 95, see also 48–49 and 93).

[45] It is important to note that this court would not have to deal with parental responsibility questions in cases where children were involved. This is because Art 15 Brussels IIbis contains a helpful provision that allows a transfer of court in matters relating to children when necessary.

jurisdiction would not be retained after the divorce is finalised. The various alternative grounds under Brussels IIbis are far from perfect,[46] and these should also be tightened, but it would be a first step towards a more coherent system. Although the court that has jurisdiction in divorce may not necessarily be the most suitable court, like in *Moore v Moore*,[47] there would have to be a close enough connection in order for the jurisdiction to be established in the first place.

Such an approach would benefit applicants in the vast majority of cases because it would increase legal certainty and decrease exorbitant proceedings. This would also be a step towards preventing irreconcilable judgments between the decision of the divorce court, which may include provisional measures for maintenance, and the decision of the court dealing with the maintenance claim. Applicants resident in all Member States would benefit from this, including those resident in the UK. To complete the picture a similar provision should be included in any future instruments on matrimonial property in order to ensure coherence in decisions on divorce and ancillary matters.[48] This is particularly important because the distinction between maintenance and matrimonial property is not always clear, and it is very unlikely that the terms will be interpreted 'autonomously' throughout the EU.[49]

[46] 'The list of seven alternative fora, which is criticized even with respect to divorce, seems inadequate in a proposal aimed at fixing the specific competent court' (Campuzano Diaz (n 40) 239). A full analysis of the grounds in Brussels IIbis is outside the scope of this book but some of the problems with the variety of alternative grounds of jurisdiction available, such as forum shopping, rush to court and failure to engage in mediation are highlighted in: S Marinai, 'Matrimonial Matters and the Harmonization of Conflict of Laws: A Way to Reduce the Role of Public Policy as a Ground for Non-recognition of Judgments' (2011) 13 *Yearbook of Private International Law* 255, 260–61; Ni Shuilleabhain (n 40); and Hodson (n 40).

[47] *Moore v Moore* [2007] EWCA Civ 361. In this case the divorce proceedings were heard before the Spanish Court. However, it was decided that the English Court could have jurisdiction to hear the other aspects relating to the division of wealth because 'the connection with this jurisdiction [is] "overwhelming". First, both the husband and the wife are English. They married and spent most of their married life here. Indeed, their marital life in Spain, before they separated, was measured not in years but in months' (503–04).

[48] The proposal on matrimonial property does attempt to coordinate jurisdiction in this area but like in the Maintenance Regulation, there is no requirement to apply the relevant Article as it contains caveats. The 'court with jurisdiction for divorce proceedings, legal separation or marriage annulment in accordance with Regulation (EC) 2201/2003 *may*, if the spouses agree, extend its jurisdiction to the liquidation of the matrimonial property following the separation procedure and to other matters concerning the matrimonial property arising from this procedure.' (Art 4 of the proposal (n 9) emphasis added.) Since the Article is not definitive then this will not fully solve the problem of characterisation of financial dissolution on divorce. In addition, although the article is designed to respect party autonomy, it may have a negative impact on the weaker party if a richer party who has sought detailed legal advice refuses to accept the jurisdiction of the divorce court for matrimonial property. For a discussion of the proposed matrimonial property regime and its coordination with respect to international jurisdiction, see Campuzano Diaz (n 40) 236–45.

[49] See ch 3 s IV. See also C Nagy, 'Love and Money: Problems of Characterisation in Matrimonial Property and Maintenance Matters in the European Union' and M Torga, 'Drawing a Demarcating Line between Spousal Maintenance Obligations and Matrimonial Property in the Context of the New Instruments of European Union Private International Law' both in Beaumont et al (eds), *The Recovery of Maintenance in the EU and Worldwide* (Oxford, Hart Publishing, 2014) at 411 and 425.

The necessary jurisdiction of the divorce court would only apply in the first instance, when that court was still determining status, as implied by the wording of Article 3(c) currently. After the divorce and related proceedings are finalised the requirement to use Article 3(c) would end. Any revision of the maintenance obligation (in cases where the award does not constitute a clean break) could be made by a different court at a later date as long as the rules on modification were complied with.[50] Therefore the problem of *perpetuatio juris* which occurred under the Enforcement Convention would not arise under the proposed formula.[51] The purpose of the proposed hierarchy is not to forever tie the parties to the jurisdiction of the divorce court, but to improve certainty for parties in respect of divorce and related proceedings. This could prevent conflicting judgments and possibly numerous proceedings in this area before different jurisdictions. It is also designed to prevent irreconcilable judgments arising either in terms of the distinction between maintenance and matrimonial property, or in relation to interim maintenance payments authorised by the divorce court which may conflict with the decision on maintenance reached by another court.

However, where the divorce involves children the numerous grounds for divorce create further problems, as these will not necessarily be applicable to parental responsibility claims. This is apparent in *EA v AP*,[52] where child support proceedings were delayed due to problems with jurisdiction. This is a very interesting case, because if the father had not seised the Italian courts, under one of the numerous grounds of jurisdiction available under Brussels IIbis, then it would be an internal decision on child support and maintenance as all parties are still resident in London. The parents are Italian, but have lived all their married life in London, and their children have always lived in London. The husband petitioned for separation, a necessary precursor to divorce, in Italy on 28 February 2012. The parties' common nationality is an acceptable divorce jurisdiction, under the numerous grounds for divorce listed under Brussels IIbis.[53]

As well as legal separation the husband also sought orders for:

- Acknowledgement of self-sufficiency so that neither party would have to pay spousal maintenance.
- Joint parental responsibility.
- Allocation of the family home.
- Quantification of the husband's liability to pay child maintenance, depending on who the family home was allocated to.
- Payment of school fees.
- An acknowledgment of the matrimonial property regime adopted.[54]

50 See below at s VIII.

51 See ch 2 at p 26.

52 *EA v AP* [2013] EWHC 2344 (Fam).

53 Brussels IIbis Art 3(b).

54 *EA v AP* (n 52) para 2.

The wife lodged similar proceedings in England and Wales on 12 March 2012, on the basis of the parties' habitual residence.[55] On 2 October 2012 the wife applied for child support from the Child Support Agency.[56] On 16 November 2012 an Italian judge, sitting alone, acknowledged that the Italian courts had jurisdiction to adjudicate the separation. Flowing from that she also said, correctly, that the Italian courts had jurisdiction to make spousal maintenance orders under the Maintenance Regulation which allows the court determining status to also determine maintenance, if the maintenance claim is ancillary to these proceedings.[57] The judge then held that the Italian Court had no jurisdiction to rule on parental responsibility as this had to be done by the courts of the children's habitual residence,[58] so England. As a result there was no jurisdiction to rule on child maintenance as this had to be done either by the courts determining parental responsibility, or the court that had jurisdiction under one of the other relevant grounds in the Maintenance Regulation. The Italian judge was correct because jurisdiction for parental child support should not be determined under Article 3(c) status, when there is no question of status in relation to the children. It is clear that the mother and father are the parents of these children and this is not in dispute. The only related question that concerns the children in this case is parental responsibility, for which the Italian courts do not have jurisdiction. Further, given that the whole family is still living in England, it seems ridiculous that the questions of parental responsibility and child support can become cross border issues when they could be dealt with internally as all parties were residing in London at the relevant time.[59]

On 27 December 2012 the father applied, to the Supreme Court of Cassation in Italy, for a review of jurisdiction.[60] This application was made on the basis that under Italian law a single judge is not allowed to rule on jurisdiction. The English judge noted that the wife could not currently seek a decision on child support in Italy because there was currently no jurisdiction there. However the judge concluded that because a new decision on jurisdiction was pending it would be better to stay proceedings in England under Article 12 until the Italian Supreme Court had given its ruling. This case indicates the difficulty with the numerous alternative grounds of divorce jurisdiction in Brussels IIbis. The decision taken by the Italian judge at first instance is sensible because if the Italian courts dealt with divorce, maintenance and the distribution of property then this would resolve any problems with characterisation. The English courts can resolve parental

[55] Ibid, para 4. This ground of jurisdiction is available under Art 3(a) Brussels IIbis, a stay has been granted in relation to this application.

[56] *EA v AP* (n 52) para 6.

[57] Maintenance Regulation Art 3(c).

[58] Art 9 Brussels IIbis. It is possible for the divorce court to hear parental responsibility proceedings, but only if the parties agree to this, Art 12 Brussels IIbis.

[59] *EA v AP* (n 52) para 1.

[60] Ibid, para 13. Under Italian law, this does not constitute an appeal but a new application.

responsibility and award child maintenance, which would be internal decisions (given and enforced in England) for as long as the whole family remains in the UK.

An alternative method of solving the problem of lack of coordination, which was suggested in the past by the Institut de droit international, is the unification of the applicable law.[61] The same law would be applied to the whole range of related issues, such as 'maintenance obligations and maintenance payments, particularly in respect of the consequences of divorce, according to which one should start with the recognition of a final divorce settlement by the parties governed by one law and recognised abroad.'[62] Either approach could reach the desired result, however coherence in jurisdiction would create a higher degree of certainty. If different courts are dealing with different aspects of a case, it is unclear how it could be ensured that each court applied the same law even if there was a Regulation which attempted to standardise this. However it would appear that unification across this area in the EU is very difficult. Rome III which only attempts to harmonise applicable law on divorce (specifically excluding maintenance and matrimonial property) and therefore unable to address the overall coordination of applicable law in family law, was initially only accepted by 14 of the Member States.[63] Applicable law in maintenance is dealt with by the Hague Protocol which applies in all Member States except the UK and Denmark,[64] and the proposed regulation on matrimonial property would regulate applicable law separately in this context along with jurisdiction and recognition and enforcement.[65] The lack of uptake of Rome III and the variety of documents available in this area suggests that the overall coordination of applicable law in family matters seems extremely unrealistic any time in the near future.[66] Further, even if harmonisation was achieved in this area and each court did apply the same law, the courts may interpret the law differently which would still lead to irreconcilable decisions if the characterisation of maintenance and matrimonial property conflicted.

[61] See, Martiny (n 10) 219. This approach is also advocated by Nagy, see C Nagy, 'Love and Money: Problems of Characterisation in Matrimonial Property and Maintenance Matters in the European Union' in Beaumont et al (eds) (n 49).

[62] Martiny, Ibid.

[63] Council Regulation (EU) 1259/2010 of 20 December 2010 on implementing enhanced cooperation in the area of the law applicable to divorce and legal separation [2010] OJ L 343/10 (Rome III) Recital 6. The regulation applies to: Belgium, Bulgaria, Germany, Spain, France, Italy, Latvia, Luxembourg, Hungary, Malta, Austria, Portugal, Romania and Slovenia. It is also noted that this only attempted to regulate applicable law on divorce. The Protocol regulates applicable law in relation to maintenance (in all Member States except for two), but there was no attempt to create coherence between the two. Further, the rules on applicable law in the Protocol do not regulate all aspects of a maintenance application such as parentage or status which creates further problems (see ch 1 s V and ch 3 s II).

[64] However in many cases this results in the application of the law of the forum (see ch 6 for more details) therefore this is not particularly helpful in this regard, further indicating that the key is resolving incoherence with jurisdiction.

[65] See the European Commission's proposal (n 9) at pp 7–9 for information on the rules relating to applicable law.

[66] For more information on the applicable law regime see Campuzano Diaz (n 40) 245–52, and Tebbens (n 22) 127–31.

Alternatively, if only one court is dealing with all the aspects of the case that court has to reach a decision that is consistent, and therefore capable of being enforced in another State. Even if that court is required to apply a different law to different aspects of the case, there cannot be two irreconcilable decisions because, the overall judgment by that one court would have to be coherent. Consequently, the most efficient way of creating legal certainty for parties is to unify jurisdiction in divorce and ancillary proceedings, by creating a hierarchy of jurisdiction across the relevant EU Regulations. The benefit of combining the different elements of such cases so that they are heard by one court has already been recognised by certain States;[67] therefore this would be a suitable amendment that should be made in the future.

## V. Choice of Court

Individuals are also given the option to designate a court.[68] This is important in order to protect the principle of party autonomy. However, the Maintenance Regulation limits this choice in an attempt to keep forum shopping to a minimum. The Regulation also prevents parties from designating a court where the maintenance obligation is in respect of a child who is less than 18 years old, in order to protect the interests of the child.[69] Under Article 4 the parties can select either a court in a country where one of the parties is habitually resident, or a court in a country where one of the parties is a national.[70] Where the maintenance obligation relates to spouses or former spouses, they can also designate the court which has jurisdiction to determine their marriage disputes, or the court of the Member State where they last had a common habitual residence, provided that that residence lasted for a year.[71] Any agreement has to be in writing.[72]

The provision for party autonomy in the Regulation should not be too problematic, as the choice of the parties is quite limited. This should prevent erroneous choices of jurisdiction. This is very different to the old position under Brussels I where the Article on prorogation of jurisdiction allowed the parties to select any court and covered child maintenance.[73] This highlights one of the reasons why

[67] See n 27 above.

[68] Maintenance Regulation Art 4.

[69] Ibid, Art 4(3). However, it has been argued that this distinction is not necessary, see P Bremner, 'The EU Maintenance Regulation: A Qualified Success for European Family Law' (2010) *Kings Student Law Review* 5, 15 and Hellner (n 1) 349.

[70] Maintenance Regulation Art 4(1)(a) and (b).

[71] Ibid, Art 4(1)(c). See, J Carruthers, 'Party Autonomy in the Legal Regulation of Adult Relationships: What Place for Party Choice in Private International Law?' (2012) 61 *International and Comparative Law Quarterly* 881, 897.

[72] Ibid, Art 4(2).

[73] Art 23 Brussels I. See the decision in *M v V* [2010] EWHC 1453 (Fam) where a jurisdiction agreement in relation to a child was upheld by the English Court.

dealing with maintenance under a regulation that was primarily designed for non-family law matters was problematic. However, it is interesting to note that under the Hague Convention there are in fact no limitations in the choice of court provision, except that it should not apply to children.[74] There is no reference in the Borrás and Degeling Report as to why this provision was left open, so that the parties could choose virtually any State.[75] The provision in the Regulation is more sensible in this respect. It can limit forum shopping and the ability of parties to make erroneous choices of jurisdiction that may benefit one party a great deal more than the other, especially when it is a court in a State that the parties have minimal or no links with.

## VI. Jurisdiction Based on the Appearance of the Defendant

Article 5 sets out a rule that is designed to prevent delays in proceedings. This provides that if 'the defendant enters an appearance before a court, and the appearance is not to contest jurisdiction, then that court will be considered to have jurisdiction for the purposes of the Regulation'.[76] This simply prevents the defendant from contesting the jurisdiction at a later date, if it appears that the defendant has already accepted the jurisdiction. The policy behind the provision is party autonomy, as it is effectively 'consent based jurisdiction.'[77] The provision should stop lengthy delays caused by disputes on jurisdiction, unless the defendant is well informed and contests the jurisdiction straight away. Potentially this is also beneficial as it could cut the cost of court proceedings. However, this may harm the most vulnerable. Those with enough money to spend on court proceedings will probably seek legal advice in the first place and be aware that they have to contest the jurisdiction straight away, whereas those with little means may just appear in court and not be aware of the consequences. Therefore, although designed to limit ongoing jurisdictional disputes this provision may have an adverse effect on the weaker party.

There is no equivalent provision in Brussels IIbis or the Hague Convention. However, the Brussels I recast contains a provision that is designed to protect the

[74] 2007 Hague Convention Art 20(1)(e).

[75] See ch 8 s III. A possible explanation is that adults were considered to be equal and therefore it was not necessary to protect a potentially weaker party, although this might not always be the case. Although compare this with applicable law, where vulnerable adults are specifically excluded from designating a law (see ch 6, nn 110 and 112).

[76] Maintenance Regulation Art 5 and see Art 24 of Brussels I.

[77] P Beaumont, 'International Family Law in Europe—the Maintenance Project, the Hague Conference and the EC: A Triumph of Reverse Subsidiarity' (2009) 73 *Rabels Zeitschrift* 509, 534.

weaker party in cases where jurisdiction is based on submission.[78] The Article applies to the policy holder, the insured or a beneficiary in insurance contracts, the injured party (in insurance contract cases) and the consumer or employee when they are the defendant. In these particular situations, a court cannot assume jurisdiction unless it has ensured that 'the defendant is informed of his right to contest the jurisdiction of the court and of the consequences of entering or not entering an appearance.'[79] This provision ensures that the most vulnerable are protected. A similar provision in the Maintenance Regulation in order to guarantee that defenders are aware of the consequences of their actions would be useful, for those who may not seek legal advice before entering an appearance in court and thus unknowingly submit to the jurisdiction.

## VII. Subsidiary Jurisdiction and *Forum Necessitatis*—No Room for National Law

The Regulation departs from the previous position under Brussels I because it removes the requirement that the defendant is domiciled in a Member State.

> In order to preserve the interests of maintenance creditors and to promote the proper administration of justice within the European Union, the rules on jurisdiction as they result from Regulation (EC) No 44/2001 should be adapted. The circumstance that the defendant is habitually resident in a third State should no longer entail the non-application of Community rules on jurisdiction, and there should no longer be any referral to national law. This Regulation should therefore determine the cases in which a court in a Member State may exercise subsidiary jurisdiction.[80]

This is done under Article 6 which provides for subsidiary jurisdiction where no court has jurisdiction under Articles 3, 4 and 5, thus neither the defendant nor the creditor is habitually resident in the EU. However, Article 6 would only apply in limited circumstances because it requires that the parties have a common nationality. Therefore, although the position has changed the defendant is still protected because the rules of the Regulation will only apply where the parties have a common nationality and it will be the court of the State that the defendant is a national of that has jurisdiction to hear the case. Brussels IIbis does not include a similar basis of jurisdiction. Instead it provides for residual jurisdiction under Article 7. This means that where no State has jurisdiction under the grounds provided then it is left to national law to determine whether that court has jurisdiction or not.

[78] Brussels I recast Art 26(2).
[79] Ibid.
[80] Maintenance Regulation Recital 15.

In addition to the rules on subsidiary jurisdiction the Regulation also includes a *forum necessitatis* rule.

> Where no court of a Member State has jurisdiction pursuant to Articles 3, 4, 5 and 6, the courts of a Member State may, on an exceptional basis, hear the case if proceedings cannot reasonably be brought or conducted or would be impossible in a third State with which the dispute is closely connected. The dispute must have a sufficient connection with the Member State of the court seised.[81]

It seems unlikely that this provision will be used very often. It is suggested that such a situation 'may be deemed to exist when proceedings prove impossible in the third State in question, for example because of civil war, or when an applicant cannot reasonably be expected to initiate or conduct proceedings in that State.'[82]

However, it is questionable whether it is appropriate to extend the provisions of the Regulation to those living in third States when neither Brussels IIbis nor Brussels I does this.[83] Brussels IIbis is in the process of being reviewed and the rules on residual jurisdiction may change in this respect. It has been suggested that the current rules on residual jurisdiction are insufficient as the law of some States protects nationals who have moved abroad while the law of other States does not.[84] Therefore the impact assessment recommended that rules on residual jurisdiction should be harmonised in order to increase legal certainty for EU citizens living in third States.[85] It has also been suggested that a *forum necessitatis* rule shall be included in Brussels IIbis in respect of disputes between adults only.[86] Since the *forum necessitatis* rule in the Maintenance Regulation includes a

[81] Ibid, Art 7. This is very different to the position under Brussels IIbis (Arts 7 and 14) and Brussels I (Art 4) where the Regulations include provisions on residual jurisdiction. This means States can then apply the national law to determine if they have jurisdiction rather than continuing to apply EU law. The Brussels I recast (Art 6) maintains the application of national law when the defendant is domiciled outside the EU and does not contain a *forum necessitatis* rule. Where the defendant is not an EU domiciliary the national law rules are only set aside in specific circumstances either where the parties have chosen a court or the case relates to a specific type of contract such as a consumer contract (Art 18), an employment contract (Art 21) or an area where the nature of the dispute requires that a certain court must have exclusive jurisdiction (Art 24). A study was carried out on residual jurisdiction under Brussels I. The main point of the report was to focus on 'which connecting factors should be retained if the rules on jurisdiction for defendants domiciled outside the EU were to be harmonized' (Professor A Nuyts, Study on Residual Jurisdiction, JLS/C4/2005/07-30-CE)0040309/00-37 (2007) 14). However, it was concluded that these rules should not be harmonised, except in relation to consumer and employment contracts, and the rules in the new Brussels I in this area remain virtually the same. '[T]he proposal to replace subsidiary jurisdiction remains on politically thin ground. Just as the Commission's argument for the necessity of the Rome II Regulation was scrutinised by Dickinson, the arguments presented by the Commission *vis-à-vis* the proposal to amend subsidiary jurisdiction rules in line with the Brussels I Regulation must be scrutinised further.' L Gillies, 'Creation of Subsidiary Jurisdiction Rules in the Recast of Brussels I: Back to the Drawing Board?' (2012) 8 *Journal of Private International Law* 489, 507.

[82] Maintenance Regulation Recital 16.

[83] There 'is no limitation in the geographic scope of the proposed Regulation.' Hellner (n 1) 347, and see n 81.

[84] See EPEC Study (n 44) 7–8 and 50.

[85] Ibid, see 79–80 and 95.

[86] See Nuyts (n 81) 10–11.

sufficient connection clause then it is recognised that the inclusion of this provision is to try and protect parties who have moved to third States. Therefore it should only apply in specific circumstances, such as, where one of the spouses is an EU national,[87] and the courts in the State they have moved to will not hear the case. Despite this it is questionable whether it is appropriate to extend rules established by the European Union in the context of maintenance to defendants domiciled in third States.

One of the reasons that such a provision was not included in the Brussels I recast was because the national law provisions are wider than those contained in the Regulation. In fact even exorbitant heads of jurisdiction are applicable.[88] Therefore the retention of national law grounds where the defendant is domiciled in a third State could actually extend to a wider application of the recognition and enforcement rules in Brussels I in these types of applications, than if harmonised European rules on jurisdiction applied. It is not clear what the correct position is. Although the Maintenance Regulation has a greater impact on national law the impact on parties resident in third States may be narrower than that under Brussels I, because some national laws may have wider grounds than the Regulation itself. A positive aspect of the rules under the Maintenance Regulation is that they increase certainty for defendants residing in third States, as it is clear in what situations the Regulation will apply. The Maintenance Regulation stands alone in this context and it is clear that in terms of Brussels I the 'Commission's proposal to fully harmonise subsidiary jurisdiction rules, in the words of Lord Mance, goes beyond what is (currently) necessary to ensure "certainty, confidence and allegiance"'.[89] Consequently, the European system of private international law is currently divided on what the most appropriate approach is in this context.

## VIII. Limits on Bringing Proceedings

The Maintenance Regulation, in light of the work completed under the Convention, introduces a provision to limit the jurisdiction of debtors if they bring proceedings to modify a decision.[90] The purpose of the provision is to prevent a debtor who moves to another State to then seek modification of a maintenance obligation in that State. The general rule is that when a decision has been given by courts in the State of the habitual residence of the creditor, proceedings

[87] Maintenance Regulation Recital 16.

[88] B Hess, 'The Brussels I Regulation: Recent Case Law of the Court of Justice and the Commission's Proposed Recast' (2012) 49 *Common Market Law Review* 1075, 1105.

[89] Gillies (n 81) 512.

[90] Maintenance Regulation Art 8 and Recital 17. These provisions are taken directly from Art 18 of the Hague Convention, and the Regulation even includes the Contracting States to the Hague Convention in the rules under Art 8.

cannot be brought in another State by the debtor for as long as the creditor remains habitually resident in the State where the decision was given.[91]

There are some exceptions to this general rule. It does not apply where the parties have designated a court to have jurisdiction to assess the dispute under Article 4.[92] This allows the debtor to approach a court in the agreed jurisdiction and the general rule in Article 8 will not apply. The exception also applies if the creditor submits to the jurisdiction,[93] which allows the rule in Article 5 to apply to these cases. If the requirements in Article 5 are met then the general rule in Article 8 will not apply. This provision may have undesirable consequences for creditors who are not well informed of the rules under the Regulation and have limited means. Therefore, it would be helpful if creditors were advised of these rules by the Central Authority in their State of habitual residence when an application for modification of a decision by a debtor was sent to them.[94] However, it is questionable whether the Central Authority will actually be aware of these rules, because in most cases they have not received adequate training and the EU has not provided a practical handbook, guide to good practice or any other form of advisory document.[95] As such, in the majority of cases, it is unlikely that Central Authorities will provide such advice and in the absence of a specific requirement for them to do so it seems even more unlikely.[96]

The information provided by the Central Authorities that completed the questionnaire indicated that there had not been many applications for modification of a decision by a debtor, at the relevant time.[97] On the basis of the information provided in respect of incoming applications, only three of these types of applications were received: one each for Hungary, Ireland, and England and Wales. The information provided on outgoing applications was slightly more interesting. England and Wales sent 43 applications under Article 56(2)(b) and (c) and the majority of these were sent to Poland.

Hungary, Ireland and Sweden sent one application each and the other States listed sent no applications.[98] All the applications, except for one, were still pending at the time the questionnaire was returned. In that one case the application for modification was refused. It is not known why the application for modification was refused. Data provided in this area is incomplete and therefore no conclusions can be drawn at this time in regard to: how many of

[91] Maintenance Regulation Art 8(1).

[92] Ibid, Art 8(2)(a).

[93] Ibid, Art 8(2)(b).

[94] Applications for modification of a decision by a debtor are covered by Arts 56(2)(b) and (c) of the Maintenance Regulation. The applications that could cause a problem would be those under Art 56(2)(c) which are for modification of a decision made in a State other than the requested State.

[95] See ch 10.

[96] See ch 7 s VII for an example of a possible error of interpretation made by Central Authorities and see ch 10.

[97] The data is based on the responses to Q1 (a) and (b) part III. However, not all Member States provided the full data requested (see the Methodology).

[98] The graph shows the information provided by the Central Authorities who filled out the relevant part of the questionnaire. Those that did not answer this question are excluded from the graph.

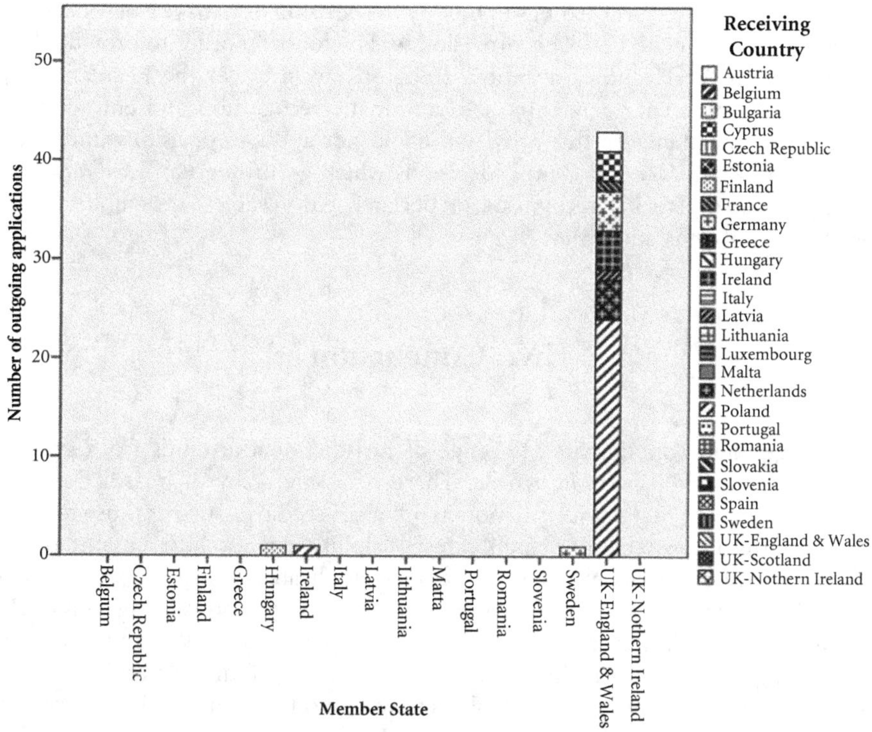


**Figure 5.1: Requests for modification by debtors**

these applications there really are, whether the rules are working and whether there have been any undesirable consequences for creditors who have unwittingly submitted to the jurisdiction.

The Regulation contains two more exceptions to the general rule. However, they are slightly more complicated because, these only apply where the State of origin is a Contracting State to the 2007 Hague Convention but not a Member State of the European Union. The first exception applies 'where the competent authority in the 2007 Hague Convention Contracting State of origin cannot, or refuses to, exercise jurisdiction to modify the decision or give a new decision'.[99] The provision refers only to a Hague Contracting State because an EU Member State could never be in a position where it cannot, or refuses to, exercise jurisdiction in such a case because Article 3(b) of the Regulation provides for jurisdiction on the basis of the habitual residence of the creditor. Therefore, if the creditor remains habitually resident in that State there is no reason why that Member State would not be able to exercise jurisdiction under the Regulation where a debtor tried to modify the decisions in that State.

The other exception is where 'the decision given in the 2007 Hague Convention Contracting State of origin cannot be recognised or declared enforceable in the

[99] Art 8(2)(c) and see Art 18(2)(c) of the Hague Convention.

Member State where proceedings to modify the decision or to have a new decision given are contemplated.'[100] This provision was included in order to provide consistency with the Hague Convention. Decisions given under the Regulation by a Member State's court are subject to automatic recognition and enforcement in the EU, and therefore this provision could not apply to decisions under the Regulation (even UK and Danish decisions which go through an *exequatur* are always capable of being recognised or declared enforceable—the public policy exception notwithstanding).

## IX. Conclusion

The Regulation contains a wide range of jurisdictional grounds from general grounds to a *forum necessitatis* rule. There is no hierarchy of jurisdiction and because the court that has jurisdiction in other proceedings, such as those relating to the status of the person or parental responsibility, can also hear a maintenance claim the rules in Brussels IIbis may also be applicable. However, because that court is not required to procure jurisdiction in both sets of proceedings this could result in a complicated situation where different courts are dealing with related proceedings. Therefore, the introduction of a hierarchy of jurisdiction in this area could ensure certainty for individuals as they would know that maintenance and divorce proceedings would be dealt with by the same court, at the same time. The hierarchy suggested would be that Article 3(c) which refers to the court determining status would be placed first. The implication of this would be that the court that has jurisdiction for divorce under Brussels IIbis would automatically have jurisdiction for maintenance. This would ensure that the court that has jurisdiction in divorce proceedings would also have jurisdiction for maintenance at the time of the divorce.

Although it is recognised that the various alternative grounds in Brussels IIbis are far from perfect and could also benefit from a review, this would be a first step towards reaching coherence and clarity in this area. This would create more certainty for parties and be more economical as they would not have different proceedings relating to the dissolution of their marriage ongoing before different courts. Any future instrument on matrimonial property should also contain a hierarchy of jurisdiction in order to complete the picture and provide coherence in this area.[101] Therefore the solution suggested in this book seeks to solve the problem of the characterisation of maintenance and matrimonial property by placing jurisdiction with the court determining status. This is especially

[100] Ibid.

[101] It is recognised that the proposed Regulation on matrimonial property does include a hierarchy of jurisdiction; however, the rules do not fix the current problem as the hierarchy provided does not necessarily relate to the other instruments.

important because there is no definition of the term 'maintenance' and therefore this could lead to conflicts of characterisation where different courts are dealing with different aspects of a related case.[102]

The indirect grounds of jurisdiction under the Convention are different from the direct grounds of jurisdiction under the Regulation partly because in some non EU States jurisdiction based on the habitual residence of the creditor is not seen as suitable. A maintenance creditor seeking maintenance from a defendant resident in such a State may need to consider, with the help of the Central Authority, whether to initiate proceedings in that State or in the State of their habitual residence. Doing the latter may run the risk that the judgment is not recognised and enforced in the non EU State, so the applicant and the Central Authority should consider which indirect grounds of jurisdiction could be applicable. This will prevent applicants and authorities from wasting time and resources on an application which may not be enforceable in the enforcing State. Unfortunately, at this stage it is very unlikely that personnel working at Central Authorities will have the initiative to provide such assistance to these types of maintenance creditors. Therefore it would be useful if a Guide to Good Practice was developed for Central Authorities, by the European Institutions, in order to assist Central Authorities with potential problems that may arise.[103]

[102] See ch 3 s III.

[103] See ch 10.

# 6

# Hague Protocol on Applicable Law

## I. Introduction

The Hague Protocol on Applicable Law[1] is a cleverly designed compromise in regard to the harmonisation of the recovery of maintenance from abroad in both the European Union and worldwide. The decision to put applicable law in a separate Protocol outside the text of the 2007 Hague Convention[2] and the Maintenance Regulation allows the widest ratification of the Convention, and the UK to opt in to the Regulation, while allowing those States that want to harmonise applicable law to apply the Protocol separately. The decision to draft a separate Protocol did not come until relatively late in the negotiating process, however even if the applicable law regime had instead been included in the main body of the Convention it would have been subject to either an opt-in or opt-out rule.[3] This alternative method should still have allowed States that prefer to apply the *lex fori* to maintenance disputes to ratify the Convention. However, the major benefit of the innovative approach taken is that this approach was followed in Europe and there is only one text on applicable law that will apply worldwide.[4] The Protocol is currently in force in the EU and Serbia.[5] This means that the Protocol applies within the EU Member States,[6] and externally in Serbia.

[1] Protocol of 23 November 2007 on the Law Applicable to Maintenance Obligations.

[2] It should be noted that the Convention (Hague Convention of 23 November 2007 on the International Recovery of Child Support and other forms of Family Maintenance) does not exclude applicable law completely but contains specific applicable law rules in Arts 36(2), 32(5) and 20(5).

[3] W Duncan, 'The New Hague Maintenance Convention and Protocol' (2008) 10 *Yearbook of Private International Law* 313, 327. (Council Regulation (EC) 4/2009 of 18 December 2008 on jurisdiction, applicable law, recognition and enforcement of decisions and cooperation in matters relating to maintenance obligations (Maintenance Regulation) [2009] OJ L7/1.)

[4] See P Beaumont, 'International Family Law in Europe—the Maintenance Project, the Hague Conference and the EC: A Triumph of Reverse Subsidiarity' (2009) 73 *Rabels Zeitschrift* 509, 519–21, for further information on the decision to use a separate Protocol internationally and in the EU.

[5] See www.hcch.net/index_en.php?act=conventions.status&cid=133, accessed 27 March 2014. The Protocol applies in all Member States except Denmark and the United Kingdom (see Declarations and Notifications, www.hcch.net/index_en.php?act=status.comment&csid=1065&disp=resdn, accessed 27 March 2014).

[6] The EU declared that it would apply the rules of the Protocol provisionally from the date of application of the Maintenance Regulation, 18 June 2011 (see Declarations and Notifications, ibid). The Protocol only entered into force officially on the 1 August 2013.

This compromise works on a wider basis as the Protocol has broader application than the Convention it accompanies. This is because the Convention only applies between Contracting States,[7] but the Protocol will always apply in a Contracting State regardless of whether it designates a law in a non-contracting State.[8] However this is not unusual and was taken from the 1973 Applicable Law Convention.[9] This approach was also considered suitable as unusually the Protocol can be ratified or acceded to by a State that has not ratified the Convention.[10]

## II. Scope

The Protocol seeks to determine the law applicable to maintenance obligations arising from 'a family relationship, parentage, marriage or affinity, including a maintenance obligation in respect of a child regardless of the marital status of the parents.'[11] The Protocol only determines the law applicable to the maintenance obligation,[12] and does not aim to address the incidental question of whether one of the relationships designated in Article 1 actually exists. Therefore this means that the law applicable to determine the existence of the family relationship can be determined in three ways.[13] The court can apply the law designated by the Protocol to the incidental question,[14] as there is nothing in Article 1 that expressly prevents this,[15] or they can apply their own law. If they apply their own law they have two options, firstly they can apply the internal law of the forum or they can apply the law designated by reference to the private international law rules of the forum.[16] It is clear that there is no coherent approach to determining how the

[7] See Arts 1 and 2 of the Hague Convention.

[8] Hague Protocol Art 2 Universal Application.

[9] A Bonomi, 'Explanatory Report on the Protocol of 23 November 2007 on the Law Applicable to Maintenance Obligations' paras 34 (Bonomi Report), available at www.hcch.net/upload/expl39e.pdf, accessed 10 June 2014.

[10] This decision was also taken late in the proceedings, see Duncan (n 3) 327. Again this is important from the European perspective as the Protocol has applied internally within the EU since June 2011, but the EU did not ratify the Convention until 2014.

[11] Hague Protocol Art 1(1).

[12] This is believed to be an important distinction which is emphasised in the Bonomi Report (n 9) para 23.

[13] M Verwilghen, 'Explanatory Report on the 1973 Hague Maintenance Conventions (1975) para 125, available at www.hcch.net/index_en.php?act=publications.details&pid=2946&dtid=3, accessed 21 May 2014 (Verwilghen Report).

[14] The Bonomi Report specifically refers to this approach however, from the wording used, this does not appear to amount to a recommendation. Rather it appears to just be an option or an obiter comment, as the term 'recommend' is not used. Instead Bonomi uses the terminology 'nothing to prevent' which creates the idea of a valid option rather than *the* recommended approach. Further, the following sentence emphasises that this approach is optional (Bonomi Report (n 9) para 24).

[15] See the Verwilghen Report (n 13) para 125 and the Bonomi Report (n 9) para 24.

[16] See the Verwilghen Report (n 13) para 125. Literature suggests that there are two main approaches, the application of the *lex fori* or the *lex causae* (AE Gotlieb, 'The Incidental Question

issue of the incidental question should be addressed.[17] Given that 'the overwhelming majority of decisions involving incidental questions … deal with matters of status',[18] this is a problem that will prevail in international family law and there is no clear way of resolving it any time soon.[19] The approach taken to determine the answer to the incidental question may alter the outcome—because if the relationship is deemed not to exist, under the *lex fori*, then no maintenance obligation will arise; despite the fact that the relationship might exist under the *lex causae*. However it is important to note that this is non-determinative because in this case even if the *lex causae* was applied to determine the incidental question, the court can still refuse the application of this law (to determine the maintenance obligation) on the basis of public policy.[20] Therefore the outcome could potentially be the same and the maintenance obligation may be deemed not to exist, either because the relationship is found not to exist or because the requirement to pay maintenance on the basis of that relationship is manifestly contrary to the public policy of the forum.

In terms of the relationships that the Protocol applies to it has more in common with the Regulation,[21] than the core mandatory scope of the Convention that it accompanies.[22] This is because the core scope of the Convention only covers child support and spousal support. Contracting States can extend the

Revisited—Theory and Practice in the Conflict of Laws' (1977) 26 *International and Comparative Law Quarterly* 734, 751 and see T Schmidt, 'The Incidental Question in Private International Law' (1992) 233 *Recueil des Cours* 315). However Gotlieb admits that these lines are blurred and others consider that 'certain types or categories of cases justify certain approaches' (Gotlieb, 752).

[17] See Gotlieb (n 16) 734.

[18] Ibid, 764.

[19] Goessl writing more recently favours a *lex fori* approach, particularly where the rules have already been harmonised, such as in the EU. This is because if parties are seising a court on the basis of grounds of jurisdiction that have been designated in law as appropriate grounds, then it is appropriate to apply the *lex fori* (she refers specifically to Brussels I (Council Regulation (EC) 44/2001 of 22 December 2000 on jurisdiction and the recognition and enforcement of judgments in civil and commercial matters [2001] OJ L012/1)). In particular she concludes 'the lex fori approach leads to a practical, foreseeable solution which advances the integration of EU law in the national systems. Therefore, no matter whether the concept occurs in a PIL or substantive rule, the lex fori approach is the better solution. An exception which leads to the application of the lex causae approach should be made only in rare cases and expressly mentioned in the EU act.' (S Goessl, 'Preliminary Questions in EU Private International Law' (2012) *Journal of Private International Law* 63, 76 and see 72–73.)

[20] Hague Protocol Art 13, see below at s IV A. Applying the *lex causae* and using public policy as a fall back is the approach favoured by Raape after deliberation either way. (Schmidt (n 16) 347–48.)

[21] In this respect the European Commission did propose that the Regulation applied to maintenance obligations deriving from 'relationships deemed by the law applicable to such relationships as having comparable effects'. (Art 1(1) of the Proposal). However this was dropped 'in order to coordinate with the Protocol, which determines its own substantive scope of application in the same terms, but also guarantees coherence with the content of Recitals 21 and 25 and of Art 22 of the Maintenance Regulation, regarding the non-application of the Regulation to the preliminary questions related to family status.' (I Viarengo, 'The Enforcement of Maintenance Decisions in the EU: Requiem For Public Policy? Family Relationships and the (Partial) Abolition of Exequatur' in Beaumont et al (eds), *The Recovery of Maintenance in the EU and Worldwide* (Oxford, Hart Publishing, 2014) 473.)

[22] See chs 3 and 4.

scope but this will only apply *inter partes*.[23] The scope is different from that of the Convention because of the desire to keep the Protocol consistent with the scope of the 1973 Applicable Law Convention.[24] This means that the Protocol can replace the 1973 Applicable Law Convention, for Contracting States. Secondly, in order to maintain flexibility, as the Protocol is optional, it was desirable not to excessively limit the text as States can ratify either the Convention or the Protocol and do not need to be party to both.[25] This results in the scope of the Regulation and the Protocol being virtually identical.[26] The difference being that the Protocol is slightly more descriptive, stating specifically that it includes 'a maintenance obligation in respect of a child regardless of the marital status of the parents'.[27] Hopefully this is also the case under the Regulation,[28] and generally the recognition of the rights of children regardless of the marital status of their parents is no longer problematic in law.[29]

Bonomi has argued that the major problem currently will be the recognition of maintenance obligations between civil or married same-sex partners.[30] Given that the Protocol does not apply to status in order to determine whether a 'family relationship' exists it will necessarily not be able to solve any of the problems in this area. The Protocol avoids specifically referring to these types of relationships in its scope in order to avoid 'running up against the fundamental opposition existing between States on these issues'.[31] This means that the text was passed and will hopefully be widely ratified but it also means that the Protocol will not be applied uniformly in the context of civil partnerships and/or same sex marriages.[32]

It is clear that the Protocol covers the law applicable to the maintenance obligation and not (directly) the law applicable to the relationship. So how does this work in terms of determining the validity of the maintenance obligation? The law applicable can be used to determine: whether, to what extent and from whom the creditor can claim maintenance.[33] Although the Protocol does not specifically apply to designate the law applicable to determine the incidental question; in order for a court to determine if there is a maintenance obligation this must to some extent imply an evaluation of the relationship between and/or the status of

[23] Arts 2(3) and 63 of the 2007 Hague Convention, and see ch 4.

[24] Bonomi Report (n 9) para 26.

[25] Ibid.

[26] They both apply to maintenance obligations arising out of a 'family relationship, parentage, marriage or affinity'. (Art 1(1) of the Maintenance Regulation and Art 1(1) of the Hague Protocol.)

[27] Hague Protocol, Art 1(1).

[28] The Regulation appears to be silent on the matter, although it is emphasised that recognition of an obligation to pay maintenance does not require the State to recognise the relationship which the obligation arises from (Recital 25 and see ch 7). Conversely, the Convention gives the same specification in Art 2(4)).

[29] See ch 2.

[30] Bonomi Report (n 9) para 31.

[31] Ibid.

[32] See s III B, *ii* and *iii* below.

[33] Hague Protocol Art 11(a).

the parties in order to determine whether there is an actual claim.[34] It is difficult to ignore this in order to determine the answer to this question. Bonomi suggests the law applicable 'determines, *without limitation*, a person's eligibility for maintenance, having regard to that person's *family relationship* with the debtor, and age.'[35] Indicating the close proximity between maintenance and the family relationship; and the difficulty of separating the question of eligibility to receive maintenance from the incidental question of whether the relationship exists. The law applicable also determines the extent to which the creditor can claim retroactive maintenance;[36] the basis for calculation of the amount of maintenance, and indexation;[37] who is entitled to initiate maintenance proceedings, except for issues relating to procedural capacity and representation in the proceedings;[38] prescription or limitation periods;[39] and the extent of the obligation of a maintenance debtor, where a public body seeks reimbursement of benefits provided for a creditor in place of maintenance.[40]

# III. Law Applicable

The applicable law is determined under the rules in Articles 3–8 of the Hague Protocol. The Protocol sets out a general rule in Article 3, but this law can be set aside for preference of the law designated by Articles 4, 5, 6, 7 or 8 if the relevant criteria are met.

## A. General Rule

The general rule is that the law applicable is that of the habitual residence of the creditor, unless the Protocol provides otherwise.[41] The Protocol further provides that where the creditor changes their habitual residence then the law of the new habitual residence will apply from the moment that the change occurs.[42] The

[34] In this respect see the text accompanying nn 17–20 above.
[35] Bonomi Report (n 9) para 168 emphasis added.
[36] Hague Protocol Art 11(b).
[37] Ibid, Art 11(c).
[38] Ibid, Art 11(d).
[39] Ibid, Art 11(e).
[40] Ibid, Art 11(f).
[41] Ibid, Art 3(1).
[42] Ibid, Art 3(2). In order to be consistent with other Hague Children's Conventions and the Brussels IIbis Regulation (Council Regulation (EC) 2201/2003 of 27 November 2003 on jurisdiction, recognition and enforcement of judgments in matrimonial matters and matters of parental responsibility, repealing Regulation (EC) No 1347/2000 [2003] OJ L 338/1), habitual residence should be interpreted as the main place of residence, of the creditor, and ascertained on the basis of objective criteria such as length and permanence of residence, as well as family, professional and social ties. For example

choice of habitual residence as the main connecting factor offers several advantages. Importantly it means that the maintenance payable is determined with regard to the 'legal and factual conditions of the social environment in the country where the creditor lives and engages in most of his or her activities.'[43] Although a disadvantage with this approach is that the factual and social environment in the debtor's State could be vastly different from that in the creditor's State, so discerning a suitable amount of maintenance could be problematic.[44]

Another stated advantage is that all creditors living in the same State should be treated the same regardless of nationality,[45] although this again has to be circumscribed by the living conditions of the debtor and his or her ability to pay. If the maintenance is set too high, so that it is impossible for the debtor to pay, the obligation may become unenforceable.[46] The final specified advantage is that it is acknowledged that several maintenance instruments (including the Maintenance Regulation and 2007 Hague Convention) use the creditor's habitual residence as the main connecting factor to establish jurisdiction.[47] Use of the 'same criterion to determine the applicable law often leads to the application of the law of the authority seized, which provides obvious benefits in terms of simplicity and efficiency.'[48] This is particularly true in relation to the Regulation which has non-exorbitant direct rules of jurisdiction. Subsequently in the majority of proceedings under the Regulation (where jurisdiction is based on one of the general rules)[49] the *lex fori* should apply, regardless of whether the proceedings are taking place in a Protocol or Non-Protocol Member State.[50] The difference is how this

see: C-532/07 *A* [2009] ECR I-02805; C-497/10 PPU *Mercredi v Chaffe* [2010] ECR I-14309 and see the 1980 Convention cases on habitual residence, summaries available at www.incadat.com/index.cfm?act=search.result&actie=search&lng=1&sl=2, accessed 2 April 2014.

[43] Bonomi Report (n 9) para 37.

[44] In this regard Hague Protocol Art 14 is also relevant, see below at s IV.

[45] Bonomi Report (n 9) para 38.

[46] See chs 7 and 8.

[47] The general rules on jurisdiction are found in Art 3 of the Maintenance Regulation (see ch 5 for more details). These point to the habitual residence of the creditor—in which case jurisdiction and applicable law would coincide; the habitual residence of the defendant—Art 4(3) of the Protocol applies instead for certain creditors, giving the same result (see below); the court that has jurisdiction to determine parental responsibility, which is the court of the child's habitual residence (Art 9 Brussels IIbis)—so jurisdiction and applicable law would again coincide; or the court that has jurisdiction to determine status. Where jurisdiction is based on the final ground there is no guarantee that jurisdiction and applicable law will coincide because Brussels IIbis contains a number of alternative jurisdictional grounds for divorce (see ch 5), and the rules on other questions of status are not necessarily harmonised.

[48] Bonomi Report (n 9) para 39. See also A Bonomi, 'The Hague Protocol of 23 November 2007 on the Law Applicable to Maintenance Obligations' (2008) 10 *Yearbook of Private International Law* 333, 342.

[49] See n 47 above. However if jurisdiction is based on Art 5 (submission), or the subsidiary jurisdictions in Art 6 or 7 it is unlikely that jurisdiction and applicable law will coincide. The parties can also designate a court under Art 4, unless the application is for child support. Where parties have designated a court, the law applicable will depend on whether they have also designated the same law, a different law or no law.

[50] Martiny notes that 'under the Hague Conventions there is a tendency that where there is jurisdiction of a competent authority it should apply its own law. This, however, is generally based on the

outcome is reached. Common law States prefer the direct application of the *lex fori* because it is swift and efficient.[51] In contrast civil law States do not like the direct application of the *lex fori*, particularly where there are indirect rules of jurisdiction,[52] and often in 'maintenance law the application of the lex fori is only the last resort.'[53] The result being that under the regime in the Regulation and the Protocol the *lex fori* is applied on the basis that it is the law of the habitual residence of the creditor; and is therefore based on the 'closest connection' principle.[54] However, where a creditor's habitual residence changes during the course of proceedings then the court should start to apply the law of the new habitual residence from that point.[55] Bonomi notes that this solution is not consistent with the advantage of the court applying forum law to the dispute.[56] However he argues that if the decision determines maintenance for the future 'it would be illogical not to take into account such a significant change in circumstances.'[57]

## B. Special Rules

Article 4 of the Protocol contains special rules that favour certain types of creditors. 'The reason for the existence of these exceptions is to provide slightly more favourable rules for certain classes of maintenance creditors in cases where application of the law of their habitual residences is found to be contrary to their interests.'[58] Articles 5 and 6 include special rules to protect debtors from any potential unfairness that might arise from the application of the general rules, in relation to certain types of maintenance obligations.

habitual residence of the parties or the protected individual.' (D Martiny, 'Objectives and Values of (Private) International Law in Family Law' in J Meeusen et al (eds), *International Family Law for the European Union* (Antwerp, Intersentia, 2007) 69, 94.)

[51] Ibid, 94 and Duncan (n 3) 327–28.

[52] Duncan (n 3) 327.

[53] Martiny (n 50) 94.

[54] 'As the habitual residence of maintenance creditors is regarded as the most favourable forum for maintenance dispute resolution, and this connecting factor is applied as the default choice of law rule, we essentially reach the point of applying the lex fori. By considering the interconnection between jurisdictional rules and choice of law rules, it appears that the philosophy that lies behind them differs. The applicable law rules serve the Savigny principle of the closest connection of a relationship and a legal system, whereas the jurisdictional rules aim at ensuring a fair and efficient judicial procedure (easy access to evidence, etc).' (M Zupan, 'Novelties of the 2007 Hague Maintenance Protocol' in Beaumont et al (eds) (n 21) 311.)

[55] Hague Protocol, Article 3(2) and Bonomi Report (n 9) para 45.

[56] However, clearly this is not what EU States, apart from Denmark and the UK, want to do as then they would not have agreed unanimously to the Council decision to adopt the Protocol, so that they could apply forum law.

[57] Bonomi Report (n 9) para 45.

[58] Ibid, para 49.

### *i. Special Rule Favouring Certain Creditors*

Article 4 benefits certain specific creditors, mainly in relation to child support,[59] and only applies to the specific relationships listed. These are parents towards their children;[60] persons, other than parents, towards persons who have not attained the age of 21 years, except for obligations arising out of the relationships referred to in Article 5;[61] and children towards their parents.[62] If you are not within these classes of creditors then you cannot benefit from Article 4 and will have to use the general rule in Article 3 or the other alternative rules in Articles 5–8 (if they apply). These classes of creditors benefit from different advantages under Article 4. However, it is important to note that this does not trump the other provisions and these can still apply, such as Article 6.[63]

#### a—Law of the Forum Replaces the Law of the Creditor's Habitual Residence

Article 4(2) of the Hague Protocol allows the creditor to use the law of the forum to obtain maintenance from the debtor, if the law of their own habitual residence does not allow them to do so.[64] This solution is designed to ensure that the creditor can obtain maintenance if this is possible under a law which is related to the dispute, in this case the law of the forum. The law of the forum is preferred to the law of common nationality because the law of the common nationality may not have much relevance to the parties' current living arrangements and conditions. It is also simpler for the court seised to apply the law of the forum, which should be quicker and less costly than applying a foreign law.[65] Article 4(2) will only apply if the creditor cannot obtain maintenance under the law designated by Article 3. The fact that the law of the habitual residence of the creditor is less favourable than the law of the forum will not be enough to invoke Article 4.[66]

The subsidiary connection to the law of the forum can only be used if the forum is not the habitual residence of the creditor, otherwise the law designated by Articles 3 and 4(2) would be the same. Article 4(2) cannot apply when the creditor initiates proceedings in the debtor's State either.[67] This is because in this specific example the rule in Article 4(3) would apply instead. Therefore Article 4(2)

[59] However, Art 4(c) also covers payments from children to their parents.

[60] Hague Protocol Art 4(1)(a).

[61] Ibid, Art 4 (1)(b).

[62] Ibid, Art 4(1)(c).

[63] This allows the debtor to argue that there is no such obligation under the law of their habitual residence. See below at s *iii*.

[64] Hague Protocol Art 4(2).

[65] Bonomi Report (n 9) para 60. See also the discussion above at nn 50–54 and the accompanying text.

[66] See the Bonomi Report (n 9) paras 61–62. Zupan argues that this 'does not leave any possibility of a real in favorem approach to the creditor—if the creditor argued that some other law is more favourable to his or her claim then the authority must reject such objections.' (Zupan (n 54).)

[67] The creditor can seise the court of the debtor's habitual residence under Art 3(a) of the Regulation, and this is also considered as a basis for recognition and enforcement under Art 20(1)(a) of the Hague Convention.

can only apply if the debtor brings proceedings before the court in their habitual residence,[68] or if the court seised is in a State in which neither party is habitually resident.[69] In all cases the first example is virtually impossible. In the case of children the latter category would still need some form of connection in order to apply, such as common nationality, so the application of Article 4(2) appears limited in relation to child support applications.[70] The provision may be useful in applications for maintenance between adults, where the parties have designated a court which has little connection to the application, if the defender has submitted to the jurisdiction or if jurisdiction is based on one of the subsidiary rules.[71]

### b—The Switch of Connecting Factors in the Case of Proceedings Instituted by the Creditor in the State of the Debtor's Habitual Residence

Article 4(3) also favours the solution that the *lex fori* should usually apply, which is one of the principles on which Article 3 is based. If the creditor has seised the courts of the debtor's habitual residence, then in that case the law of the forum will apply.[72] If the creditor is unable to obtain maintenance under this law then the Protocol refers you back to the law of the creditor's habitual residence on a subsidiary basis. 'This is a major switch of the connecting factors in Article 3 and Article 4(2).'[73] Effectively the relationship between the three provisions seems, at the most basic level, to be: if the creditor seises the courts of his or her own habitual residence then only Article 3 can apply—the law of the creditor's habitual residence which is also the law of the forum. If one of the special classes of creditor seises the courts of the debtor's habitual residence then Article 4(3) applies rather than Article 3, which also results in the application of the law of the forum. The creditor should not complain about this because they chose to initiate proceedings

[68] This is not possible under the direct rules of jurisdiction under the Maintenance Regulation (see ch 5 for more details) and is only permitted under the Hague Convention when it is not prohibited by Art 18. Therefore this would only have a possibility of working where the Protocol is being applied by a non-EU Member State and the debtor is not in breach of the limitation on where debtors can bring proceedings in Art 18 of the Convention.

[69] See nn 47 and 49. See also ch 5 for more information on the direct rules of jurisdiction in the Regulation and ch 8 for information on the indirect rules contained in the Convention.

[70] There is one caveat to this due to the rules in Brussels IIbis. Art 12 allows the parties to select the divorce court to also determine parental responsibility, if they agree on this. If the maintenance claim is ancillary to the parental responsibility proceedings then the divorce court could also have jurisdiction for child maintenance.

[71] See n 49.

[72] Pertegás considers that a reference to the law of the forum rather than the law of nationality is remarkable. However, she recognises that 'the outcome would in most cases be similar, a direct reference to the law of the forum is a clear indication that the selection of a proper forum, a swift dispute resolution and a correct application of the law are considered to be important factors to cross-border family dispute resolution.' (M Pertegás, 'Beyond Nationality and Habitual Residence: Other Connecting Factors in European Private International Law in Family Matters' in J Meeusen et al (eds) (n 50).)

[73] Bonomi Report (n 9) para 64. This provision is designed in order to produce a 'compromise between supporters of undifferentiated application of the law of the creditor's habitual residence and those of the law of the forum' (ibid).

in this State, so the application of that law should not be unfair.[74] However, if this means that no maintenance obligation arises then the Protocol reverts back to the rule in Article 3 and the law of the creditor's habitual residence applies. In such cases it would be highly beneficial if the creditor was advised to initiate proceedings in the courts of his or her own habitual residence as this would be simpler for both the creditor and the judiciary. Thirdly, if proceedings are initiated in a court where neither party is habitually resident and the law designated by Article 3 does not provide a remedy for the creditor, then the law of the forum will apply because of the rule in Article 4(2).

### c—Nationality as the Final Option

Finally, if the creditor is unable to obtain maintenance either under the law of their habitual residence or the law of the forum (in the appropriate order)[75] the Court can apply the law of the common nationality of the parties, as a last resort.[76] 'This secondary subsidiary connection completes the protection of the maintenance creditor in cases where the laws designated by the first two criteria do not provide for any maintenance obligation.'[77] This provision limits the class of creditors protected by the special rule in Article 4 further, as it will only be of use where there is a common nationality.[78] The Protocol refrains from giving guidance on what the court should do where the connection leads to a multi-unit State or the applicants have more than one nationality.[79] These matters are left to the internal rules of the State. Despite the drawbacks of this subsidiary connection it could provide a remedy for parties in a small minority of cases.[80]

[74] If the creditor opts to sue in the debtor's State instead of their own then they 'cannot complain of the application of the internal law of the debtor's country.' (Bonomi Report (n 9) para 67.) This is very solidly grounded as the basis of this jurisdictional ground is the principle of *actor sequitur forum rei*, providing clear justification for the application of the law of the forum. (See the Bonomi Report (n 9) para 67 and Zupan (n 54).)

[75] Normally the law of the habitual residence and then the law of the forum—Art 3 followed by Art 4(2) of the Hague Protocol. However if the creditor sues in the debtor's State the law of the forum will apply first followed by the law of the creditor's habitual residence (Art 4(3)).

[76] Hague Protocol Art 4(4). Art 9 of the Protocol allows States to replace the term nationality with domicile by informing the Permanent Bureau. The same rule applies to Art 6 but not to Art 8(1)(a). (See para 159 of the Bonomi Report (n 9).)

[77] Bonomi Report (n 9) para 71.

[78] This is one of the reasons for giving preference to the law of the forum over the law of common nationality (a change from the 1973 Convention) because the application of the provision is discriminatory by its very nature. (Bonomi Report (n 9) para 74.)

[79] Bonomi Report (n 9) paras 74 and 76.

[80] It should be noted that the relegation of this connecting factor to last place in the cascade system is one of the few changes made to the 1973 Convention. The new Protocol places more emphasis on the *lex fori* as this is deemed to have a closer connection to the dispute and the application of the *lex fori* is more efficient in terms of time and cost. (See Duncan (n 3) 328.)

### *ii. Special Rule with Respect to Spouses and Ex-Spouses (Article 5)*

This special rule is included because it is recognised that in the case of spouses it might not be appropriate to apply the law of the creditor's habitual residence. This rule is designed to respect the legitimate expectations of the debtor in these particular situations. Where the parties have lived all their married life in one State that does not look favourably on maintenance after divorce, the general expectation would be that their marriage and then the subsequent divorce would be managed in accordance with this law. If Article 3 were to apply in this case this would allow the creditor to move unilaterally, causing a change in their habitual residence. This would result in a new law applying to the dispute, and that law could be more favourable towards providing maintenance after divorce.[81]

In order for Article 5 to apply certain criteria have to be met. One of the parties has to *object* to the application of the law designated by Article 3 and the law of another State, most likely the law of the last common habitual residence, has to have a *closer connection* to the marriage.[82] The Protocol is novel in the sense that the escape clause in Article 5 will only be triggered if one of the parties requests it. Courts cannot of their own accord decide that another law may have a closer connection. The benefit of this solution is 'that it reduces the uncertainty inherent in any escape clause by restricting the search for the closest connections to only those cases where one party asks for it.'[83] One problem with this approach is that it is not clear at what point in proceedings the debtor would need to make this request. Agreement could not be reached in this regard,[84] so the issue is left open. Authorities need to be sensible in this area and not allow late requests when proceedings are coming to an end and the issue is almost resolved.[85]

If one of the parties does object to the application of the law designated by Article 3 this leaves the court with what could be a potentially difficult balancing act. The court will have to take into account

> all the connections of the marriage with the various countries concerned, such as the spouses' habitual residence and/or domicile during the marriage, their nationalities, the location where the marriage was celebrated and the location of the legal separation or divorce.[86]

They will then have to balance these connections against the connection of the dispute to the creditor's habitual residence, to determine which law has the closest connection. If the spouses spent all their married life in one State and have

[81] See Bonomi Report (n 9) para 78.
[82] Hague Protocol Art 5, emphasis added.
[83] Bonomi Report (n 9) para 83.
[84] Ibid, para 84.
[85] Contrast this with Art 5 of the Maintenance Regulation where an appearance in court more or less automatically deems the defendant to have submitted to the jurisdiction, with no scope for review.
[86] Bonomi Report (n 9) para 85.

moved separately since the marriage ended then the outcome should be clear.[87] If however the parties have moved regularly then determining the law with the closest connection will be much more difficult. In fact if there is no clear connection with any law then the law of the creditor's habitual residence will apply by default.

It is clear from the wording that Article 5 covers maintenance obligations both during the marriage and after the marriage has ended. The Protocol does not attempt to specify or clarify what exactly is meant by the term 'spouse' in this context. It is unclear whether it also covers situations akin to marriage such as registered partnerships.[88] It is a question for the State to determine whether this is a relationship between 'spouses', some other form of family relationship or no relationship at all. The lack of guidance produces flexibility and allows States that recognise these partnerships as equivalent to marriage to apply Article 5 to these situations. However, for States that do not recognise these relationships and would not apply Article 5, they have alternative options to determine which provision in the Protocol should apply or indeed whether the Protocol should apply at all.[89] This indicates that the application of the Protocol will not be uniform across the Contracting States, at present. Within the EU it is possible that the Court of Justice of the European Union (CJEU) may clarify both or one of these points in the future, as the Protocol has been adopted by the EU. However given the decision during the negotiations to make these provisions flexible,[90] a decision by the CJEU in this area would be controversial and a major political statement.[91]

[87] This is reflected in the fact that the Protocol refers specifically to the 'last common habitual residence' of the spouses (Art 5). Although this is in no way decisive it reflects the fact that in the majority of cases 'the law of the last common habitual residence has very significant connections with the marriage'. (Bonomi Report (n 9) para 86.)

[88] In this respect 'certain delegations (Switzerland, Israel) had suggested an express statement in the Protocol's text that this provision could, at States' discretion, apply to those institutions similar to marriage. Though that proposal did not achieve the necessary consensus, Commission II of the Diplomatic Session accepted that those States which recognise such institutions in their legal systems, or are willing to recognise them, may make them subject to the rule under Art. 5, which is equivalent to an implied admission that the Protocol may apply to them.' (Bonomi (n 48) 339.) See also the Bonomi Report (n 9) paras 92–93.

[89] Bonomi puts forward two possible solutions for States that do not recognise institutions such as civil partnerships and therefore would not include them under the special rules in Art 5 of the Protocol. He believes that the Contracting State could either consider 'that these relationships are not family relationships within the meaning of Art 1 and the Protocol is therefore not applicable to them (in such case, it will apply its own national conflicts rules), or it considers that they are indeed family relationships, but may not be treated like marriage (in that case, the applicable law will be determined on the basis of other rules in the Protocol, and in particular Arts 3 and 6). Given the silence of the Protocol and preparatory instruments, it must be admitted that both these solutions are legitimate, even though that implies that the Protocol's application will not be uniform among the Contracting States.' (Bonomi (n 48) 339.)

[90] See n 88 above.

[91] In this respect it is important to note that there are two separate proposals on matrimonial property—one for marriage and one for civil partnerships. See also ch 7 s V on internal public policy and state traditions, particularly nn 155–60.

### *iii. Special Rule on Defence*

Article 6 allows the debtor to contest a maintenance claim from the creditor on the basis that there is no such obligation to pay maintenance under both the law of the debtor's habitual residence, and the law of the common nationality (if there is one). Article 6 cannot apply to parent-child relationships,[92] or relationships covered by Article 5.[93] This clearly creates an alternative category for civil partnerships (and equivalent relationships) because if the forum treats the parties as 'spouses' then the defence in Article 6 cannot apply. If however they are not treated as 'spouses' then the defence in Article 6 can apply. This creates an anomaly in terms of legitimate expectations, because if the parties entered into a valid partnership in a State where this is legal then there has to be some expectation that rights and responsibilities will flow as a consequence of entering into the partnership.[94]

The defence in Article 6 allows the impact of the Protocol (and effectively the Regulation and the Convention) to be limited in respect of maintenance obligations that do not receive international consensus. The Bonomi Report gives some examples of when Article 6 might apply. These are:

i. Parentage in direct-line that is not a parent-child relationship—such as grandparents to grandchildren or children to grandparents.
ii. A collateral relationship—such as brother to sister.
iii. A relationship by affinity—such as step-parents to their step-children.[95]
iv. A child to his or her parents.
v. Any person other than parents or spouses towards a child under the age of 21.[96]

In the last two cases, the second of which could cover relationships listed in the first three categories, the general rule in Article 3 and the rule in Article 4 can be applied. In situations where both Articles 4 and 6 are applicable then the rules in both Articles can be applied concurrently.[97] Therefore a maintenance claim designated by a law applicable under Article 4 can be set aside if that claim cannot be made under the law designated by Article 6. In order to apply Article 6 the forum must first determine the law applicable under Articles 3 and/ or 4. They can then disapply that law if the criteria in Article 6 are met. If there is no common nationality then the court need only determine whether the obligation exists under the law of the debtor's habitual residence. If the obligation does not exist then that is

[92] Covered by the Hague Protocol Arts 3 and 4(1)(a).

[93] This is wider than the scope of the previous provision in the 1973 (Applicable Law) Convention Art 7, which only applied between parties related collaterally or by affinity.

[94] Particularly when it is clear that these expectations can be effectively managed by the Hague Protocol Art 5.

[95] Bonomi Report (n 9) para 99.

[96] Ibid, para 100.

[97] Ibid.

enough to invoke Article 6 and the defence can be raised.[98] If however, the parties do have a common nationality then the court will have to determine whether the obligation does not exist under both the law of the debtor's habitual residence and the law of the common nationality. Where there is a common nationality the provisions are cumulative and the defence can only be used if there is no obligation to pay maintenance under both laws. Commentators believe that this additional element is justified because, if the parties have a common nationality it would be inequitable not to take into account whether that law provides for the obligation.[99]

## C. Choice of Applicable Law

Articles 7 and 8 both allow the parties to designate an applicable law, subject to a variety of restrictions. Article 7 allows choice of law for the purpose of a specific proceeding. Article 8 allows an open ended choice and is therefore subject to more restrictions.[100]

### *i. For the Purpose of a Specific Proceeding*

Article 7 is restrictive in its nature and only allows parties to designate the law of the forum in relation to a particular proceeding.[101] Due to the restrictive nature of the provision, Article 7 is applicable to disputes involving adults and children. This is because it 'appeared that the possible risks connected with the introduction of party autonomy are amply counterbalanced by the benefits in terms of simplicity that arise from application of the law of the forum.'[102] However, in the context of parental child support a designation to apply forum law is unlikely to alter the law otherwise applicable under the Protocol given the rules in Articles 3 and 4(3), which would both normally result in the application of the *lex fori*.[103] Any designation is likely to have more effect where the maintenance obligation

[98] However it is not possible to review whether these provisions were applied correctly and the appropriate law or the correct defence and/or special rule was applied. This is important in relation to the automatic recognition and enforcement under the Regulation of decisions given in Protocol States. See ch 7 for a detailed discussion.

[99] Bonomi Report (n 9) para 105.

[100] Ibid, para 111.

[101] This is also known as an *accord procedural* and it 'assumes that the maintenance creditor has already brought, or is about to bring, a claim before a specific authority.' (Bonomi (n 48) 351–52.) However if the choice is made before the proceedings are instituted 'it will only be valid in so far as the parties have specified the law they intend to designate, or at least the authority before which the proceedings contemplated are to be instituted. It will not be sufficient for the parties to designate in a general fashion "the law of the forum" since until an authority has been seized, the "forum" has not been determined. Such a choice made blindly does not provide an assurance that the parties have been informed and, and are aware, of the object of their choice.' (Bonomi (n 48) 352.)

[102] Bonomi Report (n 9) para 114.

[103] See the discussion above at A and Bi. An example of where this would not be the case is where the general rule in Art 9 Brussels IIbis did not apply because the parties had chosen the divorce court to

arises from another relationship as there is slightly more chance that the *lex fori* would not be directly applicable. The main effect of a designation under Article 7 would be to prevent the special rules in Articles 5 and 6 applying, and where Article 4(3) applies it would prevent the application of the law of the habitual residence of the creditor where the *lex fori* does not allow the creditor to claim maintenance.

### *ii. Designation of Applicable Law*

Unlike Article 7, where the choice of the law of the forum only applies for the purpose of a particular proceeding, a law designated by the parties under Article 8 is intended to 'govern the maintenance obligations between the parties from the time of the choice and until when they choose to cancel or modify it.'[104] The main advantage of designating a law under Article 8 is to 'secure a measure of stability and foreseeability'[105] as that law will remain applicable regardless of any changes in the parties' living arrangements,[106] or the court seised. Traditionally party autonomy has played a limited role in family law for a number of reasons, particularly because there are State interests as well as individual interests that need to be protected in family situations.[107] However this approach is changing, as indicated by the Protocol, Regulation and Convention, and there are several reasons that justify the introduction of party autonomy.[108] One as indicated above is to ensure certainty. Another is that given the aim to solve disputes through mediation and achieve amicable solutions 'strengthening the role of party autonomy in international family law could substantially contribute to the creation of a legal environment where parties are encouraged to seek consensual solutions to their cross-border family disputes'.[109] Therefore a move towards increased party autonomy is legitimate and appropriate as long as the 'weaker' party is protected.

deal with parental responsibility. Given the wide range of jurisdictional grounds available for divorce, designation of the *lex fori* could result in a different law than that under Art 3 being applicable.

104 Bonomi (n 48) 353.

105 Bonomi Report (n 9) para 125.

106 This certainty is not possible under the general rule as the law applicable will change as soon as the creditor gains a new habitual residence (Art 3(2) of the Hague Protocol).

107 See E Jayme, 'Party Autonomy in International Family and Succession Law: New Tendencies' (2009) *Yearbook of Private International Law* 1, 2 and Pertegás (n 72) 330–31. This is also evidenced in the fact that the 1973 Applicable Law Convention did not provide for party autonomy.

108 Jayme (n 107) 2.

109 Pertegás (n 72) 329.

Article 8 aims to protect the weaker party as it does not apply to 'vulnerable' adults,[110] or to children under 18,[111] because it was considered that the benefits outweighed the risks for these groups.[112] However even consenting adults are restricted as to the law they can actually designate. They cannot just select any law, it has to have some connection to the dispute as provided for in Article 8(1).[113] The laws that can be designated according to Article 8 are: the law of the State of the nationality of either party at the time of the designation;[114] the law of the State of the habitual residence of either party at the time of the designation;[115] the law designated by the parties as applicable to their property regime, or the law in fact applied to this;[116] or the law designated by the parties as applicable to their divorce or the law in fact applied to the divorce.[117]

The first two grounds were on the whole undisputed and they appear to be relevant connecting factors for permitting the designation of a law. What is more problematic, particularly in relation to the second ground, is the express reference to the time of designation. Therefore the choice remains indefinitely regardless of a change in habitual residence, or nationality, at a later date.[118] Although this provides certainty, in contrast to the rule in Article 3(2), given that habitual residence is a flexible concept that can change easily a law designated on the basis of Article 8(1)(b) may have no real relevance to the dispute at the time the proceedings are held.

The last two options have the potential to be more problematic for the parties, and are limited to spouses and ex-spouses. Although these options aim to create consistency between the maintenance obligation and either the property

[110] Art 8(3). The Protocol refers to this group as an adult 'who by reason of an impairment or insufficiency of his or her personal faculties, is not in a position to protect his or her interest.' This definition is taken from the Hague Convention of 13 January 2000 on the International Protection of Adults (see Art 1(1) of the Convention and Bonomi Report (n 9) para 127). This conforms with the pragmatic approach in the sense that the Protocol clearly determines groups that cannot designate a law, while protecting party autonomy. However the determination of who is 'vulnerable' in family matters is not necessarily clear, and 'vulnerability' does not in itself have to be a negative state that precludes autonomy. See A Diduck, 'Autonomy and Vulnerability in Family Law: The Missing Link' in J Wallbank and J Herring (eds), *Vulnerabilities, Care and Family Law* (Oxon, Routledge, 2014) 95–114.

[111] Hague Protocol Art 8(3).

[112] Bonomi Report (n 9) para 128. For more information on the decision to exclude vulnerable adults see Beaumont (n 4) 520–21.

[113] As such State interference still prevails, by restricting the laws that can be designated in order not to disadvantage a possible 'weaker party'. This is reflected in the Regulation in the rules on choice of court where the parties choice is restricted (Art 4 of the Regulation) but not in the equivalent rules under the Convention where parties can designate any court for all disputes, unless one of the parties is a child (Art 20(1)(e)).

[114] Hague Protocol Art 8(1)(a). It should be noted that there is no requirement that the nationality is common, unlike earlier provisions. Thus where the parties have multiple nationalities they potentially have a number of laws that they could designate, which widens the scope of choice.

[115] Hague Protocol Art 8(1)(b).

[116] Ibid, Art 8(1)(c).

[117] Ibid, Art 8(1)(d).

[118] See the Bonomi Report (n 9) para 133.

regime or divorce, they are dependent on the law selected in relation to the property regime or the divorce being valid. The validity of the law designated for matrimonial property disputes or divorce is not something that the Protocol can regulate. Instead it is regulated by the private international law of the Contracting States (including any regional or international instruments that may apply). If the choice of law in relation to either the property regime or divorce is invalid (according to the relevant rules) then the designation of the law in relation to maintenance will also be invalid.[119] Consequently Zupan believes that the choices available under these provisions are

> disadvantageous, because it has unnecessarily created a very complex system and a wide choice of applicable laws; the options provided for under points c) and d) depend on the national conflict of laws rule applicable to the respective issues, thereby undermining the uniqueness of a unified instrument.[120]

Unless spouses seek appropriate advice, they might find that a designation which appears valid under the rules in the Protocol is inappropriate because of the lack of uniformity in relation to divorce and matrimonial property.

Any agreement must be formally recorded and signed, in order to provide evidence of the choice. This will normally be in writing, but the Protocol is forward looking, stating that the document shall be in writing 'or recorded in any medium'.[121] No specific forms of medium are stated so that the provision can continue to adapt to changing technologies,[122] however the need for a signature remains no matter what medium is used to record the agreement.[123]

There are further limitations on the choice of law. Article 8(4) provides that regardless of the applicable law, any decision by the creditor to renounce his or her right to maintenance will continue to be determined by the law of the State of the creditor's habitual residence.

> This provision is naturally intended to prevent the creditor, through the choice of a particularly liberal and unprotective law, from being made to renounce the maintenance to which he or she would be entitled under the applicable law if there had been no choice.[124]

The final escape clause allows the court hearing the application to set aside the choice of law in favour of another law designated by the Protocol if the court is concerned that application of the designated law will lead to manifestly unfair or

[119] 'This lack of uniformity may also occur in the case of choice of law actually applied to the property regime or divorce; as the connecting rules have not been unified in such matters, the law applied may change according to the conflict of law rules of the court seized.' (Bonomi (n 48) 355.) See also the Bonomi Report (n 9) paras 135–37 and Zupan (n 54).

[120] Zupan (n 54).

[121] Hague Protocol Art 8(2).

[122] See the preamble to the Convention, which states that the Convention seeks 'to take advantage of advances in technologies and to create a flexible system which can continue to evolve as needs change and further advances in technology create new opportunities'.

[123] Bonomi Report (n 9) para 145.

[124] Ibid, para 148.

unreasonable consequences for the parties.[125] This should only be done if it can be shown that the parties were not fully informed and aware of the consequences of their choice.[126] However, Bonomi suggests that the clause could also be triggered if the chosen law has 'only a very weak link to the parties'[127] at the time of the dispute. This provision aims to limit the power of the court to set aside the designated law but ensures that the parties are protected.

Bonomi reflects that aside from these specific questions that are addressed in their own way, there is no provision that specifies which law is applicable to determine the validity or the existence of the agreement.[128] The solution suggested is to apply the law designated by the parties to determine whether the agreement is valid under that law.[129] This would appear to be the most sensible solution and is the solution prescribed in other documents, such as Rome I.[130] From the perspective of clarity and consistency it would have been preferable if the Protocol had specifically stated this in the text. The Bonomi Report only provides guidance and technically, therefore, courts are free to apply whatever law they want to determine the validity of the agreement. The other option which may appear sensible and possibly less costly would be to apply the law of the forum. However, as Jayme indicates the Protocol should be interpreted autonomously and therefore there should be no reference to national law.[131] Despite this he recognises that 'the broad and vague language of the Protocol reduces the importance of party autonomy for maintenance obligations, given that the validity of each agreement may be questioned in a dispute.'[132] Therefore courts can revert to the law of the forum because even though the Protocol should be interpreted autonomously this is not a requirement in Article 8. Courts might also be tempted to apply the law of the creditor's habitual residence to questions of validity (if this is not the designated law or the law of the forum) due to the Protocol's preference for this law, which is clear from the text. Time will tell what approach courts take to determine the validity of an agreement which designates an applicable law.[133] The best solution, as suggested by the Bonomi Report, is to apply the designated law to determine the validity of the agreement. If the CJEU gives a ruling on this point it is likely this is the solution they will opt for as this is the approach taken in Rome I.

[125] Hague Protocol Art 8(5).

[126] Ibid, Art 8(5).

[127] Bonomi (n 48) 357.

[128] Bonomi Report (n 9) para 152.

[129] 'The preferred solution for dealing with this deficiency is to consider that these issues will be governed by the law designated by the parties.' (Bonomi Report (n 9) para 152.)

[130] Regulation (EC) No 593/2008 of the European Parliament and of the Council of 17 June 2008 on the law applicable to contractual obligations (2008) OJ L177/6, Arts 10, 11 and 13 read in conjunction with Art 3(5).

[131] Jayme (n 107) 5.

[132] Ibid.

[133] This could be a matter on which the CJEU is requested to give an interpretation. If this happens then the question of validity will be dealt with uniformly within the EU.

## IV. Other Provisions

### A. Public Policy and Determining the Amount of Maintenance

It is possible to refuse the application of the law determined by the Protocol but only if the effects of that law are 'manifestly contrary to the public policy of the forum'.[134] The most likely scenario for invoking this clause is where the applicable law would impose maintenance payments through a relationship that is not recognised by the forum. This would include same sex partnerships or polygamous marriages. However, the Bonomi Report makes it clear that Article 13 should not be used wherever possible.[135] This is because the 'determination of public policy is to be performed *in concreto*'.[136] Therefore it is not enough that the law of the forum simply does not recognise the relationship; the actual payment of the maintenance would have to be against the public policy of the State.

The provision in the 1973 Applicable Law Convention that dealt with public policy contained an additional requirement.[137] This provided that the court also had to take account of the needs and resources of the parties, even if the applicable law provides otherwise. The Protocol retains this provision but removes it from the public policy provision to a separate Article.[138] The decision to move this requirement is important. This is because when it is paired with the public policy exception the suggestion might be that it only applies to foreign law; but in its new position it should apply to whichever law is applicable, even if it is the law of the forum.[139] Unfortunately it reduces legal certainty as it allows the judge to depart from the law designated by the Protocol. The second difference is that in addition to needs and resources, the court should also take account of any compensation the creditor has been awarded instead of periodical maintenance payments.[140]

### B. Exclusion of *Renvoi*

The Protocol specifically excludes the application of *renvoi*.[141] This approach is consistent with the 1973 Applicable Law Convention and other Hague instruments. It is also consistent with the general approach of the Protocol which seeks to increase efficiency and reduce costs by making reference to the law of the forum (or the law of the habitual residence of the creditor, which will often be the

[134] Hague Protocol Art 13.
[135] Bonomi Report (n 9) para 177.
[136] Ibid. See also ch 7 at s VI A.
[137] 1973 (Applicable Law) Convention, Art 11.
[138] Hague Protocol Art 14.
[139] Bonomi Report (n 9) para 182.
[140] See ibid para 184 for more information.
[141] Hague Protocol Art 12.

*lex fori*). The exclusion of *renvoi* also reduces costs by limiting the reference to yet another law, where the law applicable is not the law of the forum. Martiny has argued that as all Member States apply the same rules, harmony should already be achieved within the EU so 'the application of the doctrine of renvoi would not make sense.'[142]

## V. Conclusion

It is clear that the Hague Protocol represents an innovative approach which seeks to compromise between wide ratification of the Convention (limit the States opting out of the Regulation) and the inclusion of applicable law rules for those States that do not agree with the automatic application of the law of the forum. The Protocol is largely based on the 1973 Applicable Law Convention, but it makes some significant changes by: introducing party autonomy, placing the law of the forum above the law of common nationality where these laws are applied as subsidiary connections, reforming the law applicable to spousal support, and improving the defence of the debtor in controversial types of maintenance. The Protocol is also novel, in the sense it is not like normal 'Protocols', because it can be ratified by States that are not party to the Convention.[143]

Within the EU, the Protocol applies to all Member States apart from the UK and Denmark. One of the main reasons for this, at least from the UK perspective, is that common law countries prefer to apply the *lex fori* and civil law countries prefer to apply applicable law rules.[144] However, a closer analysis of the rules in the Protocol suggest that when it is applied in the EU along with (most) of the general grounds of jurisdiction in the Regulation,[145] the result will be that the *lex fori* will apply in many cases, if not all parental child support cases. This is clear from the general rule in Article 3 combined with the alternative rule in Article 4(3) which will both normally result in the application of the law of the forum. It is only if for some reason these rules do not apply, either because of party autonomy, because another law would not support a maintenance obligation arising from a particular relationship, or if jurisdiction is based on Article 5, 6, 7 or 8 that an alternative law would probably apply. In itself this general favour for the *lex fori*, no matter what regime you are using, seems unproblematic. However the approach taken to recognition and enforcement in the Regulation creates two

[142] Martiny (n 50) 96.

[143] Generally in international law, additional Protocols only apply to States that are party to the main instrument.

[144] See, Duncan (n 3) 327.

[145] The cases where this will not happen is where jurisdiction is based on status—due to the number of alternative rules of jurisdiction contained in Brussels IIbis. For example see *EA v AP* [2013] EWHC 2344 (Fam).

systems—one for Protocol States and the other for non-Protocol States.[146] This means in the European context that UK courts have to automatically recognise and enforce decisions from other Member States but decisions taken in the UK are subject to review before being recognised and enforced in all other Member States.[147]Although it is clearly much easier to directly apply the *lex fori* rather than apply the rules in the Protocol, it is questionable whether the UK really wants to be in this, arguably, downgraded position where the decisions originating there are treated differently from decisions given in other Member States,[148] when in many cases—particularly child support cases—the *lex fori* will apply anyway.

[146] These two regimes are discussed in detail in the next chapter.

[147] If 'one reviews this objectively, the outcome is actually rather unjust for the UK, with almost no objection it allows the enforcement of each Member States' judgments while UK judgments are subject to additional controls in other Member States when submitted for enforcement.' (Zupan (n 54).)

[148] It is also questioned how the rules in the Protocol, which in some cases acknowledge that a different law can apply, really justify the automatic recognition and enforcement of all decisions. This is discussed in detail in ch 7 below.

# 7

# Recognition and Enforcement: Regulation

## I. Introduction

In order for foreign judgments to be recognised and declared enforceable in the enforcing State they have traditionally, in many States, had to go through a process commonly known as *exequatur*. The process means that once the judgment has been recognised and declared enforceable, it can then be enforced just like a national decision, under national enforcement laws. The *exequatur* process prevents judgments from being enforced when for certain specific reasons they are not enforceable in the State of enforcement. This process provides necessary safeguards for the parties involved. The most important exception included in the process is whether the enforcement of the decision would manifestly violate the public policy of the enforcing State.

The development of common policies and the principle of mutual trust in Europe has meant that there are now different levels of safeguards in international and regional instruments. Some instruments, in particular the international ones, have positive and negative requirements for refusing recognition and enforcement.[1] This form of instrument is known as a 'simple or indirect' treaty. In these instruments during the procedure the court has to refuse to award recognition and enforcement of the judgment if it considers that the judgment was not based on an adequate ground of jurisdiction.[2] However, if the decision was granted on an adequate jurisdictional base the Court can still refuse recognition and enforcement on one of the grounds for refusing recognition.[3] This form of instrument works well at

[1] See the Verwilghen Report (M Verwilghen, 'Explanatory Report on the 1973 Hague Maintenance Conventions (1975) para 125, available at www.hcch.net/index_en.php?act=publications.details&pid=2946&dtid=3, accessed 21 May 2014). The new Maintenance Convention (Hague Convention of 23 November 2007 on the International Recovery of Child Support and other forms of Family Maintenance) also follows this method.

[2] For example, see the Maintenance Convention Art 20.

[3] Ibid, Art 22 for the common procedure, and Art 24 for the alternative procedure.

the international level, because it means that States do not have to 'change their municipal laws.'[4]

Another form is the one used in the majority of European instruments, since the Brussels Convention. This method suggests that a 'judgment given in an EU State should be recognised without special proceedings unless the recognition is contested.'[5] There are limited grounds on which recognition and enforcement can be contested.[6] This procedure is possible because these instruments have direct rules of jurisdiction. This 'attacks the problem of conflicting jurisdictional bases among Member States by providing exclusive rules of jurisdiction from which recognition and enforcement may automatically flow.'[7] This is because the rules established 'apply independently of any procedure for recognition and enforcement, [so] the reviewing function of the recognising court is greatly reduced.'[8]

The next method, which looks like it will be the route of new EU instruments following the Brussels I recast, is to remove the *exequatur* procedure completely but to maintain safeguards at the actual enforcement stage.[9] This would mean that it would still be possible not to enforce the judgment, for one of the reasons that already exist, but the length of the process will be reduced for States that have Court proceedings at both the *exequatur* stage and the 'actual enforcement stage'. However, this could mean that some States will have to overhaul their systems if they do not provide for court proceedings at the enforcement stage. The fourth method is to have no procedure at all and to retain virtually no safeguards.[10] This effectively means that judgments from a second State are treated in exactly the same way as national decisions.

[4] LI De Winter, 'Excessive Jurisdiction in Private International Law' (1968) 17 *International and Comparative Law Quarterly* 706, 709.

[5] http://europa.eu/legislation_summaries/justice_freedom_security/judicial_cooperation_in_civil_matters/l33054_en.htm, accessed 5 June 2014. This is the procedure that is used under the Regulation, where the decision has originated in the UK (and possibly Denmark). See Arts 23 and 24 of the Maintenance Regulation (Council Regulation (EC) 4/2009 of 18 December 2008 on jurisdiction, applicable law, recognition and enforcement of decisions and cooperation in matters relating to maintenance obligations [2009] OJ L7/1 (Maintenance Regulation)).

[6] See Art 24 of the Maintenance Regulation and Arts 34 and 35 of Brussels I (Council Regulation (EC) 44/2001 of 22 December 2000 on jurisdiction and the recognition and enforcement of judgments in civil and commercial matters [2001] OJ L012/1 (Brussels I)).

[7] LS Bartlett, 'Full Faith and Credit comes to the Common Market an Analysis of the Convention on Jurisdiction and Enforcement of Judgments in Civil and Commercial Matters' (1975) 24 *International and Comparative Law Quarterly* 44, 49.

[8] Ibid, 46.

[9] See the Council of the European Union, Press Release December 2011 (19498/11) 22, and the official text of the Brussels I recast (Regulation (EU) 1215/2012 of the European Parliament and of the Council of 12 December 2012 on jurisdiction and the recognition and enforcement of judgments in civil and commercial matters (recast) [2012] OJ L351/1 (Brussels I recast)) Arts 45 and 46.

[10] This is the normal procedure under the Maintenance Regulation where only the irreconcilable judgments defence is retained with the same effect (Art 21(2)). Possible harm caused by this will be discussed below, at s III.

## II. The Procedures in the Maintenance Regulation

There are four different tracks for recognition and enforcement available under the Maintenance Regulation and Convention. Two tracks per instrument. This chapter will focus on the two tracks in the Maintenance Regulation. This chapter aims to distinguish between these tracks and identify the most suitable system for recognition and enforcement of foreign decisions. The most suitable track will be the one that aims to best fulfil the objectives of the Regulation,[11] whilst protecting the rights of the individuals who are involved in the application. Then it will be questioned how appropriate the chosen track actually is and whether this could be improved further.

Both the Regulation tracks are stricter than the Convention tracks. The first track provides for the abolition of *exequatur*. This applies to all Member States who have signed the Hague Protocol on Applicable Law.[12] There is no possibility of opposing recognition of a decision, and there is no need for a declaration of enforceability.[13] This track will apply to applications between all Member States unless the judgment to be recognised or enforced was given in the United Kingdom or Denmark. This position was taken with the intention of speeding up proceedings. However, this is possibly a step too far that could potentially violate

[11] Both instruments aim to provide an effective and prompt procedure for the recovery of family maintenance from abroad. The Regulation makes a variety of references in this regard but the overall aim is not so clear to pinpoint. Perhaps, if the United Kingdom position had not been considered carefully from the beginning, the only reference would be the one in Recital (9). 'A maintenance creditor should be able to obtain easily, in a Member State, a decision which will be automatically enforceable in another Member State without further formalities.' Unfortunately although this was the priority at the time the Regulation was concluded this could not be the system in all Member States. The alternative is covered by Recital (26). This states that where there are proceedings for recognition and enforcement, in order to accelerate proceedings 'the court seised should be required to give its decision within a set time, unless there are exceptional circumstances'. The influence appears to be the speed of procedures and unlike the Convention there is no mention of the fairness of procedures. The right of parties to be heard is mentioned briefly in Recital (12) however, this only appears to apply in relation to proceedings before administrative authorities rather than across the board. Recital (31) refers to the duties of Central Authorities (see ch 10). This mentions the rights of creditors and debtors but only in relation to their rights under the Regulation rather than their right to fair proceedings in general. This is slightly unfortunate. However, the Charter of Fundamental Rights has the same legal value as the Treaties (Art 6(1) TEU). Therefore, the rights contained in this document should have priority over the correct application of the Regulation. How this will work in practice is a different matter.

[12] Protocol of 23 November 2007 on the Law Applicable to Maintenance Obligations has been ratified by the European Community and applies to all Member States except for the United Kingdom and Denmark. 'For the purpose of this declaration the term "European Community" does not include Denmark, by virtue of Articles 1 and 2 of the Protocol on the position of Denmark, annexed to the Treaty on European Union and to the Treaty establishing the European Community, and the United Kingdom, by virtue of Articles 1 and 2 of the Protocol on the position of the United Kingdom and Ireland, annexed to the Treaty on European Union and to the Treaty establishing the European Community.' See the status table at: www.hcch.net/index_en.php?act=conventions.status&cid=133, accessed 5 June 2013.

[13] Maintenance Regulation Art 17. The irreconcilable judgments defence remains, see Art 21(2), although technically this is effective at the enforcement stage rather than the recognition stage.

the rights of individuals in the process under the Regulation.[14] One potential benefit of this for parties to the Protocol is that all applications will be treated in the same way no matter what type of document is being used to enforce the maintenance obligation.[15] However, it is noted that in the first year of operation of the Regulation the majority of obligations that were sought to be enforced originated from a decision of a court or administrative authority, rather than from a court settlement or an authentic instrument.[16]

## III. Non-Protocol States

Where a UK, or potentially a Danish judgment is being sought recognition in another EU Member State, a simplified procedure for recognition and enforcement is in place under the Regulation.[17] This procedure only applies to outgoing decisions from these States. All incoming decisions to the UK (except the ones from Denmark) have to be automatically enforced, because the decision originated in a Protocol State and the application of the Protocol is seen as a condition for the abolition of *exequatur*.[18] The simplified procedure contains only four grounds on which recognition or enforcement can be refused. These grounds are almost identical to the current grounds for refusal of recognition in Brussels I,[19] (and its predecessor the Brussels Convention). There are also additional grounds in Article 35 of Brussels I but these are not relevant in the disputes covered by the Maintenance Regulation. It is notable that this is the case for a variety of reasons. Prior to the Maintenance Regulation disputes of this sort were dealt with under Brussels I. Therefore, a direct substitution of the grounds would appear sensible.

[14] This will be discussed at s V.

[15] The system will be the same whether it is a decision of a court or an administrative authority, a court settlement or an authentic instrument. This is important because authentic instruments cannot be recognised because they do not have *res judicata* effect. This meant that under Brussels I as it stands authentic instruments had to be subject to different treatment. 'When one considers Article 57(1) together with Article 34, the contrast between the treatment of authentic instruments and judgments within the Brussels I regime is striking; Article 34 of Chapter III provides four distinct bases, each of which allow a judgment debtor to appeal against the recognition or, via Article 45(1) the enforcement of a foreign judgment. Article 57 of Chapter IV [authentic instruments] provides only one ground to resist the declaration of enforceability.' J Fitchen, 'Authentic Instruments and European Private International Law in Civil and Commercial Matters: Is Now the Time to Break New Ground?' (2011) 7 *Journal of Private International Law* 33, 69–70.

[16] Information obtained from the empirical study. Only around 2% of applications were reported as being based on a court settlement or an authentic instrument.

[17] See Maintenance Regulation Arts 23 and 24.

[18] See ss IV, V and VI.

[19] Brussels I, see Art 34. In fact, the procedure is modelled on Brussels I: 'That procedure should be modelled on the procedure and grounds for refusing recognition set out in Regulation (EC) No 44/2001. To accelerate proceedings and enable the creditor to recover his claim quickly, the court seised should be required to give its decision within a set time, unless there are exceptional circumstances'. (Maintenance Regulation Recital (26).)

Under the Maintenance Regulation, the first exception is public policy: 'if such recognition is manifestly contrary to public policy in the Member State in which recognition is sought. The test of public policy may not be applied to the rules relating to jurisdiction'.[20] The second exception relates to the right to a fair hearing in the sense that the defendant is given due notification of the proceedings.

> where [the decision] was given in default of appearance, if the defendant was not served with the document which instituted the proceedings or with an equivalent document in sufficient time and in such a way as to enable him to arrange for his defence, unless the defendant failed to commence proceedings to challenge the decision when it was possible for him to do so.[21]

The remaining two grounds can be invoked where the decision to be recognised is irreconcilable with another decision. Firstly one given in the Member State where recognition is sought; 'if it is irreconcilable with a decision given in a dispute between the same parties in the Member State in which recognition is sought'.[22] Secondly where the decision is from another State;

> if it is irreconcilable with an earlier decision given in another Member State or in a third State in a dispute involving the same cause of action and between the same parties, provided that the earlier decision fulfils the conditions necessary for its recognition in the Member State in which recognition is sought.[23]

The public policy exception, and the importance of retaining this safeguard as a safety valve, is discussed in detail below. The notification defence is also analysed below. The irreconcilable judgments defences will be discussed now. As explained in the previous chapters on scope and jurisdiction, the refusal of enforceability on the basis of irreconcilable judgments could be a problem, particularly in the context of spousal maintenance on divorce.[24] This is because there is no clear definition of the term 'maintenance'[25] and there are a number of alternative bases of jurisdiction available, which include the ability to select a different court to deal with the divorce and/or the matrimonial property.[26] Therefore, irreconcilable judgments could arise in a variety of situations. This could be from decisions where one court characterises a payment as matrimonial property and the other regards it as maintenance. The decision to pay maintenance would be difficult to enforce if the money has already been allocated as a matrimonial property payment. A decision awarding interim payment on divorce could also conflict with a final maintenance order. Judgments could also be irreconcilable with other

[20] Maintenance Regulation Art 24(a).
[21] Ibid, Art 24(b). However, is this exception really necessary? (see s VIII below).
[22] Ibid, Art 24(c).
[23] Ibid, Art 24(d).
[24] This problem exists to the same extent for both Protocol and non-Protocol States because Maintenance Regulation Art 21(2) applies where Arts 24(c) and (d) do not.
[25] See ch 3.
[26] See ch 5.

maintenance decisions made in third States, because the *lis pendens* and related actions provisions only cover proceedings in another Member State.[27]

*Hoffman v Krieg*[28] concerned the enforcement of an order for spousal maintenance that was awarded when the couple were married. The couple had subsequently divorced and the issue was whether the previous maintenance award was still enforceable, or if it was irreconcilable with the subsequent divorce decision. The maintenance order was given in Germany and the divorce decree was given in the Netherlands. The crux of the problem was that even though the maintenance award 'presuppose[d] the existence of a matrimonial relationship',[29] the award was still enforceable in the State of origin (Germany) because the divorce decree had not been recognised there.[30] The assumption in the State of origin was that the parties were still married; therefore, the award remained enforceable in that State. The Court of Justice of the European Union (CJEU) was left to determine what the solution should be in such a case. In particular could the enforcing State refuse enforcement under the irreconcilable judgments defence, or would it have to rely on public policy?[31] The Court considered that the public policy clause should only apply in exceptional circumstances and therefore should be precluded when the main issue is the compatibility of a foreign judgment with a national judgment.[32]

Once the public policy defence had been excluded, the Court then considered whether the judgments were irreconcilable, within the meaning of the Brussels Convention. In order to determine if the decisions were indeed irreconcilable the Court had to examine whether they 'entail legal consequences which are mutually exclusive.'[33] The Court held that the legal consequences of the decision were mutually exclusive because:

> The foreign judgment which necessarily presupposes the existence of the matrimonial relationship, would have to be enforced although that relationship has been dissolved by a judgment given in a dispute between the same parties in the State in which enforcement is sought.
>
> The answer to be given to the third question submitted by the national court is therefore that a foreign judgment ordering a person to make maintenance payments to his spouse by virtue of his conjugal obligations to support her is irreconcilable within the meaning of Article 27(3) of the Convention with a national judgment pronouncing the divorce of the spouses.[34]

The judgment confirms that decisions which relate to divorce and maintenance of spouses or ex-spouses often have legal consequences that are mutually exclusive

[27] See ch 5 s IV.
[28] C-145/86 *Hoffmann v Krieg* [1988] ECR 645.
[29] Ibid, para 13.
[30] Ibid, para 14.
[31] Ibid, para 7(3).
[32] Ibid, para 21. However, for a detailed analysis of the scope of the public policy defence see ss V and VIII.
[33] Ibid, para 22.
[34] Ibid, paras 24–25.

because of the nature of these judgments and the fact that maintenance orders are often related to the status of persons.[35] It highlights when the provisions on irreconcilable judgments may come into force and clarifies that decisions on maintenance are not only irreconcilable with other decisions, given in the State of enforcement, specifically on maintenance but also decisions on status covered by Brussels IIbis.[36] Martiny has argued that the decision in *Hoffmann* is complicated and the outcome is doubtful.[37] There are several reasons why he takes this stance. Firstly, because the foreign maintenance order was given when the spouses were already separated, there 'is no reason why a judgment dealing with this question should not be enforced even after a divorce.'[38] Secondly, it is contemplated that there could be situations under the relevant domestic law where a maintenance order remains enforceable; despite the fact the parties have subsequently divorced.[39] This particular point is considered by Justice Ward in *R v West London Magistrates' Court*.[40]

In the case Ward J was following the earlier decision in *Macaulay*,[41] which is very similar to the *West London* case. Both cases involved Irish maintenance orders that were sought to be enforced in England between spouses who had subsequently divorced. It should be noted that these maintenance orders concerned awards for the spouse, as well as awards for the children of the marriage. In *Macaulay*, the solicitor pointed out that:

> there is nothing inherently objectionable in the English courts enforcing against a divorced spouse an order obtained during the subsistence of the marriage for the maintenance

[35] See ch 5 ss III and IV.

[36] (Council Regulation (EC) 2201/2003 of 27 November 2003 on jurisdiction, recognition and enforcement of judgments in matrimonial matters and matters of parental responsibility, repealing Regulation (EC) No 1347/2000 [2003] OJ L 338/1 (Brussels IIbis.) This is specifically in relation to Art 24(c) and decisions in the State of enforcement, so cases akin to *Hoffmann*. However, in regard to Art 24(d) cases the situation is different, because like the rules on *lis pendens* it requires that both these decisions have 'the same cause of action'. Therefore, in situations that fall under Art 24(d) the provision is not as far reaching and is unlikely to cover such a wide range of cases (see the discussion on *lis pendens* and related actions at ch 5 s IV). It is questioned whether this distinction is ideal, because as shown in *Hoffmann* decisions do not need to have 'the same cause of action' to be irreconcilable or have 'mutually exclusive legal consequences'.

[37] D Martiny, 'Maintenance Obligations in the Conflict of Laws' (1994) 247 *Recueil des Cours* 131, 270. Conversely, Hartley appears to take no objection to the judgment, considering that the idea behind it was; 'if the divorce had been within the scope of the Convention, the German court would have been obliged either not to give the maintenance order (if the divorce had been granted first) or to rescind it (if it was granted later). If this had been the case the husband's attempt to have the maintenance order set aside in Germany would have been successful.' (T Hartley, 'Case Comment, Maintenance Orders—Irreconcilable Judgments' (1991) 16 *European Law Review* 64, 67–68.) Therefore Hartley indicates that imagining trying to enforce the two obligations under the same instrument provides greater clarification as to why this particular decision should not be enforced and indicates how this should protect parties' expectations.

[38] Martiny (n 37) 270.

[39] Ibid, 270. Hartley's analysis would also imply that the decision in *Hoffmann* should not be followed in such cases (n 37). This is because if the two elements both fell under the same instrument they would still have to be irreconcilable in order to prevent the enforcement of one of the judgments.

[40] *R v West London Magistrates' Court* [1994] 1 FCR 421, 435.

[41] *Macaulay v Macaulay* [1991] 1 WLR 179.

> of the other spouse qua spouse. An order made in the magistrates' court under the Domestic Proceedings and Magistrates' Courts Act 1978 does not automatically terminate upon the dissolution of the parties' marriage, nor do financial orders made in a suit for judicial separation or under section 27 of the Matrimonial Causes Act 1973 come to an end on divorce.[42]

As such the solicitor considered that the judgments were not mutually exclusive and therefore not irreconcilable. The judge however disagreed, considered that the case could not be distinguished from *Hoffmann*, and therefore held that the judgments were mutually exclusive and therefore irreconcilable. On the basis that like *Hoffmann*, the maintenance obligation 'was founded upon the husband's obligation to maintain the wife and that obligation was brought to an end by the English decree of divorce.'[43] In the *West London* case the judge considered that he had no option but to follow the decision in *Macaulay*, since the facts were so similar, despite the fact that he considered the decision was wrong.[44] Ward J believed that the previous decision was wrong because the cases could be distinguished from *Hoffmann* on the basis that the English law (and the Irish law) differed from German law in this area. This is because the maintenance obligation in the Irish cases did not 'presuppose the existence of the marriage' and therefore the judgments were not mutually exclusive.[45]

If the decision on maintenance did not presuppose the existence of the marriage and thereby remained enforceable regardless of personal status then it has to be assumed that they were not mutually exclusive, so not irreconcilable, and therefore capable of being enforced. This would be more in keeping with the spirit of the Convention and now the Regulation which seek to facilitate the free movement of judgments.[46] Therefore, it could be argued that the English judges erred in law by refusing to enforce judgments which were in fact enforceable under Irish and also English law.[47] If a similar case arose now, the judge could use their discretion to refer the issue to the CJEU to clarify whether the judgments could be

[42] Ibid, 185.

[43] Ibid.

[44] *West London* (n 40) 435.

[45] Ibid.

[46] See, P Jenard, 'Report on the Convention on Jurisdiction and the Enforcement of Judgments in Civil and Commercial Matters Signed at Brussels, 27 September 1968' OJ C 59, 5 March 1979 (Jenard Report). 'If a judgment is enforceable in the State of origin, it also ought to be enforceable in the State in which enforcement is sought.' (Martiny (n 37) 271.)

[47] However, in case C-80/00 *Italian Leather v WECO Postermobel GmbH & Co* [2002] ECR I-5011, it was held that where a judgment is irreconcilable then the judge in the State of enforcement has no discretion and must refuse enforcement. The ground is 'mandatory' (para 50). This is because 'it would be contrary to the principle of legal certainty, which the Court has repeatedly held to be one of the objectives of the Brussels Convention … to interpret Article 27(3) as conferring on the court of the State in which recognition is sought the power to authorise recognition of a foreign judgment when it is irreconcilable with a judgment given in that Contracting State.' (para 51). It is unclear how this interpretation would fit with the present facts. The decision implies that the court should not have power to authorise recognition where the decision is irreconcilable with a judgment given in that State. So if the judgment is reconcilable then they have to authorise recognition. However, should the logic be that the Court has no discretion and must follow *Hoffmann* where a divorce followed a

distinguished.[48] The judgments can also be distinguished from *Hoffmann* on another ground. This is because the maintenance orders in the Irish cases concerned maintenance payments in respect of children as well as spouses, unlike *Hoffmann*. The status of the parents has no effect on the maintenance obligation in respect of the children which would still arise despite the divorce. Therefore, this part of the maintenance order should still remain enforceable regardless of the other questions. This is not something that appears to have been considered at all.

Whether or not the Irish cases are in fact distinguishable from *Hoffmann*, Martiny believes that the use of the irreconcilable judgments defence in *Hoffmann* was not actually justified.[49] Following the system in the European Union if the judgment is enforceable in the State of origin it should also be enforceable in the State of enforcement. Therefore if there is a change in circumstance before the judgment is enforced, the judgment should be amended in the State of origin, not simply refused recognition in the enforcing State. This should technically not be possible while the judgment remains enforceable in the State of origin.[50] It is not clear what the correct outcome is here. The remedy given in *Hoffmann* is simple. It provided an immediate solution, thus benefiting the parties, as it meant that they did not need to get the divorce order recognised first in order to then seek a new decision in the State of origin. It also means that the decision is not passing through the recognition and enforcement stage only to be refused enforcement later on, and thus prolonging procedures.[51] However, the decision has resulted in the free movement of judgments being impeded in later cases, since *Hoffmann* was followed on the basis that the situation between the parties was the same despite the fact that the judgments were not actually 'mutually exclusive'.[52]

maintenance order or should the court be allowed not to follow *Hoffmann* on the fact that in that case the judgments were not irreconcilable.

[48] Under Art 267 TFEU, a court may raise a question before the CJEU if it considers it necessary to decide the case. Although the judge would not need to refer, unless it was a court of last resort, they could refer this question in the future, if the judge thought the case was distinguishable from *Hoffmann* (n 28), and that the decision in *Macaulay* (n 41) and *West London* (n 40) was wrong. This would clarify the position and judges would know what to do in future cases.

[49] Martiny (n 37) 270–71.

[50] Ibid, 271. He also refers to a particular German law that could have been useful in the case which could have protected the parties. However, following the decision in *Italian Leather* (n 47) if the judgments are indeed irreconcilable the judge has no choice but to refuse recognition even if the judgment is still enforceable in the State of origin.

[51] This seems to be the solution that Martiny is referring to: '[a]n action to avert execution'. If this route had been taken the decision in *Hoffmann* would have been akin to the later decision in *Prism Investments* (C-139/10 *Prism Investments v van der Meer* [2011] ECR I-09511) where *exequatur* had to be granted despite the fact that the judgment would never be enforced.

[52] See, the two English decisions above, however as noted does the fact that the judge has no discretion in these cases impede their ability to examine the differences between the cases?

The three judgments highlight the difficulty of dealing with these issues at the recognition and enforcement stage.[53] The Heidelberg Report criticises the fact that Article 34(3) (equivalent to Article 24(c)) gives priority to the conflicting judgment in the recognising State, regardless which decision was given first.[54] As a result this effectively conflicts with the *lis pendens* and related actions provisions in Articles 12 and 13.[55] The most important thing is that the system ensures certainty for individuals to the greatest extent possible. Therefore, the best solution would be to deal with these problems at the outset in the State of origin, rather than at the recognition and enforcement stage. This emphasises the importance of having a clear and coherent system of jurisdiction throughout the relevant Regulations in the EU, which is something that does not currently exist.[56] It further suggests the development of the related actions provision, which currently does not require the court second seised to stay proceedings,[57] because the case law indicates that judgments which are related may be refused recognition and enforcement if they are deemed to have consequences which are 'mutually exclusive'.

Further, the irreconcilable judgments provisions apply under both tracks.[58] Therefore they are most likely to cause problems in relation to spousal maintenance during marriage or after divorce if the status of the spouses has changed. However, the Irish/English cases above indicate that this may also affect the enforcement of a maintenance award in relation to children, where the two awards fall under the same order.[59] As a final point in relation to the link between the *lis pendens* provisions and the provisions for refusal of enforcement there is a large gap in the Regulation. This is because the *lis pendens* rules only cover proceedings in other Member States whereas the irreconcilable judgment defence covers judgments arising in third States.[60] Therefore, it will be possible for irreconcilable judgments to occur in relation to judgments from third States as *lis pendens* does not apply.[61]

[53] See, J Fawcett and J Carruthers, *Cheshire, North and Fawcett: Private International Law*, 14th edn (Oxford, Oxford University Press, 2008) 622–24, and Martiny (n 37) 271 ('it seems inappropriate to characterize these problems as recognition issues when they only concern the correct approach to enforcement proceedings.').

[54] See, B Hess, T Pfeiffer and P Schlosser, *The Brussels I Regulation 44/2001. The Heidelberg Report on the Application of Regulation Brussels I in 25 Member States* (Study JLS/C4/2005/03), Munich: Verlag CH Beck 2008 (Heidelberg Report) 252–54.

[55] Ibid, and see ch 5 s IV.

[56] See ch 5 s IV.

[57] Ibid.

[58] Maintenance Regulation Art 24(c) and Art 21(2).

[59] See *West London* (n 40) and *Macaulay* (n 41).

[60] Compare Maintenance Regulation Arts 12 and 13 with Arts 24(d) and 21(2).

[61] The Brussels I recast attempts to fix this problem by including an additional provision that applies in relation to third States, Brussels I recast Art 33.

# IV. The Abolition of *Exequatur*

At the time the Maintenance Regulation was negotiated it was argued that the *exequatur* procedure should be abolished across the board. The abolition of *exequatur* had been on the European Agenda since the 1990s, and the initial plan was to abolish it from Brussels I in the Brussels I recast.[62] The final decision was to remove the *exequatur* process from Brussels I but retain the grounds for non-enforcement, as necessary safeguards, and apply them at the enforcement stage. Consequently instead of the Maintenance Regulation being one of the first steps towards the abolition of the safeguards contained in the *exequatur* process across the majority of EU instruments, it is now going to be virtually alone in this.[63] On the whole this is a positive result because the abolition of the *exequatur* procedure, along with the limited safeguards, is a dangerous route that does not necessarily protect the rights and integrity of individuals.[64] In the context of maintenance, the abolition of *exequatur* proceedings, without the retention of safeguards, is not proportionate to the aim and other alternatives should have been considered.

# V. Possible Issues with the Abolition of *Exequatur* in EU Regulations

The main argument for the abolition of *exequatur* is to help simplify proceedings and, therefore make them more expeditious. 'The time required to obtain a

[62] See X Kramer, 'Abolition of Exequatur under the Brussels I Regulation: Effecting and Protecting the Rights in the European Judicial Area' (2011) 4 *Nederlands Internationaal Privaatrecht* 633.

[63] Other instruments are: Regulation (EC) 805/2004 of 21 April 2004 of the European Parliament and of the Council creating a European enforcement order for uncontested claims [2004] OJ L143/15 (European Enforcement Order Regulation (EEO)) abolished *exequatur* proceedings for uncontested claims, and Regulation (EC) 861/2007 of the European Parliament and of the Council of 11 July 2007 establishing a European small claims Procedure [2007] OJ L199/1. The impact of the abolition of *exequatur* in these Regulations was considered to be minimal as one Regulation only applies to uncontested claims and the other to small claims (much less than the cost of recognition and enforcement proceedings). In contrast Brussels IIbis appears to completely abolish *exequatur* in relation to a return order in the context of child abduction. The Court of Justice of the European Union (CJEU) has held that the state of refuge has a duty to enforce the decision no matter whether human rights violations have occurred. Only the state of origin has a right to review the decision. (See Art 42 of Brussels IIbis, case C-491/10 PPU, *Joseba Andoni Aguirre Zarraga v Simone Pelz* [2010] ECR I-14247, and L Walker, 'From Brussels I and the Maintenance Convention to the Maintenance Regulation: Is the Resulting Maintenance Regulation Consistent with the Other EU PIL Instruments?' (2013) *Nederlands Internationaal Privaatrecht* 167, particularly s 2.2.)

[64] See in particular *Aguirre Zarraga* (n 63) and commentary L Walker and P Beaumont, 'Shifting the Balance Achieved by the Abduction Convention: The Contrasting Approaches of the European Court of Human Rights and the European Court of Justice' (2011) 7 *Journal of Private International Law* 239–48. See also P Beaumont and E Johnston, 'Can *Exequatur* be Abolished in Brussels I whilst Retaining a Public Policy Defence' (2010) 6 *Journal of Private International Law* 249–79.

declaration of enforceability [varies] … but the slowness of this procedure and abuse of the possibility to appeal is certainly a problem.'[65] Cuniberti has noted that the *exequatur* procedure has been used as a means to delay payment, however: '[in] practice, it is true that foreign judgments are rarely denied recognition, especially under the European law of judgments.'[66] Although the abolition of *exequatur* is a method to solve the delays, other alternatives do not seem to have been considered, and the procedure could be reformed in other ways.

> This could have been done through introducing time limits and limits on appeal. The proportionality of the measure is therefore questionable since the Commission appears to be proposing a measure that goes beyond what is necessary for the attainment of the aim. It is also submitted that the Commission has failed to fulfil its duty under the 1997 protocol on the application of principles of subsidiarity and proportionality.[67]

In this context, table 7 on the impact of maintenance obligations in regard to fundamental rights is relevant.[68] In relation to the effect on Article 47 (fair trial) and Article 49 (proportionality of criminal offences and penalties), the Commission identified no positive impact in this regard, and failed to comment on the proportionality of these restrictions. In relation to mitigating measures, the Commission refers to legal aid. However, it is questionable how the provision of legal aid will act as a mitigating measure in this area because legal aid is only guaranteed for creditors, not debtors.[69] Therefore, the abolition of the *exequatur* process appears to be disproportionate to the aim, as appropriate alternatives do not appear to have been considered properly.[70] This can have a negative impact on the rights of individuals.

[65] M Hellner, 'The Maintenance Regulation: A Critical Assessment of the Commission's Proposal' in K Boele-Woelki and T Sverdrup (eds), *European Challenges in Contemporary Family Law* (Antwerp, Intersentia, 2009) 362. However, Hess notes that, the 'efficiency of the procedure for recognition under Arts 38-45 Reg. 44/2001 cannot be denied. In almost all Member States, exequatur is obtained within days, and less than 5 percent of all exequatur decisions are appealed.' (B Hess, 'The Brussels I Regulation: Recent Case Law of the Court of Justice and the Commission's Proposed Recast' (2012) 49 *Common Market Law Review* 1075, 1094.) For a review of the length of time taken for recognition and enforcement procedures under Brussels I see the Heidelberg Report (n 54) 226–27 (and the other relevant documents cited in the study).

[66] G Cuniberti, 'Recognition of Foreign Judgments Lacking Reasons in Europe' (2008) 57 *International and Comparative Law Quarterly* 25, 48.

[67] Hellner (n 65) 362. See also Kramer (n 62) s 4; L Timmer, 'Abolition of *Exequatur* under the Brussels I Regulation: Ill Conceived and Premature?' (2013) 9 *Journal of Private International Law* 129; and G Cuniberti and I Reuda, 'Abolition of Exequatur—Addressing the Commission's Concerns' (2011) 75 *Rabels Zeichshrift* 286. See also Staff Working Document, Annex to the Proposal for a Council Regulation on jurisdiction, applicable law, recognition and enforcement of decisions and cooperation in matters relating to maintenance obligations—Impact assessment, SEC/2005/1629, where the Commission itself acknowledged that 'intermediate measures do not significantly contribute to time delays in maintenance claims'.

[68] SEC/2005/1629, 27–28.

[69] Art 46 of the Maintenance Regulation.

[70] One safeguard has been retained in relation to the rights of the defendant in Art 19. However, the application of this defence appears to be limited. See below at s VI B.

The main reason for *exequatur* proceedings is to protect the rights of individuals in exceptional circumstances. This can be done by either retaining the *exequatur* proceedings, or removing them but retaining necessary safeguards at the enforcement stage. The public policy exception can be used as a method to protect the rights of individuals. As the Maintenance Regulation contains no grounds for refusing recognition and enforcement, one can see how this may violate the human rights of the parties, in particular the debtor's right to an effective remedy and a fair trial. Parties have the right to an effective legal remedy in civil proceedings.[71] In order to protect this right the *exequatur* procedure, or at least the grounds for refusing recognition and enforcement normally dealt with in *exequatur* proceedings, should be retained in EU Regulations.[72]

The EU legal order has attempted to protect the fundamental rights of individuals for many years,[73] but following the Treaty of Lisbon the EU is supposed to provide even greater protection in this area. The Charter on Fundamental Rights now has the same legal value as the Treaties (rather than just being a soft law instrument),[74] and the European Union can accede to the European Convention on Human Rights (ECHR).[75] Now that the Charter has equal legal value to the Treaties the Treaty provisions need to be balanced with human rights considerations.[76] Neither have prevalence over the other. This is of particular importance in relation to Title V—area of freedom, security and justice. Despite the fact that these provisions still require 'respect for fundamental rights and the different legal systems and traditions of the Member States',[77] reference to human rights protection in relation to provisions under this title has been minimal.[78] This is

[71] Art 47 of the Charter of Fundamental Rights of the European Union [2000] OJ C364/01 and Art 6 ECHR (cited at nn 237 and 238 below).

[72] In this respect, the situation in the Maintenance Regulation is not as bad as it is under the provision concerning access and child abduction under Brussels IIbis. This is because there are possible grounds for refusing to enforce the decision at the enforcement stage, under Arts 19 and 21(discussed at s VI).

[73] For example see P Craig and G de Búrca, *EU Law: Text, Cases and Materials*, 5th edn (Oxford, Oxford University Press, 2011) 363–98; FG Jacobs, 'Human Rights in the European Union: The Role of the Court of Justice' (2001) *European Law Review* 331 and nn 75, 76 and 156 below.

[74] Treaty on the European Union, Art 6(1). For further information see D Sarmiento, 'Who's Afraid of the Charter? The Court of Justice, National Courts and the New Framework of Fundamental Rights Protection in Europe' (2013) 50 *Common Market Law Review* 1267.

[75] Ibid, Art 6(2). See, P Gragl, *The Accession of the European Union to the European Convention on Human Rights* (Oxford, Hart Publishing, 2013); JP Jacqué, 'The Accession of the EU to the ECHR' (2011) 48 *Common Market Law Review* 995 and T Lock, 'Walking on a Tightrope: The Draft ECHR Agreement and the Autonomy of the EU Legal Order' (2011) 48 *Common Market Law Review* 1025.

[76] For examples of previous CJEU case law on the balancing of human rights with Treaty provisions see, C-36/02 *Omega Spielhallen v Oberbürgermeisterin des Bundesstadt Bonn* [2004] ECR I-9609; C-112/00 *Schmidberger Internationale Transporte und Planzuge v Austria* [2003] ECR I-5659; C-341/05 *Laval un Partneri v Svenska Byggnadsarbetareförbundet* [2007] ECR I-11767; and C-438/05 *International Transport Workers Federation v Viking* [2007] ECR I-10779.

[77] Art 67(1) TFEU.

[78] For example see J Polakiewicz, 'EU Law and the ECHR: Will the European Union's Accession Square the Circle?' (2013) *European Human Rights Law Review* 592, 602–05 and A Kornezov, 'The Area of Freedom, Security and Justice in the Light of EU Accession to the ECHR—Is the Break-Up Inevitable?'. Working Paper available at www.cels.law.cam.ac.uk/Kornezov_WorkingPaper.pdf, accessed 15 May 2014.

because measures taken under this title should be designed to 'facilitate access to justice, in particular through the principle of mutual recognition of extrajudicial decisions in civil matters.'[79] This is emphasised further in the chapter that applies specifically to civil matters, which refers to mutual recognition of judgments but not to fundamental rights.[80] However mutual recognition of judgments can be achieved without removing all safeguards. This is indicated by the Brussels I recast which retains safeguards, allowing a balance to be achieved between the Treaty provisions that require mutual recognition and those that require respect for fundamental rights.[81] Since Regulations are secondary legislation; rather than primary legislation, like Treaty provisions and the Charter,[82] they need to effectively balance the key requirements under Title V. Where they do not then the provisions in the Regulation can be set aside in order to take account of the imbalance.[83]

Taking these factors into account, this book will now explore the approach of the European Court of Human Rights (ECtHR) and the CJEU in relation to the human rights duties of the enforcing court, particularly in relation to legislation under Title V. This will focus primarily on what is required of enforcing courts in relation to fundamental rights protection. If an effective legal remedy is not provided by the courts of origin, in a cross border case, then it should be in the hands of the enforcing court to provide that remedy, where they are bound by

[79] Art 67(4) TFEU.

[80] Ibid Art 81.

[81] Brussels I (recast), Art 45. This is also in line with the interpretation of the pragmatic approach advocated by this book. In most cases mutual recognition will allow for the automatic recognition of judgments, which seeks to ensure access to justice. However, in exceptional situations substantive interests will have to prevail in order to secure justice. (G Kegel, 'Fundamental Approaches' in International Encyclopaedia of Comparative Law, Volume III, Private International Law (Tübingen, Mohr Siebeck, 1986) and see ch 1.) Conversely, Cuniberti and Reuda argue that the problem is that the policy of mutual recognition contradicts any form of human rights review. They consider that a 'genuine policy decision must thus be made: preferring mutual trust over an efficient protection of human rights, or the other way around. It is submitted that human rights must prevail'. (Cuniberti and Rueda (n 67) 312.) However a clear preference for human rights in every single case, goes beyond the pragmatic approach. Therefore an equitable balance of the two principles (mutual recognition and human rights) attained through a limited review procedure which is only invoked in exceptional circumstances, complies with the pragmatic approach and will achieve mutual recognition of judgments in the majority of cases.

[82] This is clear from the Treaties and see also Craig and de Búrca (n 73) 109–13.

[83] This happened in *Kadi* where the procedure under the Regulation was considered incompatible with human rights law and the Regulation had to be annulled in relation to the applicants. (Cases C-402/05 P and C-415/05 P *Kadi and Al Barakaat International Foundation v Council* [2008] ECR I-6351, para 372 and see C-584/10 P *Commission and Others v Kadi* ECLI:EU:C:2013:518.)

the ECHR.[84] This can be achieved through the use of a public policy safeguard,[85] which is in effect the indirect protection of rights.

The question of 'indirect' violation of rights, under the ECtHR, by a State enforcing a decision of another State which may violate fundamental rights has been a matter of debate.[86] The ECtHR has held that a Contracting State of the ECHR is in breach of the Convention if it enforces a decision from a non-contracting State that is contrary to the rights of the individual.[87] *Pellegrini* concerned a decision on nullity of marriage and maintenance given in the Holy See, under canon law, that was to be enforced in Italy. The applicant had appeared before the Ecclesiastical Court and appealed the decision. However, she was apparently not aware of what the proceedings were about when she entered her appearance and as such did not have the benefit of a lawyer. The ECtHR considered that: 'the Italian courts breached their duty of satisfying themselves, before authorising enforcement of the Roman Rota's judgment, that the applicant had had a fair trial in the proceedings under canon law',[88] therefore there had been a violation of Article 6(1) of the Convention.

In the decision it was clearly stated that the review in the enforcing court is only 'required' where the State of origin is not party to the ECHR.[89] It is assumed that the reason for only 'requiring' a review by the enforcing court in these cases, is that if the decision in *Pellegrini* originated in a State that is party to the ECHR then it is simpler to bring proceedings against the State of origin. Where that State is not

[84] For example see, *Soering v United Kingdom*, Series A, No 161 (1989) EHRR 45; *Pellegrini v Italy* (App no 30882/96) ECHR 20 July 2001 and conversely *Drodz and Janousk v France and Spain* (App no 12747/87) ECHR 26 June 1992. See also *Eskinazi and Chelouche v Turkey* (App no 14600/05) 14 December 2005 where the orders should be enforced because they did not constitute a 'flagrant denial of justice'. For commentary on these cases see, JK Škerl, 'European Public Policy (with an emphasis on *exequatur* proceedings) (2011) 7 *Journal of Private International Law* 461, 467–68, 470–72 and 475; A Schulz, 'The Abolition of Exequatur and State Liability for Human Rights Violations through the Enforcement of Judgments in European Family Law' in *A Commitment to Private International Law—Essays in Honour of Hans van Loon* (Intersentia, 2013) 515, 516–18; P Beaumont, 'The Jurisprudence of the European Court of Human Rights and the European Court of Justice on the Hague Convention on Child Abduction' (2008) 335 *Recueil des Cours* 12, 76–79; and L Walker, 'The Impact of the Hague Abduction Convention on the Rights of the Family in the Case-Law of the European Court of Human Rights and the UN Human Rights Committee: The Danger of *Neulinger*' (2010) 6 *Journal of Private International Law* 649, 676–77.

[85] See, below at s VI A, where the German Supreme Court (BGH) used the public policy safeguard to provide an effective legal remedy in respect of a German/Polish maintenance order. 'According to the case law of the *BGH*, recourse to public policy requires prior exhaustion of available remedies in the Member State of origin.' (Hess (n 65) 1094.)

[86] See JJ Fawcett, 'The Impact of Article 6(1) of the ECHR on Private International Law' (2007) 56 *International and Comparative Law Quarterly* 1.

[87] *Pellegrini v Italy* (n 84).

[88] Ibid, para 47.

[89] Ibid, para 40. However, see the concurring opinion of Judge Matscher in *Drozd* where it is suggested that 'a contracting State may incur responsibility by reason of assisting in the enforcement of a foreign judgment, originating from a contracting or a non-contracting State, which has been obtained in conditions which constitute a breach of Article 6 (art. 6), whether it is a civil or criminal judgment'. (*Drodz* (n 84) 32–33.)

party to the ECHR then this is not possible. Until recently there was no indication as to what would happen if an applicant brought proceedings before the ECtHR against an enforcing court where the court of origin is in an ECHR State.[90] One approach would be to bring proceedings against the State of origin.[91] However, this is unsuitable for both practical and theoretical reasons because all the ECtHR can do is award damages; the judgment cannot be declared unrecognisable or unenforceable,[92] unlike with the *exequatur* process.[93]

Škerl also considers that this approach is not necessarily suitable because the 'actual infringement generally occurs only when a judicial decision attains real effects, and this happens when it is recognised or enforced.'[94] Further, what if the applicant was in the middle of bringing proceedings before the ECtHR, a lengthy process, and the State of enforcement enforces the decision without regard to the human rights issues. Surely in such cases, both States could be in violation of the ECHR, as the logic in *Pellegrini* could still apply. This is because the effect of enforcing a decision that violates fundamental rights is the same whether or not the decision originated in an ECHR contracting State or not.[95]

> If the state of enforcement actually adopts this violation in its legal order, this also violates the Convention … The states must verify the compliance of the proceedings for issuing judicial decisions with Convention standards irrespective of the state that issued the judicial decision.[96]

Fawcett also endorses this approach and in fact goes further. He thinks that the English courts should do more to prevent the indirect violation of human rights through the enforcement of foreign judgments. They should carry out a more thorough review before enforcing foreign judgments with a view to invoke the public policy clause if necessary,[97] in order to ensure human rights protection is 'practical and effective.'[98]

[90] However as Schulz points out; the rationale in *Pellegrini* (n 84) implies that where *exequatur* proceedings exist, EU Member States are 'not obliged by the ECHR … to carry out any Human Rights scrutiny with regard to the foreign judgment.' (Schulz (n 84) 523.) Mills considers that ECHR States should refrain from reviewing decisions from other ECHR states on grounds of public policy 'unless the breach is so serious that the need to remedy the breach outweighs the need to respect usual procedures.' (A Mills, 'The Dimensions of Public Policy in Private International Law' (2008) 4 *Journal of Private International Law* 201, 218.)

[91] This was the approach taken in *Šneersone* and the applicant was successful, *Šneersone and Kampenella v Italy* (App no 14737/09) ECtHR 12 July 2011.

[92] Cuniberti and Rueda (n 67) 297.

[93] The Strasbourg Court has also been unwilling to be involved in these cases—a prime example being *Marco Gambazzi v Daimler Chrysler Canada Inc* [2009] ECR I-02563 (discussed below at s VIII and by Cuniberti and Rueda (n 67) 295–96).

[94] Škerl (n 84) 470–71.

[95] In *Avotinš v Latvia* (App no 17502/07) 25 February 2014, the Court indicated that *Pellegrini* (n 84) was applicable in cases between two Contracting States.

[96] Škerl (n 84) 471. However, cf *Aguirre Zarraga* (n 63) (discussed below at nn 135–43) where the CJEU considered the German authorities should enforce the decision, but the applicant could appeal in the State of origin.

[97] Fawcett (n 86) in particular 43–44. However, this seems to go beyond the pragmatic approach (see n 81 above).

[98] Ibid, 47.

Since June 2013 there have been two developments in this area, both on the enforcement of judgments under the EU regime. One case where *exequatur* is abolished (child abduction) and the other case where *exequatur* still applies (Brussels I). They both clarify the current general approach of the ECtHR where an EU Regulation applies. Both judgments hinge on the 'equivalent protection' doctrine made clear in *Bosphorus*.[99] The doctrine suggests that it can be assumed that the protection given to fundamental rights by the EU is comparable to that given by the ECHR. The doctrine generally applies to protect the sovereignty of the EU, and to emphasise that the EU is not a party to the ECHR so it is therefore difficult for the ECtHR to scrutinise EU law and hold the EU to account. As this will obviously change post accession, it is unlikely that the *Bosphorus* presumption can survive legitimately.[100] The doctrine also recognises that where the EU legislation is directly applicable States have no choice in the resulting outcome.[101] However, this doctrine is not absolute—indicating that regardless of the position post accession, the doctrine should not just be applied automatically. Costello has identified three key features of the doctrine:

i. It does not amount to an enduring assumption of compliance.
ii. It is subject to revision in those areas where the EU does not provide 'equivalent protection'.
iii. The resultant presumption is, in any event, rebuttable.[102]

The two recent cases do nothing more than confirm the *Bosphorus* doctrine. The ECtHR applied the doctrine directly because it considered there was nothing in the cases that justified rebutting the presumption.

The first decision *Povse* concerned child abduction under Brussels IIbis.[103] The Austrian courts had initially ordered the non-return of the child. The Italian courts then ordered the return of the child to Italy. Under the rules in Brussels IIbis this decision is automatically enforceable and the Austrian authorities had no choice but to enforce the order. This had already been confirmed by the CJEU in the current dispute.[104] Unfortunately, for the applicant, this links the case directly to *Bosphorus*.[105] The ECtHR applied the *Bosphorus* doctrine, and held that there

[99] *Bosphorus Hava Yollari Turizm v Ireland* (2006) 42 EHRR 1. For an analysis see C Costello, 'The Bosphorus Ruling of the European Court of Human Rights: Fundamental Rights and Blurred Boundaries in Europe' (2006) 6 *Human Rights Law Review* 87.

[100] It would be unfair if the EU continued to be treated differently post accession when it should apply equivalent standards to the other contracting parties.

[101] Therefore the doctrine by analogy should not apply to Directives as Member States are free to implement these in a form that complies with their obligations under the ECtHR. Whereas Regulations apply directly so the doctrine applies, and the ECtHR presumes that the Regulation was negotiated with human rights in mind.

[102] Costello (n 99) 103.

[103] *Povse v Austria* (App no 3890/11) ECtHR 18 June 2013.

[104] C-211/10 PPU *Povse v Alpago* [2010] ECR I-06673.

[105] 'Bosphorus was a most exceptional case due to the combination of a specific term in a directly applicable Regulation, clarified in a decisive interpretative ruling by the ECJ.' (Costello (n 99) 111.) See also H Muir Watt on Abolition of Exequatur and Human Rights, particularly s III, at http://conflictoflaws.net/2013/muir-watt-on-povse/, accessed 8 May 2014.

had been no violation of Article 8 by the Austrian authorities when enforcing the order as they had no choice but to directly apply EU Law. The ECtHR suggested that the applicant should have brought proceedings against the Italian authorities rather than the Austrian authorities.[106] This is logical in some ways but this approach would not necessarily have any practical effects and it is not particularly suitable in this case. By directly applying *Bosphorus* and relying on a CJEU judgment made exactly three years earlier, the Court failed to take into account the reality of the current situation. The Court failed to distinguish between an order, that could have been given legitimately, and the actual enforcement of that order more than four years later;[107] in what is arguably a different situation. Therefore the enforcement of that order could in itself violate human rights, regardless of whether the original order did or not. This distinction is emphasised by Skerl and Fawcett.[108] Further, this distinction is made by the ECtHR itself in *Neulinger*, where the Court suggests that the original decision did not violate Article 8 but any further attempts to enforce that decision would.[109] Therefore, the ECtHR took the easy way out by simply applying the *Bosphorus* presumption which, although perhaps adequate three years earlier,[110] failed to take account of the current situation and the actual effects that enforcing an order which entails moving a child across borders may have. This indicates that there can be a clear distinction between the legitimacy of an order and the legitimacy of enforcing that order in another State. It cannot be assumed that only the original decision violates human rights and therefore it will not always be realistic to only bring complaints against the State of origin.

The second decision where the Court applied the *Bosphorus* presumption in private international law is *Avotinš v Latvia*.[111] The decision concerned the enforcement of an order under Brussels I where *exequatur* is not abolished. Therefore, a direct application of EU law is not required to the same extent and there is room for discretion at the recognition and enforcement stage.[112] Mr Avotinš was in debt to a commercial company registered in Cyprus. On 24 May 2004 the Cypriot courts ordered Mr Avotinš to repay his debts with interest and costs, without his presence. The judgment suggested the applicant had been informed of the hearing but had not appeared. The judgment was sent to Latvia and in February 2006 the Latvian Court ordered recognition and enforcement under Brussels I. Mr Avotinš claimed that he only became aware of the Cypriot judgment and the Latvian

[106] This was the approach taken in *Sneersone* (n 91). The proceedings were brought against the State where the decision originated and the ECtHR found a violation of Art 8.

[107] The decision ordering the return of the child by the Italian courts was given on 10 July 2009. The CJEU decision was given a year later on 1 July 2010 and the ECtHR decision was given on 18 June 2013.

[108] See nn 94–98 above.

[109] *Neulinger and Shuruk v Switzerland* (2012) 54 EHRR 31.

[110] It is important to note that Brussels IIbis removes the *exequatur* procedure in an attempt to ensure the immediate return of the child. A forced return three years later fails to achieve this aim.

[111] *Avotinš* (n 95).

[112] See C-7/98 *Krombach v Bamberski* [2000] ECR I-1395 and C-341/04 *Eurofood IFSC Ltd* [2006] ECR I-3854.

enforcement order by chance on 16 June 2006. He appealed in Latvia against the enforcement order, on the basis of Article 34(2) of Brussels I.[113] In January 2007 the Latvian Supreme Court upheld the order and Mr Avotinš repaid his debt. The applicant complained before the ECtHR that by enforcing the judgment of the Cypriot court, which he considered disregarded his right to a defence, the Latvian courts had failed to comply with Article 6(1).

The ECtHR judges were split four, three on the outcome. The majority held that there had been no violation of Article 6. The Court began by referring to *Pellegrini* (suggesting it is applicable between two ECtHR Contracting States) and stated it is up to the Court to determine whether the Latvian judges acted in accordance with Article 6 when enforcing the Cypriot judgment.[114] However following this, the approach of the majority lacked precision. The majority then went on to refer to *Bosphorus*. Although the theory still remains the same this should not be directly applicable where the Member State has some form of discretion when applying a provision in a Regulation. Yes, the Supreme Court had to ensure the rapid recognition and enforcement of the judgment,[115] under Brussels I, however it was required to take into account any arguments of the parties that fell within the exceptions. It did not have to automatically enforce the decision, unlike under Brussels IIbis. In this regard the CJEU has held that although Brussels I is designed to ensure quick procedures for recognition and enforcement that objective cannot be attained by undermining the right to a fair hearing.[116] Despite this the Latvian Supreme Court rejected the applicant's arguments on the basis that he had not appealed the judgment in Cyprus.[117] This is not a requirement under Brussels I. The requirement under Article 34(2) in relation to default judgments is that either the applicant failed to challenge the decision because they did not know about it, or they were barred in some other way from challenging the decision. The applicant claimed he did not know about the decision until it was being enforced in Latvia. Therefore, he was correct to challenge the decision at the enforcement stage as he could no longer appeal the decision in Cyprus, which was already final. As such the Latvian Court had to determine whether he actually knew about the proceedings in order to decide whether Article 34(2) applied. Dismissing the application simply because the applicant had not appealed in Cyprus, is the approach required by Brussels IIbis, not Brussels I. However, the majority agreed with the Latvian Supreme Court citing *Orams*.[118]

[113] It is possible to refuse recognition on this basis see, C-283/05 *ASML Netherlands BV v Semiconductor Industry Services GmbH* [2006] ECR I-12041 and the discussion below at s VIII entitled 'Suitable Alternative Arrangements'.

[114] *Avotinš* (n 95) para 46.

[115] Ibid, para 49.

[116] *ASML* (n 113) para 24 and see s VIII below.

[117] *Avotinš* (n 95) para 50.

[118] Ibid, para 50. The ECtHR uses the term 'able'. However as there seems to be no analysis of whether Mr Avotinš was actually 'able' to bring proceedings, it is unclear how this quote actually assists with the present argument.

The approach of the minority[119] showed a greater understanding of the procedure under Brussels I. They considered that the question raised in *Avotinš* was of great importance because it allowed the Court to give a decision on the guarantees of Article 6 in the context of Brussels I.[120] As indicated by Fawcett this is not an area where the ECtHR has had much input, if any at all.[121] There has generally been a 'failure to realize the importance of human rights law in private international law cases',[122] emphasising why it was important for the ECtHR to make a thorough analysis in *Avotinš*. The minority recognised that although the Regulation is directly applicable, Brussels I provides exceptions to the automatic execution of judgments, and therefore the relevant EU law does not provide for a blind execution of judgments.[123] Overall, they considered that there was not enough analysis by the Latvian Court of whether the applicant was aware of the proceedings, or enough thought put into the majority decision by their colleagues.[124] It is certainly a case that is deserving of a thorough analysis, given the clear distinction between the procedure in Brussels I and parts of Brussels IIbis; and the general lack of human rights jurisprudence in this area.[125] A more thorough analysis may have taken place if Mr Avotinš had tried to challenge enforcement on grounds of public policy,[126] which naturally encompasses human rights arguments, rather than the more limited default defence.[127] However, the important elements to be taken from these cases are that *Pellegrini* can apply to intra EU decisions and that the presumption in *Bosphorus* is rebuttable. Therefore it can be possible and necessary for the enforcing court to review human rights allegations in certain situations. This emphasises that it is important to balance the principle of mutual trust with fundamental human rights.

The abolition of recognition and enforcement proceedings and the removal of safeguards in the Maintenance Regulation hinged on mutual trust and the mutual recognition of judgments. However, the application of mutual trust and the presumption of compliance with fundamental human rights is problematic. The mere fact that there are so many applications to the ECtHR suggests that States are not always capable of dealing adequately with their human rights obligations.[128] '[T]he case law of the ECtHR thus underlines that there are still wide differences between the Member States, and that if there was no obligation to trust

[119] Judges Ziemele, Bianku and Gaetano.

[120] *Avotinš* (n 95) dissent, para 1.

[121] Fawcett (n 86) 34.

[122] Ibid.

[123] *Avotinš* (n 95) dissent, para 4. This is contrary to what is required by Brussels IIbis in the context of child abduction—and what is required by the Maintenance Regulation for decisions originating in Protocol States.

[124] Ibid, para 5.

[125] However, at least the application was actually heard, unlike *Gambazzi* where the application was dismissed without being heard (see n 93 above).

[126] Brussels I Art 34(1).

[127] See the discussion below at s VIII.

[128] See, www.echr.coe.int/ECHR/EN/Header/Reports+and+Statistics/Statistics/Statistical+data/ for statistical information on the ECHR, accessed 5 June 2014.

other Member States, many would not.'[129] Cuniberti and Rueda argue that at the moment the ECHR is only a promise,[130] but not yet a commitment. The EU has also recognised that Member States are not always capable of complying with human rights standards. This has been written into a Directive and confirmed by the CJEU.[131] However in the context of judicial cooperation in civil matters mutual trust has been emphasised rather than human rights.[132] The principle of mutual trust has caused problems previously in the EU, two obvious examples being *Aguirre Zarraga*[133] and *Krombach*.[134]

*Aguirre Zarraga*[135] is a decision under Brussels IIbis. Under Brussels IIbis, in certain proceedings concerning the return of the child, the *exequatur* procedure has been abolished, and no necessary safeguards have been retained. In *Zarraga* the Spanish Courts were trying to force the return of the child to Spain without actually hearing the child for themselves. This went against the original non-return order of the German courts, which considered that the child should not be returned because she had a strong desire not to be.[136] The German authorities made a preliminary reference to the CJEU asking whether they did not have to return the child at this stage because the child's fundamental rights had been breached. The CJEU failed to rule directly on the human rights point,[137] but held that the child should be returned anyway because there was no possibility for the German authorities to review the order under the Regulation.[138] The only option available to the mother was to try and appeal the decision in Spain.[139] The inability of the enforcing court

[129] Cuniberti (n 66) 52.

[130] Cuniberti and Rueda (n 67) 296.

[131] This example also falls under Title V but it applies to Ch 2 rather than Ch 3. It relates to the law on asylum applications, in particular Directive 2005/85 Art 36. A third country can only be considered as a safe third country if it has both ratified and observes the provisions of the Geneva Convention and the ECHR. 'Such wording indicates that the mere ratification of conventions by a Member State cannot result in the application of a conclusive presumption that that State observes those conventions. The same principle is applicable both to Member States and third countries.' (C-411/10 *NS v Secretary of State for the Home Department* [2011] ECR I-13905, para 103.)

[132] See Art 81 TFEU.

[133] *Aguirre Zarraga* (n 63).

[134] *Krombach* (n 112).

[135] *Aguirre Zarraga* (n 63).

[136] This is one of the strict exceptions to return established by the Hague Convention of 25 October 1980 on the civil aspects of Child Abduction (Abduction Convention) Art 13(2).

[137] An important point in this case was that proceedings had not been exhausted in the State of origin and therefore it would have been possible to appeal the decision there. Because the human rights issues were left undecided it is unclear whether the outcome would have been different had domestic remedies been exhausted. (See, JJ Kuipers, 'The (Non) Application of the Charter of Fundamental Rights to a Certificate for the Return of the Child' 2012 *European Human Rights Law Review* 397.)

[138] For a full commentary of the case see, Walker and Beaumont (n 64) 239–48; P Beaumont, 'The European Court of Justice Prioritises The Abolition of Exequatur Over Fundamental Rights in Zarraga' in J Diez-Hochleitner et al (eds), *Recent Trends in the Case Law of the Court of Justice of the European Union (2008–2011)* (Madrid, Wolters Kluwer Espana, 2012) 621; G Biagioni, 'The Aguirre Zarraga Case: Freedom of Circulation of Judgments Goes One Step Further' in J Diez-Hochleitner et al ibid 605, and see also Schulz (n 84) 521–22.

[139] Cuniberti and Reuda argue that it is unrealistic to expect a Member State to review its own approach to human rights (n 67, 301–02).

to review the decision at the enforcement stage is particularly dangerous when the rights of children are at stake. This is even more questionable when the enforcing court has already ruled on the case and reached a different outcome to the State of habitual residence. The abolition of *exequatur* is not as dangerous in maintenance as it is in the context of child abduction. However, some sticky situations may arise where fundamental rights or legitimate expectations are overridden.[140]

The main point to be taken from *Zarraga*, is that placing all the power in one Member State's authorities is not the direction that EU Law should be taking. In fact such a step seems to distort the principle of mutual trust as the power and therefore the trust is not shared equally. Kramer considers that the decision in *Zarraga* is, 'an unacceptable interpretation of the principles of mutual recognition and mutual trust, and makes all the more important the proper regulation of review mechanisms'.[141] The judicial interpretation, of the mechanism in Brussels IIbis and the principle of mutual trust, given in *Zarraga* gives all the power to one State and the other State is left to accept that no matter what the impact may be.[142] Although this partly stems from the decision of the CJEU it is also considered to be an inherent problem in the principle itself, at least in the way it is used in Brussels IIbis. The principle, as used in Brussels IIbis, allows the court of origin to overturn the non-return order of the court of refuge and makes that decision final. This undermines the balancing of the Treaty provisions under Title V with fundamental human rights considerations.[143] If the principle of mutual trust really existed then the court of origin should trust the decision of the court of refuge and not be able to issue a new decision in the first place. Therefore, the rationale behind the application of this principle in Brussels IIbis is unconvincing as it seems to create a one sided effect rather than a joint or mutual trust between two or more States; which is disproportionate to the aim.

[140] See s VI below.

[141] Kramer (n 62) 640.

[142] See, Walker and Beaumont (n 64) 246–48.

[143] This position also appears to undermine the principle of *res judicata*. The non-return order is final in the State of refuge (and will always remain final in the context of the Abduction Convention) which gives the order *res judicata*. The CJEU has previously stated that: 'Community Law does not require a national court to disapply domestic rules of procedure conferring finality on a decision, even if to do so would enable it to remedy an infringement of Community law.' (C-234/04 *Kapferer v Schlank & Schick GmbH* [2006] ECR I-2605 para 21.) This indicates that a decision has *res judicata* effects if it is final in the State in which it was given, regardless of whether it breaches Community law. However, under Brussels IIbis, the authorities in the State of origin are then apparently allowed to undermine that, without the need for the case to be exceptional and without necessarily following the required procedures. (See Walker and Beaumont (n 64) and The Practice Guide on Brussels IIbis.) 'In that regard, attention should be drawn to the importance, both for the Community legal order and national legal systems, of the principle of res judicata. In order to ensure both stability of the law and legal relations and the sound administration of justice, it is important that judicial decisions, which have become definitive *after all rights of appeal have been exhausted* … can no longer be called into question.' (*Kapferer* ibid para 20, emphasis added.) It is interesting that this makes no reference to the State in which the decision was given; indicating that the procedure in Brussels IIbis technically fits with this because it allows 'rights of appeal' in a second State. Although this is a strange analogy, the outcome in *Zarraga* may not undermine the principle of *res judicata*, because technically all appeals had not been exhausted under the system in that particular Regulation, at the time the CJEU heard the case, despite the fact the jurisdiction changed.

The ongoing *Krombach*[144] saga has also called the principle of mutual trust into question. The case concerned the alleged manslaughter of a French girl in Germany. Dr Krombach was the accused. He was tried in Germany but not convicted. He was also tried in France for the same offence. However, neither he nor his representatives were heard at the French trial because Dr Krombach was not present at the hearing. He was convicted, and found liable for damages. The French authorities sought to have the civil part of the French judgment enforced in Germany under Brussels I. This was challenged on the basis that the enforcement of the judgment breached the public policy defence in Brussels I. The CJEU held that the State of enforcement could take account of the public policy defence where 'the court of the State of origin refused to allow that person to have his defence presented unless he appeared in person.'[145] This shows how the public policy safeguard has been effective in the past in order to deal with unexpected circumstances.

However, in relation to Dr Krombach this was not the end of the story. It was reported that in 2009 the girl's father had him kidnapped and taken to France.[146] A week after Dr Krombach was found in Mulhouse the Bavarian Ministry of Justice issued a press release which referred to the importance of diplomatic relations.[147] There was a whole new trial in France. The result being that on 22 October 2011 Dr Krombach was again sentenced to 15 years, by the French courts, after numerous proceedings which began in the 1980s.[148] Whether Dr Krombach was kidnapped or not, this case still highlights how uncertain and fragile the principle of mutual trust actually is given the unrepeatable scenario that transpired in this case. It also indicates that there is a long way to go before the principle is successful and veritable. An excellent summary of the whole debacle was given by Gilles Cuniberti, 'So much for mutual trust. So much for the European single

[144] *Krombach* (n 112).

[145] Ibid, para 45. See Beaumont and Johnston (n 64) 253–55, for a longer discussion on the judgment. Fundamentally, the decision in *Krombach* was not enforced because it was given in violation of Art 6 ECHR in the state of origin. (See also Hess (n 65) 1095.) This constitutes a review of the human rights questions by the state of enforcement, where the state of origin was party to the ECHR. So, although the decision in *Pellegrini* (see discussion above at nn 89–90) does not 'require' the enforcing court to review the human rights points where the state of origin is party to the ECHR (although *Avotinš* (n 95) indicates that it might), the decision in *Krombach* suggests that there is nothing to prevent the enforcing court from doing this where the enforcement would be 'manifestly contrary' to the public policy of that State. This would be constituted by a 'manifest or disproportionate breach of a fundamental right' (Hess (n 65) 1095 and see Škerl (n 84) 471 and Cuniberti and Reuda (n 67) 297). Mills considers that the conclusion in *Krombach* was strongly justified, despite the fact that he considers that States should refrain from reviewing ECHR rights in the majority of cases (Mills (n 90) 222).

[146] http://conflictoflaws.net/2009/dr-krombachs-final-contribution-to-the-european-judicial-area/, accessed 5 June 2014.

[147] www.justiz.bayern.de/ministerium/presse/archiv/2009/detail/177.php, accessed 5 June 2014. The investigation into Dr Krombach's kidnap was being led by the Public Prosecutor of the Town of Kempton.

[148] Although the subsequent criminal trial is not directly relevant to the *exequatur* process, the saga highlights the fragility of the system and the lack of mutual trust in the EU. This is problematic when one of the preconditions for the abolition of *exequatur* was the principle of mutual trust.

area of justice.'[149] Considering how this case was handled from the beginning till the end; it is unsurprising that one may be filled with so much scepticism about the abolition of the *exequatur* procedure without the retention of necessary safeguards. Therefore as indicated in Title V of the Treaty, fundamental rights remain important even where there should be mutual recognition of judgments. This is further emphasised by the decision to retain safeguards in the Brussels I recast, which appears to strike a suitable balance between the two competing notions. Consequently the argument that the decision to remove safeguards in the Maintenance Regulation and Brussels IIbis (in the context of child abduction) is disproportionate to the aim, is justified.

One beneficial reason for retaining the public policy safeguard, as indicated above, is to protect an individual from a violation of their fundamental rights. Cuniberti wrote that the 'public policy defence can only be triggered if a fundamental right is violated. Once a right has been characterized as fundamental, its breach is always an important concern, and one cannot see why it should not always be sanctioned.'[150] This is not necessarily true. The public policy defence is useful because it can be triggered whenever a fundamental right is violated.[151] However, it goes further than this and covers certain policy areas that are specific to a particular Member State.[152] It is also clear from the Treaties that measures taken under Title V should also respect the 'different legal systems and traditions of Member States.'[153] This is a further indication that the public policy exception should be retained as a safeguard.

The decision of the CJEU in *Omega* is an example of the variation in different legal systems and traditions within the EU. In *Omega*,[154] the German authorities wanted to restrict the free movement of services, because they felt that the sale of a particular video game in Germany was an affront to human dignity as protected by the German Constitution. The CJEU held that, the German Authorities were

[149] http://conflictoflaws.net/2011/krombach-sentenced-again-to-15-years/, accessed 5 June 2014. See also P Vlas, 'Public Policy in Private International Law and Its Continuing Importance' in Permanent Bureau (eds), *A Commitment to Private International Law Essays in Honour of Hans van Loon* (Antwerp, Intersentia, 2013) 621, particularly 624–25.

[150] Cuniberti (n 66) 34.

[151] The CJEU has recognised this in cases on Brussels I: 'To that extent, the Court has … established a link between the fundamental rights protected by the ECHR at international level and national public policy. Refusal of a foreign judgment will therefore satisfy the requirements of Article 34 (1) of the regulation, in any event where the requirements of national public policy are used as a basis for remedying a manifest infringement of the fundamental rights embodied in the ECHR.' Case C-420/07 *Apostolides v Orams* [2009] ECR I-03571, para 107.

[152] For example, see HP Meidanis, 'Public Policy and *ordre public* in Private International Law of the EU: Traditional Positions and Modern Trends' (2005) 30 *European Law Review*, 96. The article discusses the national character of public policy and whether there could be a common EU public policy. If public policy only covered international human rights, then there could be a common public policy based on the ECHR, or the Charter. However this would only cover minimum standards whereas the judgment in *Omega* (n 76) goes further than this. See also Beaumont and Johnston (n 64) 277 at fn 144.

[153] Art 67(1) TFEU.

[154] *Omega* (n 76).

allowed to prohibit the game as it was against German public policy because it did not respect the right to human dignity as protected by the German Constitution. The provision that Community law conflicted with arose from a constitutional tradition.[155] However, the issue here, in contrast to the provision in Title V, is that the Treaty and the case law refer to constitutional traditions common to Member States.[156] As such it has been argued that in *Omega* the CJEU departed from its previous case law, such as *Schmidberger*, and focussed on a public policy argument rather than a human rights argument.[157] The 'Court tried only half-heartedly to recast the German particularity of human dignity as a general principle of Community law before revealing a state-centric approach in its proportionality analysis.'[158] Therefore this notion of public policy which also can protect fundamental rights arguments or traditions peculiar to a particular Member State is in line with Title V of the Treaty as it does not require that the traditions be 'common'.[159]

The *Omega* case highlights two factors. Firstly that national public policy is individual to each Member State, and can be quite different from the universal fundamental human rights that are protected by international instruments.[160] In particular, national public policy does not have to be universally acceptable so it can go further than minimum standards. Fundamentally public policy is then a method for States to retain their own individuality in areas which are important in their culture. Secondly, it highlights that public policy is not a defence that applies only to Regulations and other secondary legislation. In *Omega* the CJEU considered it appropriate to allow public policy, based on a German fundamental right, to override one of the fundamental freedoms that was an original objective of the European Economic Community. The use of public policy in *Omega*, supports the notion that 'uncommon' human rights as enforced by public policy

[155] See Art 6(3) TEU and C–11/70 *Internationale Handelsgesellschaft mbH v Einfuhr- und Vorratsstelle für Getreide und Futtermittel* [1970] ECR 1125.

[156] For a full analysis see N Nic Shuibhne, 'Margins of Appreciation: National Values, Fundamental Rights and EC Free Movement Law' (2009) *European Law Review* 230.

[157] MK Bulterman and HR Kranenborg, 'What if the Rules on Free Movement and Human Rights Collide? About Laser Games and Human Dignity: The Omega Case' (2006) *European Law Review* 93.

[158] Nic Shuibhne (n 156) 254.

[159] Examples of differing public policy, that are applicable in family law, include the legality of abortion and the recognition of civil partnerships. In fact in the context of abortion the CJEU has taken a different approach to the ECtHR in relation to Constitutional rules that protect the unborn child. In *Grogan* (C-159/90 *SPUC v Grogan* [1991] ECR I-4685) the CJEU indicated that the freedom to provide services could be restricted where the service conflicted with the Irish constitution (although the Court concluded that the case was outside the scope of EU law), but in *Open Door Counselling* (*Open Door Counselling and Dublin Well Woman Centre v Ireland* (1993) 14 EHRR 244) the ECtHR held that a ban on the distribution of information on abortion in Ireland was in violation of Art 10 ECHR. For a further analysis see Nic Shuibhne (n 156) 246–50.

[160] However, it is no longer purely a national category as States are 'linked in a number of international organisations, and are also part of the international community.' (Škerl (n 84) 462.) See also Mills in a theoretical discussion on public policy where he considers that although national public policy is 'discretionary for each State' public policy can be classified in three different ways: 'internal public policy', 'international public policy and '"truly international" public policy'. (Mills (n 90) 204 and 213.)

are a matter of the Rule of Law. Therefore, given the importance of public policy in relation to the proper administration of justice and legitimate expectations,[161] which is supported by the fact that the CJEU has previously considered it justified to limit the fundamental freedoms of the European Union on this basis (in specific circumstances), the decision not to include the safeguard within the Maintenance Regulation is unjustified.[162]

# VI. The Implications of the Hague Protocol and other Methods of Mitigating the Effect of the Abolition of *Exequatur* in Maintenance Proceedings

## A. The Hague Protocol

The impact of the abolition of *exequatur* in relation to the Maintenance Regulation is not as severe as in other instruments because of the Protocol on Applicable Law.[163] The Protocol lays out rules which specify what law should be used. If the Protocol is applied correctly the assumption is that the decision in the court of origin should be recognisable and enforceable in other courts because the appropriate law has been applied. However, what does this really achieve? Two problems immediately spring to mind. Once again there is considerable emphasis on mutual trust and a reliance on the foreign court to do two things correctly. The court must apply the Protocol correctly to discover what the applicable law is (this should not be that difficult to achieve as in the majority of cases it will be the law of the habitual residence of the creditor),[164] then it has to apply that law correctly. In the clear cut cases there should not be a problem because the law of the habitual residence of the creditor should apply. In most applications for the recovery of maintenance the creditor will proceed with the application in their country of habitual residence. Therefore, the simple scenario is that the Court applies the law of the creditor's habitual residence which is the law of the forum.

[161] Kegel, a pragmatist, strongly favours the application of conflicts justice but recognises that sometimes it is necessary to set this aside to protect the interests of the parties. He considers public policy to be an example of this. (Kegel (n 81) 15 and see ch 1.)

[162] Kramer considers that 'the abolition of all grounds of refusal is—in my view, rightfully—criticised, particularly where it concerns the public policy exception.' (Kramer (n 62) 639.) See also Timmer (n 67) who considers that the removal of the *exequatur* process from Brussels I was a step too far despite the fact that safeguards are retained.

[163] Hague Protocol of 23 November 2007 on the Law Applicable to Maintenance Obligations, ratification of which was approved by the EU in Council Decision of 30 November 2009 (2009/941/EC) [2009] OJ L331/17. However, as the Protocol will not necessarily be applied uniformly (see ch 6) it is questionable how this can justify the abolition of *exequatur*.

[164] Art 3 of the Protocol. This applies unless the Protocol provides otherwise, see Arts 4–8.

However, what happens where the scenario does not play out as above? There are various other possible outcomes arising from the Protocol that are generally aimed at protecting the legitimate expectations of the parties.[165] Article 4 benefits certain specific creditors, mainly in relation to child support.[166] Article 4 allows the creditor to use the law of the forum to obtain maintenance from the debtor, if the law of their own habitual residence does not allow them to do so. If this still does not work then you can also revert to the law of the common nationality of the spouses if there is one.[167] Article 5 provides a special rule for spouses and ex-spouses. It dissapplies Article 3 where one of the spouses does not want the prescribed law to apply, and the court decides that there is another law that has a closer connection to the marriage. Article 6 is a special rule of defence that provides protection for the debtor. This allows the debtor to contest a claim from the creditor if there is no such obligation under both the law of the debtor's habitual residence and the common nationality, if any, of both the parties. This provides a necessary defence for the debtor, whereby they may not have to pay maintenance even if an obligation arises under the law applicable under Article 3 or 4. It allows the debtor to contest an obligation where the obligation would not have arisen under the law of his or her own habitual residence.[168] If the parties do not have a common nationality then this will be all that is necessary to contest the claim under Article 6. However, if the parties do have a common nationality then the obligation should not arise under the law of that State either.[169]

Finally Articles 7 and 8 allow the parties to designate an applicable law, but there are qualifications to this.[170] This highlights that there are a variety of laws that could be applied to a maintenance dispute, which does not concern parental child support.[171] When Article 3 is not used the court must first decide what the correct applicable law should be, then it has to apply that law correctly, which may be difficult if it is not the law of the forum. Therefore, there is room for error at two stages when applying the Protocol. Furthermore, even if the Protocol is applied efficiently this does not mean that the rights of individuals will be

[165] See ibid Arts 4–8 of the Protocol. 'The reason for the existence of these exceptions is to provide slightly more favourable rules for certain classes of maintenance creditors in cases where application of the law of their habitual residences is found to be contrary to their interests.' A Bonomi, 'Explanatory Report on the Protocol of 23 November 2007 on the Law Applicable to Maintenance Obligations' (Bonomi Report) para 49, available at www.hcch.net/upload/expl39e.pdf, accessed 10 June 2014.

[166] However, Art 4(c) of the Protocol also covers payments from children to their parents.

[167] See ibid Art 4.

[168] 'If, for instance, the debtor's nephew, a resident and citizen of State A, makes on the basis of that State's law a maintenance claim against his uncle, resident in State B and a citizen of State C, the latter will be able to deny any maintenance on the grounds that the law of State B does not recognise any maintenance obligation between persons related collaterally.' Bonomi Report (n 165), para 104.

[169] 'Taking the law of the common nationality into account is justified by the consideration that, if the parties have a common nationality and the law of their common nationality provides for the obligation concerned, it seems inequitable to allow the debtor to evade it on the grounds only that this obligation is unknown in the State of his habitual residence.' Ibid, para 105. For more information see ch 6.

[170] See ch 6 for more details.

[171] Ibid.

properly respected. For example, there is no guarantee that the defendant's rights to a fair trial will be appropriately respected. Therefore the retention of the public policy defence, as a safeguard, is better in all cases.

Another problem with applying the incorrect law is creating a maintenance relationship that should not be covered. For example in some States, such as Belgium and Spain, the debtor and creditor can be siblings.[172] For someone living in the UK it would come as a bit of a shock if you were suddenly expected to pay maintenance to your brother or sister. The special rule in Article 6 of the Protocol is designed to prevent such obligations being created. If the obligation does not arise from a parent-child relationship,

> the debtor may contest a claim from the creditor on the ground that there is no such obligation under both the law of the State of the habitual residence of the debtor and the law of the State of the common nationality of the parties, if there is one.[173]

This would require the State of origin to look very closely at other laws and dis-sapply the applicable law in certain circumstances so that the law of that particular debtor would now apply. There could be scope for error. If the State of origin applies the Protocol incorrectly in this instance it would appear that the main remedy for the debtor would be to appeal in that State, as the State of enforcement cannot review the decision as to the substance.[174] This may be detrimental to the unsuspecting debtor as debtors do not get legal aid under the Regulation,[175] and the proceedings are likely to be expensive. So if the Protocol is applied incorrectly in this context the debtor may have difficulty achieving the correct result. Under the system that applies to decisions originating in the UK or Denmark however, such an obligation would not be enforced if it were deemed to be contrary to the public policy of the enforcing State.

There is a public policy defence contained in the Protocol, but this only covers the application of the particular law by the forum, it does not give any leeway to the State of enforcement. 'The application of the law determined under the Protocol may be refused only to the extent that its effects would be manifestly contrary to the public policy of the forum.'[176] The most likely situation for this clause being invoked is where the applicable law would impose maintenance payments through a relationship that is not recognised by the forum. This would include same sex partnerships or polygamous marriages. However, the Bonomi Report makes it clear that Article 13 should not be used wherever possible.[177] This is because the

[172] Impact Assessment on the Proposal for a Council Regulation on jurisdiction, applicable law, recognition and enforcement of decisions and cooperation in matters relating to Maintenance Obligations, SEC(2005) 1629, 30. See Table 7.1 for a breakdown of the relationships that maintenance could arise out of in the Member States at the relevant date.

[173] Art 6 of the Protocol.

[174] See Arts 17–21 and Art 42 of the Maintenance Regulation.

[175] Ibid, Arts 46–47.

[176] Art 13 of the Protocol.

[177] Bonomi Report (n 165) para 177.

'determination of public policy is to be performed *in concreto*'.[178] This means that it is not enough that the law of the forum simply does not recognise the relationship; the actual payment of the maintenance would have to be against the public policy of the State. In relation to polygamy some European States have held that the maintenance obligations arising out of the institution are still necessary,[179]

> even though that institution cannot be recognised as such by those States, as inconsistent with fundamental principles of the law of the forum, the provision of maintenance by the husband to the various wives is not regarded as being improper.[180]

However, this is only the stance that some States have taken. All States have a different notion of public policy and they will also have varying ideas as to what is an acceptable relationship, when it is not a relationship that is recognised under their own law.[181] Therefore it seems unlikely that the defence in Article 13 of the Protocol will have much use, and it will be of absolutely no help to the State of enforcement, which may still have to enforce an obligation that conflicts with its public policy.

The failings of the Protocol as the prerequisite for the abolition of *exequatur* can be seen by looking at a German case on maintenance.[182] The case concerned a Polish decision on child maintenance that was sought to be enforced in Germany. The defendant attempted to challenge the lawsuit on the basis that he was not the child's father. The Polish Court worked on various assertions that the defendant was the father but paternity was never proved by means of a DNA test. The defendant offered to take a paternity test, but apparently the Polish Court did not accept this, and decided that the case was 'clear'.[183] The judgment was delivered orally and became final on 21 February 2005 (so before the current system came into force meaning that recognition could be challenged on grounds of public policy). The BGH refused to recognise the decision on the basis that it violated German public policy because the paternity of the defendant had not been established.[184] In particular, because the Polish Court relied on hearsay evidence rather

[178] Ibid.

[179] This is probably fair, because even if the forum does not recognise the institution of polygamous marriages, the couple are legally married in the country to which the parties to the marriage have a close connection. The husband should therefore not be able to escape maintenance payments for that reason.

[180] Bonomi Report (n 165) para 177.

[181] See ch 1 s V and chs 3 and 6, where it is shown that if a specific relationship is not recognised under the law of that State it is up to the bodies in that State to decide whether to apply the law designated under the Protocol, or to simply apply their own private international law rules.

[182] BGH 26 August 2009, Entscheidungen des BGH in Zivilsachen (BGHZ) 182, 188. See K Seihr, 'The EU Maintenance Regulation and the Hague Maintenance Protocol of 2007' in Permanent Bureau (n 149) 529, 532–37 for a discussion of the case in English.

[183] Seihr (n 182) 533. Under the new instruments there is no requirement to provide debtors with a DNA test, or a requirement that debtors should be able to provide one if they wish. However, it is hoped that States take a sensible approach in this area and take account of scientific evidence where necessary. Conversely, if the creditor wants or is required to provide a DNA test, then legal aid should be provided. (Art 46 and see Proceedings of the 21st Session, Procès verbal (PV) no 15 and Working Document no 51.)

[184] Seihr (n 182) 536.

than scientific evidence despite the fact that the defendant offered to take a paternity test.[185] Seihr, considers that the '*Bundesgerichtshof* was correct in applying the public policy clause and in declining recognition of the Polish judgment.'[186] Based on the information available, this approach appears correct. It seems ridiculous to enforce a maintenance order where paternity is not scientifically established, and the defendant tried to cooperate by offering to undergo a paternity test.

This case highlights the inadequacies of the new system. This is because if such an order was made by a Polish court after June 2011, it would have to be automatically enforced in all Member States as there would be no way of challenging recognition or enforceability under the new system. As explained above the limited public policy clause in the Protocol would only be of assistance if the German court was trying to establish maintenance by applying Polish law and wanted to dissapply that law because it was against German public policy. The German courts cannot refuse to recognise a foreign decision on the basis of public policy. It is unlikely that the rule in Article 19 on service of documents can be of assistance,[187] because the defendant was properly served with the documents shown by the fact he offered to provide the Polish courts with a paternity test. Therefore, under the new system, the German courts would have no choice but to proceed with national enforcement measures.[188]

Although the Protocol helps to introduce safeguards where *exequatur* is abolished, the procedure established under the Protocol track—which eliminates public policy completely is insufficient, as it will not necessarily protect the rights and legitimate expectations of parties, as highlighted in the German/ Polish case.[189] Therefore the retention of simplified grounds for recognition and enforcement, or necessary safeguards at the enforcement stage are better methods for protecting individuals. The UK decided that it was better to retain these grounds; however this does not help the situation for the UK. This is because all incoming judgments to the UK[190] will have to be automatically recognised and enforced because they were decided using the Protocol. However, all outgoing judgments will be

[185] Ibid, 534–35.

[186] Ibid, 539. Although it is not clear whether all domestic remedies had been exhausted in Poland, it is most likely that they were as the BGH would not normally refuse to enforce a decision unless remedies in the state of origin have been exhausted (see Hess n 65).

[187] See below, for a discussion on Art 19 of the Protocol.

[188] As acknowledged by Seihr (n 182) 537. However, if it was proved that the defendant was not the father, could the German Authorities simply refuse to enforce the order, at the national enforcement stage, on the basis that no obligation exists under the national law as there is no relationship between the child and the defendant? As the enforcement stage is not covered by EU law this could be possible (see the discussion below on Art 21, although this is not something that Seihr considers in his analysis). See, ch 9 on actual enforcement and the decision of the CJEU in *Prism Investments* (n 51) which clarifies the distinction between the two stages.

[189] Mills describes public policy as a 'mechanism to ensure justice', and considers that the doctrine 'serves a fundamentally important function in demarcating the limits of the principles of tolerance underpinning rules on the application of foreign law and the recognition and enforcement of foreign judgments.' (Mills (n 90) 205 and 235.). See also Kegel (n 81).

[190] Except for ones from Denmark. Denmark has agreed to implement the Regulation to the extent that it amends Brussels I (OJ L149/80 12 June 2009).

subject to recognition and enforcement proceedings in the enforcing State. It seems slightly obtuse that the UK courts must automatically enforce all foreign decisions under the Maintenance Regulation, despite the fact the UK wanted to retain *exequatur* proceedings.[191] The ability of other EU States to review UK decisions may work against the UK. This is because the EU States have differing bases for awarding spousal maintenance.

The English courts in particular often award high sums of money in maintenance disputes. One reason for this could be that the UK courts do not necessarily distinguish between maintenance payments and property settlements.[192] Another issue is that the assessment of maintenance in England and Wales, as well as in Scotland, is left to the court's discretion in each individual case. This can be contrasted with the approach in some other States where 'there exists a more or less standardised maintenance calculation with tables and guidelines for the courts'.[193] It is foreseeable that if the maintenance award is particularly high the enforcing court may refuse to recognise and enforce the award on grounds of public policy, if the amount is in excess of the award that would have been calculated by the enforcing State's courts. An obvious example is the decision in *Kremen*,[194] where the applicant was awarded a lump sum of £8.3 million, which the judge 'constituted as maintenance'.[195] He reached this result by applying the 'needs' principle and considered that the sum could be enforced under the Maintenance Regulation as per *Van den Boogaard*.[196] It will be interesting to see if this judgment is enforced and whether other Member States believe the 'needs' based assessment in *Van den Boogaard* can apply to such a large sum of money, or if they will put a cap on lump sum payments. However, given the peculiar situation in *Kremen*, it is likely that Ms Kremen (formally Mrs Agrest) will have to seek enforcement of the award in more than one State.[197] Therefore the award claimed in each State will be smaller, which may mean the order is more enforceable as each amount may be considered as meeting the 'needs' principle.

Another example of where the award could conflict with a Member State's public policy is in relation to the creditor's ability to work. In Bulgaria, 'the creditor spouse's employment disability is a precondition for maintenance.'[198] Conceivably, Member States may be able to refuse to recognise a UK spousal

[191] The UK agreed to this because it felt that the ability to apply forum law would be most beneficial in its case. There is also the benefit of the review clause in Art 74 of the Regulation which requires the Regulation to be reviewed within five years. For a full summary of this, see P Beaumont, 'International Family Law in Europe—the Maintenance Project, the Hague Conference and the EC: A Triumph of Reverse Subsidiarity' (2009) 73 *Rabels Zeichschrift* 509, 543–44 fn 66.

[192] However, common practice in mainland Europe appears to be to distinguish the two awards as separate payments. K Boele-Woelki et al, *Principles of European Family Law Regarding Divorce and Maintenance Between Former Spouses* (Oxford, Intersentia, 2004) 70.

[193] Ibid, 82, where a variety of examples are given.

[194] *Kremen v Agrest* [2012] EWHC 45 (Fam) and see ch 3.

[195] Ibid, para 78.

[196] Ibid, paras 76–78 and ch 3 s III.

[197] Ibid.

[198] Boele-Woelki et al (n 192) 87.

maintenance order based on public policy for reasons relating to the size of the award. Recognition could also be refused on the basis that the award would not have been made internally. Only UK orders (and potentially Danish orders) could be refused recognition on these grounds as orders from all other Member States have to be automatically recognised and enforced. Alternatively, it could also be held that such an award is for matrimonial property rather than maintenance and therefore not enforceable under the Maintenance Regulation. Only time will tell if this will be a potential cause for concern for creditors residing in the UK. Potentially there could be an answer if enforcement of the amount awarded in *Kremen* is sought. This highlights potential issues with the public policy clause and the difference between this for Protocol and non-Protocol States. The overall conclusion is that the public policy clause in the Protocol will be of little assistance to debtors who are at the mercy of spurious maintenance orders given in the State of origin. Particularly where they have either exhausted their remedies in that State or do not have sufficient means to appeal further. This is a particular worry in the system under the Maintenance Regulation because there is a creditor bias as creditors can sue in the state of their own habitual residence.[199] Further creditors should be provided with legal aid in all child support cases whereas debtors will not.[200]

## B. Articles 19 and 21

Recital 29 of the Maintenance Regulation suggests that the

> Regulation should provide for the right of a defendant who did not enter an appearance in the court of origin of a Member State bound by the 2007 Hague Protocol to apply for a review of the decision given against him at the stage of enforcement.[201]

This has been transposed into a legal obligation in Article 19 of the Regulation. This gives the defendant a right to apply for a review where he did not enter an appearance in the case where it was not possible for him to challenge the decision, because either he did not have sufficient time to arrange a defence or he was prevented from contesting the claim due to extraordinary circumstances '*without any fault on his part*'.[202] This requires that the defendant either did not know about the

[199] See ch 5 s III and cf ch 8 s III (unlike Brussels I where the 'general' rule is that the defendant is sued in their forum, Art 2). Further, debtors cannot even try to modify the award in their own State, because this is also precluded by the instruments, see ch 5 s VIII above.

[200] Maintenance Regulation Art 46.

[201] Ibid, Recital 29.

[202] See, ibid Art 19, emphasis added. This is important because the fact that the Article specifically states that there should be no fault on the defendant's part, would appear to exclude the right to apply for a review on the basis of a debarment order as in *Gambazzi* (n 93) where the defendant was at fault. In this case the CJEU stated that it could be considered whether or not the exclusion measure was a 'disproportionate infringement' (para 48). However, Article 19 of the Maintenance Regulation does not make any reference to a proportionality test and would therefore have been of no assistance to Mr Gambazzi (see below under suitable alternative arrangements).

proceedings or that he tried to challenge them if he did. This provision is very narrow, narrower than the right to a fair trial, therefore its practical relevance is questionable.[203] Cuniberti and Rueda refer to these types of protection as minimum standards reviews. They argue that they are not suitable mechanisms for replacing the *exequatur* procedure as they do not comply with human rights standards.[204]

A Member State may also refuse or suspend enforcement based on the '*grounds* of refusal or suspension of enforcement under the law of the Member State of enforcement'.[205] It is questionable at this stage how this may be interpreted by the CJEU and Member States. This is because, the text is different from that used in the other instruments where *exequatur* has been abolished. The general concept is that the 'enforcement *procedures* shall be governed by the law of the Member State of enforcement.'[206] This is different to the provision in the Maintenance Regulation, which refers specifically to national grounds of refusal. This implies that the Maintenance Regulation does allow national grounds of refusal to creep in. This is limited though to grounds that would apply to all cases and there can be no substantive review of the decision at the enforcement stage.[207] Therefore what practical effect can Article 21 have and will this protect the fundamental rights of the parties?

Article 21 will mainly operate to protect debtors who do not have sufficient funds to pay the obligation set out in the decision. This would be fair as it would apply without discrimination to all decisions (national and international). You cannot enforce a decision if it would mean the debtor would be left with insufficient means. Another example would be where the debtor had to make a one off payment and this had already been paid.[208] Unfortunately, Article 21 cannot be used to help the unsuspecting sibling or cohabitee that may have to pay maintenance if the Protocol is not applied correctly. The best remedy is through Article 19. However if they have attended the proceedings and challenged the obligation

[203] See below at s VIII for a full analysis of these types of provisions.

[204] Cuniberti and Rueda (n 67) 298–99.

[205] Maintenance Regulation Art 21(1), emphasis added.

[206] See, Art 20 of the EEO, Art 21 of the Regulation establishing a small claims Procedure and Art 21 of Regulation (EC) 1896/2006 of the European Parliament and of the Council of 12 December 2006 creating a European Order for Payment Procedure [2006] OJ L399/1 (Order for Payment Regulation).

[207] See Art 42 of the Maintenance Regulation.

[208] *Prism Investments* (n 51) where proceedings for recognition and enforcement were ongoing even though the debtor had already paid. *Prism Investments* is a case on Brussels I. In the case the Dutch Court questioned whether it could refuse recognition and enforcement on a ground other than those specified in Arts 34 and 35, notably that the order had already been enforced. The CJEU made it clear that the enforceability of a judgment is a precondition for its enforcement (see para 38). The Court went on to say that 'once the judgment is incorporated into the legal order of the Member State in which enforcement is sought, national legislation of that Member State relating to enforcement applies in the same way as to judgments delivered by national courts' (para 40). The conclusion being that recognition and enforcement can only be refused on the specific grounds listed in the legislation. These proceedings should always be separate from actual enforcement. Once a decision is recognised as enforceable in the State of enforcement it is then subject to national procedures for enforcement, equivalent to a national judgment, and enforcement can potentially be refused on any national ground where necessary.

but the case was still decided wrongly, then Article 19 will be of no help. This is especially true where all the appeals in the State of origin have been exhausted because the State of enforcement has no possibility to review the substantive decision. Could Article 21 make a difference in these cases though?

If the State of enforcement is clever when drafting or redrafting its enforcement law there may be some way it can avoid enforcing a decision which has slipped through the minimal safeguards and would previously have been caught by the public policy exception at the recognition and enforcement stage.[209] However, it is difficult to anticipate what situations may arise at this stage; therefore it is difficult to foresee how such a provision could be drafted. It would have to be very different from an overriding public policy clause if it is to be acceptable to the CJEU. It would also have to be drafted in a way that indicated there was not a full review of the substance as this would be incompatible with Article 42. However, the German legislature passed implementing legislation which allowed a specific procedure to be applied to the enforcement of orders circulated under the EEO.[210] 'As the Regulation suppressed *exequatur*, but left untouched enforcement procedures in the Member States, the German legislature argued that this procedure complies with the abolition of exequatur as it is an enforcement procedure.'[211]

Considering all these points, could Article 21 be helpful in the German/Polish scenario discussed above? If a paternity test proved that the defendant was not the father, the German authorities could argue that the obligation no longer exists (because in this case biological paternity was a prerequisite of maintenance) so therefore it does not have to be enforced. Arguing that the obligation does not exist, would be different to applying an overriding public policy clause to refuse to recognise a decision based on lack of paternity. However, would such a decision be seen as reviewing the substance of the case? Most likely yes, but since the Maintenance Regulation only covers maintenance obligations and not paternity, it could be argued that a review of the case based on paternity is different from a review of the maintenance obligation that is to be circulated under the Regulation.[212] Only time will tell how similar and more complicated situations will be resolved in the future. It is foreseeable that there will be situations where Member States will want to refuse to enforce maintenance obligations, and may be able to do this successfully through Article 21. The extent to which the CJEU will allow for national grounds to be included is subject to interpretation however.[213]

[209] See the discussion on *Prism Investments* at n 51.

[210] Cuniberti and Rueda (n 67) 310.

[211] Ibid 310–11.

[212] See ch 6, which begins to explain the distinction between paternity and maintenance. Further, this situation is relatively simple as it considers an obligation between a child and a 'biological' parent. Imagine a similar scenario in terms of adoptive parents or surrogate parents for example (see ch 1 s V for an insight into the various forms or parentage). The numerous possibilities available and the complications that could arise are further support for the need for a public policy safeguard given the scenarios that may arise in the future.

[213] Compare the CJEU's treatment of national grounds of public policy in *Omega* (n 76) where free movement of services could be restricted because the laser game was contrary to human dignity as protected by the German Constitution, with the special case of Brussels IIbis in *Aguirre Zarraga* (n 63)

## VII. Are the Separate Procedures Understood in Practice?

The discussion above highlights the differences between the two different procedures, and explains the difficulties that could be faced by the removal of the public policy safeguard. This section will now consider whether it is sensible to have two separate procedures operating in the EU under the Maintenance Regulation.[214] It will also question whether those who apply the Regulation really understand the distinction between the two procedures and how the system should work in practice.

Although there are two procedures under the Regulation, quantitative research suggests that the distinction between the two procedures is not necessarily clear and at this stage the majority of applications are still going through an enforceability process. Articles 17–19 clearly abolish the *exequatur* process, but how this fits with the various available applications in Article 56 of the Regulation is unclear. This is partly because there is a disconnection between the procedures for recognition and enforcement in Articles 17–24 and the available applications in Article 56. The text is very far away from the available applications and there is no indication in Article 56 of which applications should apply to which procedures. Further, the available applications in Article 56 are based on the applications in Article 10 of the Maintenance Convention. This is slightly concerning given that the procedures for enforceability or strict enforcement are very different under the two instruments.[215]

Article 56(1)(a) of the Regulation covers enforceability and applications under this article only need to be made in relation to outgoing applications from the UK and Denmark. Article 56(1)(b) covers applications for enforcement and all other applications, except for those mentioned above, can be made directly under this provision without any recourse to Article 56(1)(a). Article 56(1)(a) allows a creditor to make an application for 'recognition or recognition and declaration of enforceability of a decision'. The equivalent provision in the Convention covers

where a violation of a child's right to be heard was not sufficient to exclude enforcement of the decision. As we can see the weight given to national rules can vary dramatically and although in this case the Maintenance Regulation states that enforcement can be refused on grounds of national law, it will be interesting to see how much leeway will be given to Member States. It is very unlikely that the CJEU will allow public policy arguments like in *Omega* (n 76) because this exception was abolished through Art 17. However, these cases highlight the opposite ends of the spectrum and as Art 21 is different from the equivalent provisions in the other Regulations, future preliminary rulings of the CJEU could be significant in this respect. See also, M Forde, 'The "Ordre Public" Exception and Adjudicative Jurisdiction Conventions' (1980) 29 *International and Comparative Law Quarterly* 259, for an interesting discussion on whether international instruments should always be subject to an implied public policy exception. In the context of the Maintenance Regulation this seems highly unlikely as the public policy exception was specifically excluded, but it is an interesting concept to bear in mind.

[214] Not to mention a variety of other processes operating under the EU system generally.

[215] See ch 8, particularly ss V and VI.

'recognition or recognition and enforcement of a decision'.[216] The difference in the text in both instruments clarifies the position in regards to enforceability. The fact that the term 'and enforcement' was not included in the Regulation makes it clear that Article 56(1)(a) should only apply to enforceability. However, procedures for enforcement where no enforceability is required are not so clear. Article 56(1)(b) allows a creditor to make an application for 'enforcement of a decision given or recognised in the requested Member State'; the equivalent provision in the Convention covers the 'enforcement of a decision made or recognised in the requested State'.[217] The distinction here is not so clear, because the replacement of the word 'made' with 'given' makes very little difference. It would be usual to seek enforcement of a decision originally given in the 'requesting' State, rather than the 'requested' State. However, technically, the language of Article 56(1)(b) does cover all judgments from Hague Protocol States in the EU because it includes the term 'recognised' and those decisions are 'automatically' recognised in the requested EU Member States under the Regulation without the need for any procedure. Thus the application for enforcement of such a decision is for enforcement of a decision that has been automatically already 'recognised' in the requested State. However, from a statistical point of view and from the point of view of clarity for the user it would be better to divide up the different types of decisions falling within Article 56(1)(b).

> Consideration should be given to amending **Article 56(1)(b) and Annex VI** of Council Regulation 4/2009 to reduce the current risk of confusion by **separating applications** for actual enforcement of decisions given in the requested Member State (which apply to all Member States) from: a) applications for actual enforcement of decisions given in other Member States bound by the Hague Protocol 2007 which are automatically recognised in the requested State without a declaration of enforceability; and, b) applications for actual enforcement of decisions given in other Member States not bound by the Hague Protocol which have already been the subject of a declaration of enforceability in the requested State.[218]

Given the lack of clarity in this area it is unsurprising that the figures provided are slightly confusing. There is some assistance in the Recitals, but again the terminology used is not entirely clear because it is not consistent, therefore interpretation can be ambiguous. The terminology in Recital 26 on recognition and declaration of enforceability is clear enough and matches with the wording in the second part of Article 56(1)(a). 'For decisions on maintenance obligations given in a Member State not bound by the 2007 Hague Protocol, there should be provision in this Regulation for a procedure for recognition and declaration of enforceability.'

[216] Art 10(1)(a) of the Convention.

[217] Ibid, Art 10(1)(b).

[218] See conclusion 5(e) of the Heidelberg Conference (available at Annex VIII). This section was included based on the findings of the empirical study carried out for the Heidelberg project. However, there were debates between the partners whilst constructing the conclusions as to whether such an amendment would really be necessary. It was concluded that for the sake of clarity it would be preferable if there was a change in the text.

However, Article 56 also allows a creditor to make an application purely for 'recognition' and this is not mentioned in Recital 26. Recital 24 states that the

> guarantees provided by the application of rules on conflict of laws should provide the justification for having decisions relating to maintenance obligations given in a Member State bound by the 2007 Hague Protocol recognised and regarded as enforceable in all the other Member States *without any procedure* being necessary and without any form of control on the substance in the Member State of enforcement.[219]

This recital refers to recognition as referred to in Article 56(1)(a) and then says regarded as enforceable which has no connection with the wording in Article 56(1)(b). However, although the recital uses the term 'recognised' it also says 'without any procedure being necessary'. This implies that there should be no procedure for enforceability because the obligation should be automatically enforceable. The term 'recognised' is included to acknowledge that any party can make an application for recognition, although it is not necessary to do so under either route. However this could confuse practitioners because it could be interpreted as suggesting that an application under Article 56(1)(a) is required in all cases and not just applications coming from non-Protocol States. The whole procedure is slightly confusing and it may not necessarily be clear to practitioners which procedure they should use, particularly when they have neither had any specific training on the Regulation nor do they have a legal background.

The practice in the first year of operation of the Regulation suggests that the procedures in this area are not clear. It would appear that Central Authorities are generally always making an application under Article 56(1)(a). Data provided indicated that there were at least 1649 applications under Article 56(1)(a) and only 186 applications for enforcement under Article 56(1)(b).[220] If *exequatur* was abolished and there was no procedure necessary at this stage then the figures should be reversed and there should be more applications for enforcement because the majority of States are party to the Hague Protocol. In fact there were only 179 outgoing cases from the UK,[221] technically these should be the only cases under Article 56(1)(a).[222] However at this stage the procedure is still in the transitional process, so any cases decided before June 2011 still need to go through the enforceability stage as the decision was not made according to the rules of the Protocol.

219 Emphasis added.

220 A factor that contributes towards the disparity in the figures is that applications that were commenced before June 2011 still need to go through the old system. This is because the application of the law designated under the Hague Protocol is a condition for the abolition of *exequatur*. Therefore, because the Protocol did not apply previously the system under Arts 17–19 of the Maintenance Regulation cannot be used for these cases. However, it is considered that this alone cannot account for such high numbers of applications under the old system. The lack of clarity on which type of application to use could also be a factor.

221 From discussions with practitioners working at Central Authorities a misconception is that it is believed that all applications involving the UK still need to go through the *exequatur* process, when it is only outgoing applications not incoming.

222 Except for cases from Denmark, but these applications were not included in the study.

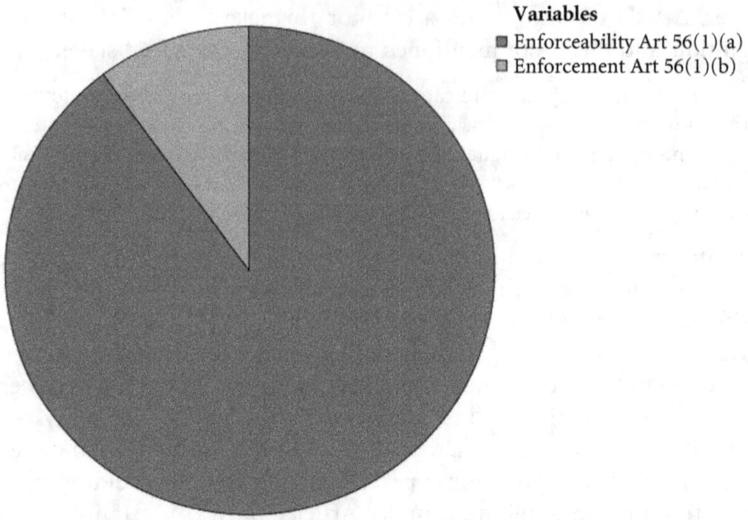


**Figure 7.1: Art 56(1)(a) and (b) applications**

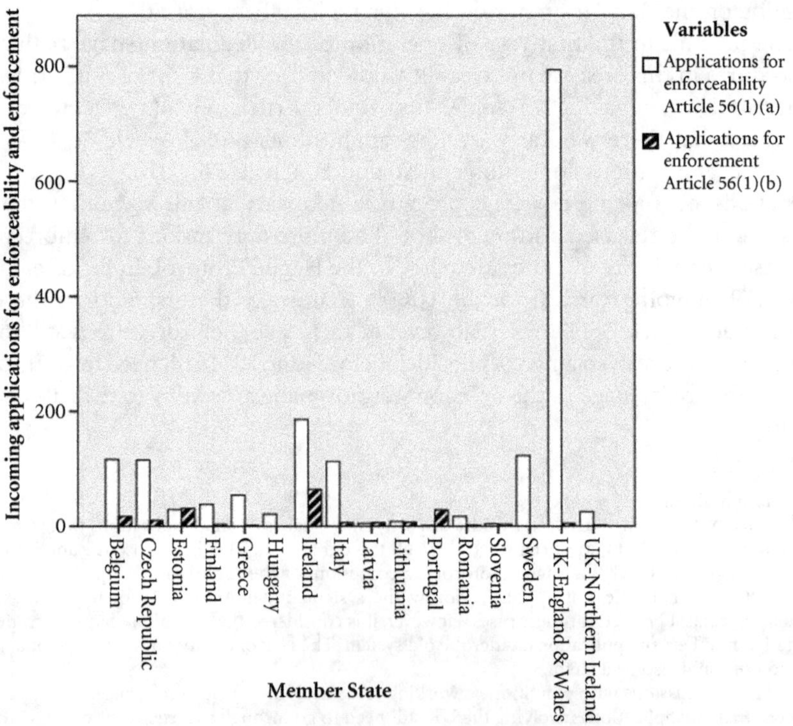


**Figure 7.2: Incoming applications for enforceability and enforcement by Member State**

Around 90 per cent of applications reported in year 1, were for enforceability and only 10 per cent were for enforcement. So, only one in 10 applications of this type were for enforcement.

However, when this matter is investigated further it can be seen that this ratio of one in 10 is not true across all the Member States. The graph below compares incoming applications for enforcement with incoming applications for enforceability in each State that completed the relevant part of the questionnaire.

As can be seen from the graph, England and Wales received a vast number of incoming applications for enforceability (99.4 per cent) and very few applications for enforcement. As they received by far the most applications, this is possibly skewing the results.[223] The high number of incoming applications for enforceability could also support the assertion that some of those working at Central Authorities believe, wrongly, that all applications involving the UK must go through the *exequatur* stage.[224] In contrast to the high number of applications for enforceability received by England and Wales, the majority of applications received by Portugal were for enforcement. Estonia received slightly more applications for enforcement than enforceability, and Latvia, Lithuania and Slovenia received similar amounts of each type of application. Numbers and percentages are displayed in Table 7.1 below.

**Table 7.1: Applications for enforceability and enforcement**

| | | **56(1)(a) enforceability** | **56(1)(b) enforcement** | **Total** |
|---|---|---|---|---|
| Estonia | Number of applications | 29 | 31 | 60 |
| | As a percentage | 48.3% | 51.7% | |
| Latvia | Number of Applications | 5 | 6 | 11 |
| | As a percentage | 45.5% | 54.5% | |
| Lithuania | Number of Applications | 8 | 7 | 15 |
| | As a percentage | 53.3% | 46.7% | |
| Portugal | Number of Applications | 1 | 28 | 29 |
| | As a percentage | 3.4% | 96.6% | |
| Slovenia | Number of Applications | 4 | 3 | 7 |
| | As a percentage | 57.1% | 42.9% | |

[223] The data from England and Wales is skewing the results slightly. If data from England and Wales is excluded then just over 80% of applications are for enforceability and around 20% for enforcement, so around 1 in 5. The figure is still much higher than one would expect given the abolition of the *exequatur* process.

[224] The Scottish Central Authority reported that incoming applications were being sent on the wrong forms and see n 221.

Although the overall figures are affected by the transitional application from the old rules in Brussels I, given that nearly all Portugal's incoming applications were for enforcement (and there are other States at around 50 per cent), this alone probably does not account for high numbers of application for enforceability overall.

A further consideration could be whether there are any patterns in relation to the States sending the applications. This could give some indication as to whether some Central Authorities seem to understand the procedure more than others. For example were applications for enforceability commonly sent by certain States and applications for enforcement sent by a different pool of States? The two graphs below indicate incoming applications split into pattern by sending State. The first graph deals with enforceability and the second graph enforcement.

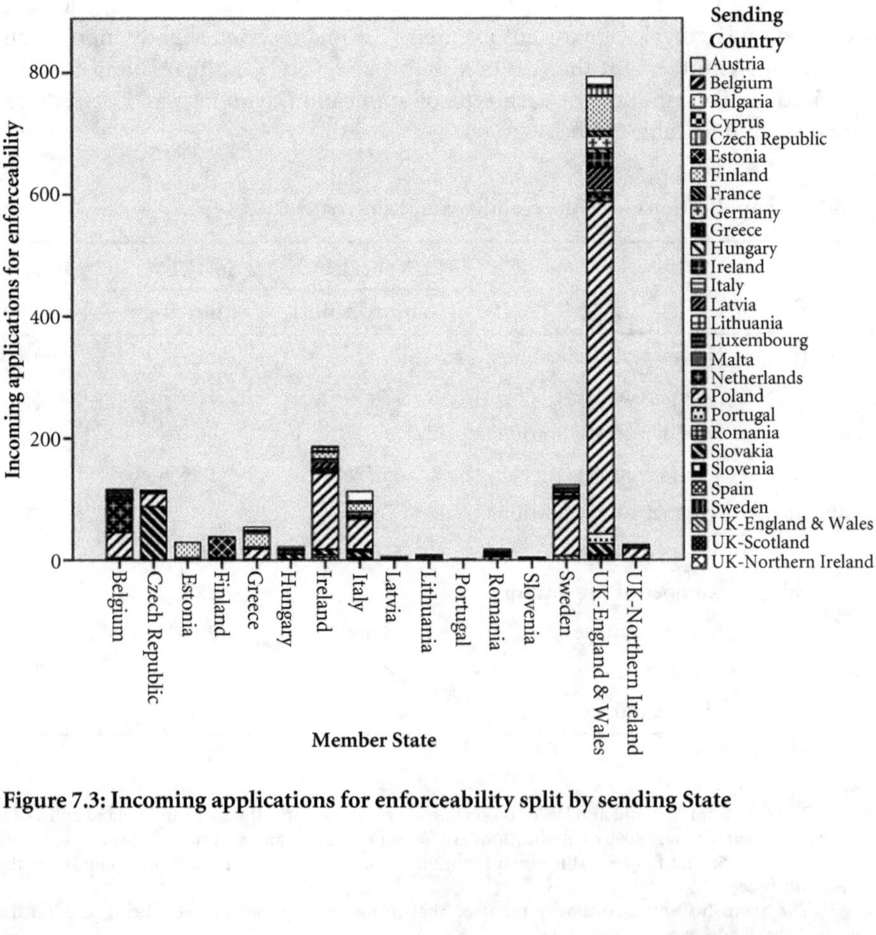


**Figure 7.3: Incoming applications for enforceability split by sending State**

In the graph above, the vast number of applications were sent by Poland, indicated in diagonal stripes. The Czech Republic received a number of applications from Slovakia, and Belgium received a few applications from the Netherlands.

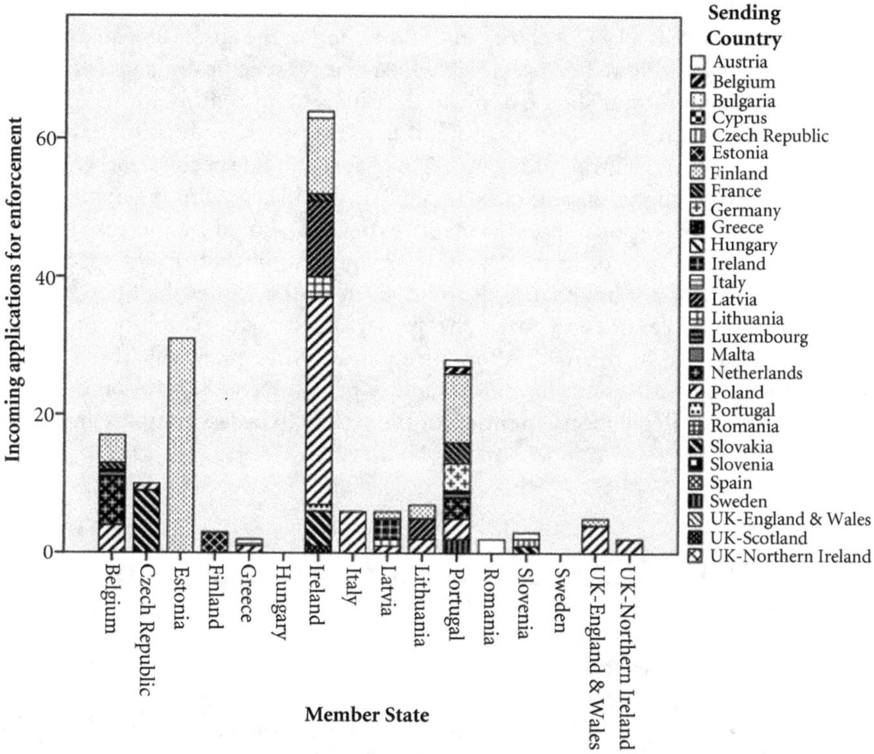


**Figure 7.4: Incoming applications for enforcement split by sending State**

In relation to enforcement, however, Poland (for the first time) is not the State that sent the most applications.[225] Notably, Sweden has received no applications for enforcement, and the vast majority of applications it received for enforceability were sent by Poland. We see a larger spread of sending Member States than in previous graphs, notably Finland, the Netherlands and Latvia. This could suggest that these Central Authorities are more aware of the new process than the Polish

[225] See Figure 2.5 and Figure 7.3 where the majority of applications came from Poland (see also Annexes II and IV).

Authority,[226] but it is not decisive. Although Finland sent more applications for enforcement than other States it still sent more applications for enforceability than enforcement (around 70 per cent of applications under 56(1)).[227]

Although there is some explanation for the disparity in the figures, the new system is slightly confusing and therefore Central Authorities could use more guidance.[228] There is a lack of clarity in this area and in the absence of an explanatory report it would have been preferable if Article 56 specifically stated which of the available applications should apply to the different procedures for recognition and enforcement. It would be very useful if the European Commission developed a Practice Guide for Central Authorities. This guide should specify clearly how the procedures for recognition and enforcement fit specifically with the applications in Article 56. The various applications in Article 56 should be increased, when the Regulation is revised, so that there is an application that relates specifically to enforcement of a maintenance decision given in the requesting State.[229] This would be a suitable amendment if the two tracks for enforceability and strict enforcement are to be retained. Alternatively it would be preferable if the Union established a unified system for enforceability or enforcement across the private international law Regulations, in order for the system to be less complex and more coherent.[230]

## VIII. Suitable Alternative Arrangements

There are many issues to be considered when debating the abolition of *exequatur* and the appropriate place for necessary safeguards. In addition to these issues, it is questionable whether it is logical to have two systems operating in the European Union between the Member States. The system is relatively complex and any further complexity is a concern. It is preferable to maintain simplicity in order to ensure the best implementation of the Regulation. Although traditional *exequatur* proceedings will undoubtedly slow down the process under the Regulation, some safeguards should be maintained in order to protect individuals where necessary.[231]

[226] According to these States shown in the graph, 980 of the applications they received under Art 56(1)(a) and (b) were sent by Poland. 926 of these (94.5%) were for enforceability and 54 were for enforcement. Further, Poland does not have a Centralised Authority but instead designates the task to the different districts (see ch 10, n 16).

[227] This means 3 in 10 of the applications sent by Finland were for enforcement, which is higher than the overall figure of 1 in 10. For a full table of the type of applications sent under Art 56(1)(a) and (b) by sending State, see Annex III.

[228] See ch 10 on administrative cooperation.

[229] See conclusions and next steps of the Heidelberg Conference, para 5(e).

[230] See below under suitable alternative arrangements, and see Walker (n 63) s 2.2.

[231] Access to justice is also a general principle of EU Law as are fundamental rights as guaranteed by the ECHR see Art 6(3) TEU.

The system in place for the UK and Denmark is better for the protection of the rights of individuals, than the system in the Protocol States, and the abolition of *exequatur* (without the retention of public policy) is not practical in the context of family law.[232] The system in Article 24 of the Maintenance Regulation is relatively uncomplex and has limited safeguards. Given the current procedures in most other European instruments it would be more consistent if the system in Article 24 applied to all proceedings under the Maintenance Regulation. Since the aim is to create a common market which allows for free movement of judgments and persons, everything should be as clear as possible. In order for there to be uniformity and certainty within the Union, the ideal approach would be for all the instruments to have the same procedure for recognition and enforcement.

Although Article 24,[233] as it currently stands, is in line with procedures for recognition and enforcement in other European legislation, in particular Brussels I, this will no longer be the case following the Brussels I recast.[234] This is because the recast will retain all the safeguards contained in Brussels I and Article 24 of the Maintenance Regulation, but these will be applied at the enforcement stage.[235] As the procedures are due to change, Article 24 of the Maintenance Regulation could be improved and the grounds could be reduced further. On the basis of the experiences under Brussels I, the exception in Article 24(b) is unnecessary.

> where it was given in default of appearance, if the defendant was not served with the document which instituted the proceedings or with an equivalent document in sufficient time and in such a way as to enable him to arrange for his defence, unless the defendant failed to commence proceedings to challenge the decision when it was possible for him to do so.[236]

The main premise for this is that any breach of fundamental rights will fall within the public policy exception in Article 24(a). This would include the

[232] For possible consequences of the rights of individuals see *Aguirre Zarraga* (n 63). See also I Viarengo, 'The Enforcement of Maintenance Obligations in the EU: Requiem for Public Policy? Family Relationships and the (Partial) Abolition of Exequatur' in Beaumont et al (eds), *The Recovery of Maintenance in the EU and Worldwide* (Oxford, Hart Publishing, 2014) 473.

[233] Maintenance Regulation.

[234] The Brussels I recast will remove the declaration of enforceability stage as a precondition for the enforcement of the judgment. However, it will retain the grounds for non-recognition as necessary safeguards which will now be applied at the enforcement stage. This will cut out the issue in *Prism Investments* (n 51) as there will only be one stage. This means that at the enforcement stage enforcement can be refused on national grounds or for one of the common grounds, previously found at the declaration of enforceability stage. In some States this will make the process shorter and the time for proceedings should be reduced. However, some States, such as the UK, will have to create an extra procedure in national law, because previously there was no court procedure at the enforcement stage.

[235] Brussels I recast Arts 45 and 46. See, Timmer (n 67) 129; Hess (n 65) s 3.1 and Walker (n 63) s 2.2.

[236] Art 24(b). This defence appears to have originated from the concept of natural justice. 'No foreign judgment which offends against "natural" or "substantive" justice will be enforced.' M Borm-Reid, 'Recognition and Enforcement of Foreign Judgments' (1954) 3 *International and Comparative Law Quarterly* 49, 80, and see 80–82. See also, K Lipstein, 'The Hague Conventions on Private International Law, Public Law and Public Policy' (1959) 8 *International and Comparative Law Quarterly* 18, 29–30.

rights of the defence in Article 24(b). The Article 24(b) exception covers only one aspect of the right to a fair trial as composed in Article 47 of the Charter[237] and Article 6 of the ECHR.[238] The main concept being that you must have a fair trial. If you are not served the document warning you of the proceedings against you in sufficient time, then the State cannot argue that the proceedings were fair. Primarily because the defendant will unlikely be able to prepare a proper defence and gain sufficient advice. This will undoubtedly be in violation of the second State's public policy because all Member States are parties to the ECHR, which constitutes general principles of EU Law, and they also have to abide by the rules in the Charter.[239] The defence as worded is very limited anyway so its added value is questionable.

A previous example of the right to a fair trial falling under the public policy exception is the famous case of *Krombach*.[240] When deciding whether recognition could be refused on the basis of public policy, the Court referred to the right to a fair trial.

> With regard to the right to be defended, to which the question submitted to the Court refers, this occupies a prominent position in the organisation and conduct of a fair trial and is one of the fundamental rights deriving from the constitutional traditions common to the Member States.[241]

The Court went on to say that, 'a national court … is entitled to hold that a refusal to hear the defence of an accused person who is not present at the hearing constitutes a manifest breach of a fundamental right.'[242] The Court concluded that

> even though the Convention is intended to secure the simplification of formalities governing the reciprocal recognition and enforcement of judgments of courts or tribunals, it is not permissible to achieve that aim by undermining the right to a fair hearing … [therefore] recourse to the public-policy clause must be regarded as being possible in exceptional cases where the guarantees laid down in the legislation of the State of origin and in the Convention itself have been insufficient to protect the defendant from a

[237] 'Everyone whose rights and freedoms guaranteed by the law of the Union are violated has the right to an effective remedy before a tribunal in compliance with the conditions laid down in this Article. Everyone is entitled to a fair and public hearing within a reasonable time by an independent and impartial tribunal previously established by law. *Everyone shall have the possibility of being advised, defended and represented.* Legal aid shall be made available to those who lack sufficient resources in so far as such aid is necessary to ensure effective access to justice.'

[238] 'In the determination of his civil rights and obligations or of any criminal charge against him, everyone is entitled to a fair and public hearing within a reasonable time by an independent and impartial tribunal established by law. Judgment shall be pronounced publicly but the press and public may be excluded from all or part of the trial in the interests of morals, public order or national security in a democratic society, where the interests of juveniles or the protection of the private life of the parties so require, or to the extent strictly necessary in the opinion of the court in special circumstances where publicity would prejudice the interests of justice.'

[239] See Arts 6(1) and (3) of the TEU.

[240] *Krombach* (n 112).

[241] Ibid, para 38.

[242] Ibid, para 40.

manifest breach of his right to defend himself before the court of origin, as recognised by the ECHR.[243]

From this it is clear that the right to a fair trial is covered by the public policy defence.[244] This conclusion is perfectly logical and this is a clear example of why the public policy defence is necessary.

Although the issue in *Krombach* was not covered by the element of the right to a fair trial that is covered by the defence in Article 24(b) (Article 34(2) of Brussels I), it would be reasonable to conclude that all violations of the right to a fair trial would fall within the public policy defence for the reasons cited by the CJEU in *Krombach*.[245] Further evidence for this can be seen in *Gambazzi*,[246] where the defendant entered an appearance but was precluded from appearing in the main proceedings because he had not complied with obligations imposed by an earlier order. The CJEU considered that the enforcing court could refuse to enforce the order based on the public policy defence if 'following a comprehensive assessment of the proceedings and in light of all the circumstances, it appears to it that that exclusion measure constituted a manifest and disproportionate infringement of the defendant's right to be heard.'[247] Again, the issue here is whether the rights of the defence were violated. The problem once again is outside the defence in Article 24(b) because the defendant knew about the proceedings and in fact did enter an appearance.[248]

Therefore, the defence in Article 24(b) does not in reality add any extra benefit because any violation of the rights of the defence would be caught by the public policy clause.[249] In fact one could go further and say that on the basis of the preliminary rulings of the CJEU, on the 'default of appearance' exception as appears in the Brussels Convention and developed in Brussels I, the precise meaning of

[243] Ibid, paras 43–44.

[244] 'In light of the importance given to Article 6 of the ECHR in *exequatur* proceedings, it is interesting to note that Article 47 of the Charter, which is now hierarchically higher than the EU regulations regarding the "free movement of judgments", even broadens the procedural protection of individuals.' (Škerl (n 84) 466.) See also n 237.

[245] See above, and Cuniberti: 'In *Krombach*, the ECJ borrowed not only Article 6 itself, but also the interpretations of the Strasbourg Court on the content of the right to a fair trial. So, if Article 6 was interpreted as requiring courts to give reasons, it seems that this law is borrowed and ought to be used to define the meaning of public policy in Article 34.' Cuniberti (n 66) 33.

[246] *Gambazzi* (n 93).

[247] Ibid, para 48. As noted above (n 202), it is clear that the special defence for Protocol countries in Article 19, would have been of no benefit in such a case either, despite the fact that it goes further than the defence in Article 24(b). The CJEU failed to take a decisive position in *Gambazzi*, but we can see that the Court would be accepting if the national court did refuse to enforce the decision for reasons of public policy. In fact the Italian court subsequently decided that it would enforce the decision and that the public policy defence had not been met, because the sanctions were proportionate to the aim. (See, Škerl (n 84) 473 and Hess (n 65) 1097). Further, the ECtHR dismissed a subsequent application by Gambazzi before them as manifestly unfounded, meaning that 'the CJEU has shown more sensibility regarding the possible human rights violations than the ECtHR' (Škerl (n 84) 474). See also Beaumont and Johnston (n 64) 255–56 and Cuniberti and Reuda (n 67) 296.

[248] These situations would also fall outside of the limited defence in Art 19 of the Maintenance Regulation.

[249] See s V above.

the exception is unclear to Member States and adds unnecessary confusion. Hess notes that the defence as it appears in Article 34(2) of the Brussels I Regulation is 'in practice, the most important provision for objecting to the recognition of a foreign judgment.'[250] This would suggest that the defence is used more often than the other exceptions, and applicants think that they may be successful where they raise the defence. Default judgments occur frequently within the EU, and the problems mainly arise in relation to the service of the document instituting the proceedings.[251] However, this does not mean that defendants are likely to be successful when they raise the defence.[252]

In *Debaecker*,[253] the letter notifying the defendant of the proceedings against him had been sent to his former address. The questions referred to the Court were about what would be sufficient time and the circumstances in which the document was served.[254] The Court began by clarifying that

> [a]lthough the Convention is … intended to 'secure the simplification and formalities governing the reciprocal recognition and enforcement of judgments of courts or tribunals', that aim cannot, according to a series of decisions of the Court, be attained *by undermining in any way the right to a fair hearing*.[255]

The United Kingdom and the Federal Republic of Germany also relied heavily on the right to a fair trial, in particular the right to prepare a defence in their arguments.[256] The Court summarised that 'Article 27(2) … seeks to enable a defendant to defend himself effectively'.[257] It is clear from the foregoing that the aim of Article 27(2) (and subsequently Article 34(2) of Brussels I and Article 24(b) of the Maintenance Regulation) is to allow the defendant to defend himself effectively and therefore not undermine the right to a fair trial. It is clear that everything

[250] Heidelberg Report (n 54) para 539, see paras 539–42.

[251] Ibid.

[252] Ibid, paras 541–42 and see C-619/10 *Trade Agency Ltd v Seramico Investments Ltd*, 6 September 2012. The case concerned a default judgment and it was questioned whether recognition could be refused on the grounds of either public policy or default of appearance. The decision was adopted in default because it was believed that the claim was uncontested. The CJEU considered that fundamental rights were not absolute and could be subject to restrictions (para 55). It concluded that Member States can only refuse to enforce a judgment where it 'it appears to the court, after an overall assessment of the proceedings in light of all the relevant circumstances that judgment is a manifest and disproportionate breach of the defendant's right to a fair trial referred to in Article 47(2) of the Charter' (para 62). This supports the assertion that the two defences ultimately do the same thing in this context.

[253] C-49/84 *Debaecker, Plouvier and Bouwman* [1985] ECR 01779. Although this case was decided under the Brussels Convention and the defence was worded slightly differently from the one that now appears in Brussels I and the Maintenance Regulation, the part of the ruling referred to is still relevant now because the idea behind the defence is the same.

[254] Ibid, see para 5.

[255] Ibid, para 10, emphasis added. Cited by the Court in para 43 of *Krombach* (n 112).

[256] Ibid, 'the purpose of Article 27(2) is to guarantee not merely a formal service but the right to be heard and thus the opportunity of presenting a defence. They therefore consider that every effort must be made to prevent judgment from being given against a defendant without his having had an opportunity of defending himself' (para 26).

[257] Ibid, para 31.

that is intended to be caught by this defence will also fall under the public policy defence.[258]

A further example is *ASML*.[259] In *ASML* the CJEU was interpreting the defence as it appears in Article 34(2) of Brussels I which is identical to the defence in the Maintenance Regulation. The difference between the defence in the Convention and the Regulation is very small and the common aim remains that 'the rights of the defence are effectively respected.'[260] The Court repeats that even though the Regulation aims to secure simple and rapid procedures for recognition and enforcement, 'that objective cannot be attained by undermining in any way the right to a fair hearing'.[261] The questions referred asked at what stage the defendant should have become aware of the proceedings against him.[262] The law suggests that the defendant needs to have sufficient notice in order to prepare a defence, so that his rights to a fair trial are not violated:

> [o]nly knowledge by the defendant of the contents of the default judgment guarantees, in accordance with the requirements of respect for the rights of defence and the effective exercise of those rights, that it is possible for the defendant, within the meaning of Article 34(2) of Regulation No 44/2001, to commence proceedings to challenge that judgment before the courts of the State in which the judgment was given.[263]

The Court concluded that 'in order to justify the conclusion that it was possible for the defendant to challenge a default judgment against him, within the meaning of Article 34(2) Regulation No 44/2001, he must have been aware of the contents of that decision, which presupposes that it was served on him.'[264] This also supports the notion that any proceedings caught by this defence should also be caught by the public policy defence.[265]

[258] In this respect see the English Court of Appeal decision in *Maronier v Larmer* [2002] EWCA Civ 774. In the case the proceedings were reactivated after 12 years and the defendant knew nothing about this until it was too late. The English Court considered that the facts were similar to those in the *Debaecker* case (n 253). However, apparently the Dutch procedure allowed the action to be reactivated without requiring a fresh service of documents, and because there was no requirement for the documents to be served, the defence in Art 27 (2) of the Brussels Convention presumably could not apply. The English courts refused to enforce the judgment based therefore on the public policy defence even though the issue was lack of knowledge of the proceedings. Although this is a national judgment and might not be entirely representative of the CJEU's views, it once again shows the limited application of the default of appearance defence, and how the public policy defence is more effective in protecting the defendant's right to a fair hearing.

[259] *ASML* (n 113).

[260] Ibid, para 20.

[261] Ibid, para 24.

[262] Ibid, para 15.

[263] Ibid, para 36.

[264] Ibid, para 40. Contrast this with the approach of the ECtHR in *Avotinš* (n 95), discussed in s V above.

[265] See also Hess when discussing the decision of the Oberlandesgericht Zweibrücken, on 5 October 2005—3 W 165/04, where the German Court declared that the judgment was unenforceable on the basis of Art 34(2) of Brussels I. However, it was also stated that recognition of the judgment would also be in violation of Art 34(1)—public policy. (Heidelberg Report (n 54) para 546 and fn 765).

The default of appearance defence is not particularly clear and therefore does not effectively assist with a simplified procedure for recognition and enforcement. National courts are referring questions about the timing of the service of documents. However, the crux of the defence is whether or not the defendant has a right to a fair hearing. Unfortunately, the defence is not in itself capable of ensuring that the defendant's right to a fair hearing is respected.[266] All violations of the right to a fair hearing are clearly within the scope of the public policy defence. One argument for having two separate defences is that the 'public policy clause ought to operate only in exceptional cases'.[267] Despite this, it has already been shown that public policy is sometimes used to protect the rights of the defendant, but in doing so can still retain its 'exceptional nature'. Therefore, as the public policy defence is capable of capturing all the exceptional cases but the default of appearance defence cannot, the situation would be a lot clearer if the defence was eliminated.

The most effective way to progress in the future would be for all instruments to contain a simplified procedure, which would contain a public policy defence either at a recognition and enforcement stage or at the actual enforcement stage as proposed in the Brussels I recast. There are certainly benefits to dealing with everything at one stage and thereby reducing the number of court proceedings that may be required. This would eliminate the problem in *Prism Investments*, whereby a decision that was ultimately unenforceable had to be declared enforceable, because the reason for non-enforcement was not one of the grounds for refusal of enforceability.[268] The solution proposed in the Brussels I recast could be ideal in maintenance cases. This is because even though the *exequatur* procedure does not generally cause serious delays, 'litigants seeking cross-border recovery of debts in the internal market face an additional intermediate procedure which causes delays and additional (mostly non-recoverable) costs.'[269] Where maintenance payments are in arrears this would constitute a debt. Given that in most cases the payment will probably be quite low it may be useful to eliminate the court procedure for *exequatur* but retain safeguards at the enforcement stage, which would be necessary in a small minority of cases.[270]

However although the procedure in the Brussels I recast has its benefits, there are also some drawbacks. For example where States do not currently have designated procedures for enforcement, such as the UK, they will need to create

[266] See in particular, *Krombach* (n 112), *Gambazzi* (n 93), *Avotinš* (n 95—where the defence does not appear to have been considered properly) and the German/Polish maintenance decision (n 182) discussed above.

[267] See the Jenard Report (n 46).

[268] See n 234, and ch 8 s V below.

[269] Hess (n 65) 1094.

[270] Although the majority of maintenance obligations, particularly child support, will not raise any issues, there will be a small minority of cases where difficulties arise that could violate the rights and expectations of the parties, and in these cases a safeguard will be necessary.

new procedures in order to comply with the Regulation.[271] One of the reasons for abolishing the *exequatur* process has been to shorten proceedings. However studies have shown that *exequatur* proceedings are generally dealt with quickly,[272] the delay is generally at the enforcement stage.[273] Since the enforcement stage is delayed anyway, is it sensible to increase the possibility of challenging enforcement which could ultimately increase delays at this stage? However, this change now means that EU Law begins to impact on the actual enforcement stage, which was traditionally left completely to the law of the enforcing State.[274] The Regulation specifies that the 'court shall decide on the application for refusal of enforcement without delay.'[275] Despite this the procedures for enforcement are primarily still left to the law of the Member State addressed,[276] and therefore there is potential for delay at this stage. The Brussels I recast does not attempt to provide suitable time limits, it simply states without delay. Therefore although there are undoubtedly benefits to combining the enforceability and enforcement stage, potential downsides have also been highlighted.

Timmer considers that the abolition of *exequatur* in the Brussels I regime is 'problematic, both from a practical as well as from an ideological perspective.'[277] His main objection to the removal of the system seems to be that the Commission has not demonstrated the need for such a radical change.[278] This suggests that even with the retention of the safeguards, unlike the Maintenance Regulation, the step is still disproportionate to the aim.[279] It is difficult to predict how effective the new procedures will be in practice, and how simple they are to implement, until the Brussels I recast enters into force. Therefore, judgment is reserved on whether the current procedures for enforceability in Brussels I and Article 24 of the Maintenance Regulation are preferable to the merged procedure in Brussels I recast or vice versa.

Ultimately there should be a coherent procedure that is identical across all the Member States and preferably also across all the relevant Regulations. The defences that should be retained as necessary safeguards are the public policy

[271] However it is noted that other States already have procedures in place that can accommodate this, see Cuniberti and Reuda (n 67) 310–11.

[272] Heidelberg Report (n 54) 126–67. See also the Report from the Commission to the European Parliament, the Council and the European Economic and Social Committee on the Application of Council Regulation (EC) No 44/2001 on jurisdiction and the recognition and enforcement of judgments in civil and commercial matters, COM(2009) 174 final.

[273] See ch 9.

[274] Ibid and see Walker (n 63) s 2.3.

[275] Brussels I recast Art 48.

[276] Ibid, Arts 41 and 47(2).

[277] Timmer (n 67) 147. Hess admits that at first sight the proposal to abolish the procedure 'appears ambitious' but concludes that in certain respects 'the replacement of the formal declaration of enforceability by a simple form constitutes an appropriate simplification of the present proceedings.' (Hess (n 65) 1102.)

[278] Timmer (n 67) 145.

[279] See, Hellner (n 65) and Kramer (n 62) who consider that the complete abolition of *exequatur* without the retention of safeguards is disproportionate to the objective (see n 67).

defence and the irreconcilable judgment exception as contained in Article 24 of the Maintenance Regulation and Article 34 of Brussels I. The rights of the defence safeguard is no longer required as violations of these rights can be more adequately protected by the public policy defence which would include the protection of the right to a fair trial. The public policy defence is necessary as it can safeguard against the enforcement of a decision that is in violation of one of the fundamental rights of the party as 'embodied in the ECHR.'[280] The public policy defence can also prevent the enforcement of a decision that violates national public policy for a reason that is particular to that State. This could include the enforcement of an obligation towards a relation (or even a non-relation) that you would not expect to occur.[281] Seihr considers that the public policy exception is a necessary safety valve and recommends 'that there should be a public policy exception with respect to the recognition and enforcement of all foreign decisions in maintenance obligations.'[282]

## IX. Conclusion

This is an area where the developments made by the new regime are negative. The abolition of *exequatur* without the retention of necessary safeguards is a step too far, which is disproportionate to the aim.[283] The retention of the public policy defence does not create any major problems but provides a safety valve that can operate in exceptional cases. Such a defence could increase trust between Member States and the European institutions and between the Member States themselves. Member States will be less concerned about judgments originating in other Member States if they know a safety valve is available where necessary. Therefore, there are many reasons for retaining such a safety valve and this could in fact increase mutual trust rather than creating spurious interpretations of the principle and a one sided regime.[284]

The system for recognition and enforcement under the Regulation that applies to non-Protocol countries is the most suitable. This is because it is important to maintain human rights protections in European instruments, and this is permissible under Title V. Although generally, public policy concerns are not such a big factor in relation to maintenance obligations as they are in other areas this does not mean that they do not exist. A concern could be in relation to the determination of parentage. Even though parentage is not strictly covered

[280] See *Apostolides* (n 151) para 107.
[281] See above at s VI A.
[282] Seihr (n 182) 540.
[283] See ch 2, n 104 above, where the Commission recognised that the *exequatur* procedure does not significantly contribute to time delays.
[284] See the discussion on *Aguirre Zarraga*, at s V.

by the Regulation, this is a caveat in the instrument, because parentage is a prerequisite for child support. The willingness of a State to enforce a maintenance obligation could rest heavily on the question of 'parentage' in certain situations. This becomes a bigger concern as there are more advances in reproductive technology, which create a wider scientific variation of parentage (possibly up to six people). There are various laws on parentage which differ in how they distinguish between intended, legal and biological parents in an attempt to adapt to these scientific developments.[285] An obligation to pay maintenance to another family member, other than your child or your spouse, may also raise public policy questions. This is dependent on the reasonable expectations of the parties which are usually based on the content of the legal systems that they are most familiar with. The final concern is a violation of the parties' right to be heard under Article 6 of the ECHR or Article 47 of the Charter. Even where the requirements in Article 19 were complied with, that does not mean that the right to a fair trial will be protected under the new system.

In addition to there being problems with the Protocol track, it is also questioned whether it is sensible to have two different systems operating. This is especially true when many Central Authorities have not been provided with training specifically on the Regulation. This is even more concerning where the procedures in the Regulation are not necessarily clear in this area and there is no Practice Guide available at this time. Data collected in this area indicated that most applications are still going through the enforceability stage. Although there are some reasons for this, particularly the transitional period, this alone may not account for such a high disparity between the figures. Therefore, because Central Authorities are not provided with efficient training it is not really suitable to have separate procedures. One clear procedure would be more effective in relation to both coherence and clarity, which would benefit both practitioners and parties seeking to have their obligations enforced. This in turn should assist with the proper administration of justice through the enforcement of cross border judgments.

Of the two current systems, the one that applies to non-Protocol countries is selected as the most suitable. However, this system could be improved further. The exception based on default of appearance is irrelevant as true violations of the rights of defendants are only efficiently covered by the public policy defence. The elimination of this defence should provide further clarity as there are some issues with the defence. The defence is too narrow to cover all aspects of the right to a defence and questions will still be asked in relation to whether the defendant knew about the proceedings in order to prepare a defence. Therefore, the retention of

[285] See ch 1 s V and K Boele Woelki, '(Cross-Border) Surrogate Motherhood: We Need to Take Action Now!' in Permanent Bureau (n 149) 47, 53 on Janita where the question of parentage and in-family adoption is considered and p 55–56 on Eric and Hein and how the problems faced by them differ slightly depending on which State the surrogate mother resides in. See also, Council of Europe, *Legal Problems Relating to Parentage* (1999, Council of Europe, Germany) 40–41.

the regular public policy defence, at the recognition and enforcement stage would assist in simplifying the procedure and would ensure that the rights of debtors are protected in exceptional cases.

In terms of eliminating the recognition and enforcement stage but retaining safeguards at the enforcement stage, as the Brussels I recast will do, it is yet to be determined how effective and efficient this change will be in practice. What is clear is that certain safeguards should be retained at some point. These are the public policy and irreconcilable judgments defence. It is also highlighted that having two separate procedures operating under one Regulation is not necessarily the best way forward, and the system would be clearer and more practical if there was one procedure that applied in all cases.

# 8

# Recognition and Enforcement: Convention

## I. Introduction

If the procedure for recognition and enforcement within Europe was not already complex enough, the Maintenance Convention adds further to this complexity. Under the Convention there are another two systems for recognition and declaration of enforceability, which are both different to the procedures discussed above. There is a mainstream procedure that most Contracting States should follow and an alternative procedure.[1]

The procedures under the Convention are much more complicated than those under the Maintenance Regulation because there are both positive and negative requirements for refusing recognition and enforcement.[2] Under the Convention, the court must refuse to award recognition and enforcement of the judgment if it considers that there was an inadequate basis of jurisdiction in the State of origin.[3] The Convention has indirect rules of jurisdiction, because direct rules of jurisdiction would not have been agreed at the international level.[4] Indirect rules were preferred because they 'do not limit the diverse jurisdictional bases of the various rendering courts'.[5] The States negotiating the Convention had a range of

[1] Hague Convention of 23 November 2007 on the International Recovery of Child Support and other forms of Family Maintenance (Maintenance Convention). The alternative procedure requires a declaration in accordance with Art 63.

[2] See M Verwilghen, 'Explanatory Report on the 1973 Hague Maintenance Conventions (1975) para 45, available at www.hcch.net/index_en.php?act=publications.details&pid=2946&dtid=3, accessed 21 May 2014 (Verwilghen Report). (Council Regulation (EC) 4/2009 of 18 December 2008 on jurisdiction, applicable law, recognition and enforcement of decisions and cooperation in matters relating to maintenance obligations (Maintenance Regulation) 2009] OJ L7/1.)

[3] Maintenance Convention Art 20. This is in contrast to the procedure under the Maintenance Regulation, where although there are rules on jurisdiction in Arts 3–14, both procedures for recognition and enforcement automatically presume these have been complied with. Art 10 of the Regulation simply relies on the Court seised to 'declare of its own motion that is has no jurisdiction'.

[4] W Duncan, 'Jurisdiction to Make and Modify Maintenance Decisions – The Quest for Uniformity' in T Einhorn and K Siehr (eds), *Intercontinental Cooperation through Private International Law Essays in Memory of Peter E. Nygh* (The Hague, TCM Asser Press, 2004) 89, 98–105.

[5] LS Bartlett, 'Full Faith and Credit comes to the Common Market an Analysis of the Convention on Jurisdiction and Enforcement of Judgments in Civil and Commercial Matters' (1975) 24 *International and Comparative Law Quarterly* 44, 46.

different policies that they wanted to protect so it was easier to opt for indirect rules of jurisdiction, unlike in the EU instruments where it is common to have direct rules of jurisdiction.

Therefore, recognition and declaration of enforceability (recognition and enforceability) can be refused under the Convention, if the court of origin did not have jurisdiction under one of the indirect grounds of jurisdiction. It can also be refused where one of the positive grounds for refusal of recognition and enforceability exist. Finally, a Contracting State may be able to refuse recognition and enforceability if it is considered that the decision does not fall within the scope of the Convention.

## II. Scope

Article 2 of the Convention covers the overall scope of the instrument, and this is primarily dealt with in the chapter on scope.[6] Article 19 refers specifically to the scope of the chapter on recognition and enforceability. Article 19 requires that the chapter applies to 'decisions' in respect of 'maintenance obligations'. The term decision is meant to be interpreted broadly to encompass; court settlements, administrative agreements, and alterations to current orders by a variety of means including increases or decreases by index scale.[7] Article 19 also specifies that where a decision does not relate solely to a 'maintenance obligation', the chapter should only apply to the part of the decision that concerns 'maintenance obligations'.[8]

It is clear that the chapter on recognition and enforceability only applies to 'maintenance obligations', which can arise from a wide range of variations on what constitutes a 'decision'. What is unclear is whether this only applies to 'maintenance obligations' as prescribed under Article 2 that fall within the overall scope of the Convention, or if it applies to 'maintenance obligations' generally.[9] The Borrás and Degeling Report provides further insight, but does not give a definitive answer. Article 19(2) was introduced as a safeguard in relation to ancillary or preliminary questions. This means that 'if a maintenance decision also includes a decision in relation to the establishment of parentage, this latter decision would not necessarily have to be recognised and enforced under the Convention.'[10] This

[6] See ch 4 above, for a discussion of the obligations which should fall within the scope of the Convention.

[7] See Art 19(1) of the Convention and paras 430–33 and 435–37 of A Borrás and J Degeling, 'Explanatory Report on the Convention on the International Recovery of Child Support and other Forms of Family Maintenance (HCCH, 2009) (Borrás and Degeling Report).

[8] Maintenance Convention Art 19(2).

[9] As explained in ch 4 above, the Convention may apply to different 'maintenance obligations' depending on which States are concerned.

[10] Para 438 of the Borrás and Degeling Report (n 7). The Report goes on to explain that this can be 'very important because in some States it would be contrary to public policy to recognise the

indicates why judgments can be severable, but it does not clarify what is meant by the term 'maintenance obligation' in Article 19. Further information is given in paragraph 434, but this paragraph is slightly ambiguous as it is not entirely clear what it is referring to. The paragraph only contains one sentence which states: 'The decision that would fall under the scope of the Convention "may" also include other elements.'[11] This could be taken to imply that the term 'maintenance obligation' in Article 19 only includes maintenance obligations that fall within the overall scope of the Convention. This would be the sensible approach but the wording contained in Article 19 does not necessarily support this.

The wording in Article 19 might be vague due to the fact that different 'maintenance obligations' are covered depending on the reservations and declarations made by particular States.[12] Despite this there was nothing to prevent Article 19 from referring to 'maintenance obligations' as covered by the Convention. Therefore, the approach taken in Article 19 could mean that cross border 'maintenance obligations' are recognised and enforced in the future, that are outside the designated scope of the Convention in Article 2(1). This could be beneficial in some situations and could result in the Convention potentially covering as many different obligations as the Regulation, even where a State has not made a declaration in respect of Article 2(3),[13] but is happy to recognise and enforce a 'wider' maintenance obligation in a particular circumstance.

## III. Jurisdiction

Article 20 of the Convention lays down the grounds on which the jurisdiction of the State of origin must be based, in order for the decision to be recognised and enforceable in the State of enforcement. The grounds are: 'the respondent

establishment of parentage only for purposes of maintenance where their domestic law would require that the recognition of parentage could only be done *erga omnes*. Therefore, through this provision it would be possible for such States to recognise and enforce only the part of the decision that deals with the maintenance payment without giving effect to the establishment of maintenance *per se*.' From this perspective it is sensible to separate the order so that the maintenance obligation can be recognised and enforced for both moral and legal reasons, where the decision establishing parentage cannot be recognised for reasons particular to that State. However, there has to be a distinction drawn between the inability to recognise a parentage order in a particular State and situations where an order on parentage is given but parentage does not actually exist. In the latter case it would not be suitable to recognise and enforce the maintenance obligation separately, because in that situation no moral or legal duty to pay maintenance should arise. Therefore, the separate recognition and enforcement of the two orders is not ideal in all situations, since ultimately parentage is usually a prerequisite for child support. See ch 7 s VI above.

[11] Para 434 of the Borrás and Degeling Report (n 7).

[12] See ch 4 above. The designated applicable law may also impact on the obligations covered when the decision is given in the State of origin.

[13] See ch 4 s IV above.

was habitually resident in the State of origin at the time the proceedings were instituted';[14] 'the respondent has submitted to the jurisdiction either expressly or by defending on the merits of the case without objecting to the jurisdiction at the first available opportunity';[15] 'the creditor was habitually resident in the State of origin at the time proceedings were instituted';[16] 'the child for whom maintenance was ordered was habitually resident in the State of origin at the time the proceedings were instituted, provided that the respondent has lived with the child in that State or has resided in that State and provided support for the child there';[17] 'except in disputes relating to maintenance obligations in respect of children, there has been agreement to the jurisdiction in writing by the parties';[18] and 'the decision was made by an authority exercising jurisdiction on a matter of personal status or parental responsibility, unless that jurisdiction was based solely on the nationality of one of the parties'.[19] Each ground is alternative and the list is closed, there are no other grounds of jurisdiction available.

## A. Habitual Residence of the Respondent and the Creditor

The first ground relates to the habitual residence of the respondent, usually the debtor. There is an alternative rule that allows jurisdiction to be based on the habitual residence of the creditor; however this ground cannot always be used as States may make a reservation in this respect.[20] The earlier Hague Convention does not explain why some States do not allow for creditor based jurisdiction. The Enforcement Convention lists both as equal alternatives: 'if either the maintenance debtor or the maintenance creditor had his habitual residence in the State of origin at the time when the proceedings were instituted'.[21] However, the Verwilghen Report highlights that there may be difficulties with this head of jurisdiction.

> Jurisdiction based on the habitual residence of the maintenance creditor does, however, raise difficulties. Jurisdiction based on *the domicile of the plaintiff* has always been recognised as quite improper in patrimonial questions. This explains the mistrust with which numerous States regard this head of jurisdiction. But, in maintenance obligation questions, humanitarian reasons give sufficient cause for an *exception* being made to the above-mentioned principle. The rules of jurisdiction of an ever-increasing number of countries thus acknowledge that a maintenance creditor—who is considered to be the

[14] Maintenance Convention, Art 20(1) a), this is the same as Art 3(a) of the Regulation (see ch 5 s III above).
[15] Ibid, Art 20(1) b), mirrored in Art 5 of the Regulation (see ch 5 s VI above).
[16] Ibid, Art 20(1) c), this is the same as Art 3(b) of the Regulation (see ch 5 s III above).
[17] Ibid, Art 20(1) d).
[18] Ibid, Art 20(1) e), this is wider than the provision in Art 4 of the Regulation (see ch 5 s V above).
[19] Ibid, Art 20(1) f), mirrored in Arts 3(c) and (d) of the Regulation (see ch v s III above).
[20] Ibid, Art 20(2).
[21] Hague Convention of 2 October 1973 Convention on the Recognition and Enforcement of Decisions Relating to Maintenance Obligations (Enforcement Convention), Art 7(1).

> weaker party—should have the right to appear in court in the place of his residence or of his own domicile. On the international level too, this head of jurisdiction has penetrated little by little. Although this idea appeared revolutionary and was sharply criticised in the discussions of the Eighth Session of the Hague Conference, it was finally included in the 1958 Enforcement Convention.[22]

The Enforcement Convention was not ratified by the United States. This was one of the main reasons for its failure. One reason why the Convention was not ratified by the United States is that the rules on due process were not compatible with the Convention because it allowed indirect jurisdiction to be based on the habitual residence of the creditor.[23] 'The Due Process Clause of the Fourteenth Amendment operates as a limitation on the jurisdiction of state courts to enter judgments affecting rights or interests of non-resident defendants.'[24] This means that the defendant has to have some connection with the forum in order for the US courts to recognise the judgment.[25] If the reservation had not been approved in this area there would not have been sufficient improvement on the Enforcement Convention and the US would again have been unable to ratify the new Convention. This would have been highly unfortunate;[26] as it would have impeded the proper administration of justice because creditors seeking maintenance from a defendant in the US would not be able to get their order enforced.[27] However, the result of this is that the US courts may refuse to recognise foreign decisions where the decision originated from a jurisdiction that was based on the habitual residence of the creditor. This could be undesirable, if the US courts abused this position, because

[22] Verwilghen Report (n 2) para 50.

[23] This is an example of why the previous system of majority voting did not work in The Hague, as the majority of other States are happy with the jurisdiction being decided on the habitual residence of the creditor, since it is considered that the creditor is the weaker party in maintenance disputes.

[24] *Kulko v Superior Court of California* 436 US 84 (1978) 91.

[25] The first case where the Supreme Court analysed this clause was *International Shoe Co v State of Washington* 326 US 310 (1945), where it was stated that 'due process requires only that in order to subject a defendant to a judgment in *personam,* if he not be present within the territory of the forum, he have certain minimum contacts with it such that maintenance of the suit does not offend 'traditional notions of fair play and substantial justice'.' (316). See TC Hartley, 'The Modern Approach to Private International Law International Litigation and Transactions from a Common Law Perspective' (2006) 319 *Recueil des Cours* 9, 60–71, and AT von Mehren, 'Theory and Practice of Adjudicatory Authority in Private International Law: A Comparative Study of the Doctrine, Policies and Practices of Common and Civil Law Systems' (2002) 295 *Recueil des Cours* 9, 117–39.

[26] Although, the due process clause is highly important and needs to be complied with in order for the US participation it is very interesting that the US appeared to be pushing two very different political agendas through the proceedings. In relation to jurisdiction they are pushing for the protection of the defender. Contrast this with the position on legal aid, where the US advocated heavily for the provision of legal aid for all creditors; primarily because the creditor is the weaker party in maintenance proceedings. However, maybe the protection of both the creditor and the debtor for different reasons is the most sensible approach when considering how little protection debtors have under the Maintenance Regulation in States where the Protocol is applied (see above at ch 7 s VI).

[27] The USA has still not ratified the Maintenance Convention but they have signed it, and it is hoped that they will ratify the Convention soon (www.hcch.net/index_en.php?act=conventions.status&cid=131, accessed 6 June 2014).

the maintenance creditor is usually considered the weaker party.[28] Article 20 contains various provisions to try and prevent the non-recognition of judgments for this reason.

Firstly, States are encouraged to recognise and enforce the decision if 'its law would in similar factual circumstances confer or would have conferred jurisdiction on its authorities to make such a decision.'[29] This provision is designed to encourage the recognition and enforcement of foreign judgments because the decision should be recognised on a 'factual basis'. It is argued that this means that 'the ground of direct jurisdiction on which the judge of origin acted is disregarded and attention is only paid to the links of factual proximity.'[30] However, this is problematic. Whatever the factual basis is, the US courts will still only be able to recognise the decision if it complies with the rules on due process which suggest that 'personal jurisdiction over the parties, especially the obligor [is] constitutionally necessary to sustain a child support order.'[31] Therefore the facts must link the defender to the chosen jurisdiction. The Borrás and Degeling Report states that; the American delegates indicated that this approach would mean that 'very few foreign decisions on maintenance are not recognised in the United States of America.'[32] This may be true to an extent, but there are still decisions that will not be recognised.

The implications of the factual circumstances approach are that the US would recognise a maintenance judgment where 'the facts of the case indicated that jurisdiction could have been predicated on any of the grounds specified in the Uniform Interstate Family Support Act.'[33] The decision in *Kulko*[34] gives some indication of when a connection would or would not be satisfied. In *Kulko* the defendant lived and was domiciled in the State of New York. His ex-wife lived in

[28] See D Martiny, 'Maintenance Obligations in the Conflict of Laws' (1994) 247 *Recueil des Cours* 131, 179.

[29] Maintenance Convention Art 20(3).

[30] Borrás and Degeling Report (n 7) para 463.

[31] JJ Sampson, 'Introductory Note to the New Hague Maintenance Convention' (2008) 47 *International Legal Materials* 255, 255.

[32] Borrás and Degeling Report (n 7) para 463.

[33] RG Spector, 'Toward an Accommodation of Divergent Jurisdictional Standards for the Determination of Maintenance Obligations in Private International Law' (2002) 36 *Family Law Quarterly* 273, 279. Under s 201 of UIFSA, a State may exercise jurisdiction over a non-resident defendant where: (1) the individual is personally served with a legal citation within the State; (2) the individual submits to the jurisdiction of the State by consent, by entering a general appearance, or by filing a responsive document that has the effect of waiving the objection to the State's jurisdiction; (3) the individual resided with the child in the State; (4) the individual resided in the State and provided prenatal expenses or support for the child; (5) the child resided in the State as a result of the acts or directives of the individual; (6) the individual engaged in sexual intercourse in the State and the child may have been conceived by that act of intercourse; (7) the individual asserted parentage in the state's putative father registry. See, RG Spector, 'Maintenance in Private International Law in the United States: Harmonization of Divergent Rules and the Proposed Hague Maintenance Convention' (2005) 7 *Yearbook of Private International Law* 63, 63–72 and JJ Sampson and BJ Brooks, 'Uniform Interstate Family Support Act (2001) With Prefatory Note and Comments (With Still More Unofficial Notations) (2002–2003) 36 *Family Law Quarterly* 36, at 357–64, in particular.

[34] *Kulko* (n 24).

California (but was also domiciled in New York). Both children lived in California. The couple were married in California, but they never lived there as a family. The wife sought to amend the divorce judgment in the State of California. The lower Court in California accepted jurisdiction, but this was reversed on appeal because of the due process clause. Both courts were agreed on the fact that

> two New York domicilliaries, for reasons of convenience, marry in the State of California and thereafter spend their entire married life in New York, the fact of their California marriage, by itself, cannot support a California court's exercise of jurisdiction over a spouse who remains a New York resident in an action relating to child support.[35]

The mother and the children lived in California and wanted to seise the courts in that State, for modifying the arrangements. This was not permitted as the State of New York had to have jurisdiction so as not to violate the rules on due process. Based on the 'facts' many other Contracting States would probably accept the Californian jurisdiction as the family had a connection there. However, it is hard to see how this would pass the fact based approach in Article 20(3) in the US because the facts still do not sufficiently connect the debtor with the chosen jurisdiction, and appear to be outside the requirements in UIFSA,[36] so the rules on due process would still be violated. It is unclear what the true benefit of Article 20(3) will be, but it is clear that the judgment will not be recognised where the jurisdiction is based purely on the habitual residence of the creditor.

In the context of child support the provision in Article 20(5) may add some value. This provides that a

> decision in favour of a child under the age of 18 years which cannot be recognised by virtue only of a reservation in respect of paragraph 1 c), e) or f) shall be accepted as establishing the eligibility of that child for maintenance in the State addressed.[37]

It is unclear what effect this provision will have, but it should ensure that the original child support order is not entirely futile. This should make a difference in cases where it was not clear who the biological father of the child was. Once it is established under one law that that child is eligible for maintenance some aspects of the process should not have to be repeated as the second State should recognise that the child is eligible. Any alterations or fresh decisions should only relate to the amount of maintenance, and when that should be paid, but the provision of child support in such cases should be guaranteed. It is imperative in these situations that any fresh assessment of the order should be kept to a minimum and recognition should be encouraged.[38] In addition, the creditor may have to institute

[35] Ibid, 93.

[36] See n 33 above.

[37] Maintenance Convention Art 20(5). In this respect the decision should be able to be recognised in the US anyway, because it complies with para (c) of UIFSA.

[38] In these types of cases, it has been suggested that lawyers will not advise the client to seek a new judgment in the American courts when he will have to pay maintenance anyway. This is because it is likely that the maintenance or child support awarded by the American court will be higher than the award given by, for example, a European court. Therefore, it would be more beneficial for the debtor

proceedings in a State with which they have no connection, which as the weaker party seems slightly unfair. The other alternative is that a

> Contracting State shall, if recognition is not possible as a result of a reservation under paragraph 2, and if the debtor is habitually resident in that State, take all appropriate measures to establish a decision for the benefit of the creditor.[39]

This rule should provide protection for creditors where jurisdiction was based solely on the jurisdiction of the creditor, and there was no personal nexus between the forum and the defendant. Although the original decision cannot be recognised and enforced, this provision requires the enforcing State to establish a new decision that can be easily enforced under national procedures.

## B. Habitual Residence of the Child

The next indirect ground of jurisdiction also solves some problems in relation to the ability of States to make a reservation in relation to the provision in c). This states:

> [T]he child for whom maintenance was ordered was habitually resident in the State of origin at the time proceedings were instituted, provided that the respondent has lived with the child in that State or has resided in that State and provided support for the child there.[40]

This ground was included as it appeared to be acceptable to all States. Jurisdiction based on the habitual residence of the creditor, in child support cases, will be acceptable if the debtor also has a strong link to that jurisdiction. This appears to be compatible with the US rules on due process. Article 20(1)d) will work to the benefit of creditors who remain in the jurisdiction where the family lived, but the debtor has moved away. In this context the defendant would presumably have 'relevant contact with the State'[41] so the due process clause would not be violated.

## C. Party Autonomy

Parties can also designate a court, as long as this is in writing.[42] This ground is fairly unproblematic as the protection of party autonomy is widely accepted.[43] Although child support is excluded from this provision, beyond that this ground

to agree that the original order should be recognised rather than seeking a new order. (Discussion at the Heidelberg Conference in the Workshop, Interstate Recovery of Child Support in the United States: A Blueprint for International Change.)

39 Maintenance Convention Art 20(4).
40 Ibid, Art 20(1)d).
41 *Kulko* (n 24) 101.
42 Maintenance Convention Art 20(1)e).
43 See above at ch 5 s V.

is not restricted in any way (unlike the equivalent ground in the Regulation).[44] Therefore parties could successfully designate any jurisdiction even if that jurisdiction is completely unrelated to the relationship. In relation to commercial matters this is not unusual,[45] but it seems rather strange to have such wide scope for party autonomy in a family law instrument.[46] It is noted that States can make a reservation in respect to this provision but again there is no explanation why.[47] It was difficult to gain consensus in this area and it 'was discussed at length during the meeting whether or not party autonomy provided an adequate basis for jurisdiction in maintenance.'[48] Therefore, consensus was reached by giving full respect to party autonomy in adult maintenance cases but retaining a reservation for States that do not agree to this. It is unclear whether States or regional bodies will be able to make a reservation restricting this (so the EU could restrict the ground so it appeared as it does in the Regulation, but it has not)[49] or whether any reservations would just exclude the use of party autonomy completely. This provision could cause difficulties at the recognition and enforceability stage where Contracting States accept party autonomy to a different extent.

## D. Personal Status

The final ground of indirect jurisdiction allows an authority exercising jurisdiction on a matter of personal status or parental responsibility to take jurisdiction in relation to maintenance. However this option cannot be used where the jurisdiction is based solely on the nationality of one of the parties.[50] It is also possible to make a reservation in relation to this ground.[51] The use of this indirect ground of jurisdiction in the Maintenance Convention is completely different to the equivalent direct ground of jurisdiction in the Maintenance Regulation. This is because the status of parties is regulated to an extent under EU law and therefore

[44] There is no explanation why this provision was left open in the Borrás and Degeling Report (n 7) para 455.

[45] See, Art 23 of Brussels I (Council Regulation (EC) 44/2001 of 22 December 2000 on jurisdiction and the recognition and enforcement of judgments in civil and commercial matters [2001] OJ L012/1).

[46] Brussels IIbis (Council Regulation (EC) 2201/2003 of 27 November 2003 on jurisdiction, recognition and enforcement of judgments in matrimonial matters and matters of parental responsibility, repealing Regulation (EC) No 1347/2000 [2003] OJ L 338/1) contains no provision for party autonomy on divorce, and choice of court under the Maintenance Regulation is limited.

[47] Borrás and Degeling Report (n 7) paras 455, 461 and 462.

[48] A Borrás, 'Reservations, Declarations and Specifications: Their Function in the Hague Convention on the International Recovery of Child Support and other Forms of Family Maintenance' in G Venturini and S Barriati (eds), *Liber Fausto Pocar: Vol. II, Nuovi instrumenti del diritto internazionale private-New Instruments of Private International Law* (Milano, Giuffrè, 2009) 127, 133.

[49] See www.hcch.net/index_en.php?act=status.comment&csid=1109&disp=resdn, accessed 6 June 2014.

[50] Maintenance Convention Art 20(1)f), see ch 5 s III for a discussion of the equivalent provisions in the Regulation.

[51] Ibid, Art 20(2).

the ground can provide coherence and consistency.[52] The inclusion of this provision at an international level is slightly different. Although it is still important for the parties to have clarity and consistency, and it is understandable that they would want divorce and maintenance decided by the same court, unfortunately jurisdiction on divorce is not necessarily regulated.[53] Therefore the initial jurisdiction could be based on national rules, which may be spurious and therefore not acceptable.[54] One way of preventing this was to include the requirement that the jurisdiction was not based solely on the nationality of one of the parties, but this was not deemed to go far enough for some States so a reservation was also included.[55]

## IV. Grounds for Refusal

Where jurisdiction falls under one of the indirect grounds then the order can be enforced. However, the court may still refuse recognition and enforceability if the order violates one of the requirements in Article 22. Article 22 provides the mainstream procedure for recognition and enforcement under the Convention. This procedure has similar grounds to those that apply under the Regulation when the UK or Denmark is the State of origin.[56] However, there are additional grounds for refusing recognition.

### A. *Ex Officio* Review

The procedures for recognition and enforceability that are set out in the 2007 Maintenance Convention represent considerable progress from previous Conventions in this area. This is because in the past procedures for recognition

[52] See ch 5 ss III–IV above.

[53] For example the Hague Convention of 14 March 1978 on Celebration and Recognition of the validity of marriages (Marriage Convention) only applies in three States (www.hcch.net/index_en.php?act=conventions.status&cid=88, accessed 6 June 2014) and the Hague Convention of 1 June 1970 on the recognition of divorces and legal separations (Divorce Convention) only applies in 20 States (www.hcch.net/index_en.php?act=conventions.status&cid=80, accessed 6 June 2014). In relation to parental responsibility the Hague Convention of 19 October 1996 on jurisdiction, applicable law, recognition, enforcement and co-operation in respect of parental responsibility and measures for the protection of children, applies in 39 States (www.hcch.net/index_en.php?act=conventions.status&cid=70, accessed 6 June 2014).

[54] '[T]here is a risk that the authority of origin has exercised an exorbitant jurisdiction on a matter of personal *status*.' (Borrás (n 48) 133.)

[55] See, Ibid, 133 and A Borrás, 'The Necessary Flexibility in Applying the New Instruments on Maintenance' in K Boele-Woelki, T Einhorn, D Girsberger, S Symeonides (eds), *Convergence and Divergence in Private International Law, Liber Amicorum Kurt Siehr* (Eleven International Publishing & Schulthess, 2010) 173, 185.

[56] See ch 7 s III above.

and enforceability were 'left to be regulated largely by the law of the State addressed.'[57] This is no longer the case and there are now uniform rules for recognition and enforceability. This brings the Convention into line with the developments in Europe, the USA and Canada. However, as discussed above the procedure in Europe is now different. These procedures minimise *ex officio* review and the burden of raising any objection is placed with the defendant. This is highly beneficial because maintenance decisions are generally uncontested, so there is little point in insisting on a review if none of the parties contest the order. The procedure in the Maintenance Convention:

> limits ex officio review to the ground of public policy; it rules out submissions by the parties at the initial stage when the foreign decision is registered or declared enforceable; it allows for challenge by either party to the decision on registration, but within a strict time period and on limited grounds; it also supports, as a general principle, the idea that any further appeal should not have the effect of staying enforcement.[58]

## B. Review by the Defendant

In addition to *ex officio* review of public policy, there are various grounds which a defendant can use to challenge recognition and enforceability of a decision. These are set out in Article 22.

### *i. Public Policy*

Recognition and enforceability may be refused if this 'is manifestly incompatible with the public policy of the State addressed'.[59] This exception is usually used in international instruments, and its inclusion is imperative in order to provide protection for the parties where necessary.[60] However, there were concerns that this exception may be used too often. The misuse of the public policy exception is in general unlikely as States are used to having this exception included in international instruments and therefore judges should be capable of applying it correctly. It is interesting to note that when the Enforcement Convention was agreed the Special Commission considered that exactly the same exception,[61] 'would necessarily cover cases in which the maintenance decision was rendered following proceedings which were incompatible with respect for the rule of "due process of

[57] W Duncan, 'The New Hague Child Support Convention: Goals and Outcomes of the Negotiations' (2009) 43 *Family Law Quarterly* 1, 12.

[58] Ibid, 12. See also P Beaumont, 'International Family Law in Europe – the Maintenance Project, the Hague Conference and the EC: A Triumph of Reverse Subsidiarity' (2009) 73 *Rabels Zeichschrift* 509, at 537–38.

[59] Maintenance Convention Art 22(a), similar to Art 24(a) of the Regulation.

[60] See ch 7 s V above.

[61] Art 5(1) of the Enforcement Convention.

law" or the rights of the defence.'[62] This is particularly interesting in relation to the discussion above. It is unclear why, after having ascertained that the public policy exception can effectively protect the rights of the defence, a separate ground pertaining to the rights of the defence but in a narrower context needs to be included in international instruments.[63]

### *ii. Procedural Fraud*

Recognition and enforcement can also be refused if 'the decision was obtained by fraud in connection with a matter of procedure'.[64] This provision is carried over from the Enforcement Convention. It is explained as follows:

> This second negative condition sparked some controversy within the Commission. Some persons felt that it was useless, since it was included anyway in the concept of public policy, while others preferred to mention it expressly since they saw in it a condition very different from the first one. As a result of discussion, it appeared that cases of fraud were not necessarily covered by the public policy condition. Fraud, as Mr Fragistas reminds us …, presupposes the existence of a *subjective element*, that is to say, of wilful misrepresentation or fraudulent machinations (and not simply a mistake or negligence) on the part of the person asking for recognition or enforcement of a decision. This element is discovered in the proceedings which resulted in the handing down of a maintenance decision, the recognition and enforcement of which is being requested. This is the case, for example, when the applicant for recognition and enforcement has falsified documents or given false evidence. As can be seen, the problems are very different to those relating to public policy.[65]

Despite the fact that fraud is different to public policy, the added value of this exception is questionable. This is because, firstly, if a decision is produced in fraudulent circumstances it is presumed that 'fraud' would be the same concept in all Contracting States, whereas public policy is not. If fraud has arisen the offended party would have the chance to appeal in the State of origin. In addition a review of a decision to establish whether there was fraud would require a review of the substantive part or the merits of the judgment,[66] unless it related to the

[62] Verwilghen Report (n 2) para 63.

[63] See the discussion at ch 7 s VIII above. The exception pertaining to the rights of the defence was worded and applied somewhat differently in the Enforcement Convention. This will be discussed below in the section on the rights of the defence. It is notable that in his paper on maintenance that refers heavily to the Enforcement Convention, Martiny only refers to public policy and conflicting judgments, but not fraud (Art 5(2)) or default of the defendant (Art 6). (Martiny (n 28) 268–74.)

[64] Maintenance Convention Art 22(b), there is no equivalent in the Regulation. However, this ground is also found in Art 5 of the Enforcement Convention.

[65] Verwilghen Report (n 2) para 65.

[66] This is particularly true in the case of substantive fraud, although not in relation to procedural fraud. A suggestion that this is correct can be found in relation to an arbitration court reviewing a contract for grounds of illegality. It is considered that if the word illegal was substituted by the word fraudulent you would have the same outcome. It is also considered that although this pertains to a public policy exception it highlights that fraud could indeed be covered by public policy. Either way a review of the merits or the substantive public policy would be required in order to determine whether there was fraudulent behaviour. 'However, merits review seems unavoidable when illegality or other

authenticity of a document.[67] The Hartley and Dogauchi Report identifies some examples of what could be considered as procedural fraud. These are:

> where the plaintiff deliberately serves the writ, or causes it to be served, on the wrong address; where the plaintiff deliberately gives the defendant the wrong information as to the time and place of the hearing; or where either party seeks to corrupt a judge, juror or witness, or deliberately conceals key evidence.[68]

It is clear that the first two points could easily be covered by the rights of the defence exception.[69] The latter point which covers corruption would, at least one would have thought, be covered by the public policy exception.

Hartley and Dogauchi recognise the overlap between these exceptions which all relate to 'procedural fairness'.[70] It is believed that there is a need to place so much emphasis on procedural fairness, because in some countries the principles of procedural justice are 'constitutionally mandated'.[71] Presumably therefore, in order to comply with national constitutions State bodies prefer that the grounds are listed separately to provide coherence. However, if the fraudulent act was so obvious to the enforcing State without having to review the substantive part of the judgment, they would not have to enforce it anyway on grounds of public policy because no State agrees with a judgment based on fraud. Hartley and Dogauchi suggest that procedural fraud has to be distinguished from public policy because there are 'some legal systems in which public policy cannot be used with regard

substantive public policies are concerned. For example, assume an award has been rendered pursuant to an allegedly illegal contract. If the arbitrator has decided or otherwise considered the illegality issue, then the enforcement court would need to examine the arbitrator's reasoning in order to determine whether or not to reopen the arbitrator's decision. If the award is silent on the illegality issue, then the court would need to examine the relevant contents of the allegedly illegal contract, which the award may or may not contain, in order to determine whether or not the contract is indeed illegal; and if so, whether the award is tainted by such illegality so as to make its enforcement contrary to the enforcement state's public policy. The enforcement court cannot properly determine whether the enforcement of an award based on an allegedly illegal contract would be contrary to public policy, unless it is satisfied that the contract is indeed illegal.' W Ma, 'Recommendations on Public Policy in the Enforcement of Arbitrarial Awards' (2009) *Arbitration* 14, 20. See also *AJT v AJU* [2010] SGHC 201, Singapore High Court and case comment, P Megens and D Finch, 'Setting Aside an Award on Public Policy Grounds: *AJT* v *AJU*' (2011) *Arbitration* 155, in particular 157.

[67] This is an example of procedural fraud.

[68] T Hartley and M Dogauchi, 'Explanatory Report on the 2005 Hague Choice of Court Agreements Convention' (HCCH, 2007) (Hartley and Dogauchi Report) para 188. Kessedjian considers that procedural fraud can be split into four categories. These are: fraud as to the jurisdiction of the court of origin, fraud as to the applicable law, fraud concerning prior notification to the defendant in the original proceeding (which she recognises 'will be caught and sanctioned at the same time as the review of the notification') and fraud committed in the submission of evidence to the court of origin. (C Kessedjian, 'Synthesis of the Work of the Special Commission of March 1998 on International Jurisdiction and the Effects of Foreign Judgments in Civil and Commercial Matters' paras 40–45 and see also the Nygh and Pocar Report, Preliminary Document no 11 of August 2000, 113.)

[69] See the discussion at ch 7 s VIII above and the analysis of the equivalent provision in the Convention below at s IV B, *v*.

[70] Hartley and Dogauchi Report (n 68) para 190.

[71] Ibid.

to procedural fraud.'[72] Such a distinction seems somewhat artificial, because if the fraudulent behaviour creates such an adverse outcome surely it would have to be manifestly contrary to public policy to enforce such an order.[73] In relation to instruments that do not contain separate provisions on fraud, it has been argued that although 'fraud cannot in itself constitute a ground of non-recognition, … there may be situations in which a court would regard it as being contrary to its public policy to recognize a judgment obtained by fraud.'[74]

If it is true that States will operate such an artificial distinction, eg recognise a decision that was obtained through procedural fraud even if the outcome is manifestly contrary to the public policy of that State, because they can only refuse to recognise such a decision on grounds of fraud then it is important to maintain this exception in the international context in order to ensure the proper administration of justice. It is recognised that it is important that the Convention appeals to as many States as possible, in order to secure the cross border enforcement of maintenance obligations worldwide. However, it is hoped that in the future differences in this area can be set aside so that a new instrument can contain a simplified procedure for recognition and enforceability that does not contain an exception based on procedural fraud. This is because the public policy exception is a necessary safeguard that should be capable of being applied to cover any abuses of procedure that affect one of the parties.

### *iii. Proceedings Already Ongoing in the State Addressed*

Recognition and enforceability can also be refused if other 'proceedings between the same parties and having the same purpose are pending before an authority of

[72] Ibid, fn 228.

[73] For example consider the German/ Polish order discussed above at ch 7 s VI. The mother 'fraudulently' asserted that the defendant was the father. Taking this further she could have obtained fake DNA evidence 'proving' that he was the father. This would have been procedural fraud because the evidence would have been corrupt. But surely the outcome would still have been the same because it is the order which is against the public policy of the State because the defendant had no moral or legal obligation to support the child. Kessedjian recognises that of the four types of fraud the one that relates to evidence is the 'most serious'. (Kessedjian (n 68) para 44.) The report suggests that several experts did not want the Judgments Convention to be weighed down by a provision on procedural fraud. It also raised the issue of whether such a provision should contain a requirement that the defendant tried to contest the fraud in the State of origin if he was aware of the fraud during the proceedings. The analogy being if you did try to contest the fraudulent evidence and this was unsuccessful or you were barred from doing this, this would most likely be a violation of public policy in the enforcing State. (See Kessedjian (n 68) para 45.) However the experts that opposed an exception on the basis of fraud were unsuccessful and the exception made it into the 2005 Convention (following the 1971 Convention) and then also the Maintenance Convention. None of the exceptions require that the defendant challenged the fraud in the State of origin. In this respect consider the English case law at common law such as *Owens Bank v Bracco* [1992] 2 AC 443, where the line of thought is that 'a foreign judgment cannot be enforced if it was obtained by fraud, even though the allegation of fraud was investigated and rejected by the foreign court' (*Owens Bank*, 468).

[74] Hartley (n 25) 307. See, Schlosser Report on the Brussels Convention [1998] OJ C 59/71, para 192 (Schlosser Report).

the State addressed and those proceedings were the first to be instituted'.[75] This is equivalent to the *lis pendens* clause in Article 12 of the Maintenance Regulation.[76] As the Regulation has direct rules of jurisdiction there was no need to include such an exception at the recognition and enforcement stage. However, because the Convention only contains indirect rules of jurisdiction it was felt that some form of protection was needed at the recognition and enforcement stage. The exception is slightly different to *lis pendens* however; because it requires that the proceedings are for the same purpose, whereas, the *lis pendens* rule covers the same cause of action.[77] It has been argued that

> the term 'purpose' of the complaint must be understood as referring to the claim ('prétention') which the plaintiff has asserted in defending a disputed right. The 'cause of action', on the other hand, refers to the *legal basis* of the contested right.[78]

An exception based on these principles is necessary at this stage because it is best to avoid the situation where there are two conflicting decisions arising in two different States.

### *iv. Irreconcilable Judgments*

Recognition and enforceability may also be refused where the

> decision is incompatible with a decision rendered between the same parties and having the same purpose, either in the State addressed or in another State, provided that this latter decision fulfils the conditions necessary for its recognition and enforcement in the State addressed.[79]

This is similar to Article 24(d) of the Regulation.[80] The provision is quite wide because it covers a decision from any State; however it only applies to 'maintenance' decisions. The decision does not have to originate from a State that is party to the Convention. This is not highlighted as such but it is clear from the fact that the word 'contracting' before State is omitted.[81] The Borrás and Degeling Report simply refers to the Enforcement Convention, which contained the same exception and states that it should be 'left to the wisdom of the judge

[75] Maintenance Convention Art 22(c).

[76] See ch 5 s IV above.

[77] See, *The owners of the cargo lately laden on board the ship 'Tatry' v The owners of the ship 'Maciej Rataj'* [1994] ECR I-5460.

[78] Verwilghen Report (n 2) para 66.

[79] Maintenance Convention Art 22(d).

[80] There is no equivalent to Art 24(c) which rests on the mutual exclusivity of judgments (eg C-145/86 *Hoffmann v Krieg* [1988] ECR 645) because this provision requires that the actions have the same 'purpose', which it is presumed is equivalent to 'the same cause of action' and would not extend to related proceedings such as divorce (see the discussion at ch 5 s IV and ch 7 s III above).

[81] In this respect the Verwilghen Report (n 2) says: 'If the Convention uses the expression "or in another State" without giving further clarification, then there is nothing to stop one thinking that the State can be a *non-contracting* State, and the logic of the instrument itself allows of such interpretation' (para 67). This was taken from the General Enforcement Convention but was given more clarity in the 1973 Enforcement Convention.

or the authority to decide in each individual case which of the incompatible decisions has priority.'[82]

## *v. Rights of the Defence*

The Convention also contains an exception that covers the right to a defence which was discussed in detail above,[83] (because within the EU this defence is unnecessary and creates extra confusion). In some respects this is even more important in the context of the Convention because it was difficult to reach agreement on the exact wording of the exception as it had to work for administrative systems as well as judicial systems. The problem being that in administrative systems 'the merits of a matter are initially considered in the absence of the defendant.'[84] As a result the agreed text had to be split into two parts that apply either or:

> in a case where the respondent has neither appeared nor was represented in the proceedings in the State of origin—
>
> i) when the law of the State of origin provides for notice of proceedings, the respondent did not have proper notice of the proceedings and an opportunity to be heard; or
>
> ii) when the law of the State of origin does not provide for notice of proceedings the respondent did not have proper notice of the decision and an opportunity to challenge or appeal it on fact and law;[85]

In the context of the Regulation this exception is virtually pointless because it is too narrow and true violations of the rights of the defence will generally always be caught by the public policy exception.[86] However, the provision may have more use in the international context and although it is still not strictly necessary, its inclusion at the international level does have more relevance. This is because, all the European States are expected to comply with fundamental rights, in particular the right to be heard.[87] Conversely, Contracting States to the Maintenance Convention might be party to the International Covenant on

[82] Borrás and Degeling Report (n 7) para 485.

[83] See ch 7 s VIII above.

[84] Borrás and Degeling Report (n 7) para 486.

[85] Maintenance Convention Art 22(e). This is similar to Art 24(b) of the Regulation, in particular part i). However, part ii) is added for States with administrative systems, where 'decisions are rendered *ex-parte* and due process is respected by allowing the defendant to challenge the decision on fact and law after the decision is rendered' (see para 488 of the Borrás and Degeling Report (n 7)). However, this double option was not necessary in the EU because the States that rely heavily on administrative systems are Australia and Norway. As Norway is not part of the European Union a consideration of administrative systems was not necessary.

[86] See ch 5 s VIII above.

[87] They are party to the ECHR, there are human rights requirements under Art 6 of the Treaty on the European Union, and they are required to comply with the Charter on fundamental rights when applying EU law, which now has the same legal value as the treaties (see Art 6 TEU). The compliance with these rights can be monitored by both the European Court of Human Rights (ECtHR) and the Court of Justice of the European Union (CJEU), see ch 7 s VIII above.

Civil and Political Rights (ICCPR), which also includes a provision on the right to a fair trial,[88] but they will not all be even though the Treaty is quite widely ratified.[89] Therefore, although the majority of States will protect the right to be heard as part of their public policy it cannot be certain at the international level; unlike the European region where it can be argued that there is a European notion of public policy which would include the rights protected by the ECHR and the Charter.[90]

A great deal of time was spent in the negotiations agreeing on the wording of the defence.[91] This was even more apparent because this exception could not be taken directly from the Enforcement Convention since the equivalent provision was designed to apply in a completely different way. Rather than the provision being an optional reason for the enforcing court not to declare the decision recognisable and enforceable, it was in a separate article from the other grounds and implied that the Court should not recognise a decision that had been given in default of appearance.[92] This was kept separate because the Commission 'felt that it had to be more exacting when dealing with the recognition and enforcement of judgments rendered by default than in relation to other foreign decisions.'[93] This is somewhat confusing when the same report suggests earlier that the public policy exception 'would necessarily' cover the rights of the defence. Unfortunately, the position at the international level is not as clear cut as at the European level. Further, since the Convention will not be reviewed for some time the two separate defences contained in the current Convention will remain for many years. It is hoped, as with the provision on procedural fraud, that national courts use both

[88] ICCPR, Art 14(1): 'All persons shall be equal before the courts and tribunals. In the determination … of his rights and obligations in a suit at law, everyone shall be entitled to a fair and public hearing by a competent, independent and impartial tribunal established by law.'

[89] http://treaties.un.org/pages/ViewDetails.aspx?src=TREATY&mtdsg_no=IV-4&chapter=4&lang=en, accessed 6 June 2014.

[90] See ch 7 s V above. A further issue is the distinction between procedural and substantive public policy. Although both types of public policy are protected at the European level (B Hess, T Pfeiffer and P Schlosser, *The Brussels I Regulation 44/2001 Application and Enforcement in the EU (the Heidelberg Report)* (Munich, Verlag C H Beck, 2008) paras 555–59) at the international level some States might only protect substantive public policy. This was the case in the US under the Uniform Foreign Money-Judgments Act 1962. However the revised act, the Uniform Foreign-Country Money Judgments Recognition Act 2005 removed this limitation and the public policy defence can now cover procedural as well as substantive public policy.

[91] See in particular Procès verbal no 10, 7–8 and Procès verbal no 16, 6. There was also discussion as to what law the defence should be based on, however the defence should be determined by a fact based approach, therefore the 'law of the State of origin was not determinative.' (Procès verbal no 10, 8.)

[92] 'Without prejudice to the provisions of Article 5, a decision rendered by default shall be recognised or enforced only if notice of the institution of proceedings, including notice of the substance of the claim, has been served on the defaulting party in accordance with the law of the State of origin and if, having regard to the circumstances, the party has had sufficient time to enable him to defend the proceedings' (Art 6 Enforcement Convention). See also P Beaumont in Procès verbal no 16 at page 6, 'Article 6 of the 1973 Maintenance Convention had been drafted in a different way to Article 19 of the current revised preliminary draft Convention [it] was a default provision, which only applied where a decision against a debtor had been given in default of appearance.'

[93] Verwilghen Report (n 2) para 68.

these exceptions sparingly and only refuse to grant recognition and enforceability where there is a clear violation of the rights of the defence so as to ensure the enforcement of cross border judgments which should in turn secure the proper administration of justice.

### *vi. Limitation on the Jurisdiction of Debtors*

Finally, recognition and enforceability can be refused if 'the decision was made in violation of Article 18.'[94] Article 18 places constraints on the jurisdiction of debtors, when they are attempting to modify proceedings. The provisions are necessary. Since there are no direct rules on jurisdiction 'the Convention cannot address fully the problem of conflicting decisions which may arise out of modification proceedings.'[95] Therefore the Convention operates on negative rules of jurisdiction which limit the jurisdiction of debtors.[96] The general rule is that when

> a decision is made in a Contracting State where the creditor is habitually resident, proceedings to modify the decision or make a new decision cannot be brought by the debtor in any other Contracting State as long as the creditor remains habitually resident in the State where the decision was made.[97]

The positive aspects of such rules are that they benefit the creditor who chooses to remain in the same jurisdiction, and it is a guarantee for the administrative or judicial authority that deals with the payments. This is useful as the unsuspecting creditor will not suddenly be sent notice of a modification to their maintenance order from a completely different State. However as Duncan points out, the provision is rather limited. 'The Convention does contain one helpful general rule which in effect requires a maintenance debtor to seek modification in the country of origin of the decision, provided the creditor was and remains resident there.'[98] Therefore, as soon as the creditor moves, this provision will no longer protect that particular creditor.

## C. Summary

This highlights the grounds on which recognition and enforceability may be refused under the main route for recognition and enforceability under the Convention. The first main difference between this and the process under the Regulation is that a decision can be refused recognition on grounds of jurisdiction.

[94] Maintenance Convention Art 22(f). Art 18 concerns restrictions on bringing proceedings. This is very similar to Art 8 of the Regulation (see ch 5 s VIII above).

[95] Borrás and Degeling Report (n 7) para 415.

[96] Art 18 of the Maintenance Convention.

[97] Ibid, Art 18(1). See Beaumont (n 58) 532–33.

[98] Duncan (n 57) 15 and see the following sentences.

This is because no agreement could have been reached on direct rules of jurisdiction, so indirect jurisdiction was the preferred option. The Convention then contains several other grounds on which recognition and enforceability can be refused. Some of these are similar to those in the Regulation and others are additional. The first ground of public policy causes no problems and is a sensible safety valve in international instruments. The second ground which relates to procedural fraud may not really be necessary as the recognition of such judgments should really raise questions of public policy. It is unfortunate that it has not been possible to eliminate this exception thus far, but it is hoped that it will not be necessary in the future. Although the third ground does not appear in the Regulation at the recognition and enforceability stage, its inclusion is not an issue as it is more or less equivalent to *lis pendens*. The fourth ground is equivalent to the irreconcilable judgments provision and its inclusion creates no major problems. The next ground is the one that relates to the rights of the defence, which is more important at the international level than the European Union level because the correlation between this and public policy is not so clear cut. The final exception applies in relation to modification of decisions. Although a general rule to limit the jurisdiction of debtors is useful, the rule in Article 18 is quite narrow, so its overall benefit may be limited.

## V. Procedure for Recognition and Enforcement

Article 23 sets out a rapid and simple procedure for the recognition of a foreign decision and the declaration of enforceability. The procedure excludes submissions from the parties and allows only limited *ex officio* review. The onus of raising objections to the registration of the foreign decision is placed on the debtor whose right to challenge or appeal is limited in respect of grounds that can be raised and is time barred, because any challenge or appeal has to be raised within either 30 or 60 days.[99]

The Central Authority can either refer the application to the competent authority or deal with the process itself depending on the competence of the authority in that particular State. The designated competent authority should then declare 'without delay' that the decision is enforceable and register it for enforcement.[100] However there are no actual time limits set. It was 'not considered advisable to set a time limit'[101] for this section because different States have different procedures so an express time limit was not considered to be suitable.[102] The terminology used should encourage States to deal with this matter expeditiously. Where the

[99] Maintenance Convention Art 23(6).
[100] Ibid, Art 23(3).
[101] Borrás and Degeling Report (n 7) para 498.
[102] See ch 10 below for a discussion on issues with time limits.

competent authority is the Central Authority the process may be quicker because the documents do not have to be sent to another body, but no conclusions can be made at this stage.

The first stage of the procedure is covered by Article 23(4). This states that recognition and enforceability of the decision may only be refused by the competent authority on grounds of public policy. Neither party is allowed to make any submissions at this stage. '[T]he reason for this is that the procedure has to be as fast and as simple as possible and, probably, in the great majority of cases, no further submissions would be made.'[103] This is a significant step forward from the Enforcement Convention which did not contain uniform procedures for recognition and enforceability. It also goes further than the Brussels Convention which allowed a broader *ex officio* review that was not limited to public policy. However, the Brussels I Regulation does not allow *ex officio* review at the first stage.[104] This is the same as the procedure under the Maintenance Regulation where recognition and enforcement procedures apply. If the defendant does not challenge the recognition then there is absolutely no review at all and enforcement should be virtually automatic.

At the second stage the applicant or respondent has to be duly notified of the declaration or registration of the decision and either party may bring a challenge or an appeal.[105] There is a time limit for this. This is an easier place to put a time limit as the time limit will not affect States' procedures. The time limit for bringing an appeal is 30 days.[106] This limits the time that the challenger has to launch an appeal, so it does not affect the procedures in the State. If the contesting party is not resident in the State he has 60 days to raise the appeal.[107] In relation to these respective periods, the Japanese delegation actually considered them to be too long and did in fact suggest they were shortened.[108] The challenge or appeal may be raised on any of the grounds in Article 20[109] or Article 22.[110]

Article 23 also introduces an additional ground on which recognition and enforceability can be refused. This is 'the fulfilment of the debt to the extent that the recognition and enforcement relates to payments that fell due in the past.'[111] Effectively this is to ensure that a particular payment will not be paid twice. Under the Regulation this is dealt with at the 'actual enforcement' stage because it is presumed that national enforcement law will not allow the enforcement of an obligation that has already been enforced.[112] This extra ground for non-recognition of judgments is useful, because it seems ridiculous for States

103 Borrás and Degeling Report (n 7) para 501.
104 See Brussels I Arts 41–43, and Beaumont (n 58) 536–38.
105 Maintenance Convention Art 23(5).
106 Ibid, Art 23(6).
107 Ibid.
108 Mr Hayakawa, Procès verbal no 5, 5.
109 Maintenance Convention Art 23(7)b).
110 Ibid, Art 23(7)a).
111 Ibid, Art 23(8).
112 See Case C-139/10 *Prism Investments v van der Meer* [2011] ECR I-09511.

to waste time and money in establishing a declaration of enforceability, where even though this exists the decision will never be enforced. Although, on the other hand it is questionable whether this provision is really necessary because the enforcing State would be unlikely to enforce an obligation that had already been discharged. States should not enforce a decision that has already been enforced, or one which would leave the debtor with no means because this would be unfair to the debtor. This must go beyond simple unfairness, if the proper administration of justice is to be secured, as one could argue that any decision or award is unfair. Therefore, better language could be 'unjustifiable', or the enforcement of the order could be 'repugnant' to that State's ethical and moral values. If it is practically certain that a State would not enforce an order that had already been enforced because this is repugnant to certain values, such as moral and ethical considerations, is this in fact the same as saying that the double enforcement of a decision or double enforcement of an award would be in violation of public policy?[113]

In a recent reference to the CJEU, the Hoge Raad considered that

> the defence that there has already been compliance with the judgment delivered in a Member State is not covered by the grounds of refusal set out in Articles 34 and 35 of Regulation No 44/2001, in particular the ground of refusal relating to infringement of public policy.[114]

Therefore the questions referred for a preliminary ruling did not address this point but simply whether recognition and enforcement could be refused on a ground that is not listed in Article 34 or 35.[115] In its decision the CJEU answered the question directly, which meant that it did not need to address the potential public policy question in this respect. It is considered that there is little clarity in this area because it is unclear on what grounds exactly a court would refuse enforcement, and therefore why one can assume that a court would not 'actually enforce' a decision that had already been enforced. It is assumed that it would not be enforced twice because this would not respect the moral and or ethical values of a State, which therefore leads to the conclusion that to enforce the same decision twice would therefore be contrary to the public policy of a State, despite the Hoge Raad's divergent views.[116]

It is also unclear why this provision is contained separately and is not included with the other grounds for non-recognition in Article 22. There does not appear to be a similar provision in any of the other relevant documents, in particular the Enforcement Convention, and *Prism Investments* clarifies that

[113] 'As the Germans say [ordre public] is a *Vorbehaltsklausel*, a reservation for the avoidance in extraordinary circumstances of a result which would be shocking because it is contrary to fundamental policies in a country or principles on which society are built, be they of a legal, *moral, ethical*, social economic, or political character.' A Philip, 'General Course on Private International Law' 1978 (II) *Recueil des cours* 9, 56–57, emphasis added.

[114] *Prism Investments* (n 112) para 24.

[115] Ibid, see para 26.

[116] See, Philip (n 113) 56–57 (fn 74).

there is no equivalent provision in the European Union documents. The brief explanation in the Report states: '[if] the respondent has discharged the debt, this is a clear reason for opposing recognition and enforcement in so far as the decision concerns past debt.'[117] This short sentence does nothing to clarify any of the above questions.

Recognition and enforceability can also be refused on the basis of the authenticity or integrity of any of the documents transmitted in accordance with Article 25(1) a), b) or d) or (3) b).[118] The documents covered are: the complete text of the decision; a document stating that the decision is enforceable in the State of origin; a document clarifying the amount of arrears (where necessary); or an abstract or extract of the decision, drawn up by the competent authority where the full decision is unavailable. According to the Explanatory Report the

> ground for challenge or appeal under Article 23(7) c) serves as a safeguard against, for example, documents the origin of which may be disputed (authenticity) or documents that may have been tampered with, for example, the text of which could have been truncated or deleted (integrity).[119]

Although it is not necessary for these documents to be provided in all cases it is uncertain whether this added ground is really necessary. This is different to the ground in Article 22(b), which refers to fraud in the procedure, and not tampering with documents (which is a form of fraud) after the procedure is finished. However any major allegations of fraud or authenticity can be dealt with by the public policy clause. Further, it will not always be necessary to refuse to recognise a decision because the document has been tampered with. The alteration may not make any difference to the outcome, or if the amount of money due has been altered then the original decision for the correct amount should still be enforceable. States should be very careful about refusing to recognise and enforce an entire decision for this reason.

## VI. Alternative Procedure for Recognition and Enforcement

Not all the States participating in the negotiations were happy with the procedure set out in Article 23, so an alternative procedure for recognition and enforceability

[117] Borrás and Degeling Report (n 7) para 512.

[118] Maintenance Convention Art 23(7) c). This was included because the previous requirement to provide certain documents at the first stage of the application was not included in the Maintenance Convention (see para 510 of the Borrás and Degeling Report). However, a Contracting State may still specify under Art 57 that a complete copy of the decision certified by the competent authority in the State of origin must accompany the application.

[119] Borrás and Degeling Report (n 7) para 510.

had to be established. It was hoped that the greater flexibility would allow more States to ratify the Convention, therefore leading to more success in terms of greater circulation and enforcement of cross border maintenance obligations. The alternative procedure is found in Article 24.[120]

Article 24 was necessary as it appears that not all States have an *exequatur* stage in relation to foreign judgments and some rules go directly to a procedure of actual enforcement. Certain systems currently have 'a single-stage procedure, not involving a separate registration or declaration of enforceability, but rather a single application to the court for enforcement of a foreign decision.'[121] This suggests that the procedure will be similar to the new procedure in the Brussels I recast, allowing for a review at the enforcement stage rather than a two stage procedure.[122] However, the safeguards are maintained unlike the Protocol procedure under the Maintenance Regulation.

Although having one procedure that covers both recognition and enforceability as well as actual enforcement would appear to create a more simplified procedure. The procedure is less strict than the one in Article 23, and much more lenient than the procedure in the Brussels I recast. The procedure in Article 23 only allows for *ex officio* review at the first stage and this is limited to public policy. However, the procedure under Article 24 allows *ex officio* review of the public policy ground, review to decipher whether or not proceedings having the same purpose are ongoing in another State, and the competent authority can also review whether an incompatible decision exists.[123] Not only are there additional grounds on which the competent authority may review the decision, but the parties can also challenge at the first stage. This provision has been included to protect the parties' right to be heard.[124]

[120] Norway has opted to use the recognition and enforcement procedure in Maintenance Convention Art 24. (Albania, Ukraine, the EU and Bosnia and Herzegovina will use the procedure in Art 23 as they have not made any declarations to the contrary.) See www.hcch.net/index_en.php?act=status.comment&csid=1067&disp=resdn, accessed 6 June 2014.

[121] Borrás and Degeling Report, para 516.

[122] Regulation (EU) 1215/2012 of the European Parliament and of the Council of 12 December 2012 on jurisdiction and the recognition and enforcement of judgments in civil and commercial matters (recast) [2012] OJ L351/1 (Brussels I recast) and see above at ch 7 s VIII.

[123] See Maintenance Convention Art 24(4).

[124] 'At the first stage of recognition and enforcement proceedings, Ms … Ferreira emphasised that a debtor had no right to be heard and that it was an automatic process of recognition and enforcement. She believed that this went against the fundamental rights of a debtor because from a procedural view there was a need to enable people to make their submissions and respond to an application. She observed that perhaps it could be acceptable not to hear from the debtor at all at the first stage of proceedings as long as that person had the opportunity to challenge any recognition of a decision made against him and then to be heard as to his arguments. She considered it strange that whilst the meeting suggested that the needs of a child must be protected, the needs of a debtor are not also considered. If no balance were struck then Ms … Ferreira stated that the Chinese delegation would support the entire deletion of all of Article 20.' Procès verbal no 5, 20.

Below is a simple diagram which demonstrates the difference at comparable stages:

| Article 23 | Article 24 |
|---|---|
| The competent authority can review on public policy grounds only. | Authorities can review three points and the defendant can appeal. |
| The defendant can then appeal for a review under any of the provisions in Article 22 or Article 20. If the defendant does not raise an appeal, recognition and enforcement will be granted. | If there is no appeal or the appeal fails and *ex officio* review is passed the decision will be enforced directly. |
| Actual enforcement proceedings. | |

Although there are fewer stages in the Article 24 procedure, there are additional methods for reviewing the decision. Therefore, just because the procedure has less stages this does not necessarily mean that the decision will be enforced more expeditiously.

> For these States it is likely that the first stage will be more protracted than under the Art. 23 system and therefore in the vast majority of cases it may mean that it takes a longer time for the maintenance creditor to get his money. On the other hand, in the difficult cases that go to appeal the Art. 24 system has advantages over the Art. 23 procedure that there is only one appeal and that during that appeal the enforcement of the decision will only be stayed in exceptional circumstances.[125]

The decision on recognition and enforcement under Article 24 can only be given after the respondent has been informed of the proceedings and both parties have been given an adequate opportunity to be heard.[126] The competent authority can review any of the grounds in Article 20, 22 and 23(7) c),[127] if an appeal is raised

[125] Beaumont (n 58) 73.
[126] Maintenance Convention Art 24 (3).
[127] This refers to the authenticity or integrity of any document in accordance with Art 25(1).

by the defendant.[128] The competent authority can also refuse to recognise and enforce the decision if it relates to payments that were due in the past.[129]

The alternative procedure in Article 24 was necessary in order to achieve consensus. The provisions in Article 24 did not appear until the very end and this was a major sticking point at the final negotiations in November 2007. The previous draft Convention, of June 2007, that was worked from at the meeting only contained one procedure for recognition and enforceability that was contained in Article 20 of the draft. This was very similar to the procedure that is now contained in Article 23. The States that had a particular problem with Article 20 as it stood at the final negotiations were China,[130] and Russia.[131]

Working document 62 was produced by an informal working group, to try to negotiate a suitable compromise.[132] This provided the option of an Article 20 *bis*, which gave an alternative option for recognition and enforcement.

Article 20 bis Alternative procedure on an application for recognition and enforcement

1. Notwithstanding Article 20, a State may declare in accordance with Article 58 that it will apply the procedure for recognition and enforcement set out in this Article.
2. Where an application for recognition and enforcement of a decision has been made through Central Authorities in accordance with Chapter III, the requested Central Authority shall promptly either—
   *a)* refer the application to the competent authority which shall decide on the request for recognition and enforcement; or
   *b)* if it is the competent authority take such a decision itself.
3. A decision on recognition and enforcement shall be given by the competent authority after the respondent has been promptly notified of the proceedings and both parties have been given an adequate opportunity to be heard.
4. The competent authority may review the grounds for refusing recognition and enforcement set out in Article 19 *a), c)* and *d)* of its own motion and all other grounds listed in Articles 17, 19 *b), e), f)* and 20(7) *c)* if they are raised by the defendant or if concerns relating to those grounds arise from the face of the documents submitted in accordance with Article 21.
5. A refusal of recognition and enforcement may also be founded on the fulfilment of the debt to the extent that the recognition and enforcement relates to payments that fell due in the past.

[128] Maintenance Convention Art 24 (4).

[129] Ibid, Art 24 (5). See above for a discussion on the equivalent provision in Art 23 (8).

[130] The principal problem was there was not enough emphasis on the rights of the debtor. They wanted 'more equitable rules'. Procès verbal no 5, 21.

[131] Procès verbal no 5, 20. The issue here was the applicability of the Article to their system.

[132] The delegations participating in the informal working group were: Canada, China, the European Community, Japan, Russian Federation, Switzerland and the USA (see Procès verbal no 17, 10).

6. Any appeal, if permitted by the law of the State addressed, shall not have the effect of staying the enforcement of the decision unless there are exceptional circumstances.
7. In taking any decision on recognition and enforcement, including any appeal, the competent authority shall act expeditiously.'[133]

When the document was submitted for review by all the participants it was stated that the delegations had 'made a big concession because there was now a genuine alternative to the procedures for recognition and enforcement that was set out in Article 20'.[134] It was hoped that the new text would be acceptable. The Latin American States were not happy because they had no representatives in the working group. Working document no 64 was then produced, which was virtually the same. Neither of these documents allowed the defendant to raise all the points in Article 22(19) for review as he would be able to under the normal procedure for recognition and enforceability. This point was raised by the Israeli delegate who considered that, 'the defendant should be empowered to raise all grounds of review, including those grounds that the competent authority could raise of its own motion.'[135] The view of the delegate was accepted and the provision was referred to the drafting committee to alter in order to incorporate this.[136]

This is sensible as it does not appear reasonable to limit the debtor's chances of appeal just because the authorities can review the other grounds of their own motion. Simply allowing the competent authority to review the grounds does not mean they will necessarily do so. In the main system under Article 23 the debtor can still raise an appeal under all grounds even though there is *ex officio* review of public policy. It therefore would have been unfair to limit the rights of debtors in the Article 24 procedure, when this was not done in the Article 23 procedure. The final text which allows the debtor to raise an appeal on all the grounds listed in Article 22, after these had been decided on, is much more appropriate than the more limited approach that was contained in Working Documents 62 and 64. As a result there are two procedures for recognition and enforceability under the Convention. States must choose which method they are going to use and make a declaration under Article 63 if they wish to opt for the procedure in Article 24. Both procedures allow an appeal by the debtor on the grounds laid out in Article 22.

133 Working Document no 62. This was reworded in Working Document no 64, but the only change was made to part 1. This still leaves para 4 different from the final text. Art 19 is equivalent to Art 22 in the final text. As seen previously the defendant can appeal on any of the points in Art 22 in the final text of Art 24, but here they have been limited to three grounds of appeal.

134 Ms Lenzing Procès verbal no 17, 10.

135 Procès verbal no 22, 5.

136 Ibid, 6–7.

## VII. Conclusion

There were various obstacles that had to be overcome to reach consensus in the Maintenance Convention. It is unfortunate that the Convention only contains indirect grounds of jurisdiction that can be reviewed at the recognition and enforceability stage. However it is recognised that direct rules of jurisdiction at the international level are still a long way off. It is also unfortunate that there are two different systems for recognition and enforceability. As identified above the two different procedures under the Regulation are proving difficult to apply in practice.[137] From August 2014, when the Convention entered into force in the EU, these Central Authorities have to manage the four different systems and be aware of what forms they should send to each State.[138] In terms of both clarity and simplicity, which can assist in achieving the proper administration of justice, it would be preferable if any future instruments contain fewer procedures for recognition and enforceability. Since the Convention is unlikely to be reviewed for many years the focus should be on providing efficient training systems for Central Authorities at both the national and international level. The Hague Conference has recently published a Practical Handbook for the Maintenance Convention which should be of assistance to Central Authorities.[139]

It is clear that there is greater chance of recognition and enforceability being refused at the international level than at the European Union level. The Convention covers indirect grounds of jurisdiction which leave scope for a variety of different reservations to be placed, in addition to a long list of grounds for refusal. It is hoped that judges in enforcing States take a robust approach to decisions circulating under the Maintenance Convention and seek to enforce them as far as possible. Judges should interpret the provisions strictly and only refuse recognition and enforceability in exceptional cases, in order to ensure the proper administration of justice. In relation to the complex rules on indirect jurisdiction, this is an area where cooperation between judges and practitioners is essential. Judges should aim to accept the original jurisdiction through the methods available, but inform practitioners and judges in other Contracting States in what circumstances it would be impossible to accept a particular jurisdiction. This should assist judges and practitioners in the State of origin when deciding whether it would be suitable for them to take jurisdiction in a particular case, or whether the creditor would be better to seek an order in a different State under a different ground of indirect

[137] See ch 7 s VII above.

[138] For example, Norway will use the alternative track and it is expected that there will be traffic between some EU Member States and Norway (www.hcch.net/index_en.php?act=status.comment&csid=1067&disp=resdn, accessed 5 June 2013).

[139] 'Practical Handbook for Caseworkers under the Hague Child Support Convention' (HCCH, 2014) available at www.hcch.net/index_en.php?act=publications.details&pid=6095&dtid=3, accessed 6 June 2014.

jurisdiction. Therefore efficient judicial and administrative cooperation will be a key factor in the enforcement of decisions under the Convention, in particular.

Judges should also be careful when declining recognition and enforceability on the basis of either fraud, the rights of the defence or tampering with documents. They should interpret each of these provisions restrictively and should only decline recognition and enforceability on one of these grounds where there has been a clear failure to comply with these provisions that would result in a violation of the administration of justice.

# 9

# Actual Enforcement

## I. Introduction

Historically, actual enforcement has been one of the most difficult aspects of private international law,[1] as it has generally been left as a national law matter. This is extremely unfortunate as it does not matter how effective and efficient the provisions are on other aspects such as, administrative cooperation, jurisdiction and recognition and enforcement, if the ultimate task of getting an obligation actually enforced is not fulfilled. One of the objectives of the Maintenance Convention is to require 'effective measures for the prompt enforcement of maintenance decisions.'[2] The relevant provisions in the Maintenance Regulation suggest that formal requirements for enforcement be limited so that costs are kept to a minimum. Further, creditors should not be required to have a postal address or a representative in the Member State of enforcement. It is also recommended that translation of documents should not be required unless the obligation is contested.[3]

Traditionally, actual enforcement is left to the national law of the State addressed. This is because enforcement has always been considered a matter of national procedure. Once a decision has gone through the *exequatur* process, it should then be enforced under national law as if it were a national decision. As a result, it was considered that it would not be possible to include detailed provisions on enforcement in the new instruments as enforcement is a matter for national law and not ripe for detailed regulation at an international level as all States have very different procedures.[4] Effectively any other work will be

[1] See W Duncan, 'The New Hague Maintenance Convention and Protocol' (2008) 10 *Yearbook of Private International Law* 313, 326. 'Lack of effective enforcement procedures or measures under national law has proved to be something of an Achilles' heel in relation to certain Hague Conventions' and D Cavers, 'International Enforcement of Family Support' (1981) 81 *Columbia Law Review* 994.

[2] Art 1(d) of the Hague Convention of 23 November 2007 on the International Recovery of Child Support and other Forms of Family Maintenance.

[3] See Recitals 27 and 28 of the Maintenance Regulation (Council Regulation (EC) 4/2009 of 18 December 2008 on jurisdiction, applicable law, recognition and enforcement of decisions and cooperation in matters relating to maintenance obligations [2009] OJ L7/1). It is also suggested that enforcement should be simpler due to the abolition of *exequatur*. See Recital 5 and ch 7 above.

[4] In November 1997, the Commission published a communication on free movement of judgments (Com (97) 609 final, OJE). The Commission expressed a view in favour of the further harmonisation

rendered pointless if the outstanding maintenance obligation is not discharged, and because of this 'actual enforcement' is probably the most important part of the process. Therefore, it is unfortunate that the provisions on enforcement in the Regulation are minimal.[5]

## II. Convention

The Hague Maintenance Convention is unique in this area because it is the first Hague Convention to include a specific chapter on enforcement in the requested State.[6] This is a new approach and it will most likely be important for the future success of the Convention that this step was taken by the Conference. This is because there have been problems with the actual enforcement of decisions under earlier Hague Conventions.[7] Therefore, it was recognised that some regulation at the actual enforcement stage was necessary. The Convention 'seeks truly to facilitate the execution of the decision, thereby making it effective.'[8] The Convention does this by inserting a non-discrimination clause which requires that 'at least' the enforcement measures available under national law are also available under the

of enforcement procedures, but did not propose an extensive or immediate harmonisation of enforcement procedures. An attempt was made to harmonise these procedures in the Maintenance Regulation but this failed (see Staff Working Document, Annex to the Proposal for a Council Regulation on jurisdiction, applicable law, recognition and enforcement of decisions and cooperation in matters relating to maintenance obligations—Impact assessment, SEC/2005/1629). However it is noted that there is nothing in the Treaty on the Functioning of the European Union itself which prevents the regulation of actual enforcement, Art 81 TFEU. The EU has instead tried to address the problems mainly through the abolition of *exequatur* in the EEO (see n 66) and the Maintenance Regulation, but there is still limited or no harmonisation of actual enforcement procedures. The Convention provides limited provisions on enforcement, but 'the wording of this provision cannot go further, as specific enforcement measures are not required by the Convention. The precise enforcement measures necessary to meet the broad requirements of effectiveness and promptness are a matter for individual Contracting States' (A Borrás and J Degeling, 'Explanatory Report on the Convention on the International Recovery of Child Support and other Forms of Family Maintenance (HCCH, 2009) (Borrás and Degeling Report) para 44).

[5] This need for enforcement procedures was recognised by the Commission in its Impact Assessment. 'Merely abolishing the exequatur would not be sufficient to remove all obstacles regarding the recovery of maintenance claims in the European law-enforcement area. Other measures would have to be put in place. The need for a judicial procedure for enforcement and the redress procedures and remedies available to the defendant are probably serious obstacles in the way of the successful enforcement of the judgment, not only because enforcement can be suspended during the proceedings but also because of the length of time taken by proceedings in some Member States' (Staff Working Document (n 4), s 3(iii)).

[6] See the Borrás and Degeling Report (n 4) para 570, and the earlier Conventions of the Hague Conference at http://www.hcch.net/index_en.php?act=conventions.listing, accessed 9 June 2014.

[7] In particular the Hague Convention on Child Abduction, where in recent years the European Court of Human Rights (ECtHR) has generated a fair amount of case law in this respect. See, www.incadat.com/index.cfm?act=search.result&actie=next&lng=1 where many of these cases are summarised, accessed 9 June 2014 and see s V below.

[8] Borrás and Degeling Report (n 4) para 44.

Convention.[9] The Convention also requires that these measures are 'effective'.[10] Further, it lists possible enforcement measures that should be made available to enforcement authorities, and extends the duties of Central Authorities to the enforcement stage. These provisions are imperative because the success and effectiveness of the new Convention would be greatly reduced if the obligations created under it were not actually being discharged.

The procedure for enforcement created under the Convention should ensure that once the decision has been declared enforceable or is registered for enforcement, the applicant will not have to make any further applications.[11] The purpose of this is to help ensure the procedure is prompt and simple for the creditor. This should help to simplify proceedings and therefore is a necessary step in the process to help ensure 'effective measures for the prompt enforcement of maintenance decisions.'[12] The provision should mean that 'the whole procedure for recognition and enforcement including *exequatur* and enforcement under internal law, is treated as a continuum, not requiring further applications at different stages',[13] because a step in the process has been removed. However this only applies where the application has been made through the Central Authority, because the authority is 'involved on behalf of the applicant to oversee the proceedings and guarantee their continuation.'[14] This could encourage the use of Central Authorities rather than private bodies, and it should also encourage more cooperation between Central Authorities as they must coordinate effectively between each other to make sure the obligation is discharged. Once the Central Authority has been approached under the new instruments, it is up to them to ensure that the case is dealt with effectively from the beginning until the end.

The Convention requires that Contracting States have effective measures available under their internal law to ensure the enforcement of decisions under the Convention. The Convention gives a list of possible measures, however the list

[9] Maintenance Convention Art 33. 'The use of the expression 'at least' suggests that the requested State may discriminate positively in favour of foreign decisions by applying to them a broader range of enforcement methods than apply to internal decisions. This is unlikely to be a common occurrence. However, the peculiar characteristic of international maintenance claims may sometimes require the application of special techniques of enforcement.' (Borrás and Degeling Report (n 4) para 580). However, in the context of EU law Advocate Generals have warned against this reverse form of discrimination. Conversely, in this context reverse discrimination would be reached by an over emphasis on the effective protection of EU rights rather than a reliance on the equivalence/ non-discrimination provision. (See, for example AG Jacobs in C-430 & 431/93 *Van Schijndel and Van Veen v Stichting Pensioenfonds voor Fysiotherapeuten* [1995] ECR I-4705 and AG Léger in C-66/95 *R v Secretary of State for Social Security, ex p Eunice Sutton* [1997] ECR I-2163.)

[10] Maintenance Convention Art 34 and see para 582 of the Borrás and Degeling Report (n 4) and n 18 below.

[11] See Maintenance Convention Art 32(3) and see the earlier decision in *Romańczyk v France* (App no 7618/05) ECHR 18 November 2010, discussed below at s V.

[12] Maintenance Convention Art 1(d).

[13] Ibid, Art 32(3), and see the Borrás and Degeling Report (n 4) para 573.

[14] Ibid.

is non exhaustive, and there is no requirement that these particular measures be available.[15] The possible measures listed in the Convention are:

— Wage withholding.
— Garnishment from bank accounts and other sources.
— Deductions from social security payments.
— Lien on or forced sale of property.
— Tax refund withholding.
— Withholding or attachment of pension.
— Credit bureau reporting.
— Denial, suspension or revocation of various licenses.
— The use of mediation, conciliation or similar process to bring about voluntary compliance.[16]

Some of these measures are directly effective such as garnishment or forced sale of property, as the money would directly be used for the maintenance payment. However, other methods such as the suspension of a driving license would only be used in an attempt to compel the debtor to pay. In relation to the possible methods listed in Article 34, the Convention contains a non-discrimination provision.[17] International decisions must be treated the same as national decisions and any measures that are available as a method of enforcing national decisions have to be available for international decisions also.[18] Enforcement should be more effective where the body responsible for enforcement has as many mechanisms available to them as possible. The more effective enforcement mechanisms are available the easier it should be for enforcement bodies to fulfil the aim in Article 1(d) of the Convention. It will make it simpler to fulfil their job in general if they have a wide range of resources and mechanisms available under the internal law of the State. However where enforcement mechanisms do exist it is important that these are all as effective as possible in order to ensure the appropriate administration of justice. Enforcement mechanisms should not be easy for debtors to avoid or simple to get

[15] 'However, the Convention does not go so far as to stipulate that specific measures of enforcement should be made available. Instead it takes the unusual course of providing an illustrative list'. Duncan (n 1) 326.

[16] Maintenance Convention Art 34. It is recognised that the final points are not enforcement mechanisms as such but these methods could assist with the initial enforcement and hopefully the ongoing enforcement of maintenance obligations.

[17] Ibid, Art 33.

[18] However, any enforcement measures that are available should be beneficial rather than detrimental. Just because enforcement measures exist does not always mean they are useful. For example in the past in the UK, attachment only happened after the debtor defaulted in payments four times in a row. Therefore, if he made the third payment the enforcement mechanism would not operate. That payment would be made then it would go back to the start meaning that the debtor only had to make one in every four payments. (See *HC Deb 08 December 1967 vol 755 cc1837–95, 1850.*) Further, States should be careful not to include imprisonment as an enforcement mechanism unless this is a final resort. The first issue is that this wastes public funds that could be used in a better way. Secondly, where imprisonment is used this should not be seen as discharging the debt, which could happen especially as the debtor will probably not have any earning capacity while in jail. (See *HC Deb 05 February 1968 vol 758 cc85–107, 91.*)

round.[19] They should be virtually automatic. For example in effective administrative systems such as Australia and Norway, the money will always be taken directly from the debtor's wage where this is possible.[20] This should not be seen as an imposition on the debtor's privacy or private life it is just an automatic interception of a payment that he has a moral duty to make, equivalent to income tax, national insurance payments (or equivalent) and mortgage or rental payments.

This is obviously more problematic where the debtor is self-employed or is not registered as PAYE for some other reason. In these situations States need alternative enforcement mechanisms that are effective. This is where mechanisms that relate to attachment of property or assets or attachment or withholding of other forms of payment are important. Finally, where none of these mechanisms prove effective States should seek to suspend or revoke documents such as driving licenses or passports in the hope that this inconvenience to the debtor will act as an incentive to pay.[21]

## III. Common Provisions on Central Authorities

In addition to the provisions on actual enforcement some of the duties of Central Authorities are also relevant to actual enforcement. These provisions are identical in both the Regulation and the Convention. The relevant provisions state that Central Authorities should take all appropriate measures:

- To facilitate the ongoing enforcement of maintenance decisions, including any arrears,[22]
- To facilitate the collection and expeditious transfer of maintenance payments,[23] and
- To initiate or facilitate the institution of proceedings to obtain any necessary provisional measures that are territorial in nature and the purpose of which is to secure the outcome of a pending maintenance application.[24]

[19] Ibid.

[20] Information gathered at the Heidelberg Conference March 2013, Plenary session on Administrative Systems.

[21] The USA has an efficient system whereby each enforcement mechanism comes in at a certain stage. Revocation of licences is used as a last resort whenever the debtor has defaulted on a certain number of payments or more (Heidelberg Conference, workshop on UIFSA).

[22] Art 6(2)(e) of the Convention and Art 51(2)(e) of the Regulation.

[23] Art 6(2)(f) of the Convention and Art 51(2)(f) of the Regulation.

[24] Art 6(2)(i) of the Convention and Art 51(2)(i) of the Regulation. Although this Article is not directly related to enforcement, certain provisional measures such as the seising of assets may ultimately assist with the actual enforcement of the final order.

In fulfilling these duties Central Authorities are expected to take 'all appropriate measures'.[25] The requirement under the Regulation is the same.[26] However, the terminology used of 'all appropriate measures' is slightly ambiguous and it is unclear exactly how far the Central Authorities should actually go.[27] The term was taken from the Abduction Convention and

> has been clearly understood … to mean any measures that a Central Authority could take to achieve the required result, depending on its own powers and resources, and providing those measures are permitted by the internal laws of the Contracting State.[28]

Therefore, in order for the Central Authority to facilitate the enforcement of maintenance decisions effectively, it is reliant on having appropriate powers and resources to discharge this duty. Central Authorities should be given sufficient powers and resources by their States,[29] and as many of the measures listed in Article 34 as possible should be available to the Central Authorities if enforcement is to function effectively. This would be the simplest and most effective method of ensuring that maintenance obligations were actually enforced, and therefore fulfilling the purpose and aim of both documents. At this stage it is unclear how effective the provisions on actual enforcement in relation to Central Authorities will be. But it is clear from lessons learned under the Abduction Convention that their effectiveness will be significantly hampered where the powers of the Central Authorities or other bodies are limited.[30]

[25] Maintenance Convention Art 6(2).

[26] See, Maintenance Regulation Art 51(2).

[27] Case law of the ECtHR in relation to actual enforcement under the Abduction Convention (Hague Convention of 25 October 1980 on the Civil Aspects of Child Abduction) would suggest that the exact meaning of the term 'appropriate measures' is not as simple as described in the Borrás and Degeling Report. In the case of *Iosub Caras v Romania* the Human Rights Court went as far to say that 'authorities have the obligation to take all *necessary* measures' (*Iosub Caras v Romania* (App no 7198/04) (2008) 47 EHRR 35, para 34 (emphasis added)). Conversely, see the earlier case of *Monory* where the authorities were required to take 'all provisional measures' (*Monory v Romania and Hungary* (App no 71099/01) (2005) 41 EHRR 77, para 79). See also L Walker, 'The Impact of the Hague Abduction Convention on the Rights of the Family in the Case-Law of the European Court of Human Rights and the UN Human Rights Committee: The Danger of *Neulinger*' (2010) 6 *Journal of Private International Law* 649, 659–60, and ch 10 below.

[28] Borrás and Degeling Report (n 4) para 121.

[29] See ch 10 s IV below. However, under EU law Member States should not alter or dilute the requirements of a Regulation. (For example see, *Commission of the European Communities v Italian Republic* [1973] ECR 00101.) If Central Authorities are not provided with sufficient powers and resources to fulfil their duties the effect of the Regulation will be diluted and States could be liable under EU law.

[30] See for example, *Maire v Portugal* (App no 48206/99) (2006) 43 EHRR 13, where the power given to the enforcement officers in the warrant was nowhere near sufficient to ensure the return of the child. For a summary see Walker (n 27) 654–56. See also, P Beaumont, 'The Jurisprudence of the European Court of Human Rights and the European Court of Justice on the Hague Convention on International Child Abduction' (2008) 335 *Recueil des Cours* 9 at 27–47. For a general report on enforcement under the 1980 Convention see N Lowe, 'A Statistical Analysis of Applications Made in 2008 under the Hague Convention of 25 October 1980 on the Civil Aspects of International Child Abduction', available at www.hcch.net/upload/wop/abduct2011pd08c.pdf, accessed 9 June 2014.

The duties of Central Authorities that are relevant to the aim of achieving enforcement of decisions will now be examined. The term 'facilitate' is used in each of the relevant provisions. This is used to show that even if the Central Authority cannot actually perform the function, they take whatever steps are necessary to assist with enforcement, usually by requesting another body to perform the task.[31]

## A. The Ongoing Enforcement of Maintenance Obligations

Central Authorities are responsible for facilitating 'the ongoing enforcement of maintenance decisions including any arrears'.[32] This is a general obligation on Central Authorities to take sufficient steps in order to guarantee that regular maintenance payments are actually made to creditors. In order to do this Central Authorities should 'ensure that the initial methods to collect payments or to enforce the maintenance decision will be effective.'[33] This would suggest that Central Authorities are expected to monitor the body that has been charged with the actual enforcement until they are sure that the obligation has been discharged. This would also imply that if the enforcement measures are not working the Authority should be well placed to suggest other suitable enforcement measures. The Borrás and Degeling Report merely states that '[s]ome effective enforcement measures are listed in Article 34.'[34] The only implication that can be taken from this is that Central Authorities should have at least some of the options listed in Article 34 available to them as a minimum. However, even though the Convention attempts to ensure enforcement by placing important duties on Central Authorities, these authorities are only capable of fulfilling these duties to the extent that the powers designated to them by State bodies allow.

It is envisaged that this provision will be used primarily in 'cases of repeat "defaulters".'[35] Where there is a problem case Central Authorities should be aware of this and closely monitor the situation. Steps the Central Authority could take in such a situation are: to provide the creditor with advice and assistance; or in cases where the problem is persistent, remove the debtor's chance to pay voluntarily by instituting wage withholding, where this option is available. Once again the ability of the Central Authority to discharge their duty is dependent on the powers accorded to it under national law. However, the Central Authority has a duty to help actual enforcement to happen by making use of the Convention and EU law principles of 'equivalence' and effectiveness'.[36]

[31] Not only are Central Authorities required to cooperate with each other but also the other relevant bodies in their States (see ch 10 s III below).

[32] Art 6(2)(e) of the Convention and Art 51(2)(e) of the Regulation.

[33] Borrás and Degeling Report (n 4) para 155.

[34] Ibid, para 155.

[35] Ibid, para 156.

[36] See P Craig and G de Búrca, *EU Law Text, Cases and Materials*, 5th edn (Oxford, Oxford University Press, 2011) 223–41 for a discussion of the principles.

There was some discussion of this provision during the negotiations to the Convention. The earlier draft also referred to the monitoring of decisions, 'to facilitate the ongoing enforcement of maintenance decisions, including the monitoring of payments'.[37] However, by the time the next draft was produced around seven months later, the provision was the same as the one that made it into the final Convention.[38] The term 'monitoring' was removed because 'it implied to some experts an impossible burden on Central Authorities to monitor and review every case, whether or not enforcement problems arose.'[39] Although the term monitoring may be too strong, Central Authorities will need to be aware of what is going on in cases where ongoing payments are made. They cannot efficiently facilitate the ongoing enforcement of maintenance if they do not have some awareness of when the payments should be made and if they are being made. Therefore they will effectively have to monitor individual situations to some extent. They should have access to a suitable database which could assist with this.[40] Further, creditors should be informed that if they are having problems receiving payments, they should contact the Central Authority again, as the Central Authority should assist with this.

## B. Collect and Transfer Payments

Central Authorities are expected to 'facilitate the collection and expeditious transfer of maintenance payments'.[41] There will also have to be some kind of monitoring of individual cases by Central Authorities to ensure that the payments are

[37] See, Preliminary Document no 13 of January 2005—Working draft of a Convention on the international recovery of child support and other forms of family maintenance, Art 6(1)(e), available at www.hcch.net/index_en.php?act=publications.details&pid=4119&dtid=35, accessed 9 June 2014.

[38] See, Preliminary Document no 16 of September 2005, Tentative draft on the international recovery of child support and other forms of family maintenance, Art 6(2)(e), available at www.hcch.net/index_en.php?act=publications.details&pid=4122&dtid=35, accessed 9 June 2014.

[39] Borrás and Degeling Report (n 4) para 157. However, the effective monitoring or awareness of applications appears to be a fundamental part of the Central Authority's role. The need to have some awareness at least in order to meet the designated time requirements and check that the payments continue to be made (see below at s VI and ch 10 s XV B). Other researchers' 'discussions with Central Authorities reveal a reluctance to burden Central Authorities with case management tasks. In many countries, eg. Sweden, Denmark and England and Wales, the payment occurs completely outside the oversight of the Central Authority.' I Curry-Sumner, 'Administrative Co-Operation and Free Legal Aid in International Child Maintenance Recovery: What is the Added Value of the Regulation? (2010) 3 *Nederlands Internationaal Privaatrecht* 611, s 3.3.3(d)). Even where the payment takes place outside the Central Authority they need to be aware what the situation is.

[40] For example in the Borrás and Degeling Report (n 4) it is recognised that 'some countries have computerised systems which allowed faster, more efficient review of case records. Where maintenance payments are being collected and distributed by a public authority, any occurrences of non-payment will be apparent immediately through a computerised system' (para 159). If all Contracting States had effective systems then this would make it much simpler for Central Authorities to discharge their duties in relation to enforcement. It would also mean that any actual monitoring would be kept to a minimum as effectively it would be the system that would be monitoring whether the payments were made. See below at s VI.

[41] Art 6(2)(f) of the Convention and Art 51(2)(f) of the Regulation.

being collected effectively and, where they are not, that they take suitable steps to facilitate this. For example, they may think there are effective measures in place but unless they check that the payments have actually been made then they cannot say that they have facilitated the collection and expeditious transfer of an obligation. It is suggested that the provision is 'intended to address existing problems of inefficient methods of collecting and transmitting payments by debtors.'[42] The report considers that inefficiencies that may arise could be bank charges and currency conversion fees. However, the wording of the provision does not really clarify this. Instead it seems to be a much more general provision designed to ensure funds are collected, and that Central Authorities are aware of whether they are collected expeditiously. It is Article 35 that focuses on the fact that any payments should be made efficiently and cost effectively.[43]

### C. Provisional Measures

Finally, Central Authorities are expected 'to initiate or facilitate the institution of proceedings to obtain any necessary provisional measures that are territorial in nature and the purpose of which is to secure the outcome of a pending maintenance application'.[44] Although these provisional measures will be taken before the actual enforcement stage, they can assist with actual enforcement. Measures that would be important to ensure the enforcement of any obligations arising are measures to prevent the dissipation of assets, including the freezing of the debtor's assets.[45] If the assets are already frozen, the authorities already have a hold over them so then it could be easier to force the debtor to pay when the obligation is meant to be discharged. This shows how this provision can assist with actual enforcement.

## IV. Enforcement in Europe

### A. The Procedure

Unlike the provisions on Central Authorities that are almost identical, the provisions in the Regulation on actual enforcement are less detailed than the provisions in the Convention. They simply state that enforcement should be governed by the

[42] Borrás and Degeling Report (n 4) para 160.

[43] See Art 35 of the Convention. There does not appear to be an equivalent provision in the Regulation.

[44] Art 6(2)(i) of the Convention and Art 51(2)(i) of the Regulation.

[45] This is discussed below at ch 10 s XIII.

national law of the State. It does not give a list of potential methods for enforcement like the Convention.

1. Subject to the provisions of this Regulation, the procedure for the enforcement of decisions given in another Member State shall be governed by the law of the Member State of enforcement. A decision given in the Member State of enforcement shall be enforced there under the same conditions as a decision given in that Member State of enforcement.
2. The party seeking the enforcement of a decision given in another Member State shall not be required to have a postal address or an authorised representative in the Member State of enforcement, without prejudice to persons with competence in matters relating to enforcement proceedings.[46]

It is disappointing that the provisions in the Regulation are not as detailed as those in the Convention. In one respect the provisions are less detailed due to the abolition of *exequatur*. This means there was no need for an equivalent provision to the one in Article 33(2), because the majority of decisions do not need to be declared enforceable, so the procedure should be automatic anyway.[47] However, in relation to decisions from States not bound by the Hague Protocol the Regulation simply states:

> A decision given in a Member State not bound by the 2007 Hague Protocol and enforceable in that State shall be enforceable in another Member State when, on the application of any interested party, it has been declared enforceable there.[48]

This is not as transparent as Article 33(2) of the Convention which clearly states that once there is a declaration of enforceability there should be enforcement without the need for the applicant to make any further applications. Article 26 of the Regulation simply states that it will be enforceable but is ambiguous in clarifying any procedural requirements. Since the EU sought to simplify the recognition and enforcement procedure, and achieved it, to the extent that it is virtually non-existent,[49] it seems peculiar that the provisions on actual enforcement then fall short of those in the Convention.[50] It was perhaps considered that because the provisions on recognition and enforcement were so advanced enforcement would be virtually automatic. However, just because these provisions exist they will probably not assist with the actual enforcement stage.[51] This is because delays at

[46] Art 41 of the Maintenance Regulation.

[47] See ch 7 above.

[48] Art 26 of the Maintenance Regulation.

[49] See ch 2 s V and ch 7 ss IV and VI above. However, in reality the removal of this procedure has meant that irreconcilable judgments can now be reviewed at the enforcement stage, which could also add to the delays. Article 21 also covers prescription and limitation, and the provision correctly focuses on the procedure with the longer period. Even though this means there is partial regulation at the enforcement stage, these provisions exist to prevent enforcement rather than to assist with the enforcement of cross border decisions.

[50] See the thoughts of the Commission at ch 2 nn 105–106 above.

[51] Lack of effective enforcement mechanisms may also mean that in the case of defaulting debtors, the money will then have to be paid by the State. See Case C-85/99 *Vincent Offermans and Esther Offermanns* [2001] ECR I-02261, where the State was required to make advance maintenance payments

the recognition and enforcement stage and delays at the actual enforcement stage are not necessarily interlinked. Therefore the existence of detailed and hopefully efficient provisions at the recognition and enforcement stage only, will not necessarily ensure a prompt procedure through the entire process and a more cohesive approach is required.

Had the Regulation contained a list of possible enforcement measures, similar to those in the Convention, this would have provided a starting point for Member States to work with. Recital 30 of the Regulation refers to enforcement but does not consider mechanisms specifically. It suggests that enforcement should be quick and that States should not allow additional obstacles to hinder enforcement.

> In order to speed up the enforcement in another Member State of a decision given in a Member State bound by the 2007 Hague Protocol it is necessary to limit the grounds of refusal or of suspension of enforcement which may be invoked by the debtor on account of the cross-border nature of the maintenance claim. This limitation should not affect the grounds of refusal or of suspension laid down in national law which are not incompatible with those listed in this Regulation, such as the debtor's discharge of his debt at the time of enforcement or the unattachable nature of certain assets.[52]

It is beneficial that this recital takes these issues into account, but it would have been better if enforcement mechanisms had also been considered. Member States have used different enforcement mechanisms in the past that have been effective. For example, the Belgian authorities have taken deductions from salaries as an interim measure in relation to maintenance payments.[53]

The Regulation requires that information is made available to the public on the measures taken to meet the obligations in Article 51. It also requires that a description of the national enforcement rules and procedures, including any limitations on enforcement, is made available.[54] However, information on the enforcement of judgments in the EU, in general terms, is more detailed in some Member States than others.[55] The information contained on the civil justice

for the children because the father had defaulted. 'The advances in question are not simply intended to speed up the procedure for enforcing maintenance obligations but are also intended to relieve the financial burden borne by the parent awarded custody of the children' (para 45). See also, Case C-363/08 *Romana Slanina v Unabhängiger Finanzsenat, Außenstelle Wien* [2009] ECR I-11111. Therefore in many cases where States do not secure the enforcement of maintenance obligations they will have to bear the burden of the costs themselves. However the Court has also ruled that where a public body has paid maintenance where the spouse has not, the public body can then recover that money under the Brussels Convention, because this would fall within the meaning of a civil matter in Art 1 (Case C-271/00 *Gemeente Steenbergen* and *Luc Baten* [2002] ECR I-10508, para 37). This is confirmed in the new Regulation where public bodies are included in the term 'creditor' whether they are acting in place of the creditor or seeking reimbursement of money they have paid (Art 64). However, it is likely that more costs will be incurred, where this route is taken instead of direct enforcement, especially if reimbursement cases are appealed and procedures will take longer as an extra party is involved.

52 Recital 30 of the Maintenance Regulation.

53 Case C-323/06 P *Theodores Kallianos v Commission of the European Communities*, 20 March 2007.

54 See Maintenance Regulation Art 70(b) and (d).

55 See http://ec.europa.eu/civiljustice/enforce_judgement/enforce_judgement_ec_en.htm, accessed 9 June 2014.

website on maintenance, in general, is outdated and does not cover the new Regulation. Therefore there is no up to date information on how the duties in Article 51 will be fulfilled.[56] The information contained on the judicial atlas is slightly better as there is a page for the new Maintenance Regulation.[57] However, although information on the contact details of Central Authorities is provided; there is still no information on how the duties in Article 51 will be fulfilled,[58] or on enforcement procedures.

It could be argued that there is no need for any provisions on enforcement in the Regulation due to the EU principles of equivalence and effectiveness. These provisos arise from the principle of 'sincere cooperation', and are underpinned by Article 4(3) of the Treaty on European Union (TEU).[59] The overarching proposition is that States must take measures to ensure their obligations under the Treaties or any other legislation are fulfilled.

> The Member State shall take any appropriate measure, general or particular, to ensure fulfillment of the obligations arising out of the Treaties or resulting from the acts of the institutions of the Union. The Member State shall facilitate the achievement of the Union's tasks and refrain from any measure which could jeopardise the attainment of the Union's objectives.[60]

It is clear that Member States must fulfil duties that arise out of EU law instruments which would include the enforcement of decisions under EU Regulations. However, the Court of Justice of the European Union (CJEU) has shifted its emphasis from a firm requirement to ensure the effectiveness of EU law regardless of national procedural law, such as in *Factortame*,[61] to a more cautious approach which now requires a 'context-specific balancing approach'.[62] This requires national courts to weigh the importance of the EU right against the scope and purpose of any conflicting rule of national law. However, it is clear from the reasoning in *Weber*, that the national rule considered must not preclude the exercise of EU law entirely. 'The principle of effectiveness precludes national legislation or a *national administrative practice* which makes the exercise of the rights conferred by the Community

[56] See http://ec.europa.eu/civiljustice/maintenance_claim/maintenance_claim_ec_en.htm, accessed 9 June 2014. At this point the main page was last updated in February 2008. The individual country pages are also of no help as these were all last updated between 2004 and 2007. The judicial atlas is not helpful in this area either. It provides information on appeals available and the languages that should be used in Member States but at this stage there is no information on national laws and procedures, which should include information on enforcement laws eventually (http://ec.europa.eu/justice_home/judicialatlascivil/html/mo_communications_it_en.htm, accessed 9 June 2014).

[57] http://ec.europa.eu/justice_home/judicialatlascivil/html/mo_information_en.htm, accessed 9 June 2014.

[58] For example, http://ec.europa.eu/justice_home/judicialatlascivil/html/mo_centralauthorities_uk_en.htm, accessed 9 June 2014.

[59] See Craig and de Burca (n 36) 223–41 for a discussion of the principles.

[60] TEU Art 4(3).

[61] C-213/89 *R v Secretary of State for Transport, ex parte Factortame Ltd and Others* [1990] ECR I-2433.

[62] Craig and de Búrca (n 36) 239 and see 231–37.

legal order *impossible* in practice or *excessively difficult*.'[63] Although these principles exist and they can assist with the cross border enforcement of maintenance orders, it is not clear to what extent they will really help with this stage especially where national maintenance orders are not necessarily enforced.[64] The Commission was clear in its proposal that they thought enforcement methods should be improved, but this was not dealt with in the final text of the Regulation.[65] It is impossible to 'eliminate all obstacles' to the recovery of maintenance without setting out requirements in this area. Therefore the introduction of time limits for enforcement would create minimum standards, which would set a goal post in order to measure the principles of 'equivalence and effectiveness' against.

There is also the benefit of additional Regulations that may help with the enforcement of orders made under the Maintenance Regulation. The main instrument that may assist with enforcement is the European Enforcement Order (EEO).[66] The EEO applies to uncontested claims. It lays down minimum standards in which judgments, court settlements and authentic instruments that are uncontested can circulate freely. There are no immediate grounds for refusal of enforcement.[67] So where the maintenance claim is uncontested the judgment may then circulate under the EEO rather than the Regulation. It is stated that the system is possible because of mutual trust.[68]

> *Mutual trust in the administration of justice* in the Member States justifies the assessment by the court of one Member State that all conditions for certification as a European Enforcement Order are fulfilled to enable a judgment to be enforced in all other Member States without judicial review of the proper application of the minimum procedural standards in the Member State where the judgment is to be enforced.[69]

The Regulation lays down minimum standards that have to be met in the State of origin in order for the judgment to be certified there.[70] However, it does not list specific measures for enforcement and again assumes that the enforcement order will just be enforced under national law.

> Without prejudice to the provisions of this Chapter, the enforcement procedures shall be governed by the law of the Member State of enforcement. A judgment certified as a

[63] *Weber's Wine World Handels-GmbH and Others v Abgabenberufungskommission Wien* [2003] ECR I-11365, 11418 (emphasis added). See, ch 10 s XV, B below and the administrative practice in Belgium which makes it excessively difficult for that authority to meet the time requirement in Art 58(3).

[64] See ch 1 s V above.

[65] See ch 2 s V above. At the time of the study not many orders had been enforced highlighting that more should and could have been done in this area (see s IV B) without regulating enforcement completely.

[66] Regulation (EC) 805/2004 of 21 April 2004 of the European Parliament and of the Council creating a European enforcement order for uncontested claims [2004] OJ L143/15 (EEO).

[67] See ch 7.

[68] However, many are sceptical when it comes to 'mutual trust', especially in terms of what it can achieve, whether previous interpretations of it are correct and whether this principle alone is sufficient to justify the abolition of *exequatur* (see ch 7 s V above).

[69] Recital 18 of the EEO (emphasis added) and ibid.

[70] See Arts 12–19 of the EEO.

> European Enforcement Order shall be enforced under the same conditions as a judgment handed down in the Member State of enforcement.[71]

This is virtually identical to the first paragraph of Article 41 of the Maintenance Regulation. Both instruments aim to ensure quicker and more effective enforcement by removing the *exequatur* procedure, but this may not be sufficient because there are also problems with the actual enforcement procedure. Therefore, it would have been more effective if the instruments had actively tried to deal with actual enforcement in a more robust way, by setting time requirements or listing possible enforcement mechanisms like in the Maintenance Convention.[72]

A decision of the Cour de Cassation involving an EEO illustrates that just because there is no longer a procedure for recognition and enforcement, actual enforcement is in no way automatic. The Cour de Cassation gave a ruling under the EEO, in a case that involved a maintenance claim.[73] In the case the husband was paying maintenance to his ex-wife. In 2005 the wife argued that he was not paying her enough maintenance. In October 2005 a Stuttgart Court issued a judgment ordering payment of one million Euros. In January 2006 the Court certified the earlier judgment as an EEO. A bank account and a house located in France were also attached to the EEO at a later date. The husband then challenged the EEO. He managed to get the order set aside in Germany and he obtained a stay of proceedings in France. Following this the husband petitioned in the French enforcement Court for all enforcement measures to be lifted. The wife argued that this could not be done as she had a valid EEO certificate.

The Cour de Cassation had to decide whether the EEO certificate could stand autonomously on its own, or if the certificate was only there to facilitate the circulation of judgments and once the judgment disappears the EEO cannot stand anymore. The Cour de Cassation took account of Article 11 of the EC Regulation. This states that the 'European Enforcement Order certificate shall take effect only within the limits of the enforceability of the judgment.'[74] Therefore the Court found that the certificate could not be used as an enforcement mechanism in France after the German Court had ruled that the certified judgment was no longer enforceable. Any existing enforcement measures had to be lifted.[75] Based on the text of the Regulation, logic and the proper administration of justice, this would appear to be the sensible approach. Even though the EEO was created to assist with the free movement of judgments in the EU, it is not sensible to use

[71] Art 20 of the Maintenance Regulation.

[72] See L Walker, 'From Brussels I and the Maintenance Convention to the Maintenance Regulation: Is the Resulting Maintenance Regulation Consistent with the Other EU PIL Instruments?' (2013) *Nederlands Internationaal Privaatrecht* 167, s 2.3.

[73] January 6 2012, www.legifrance.gouv.fr/affichJuriJudi.do?oldAction=rechJuriJudi&idTexte=JURITEXT000025119488&fastReqId=443704565&fastPos=2, accessed 9 June 2014.

[74] Art 11 of the EEO.

[75] See G Cuniberti, 'French Supreme Court Rules on European Enforcement Order' at http://conflictoflaws.net/2012/french-supreme-court-rules-on-european-enforcement-order/, accessed 9 June 2014.

a certificate to enforce a judgment that is no longer enforceable in the State of origin. The issue is not the outcome of the judgment but the length of the procedure. The certificate was issued in January 2006. A final decision setting aside the original judgment was given in Germany in 2008, and the final decision in France was not given until January 2012. This was a difficult case where it appears that the judgment was originally uncontested because the husband was not aware of it. However it highlights that the enforcement of the certificate before the husband became aware of the situation was not quick or automatic. In fact 11 months passed between when the certificate was first issued until the house in France was attached and it was not until after this that the husband became aware of the situation. Therefore even with the abolition of *exequatur* there will still be delays in the process at the enforcement stage.

There has been a study on the efficiency of enforcement within the European Union.[76] The most important aspects of the study in respect of maintenance are those on the transparency of the debtor's assets and the attachment of bank accounts. The study recognises that enforcement is necessary for the free movement of judgments around the EU. Where there are problems getting information on the debtor, or where the creditor does not have sufficient knowledge of their chances of recovering the debt, 'the free movement of judgments within Europe is seriously impaired [if] creditors don't enforce their claims in other member States, but write them off.'[77] When the report was written bodies had been arguing that there was a need to improve the opportunities for creditors to obtain information about debtors and that cross border garnishment proceedings also needed to be improved.[78] The system in the Maintenance Regulation places the responsibility to gain all the necessary information upon the Central Authority, so that the creditor is not prevented from claiming maintenance due to a lack of information.[79] The Maintenance Regulation does little to resolve problems with garnishment however, as it leaves enforcement mechanisms entirely to national law.

One of the two additional instruments that can also be of help in these areas, is the Taking of Evidence Regulation.[80] The Evidence Regulation can be relied upon for obtaining information on the whereabouts of debtors' assets. The Central Authority can resort to this in cases where it is having difficulty obtaining this information.[81] This creates a system whereby it can make an application to the

[76] Study no JAI/A3/2002/02 on making more efficient the enforcement of judicial decisions within the European Union: Transparency of a Debtor's Assets, Attachment of Bank Accounts and Provisional Enforcement and Protective Measures, Version of 18/2/2004 (Efficiency of enforcement study).

[77] Ibid, 15.

[78] Ibid.

[79] Maintenance Regulation Art 51(2)(b) and (c). See ch 10 below. See also pp 24–28 of the Efficiency of Enforcement Study (n 76) where in the past creditors sometimes had to locate debtors themselves.

[80] Council Regulation (EC) 1206/2001 of May 2001 on cooperation between the courts of the Member States in taking of evidence in civil or commercial matters [2001] OJ L 174/1 (Evidence Regulation).

[81] See Art 51(2)(c) of the Maintenance Regulation, Art 6(2)(c) of the Convention, and ch 10 below.

court to obtain the necessary information. The other Regulation that can be of assistance is the Service Regulation.[82] It enables national bodies to serve documents to those residing in another State. This can be used in relation to monetary claims where a garnishment order is served to a garnishee. This is extremely important since in 'all Member States, garnishment of a bank account and of salaries has become the most important type of enforcement proceeding.'[83] There is more and more need for this as all banking becomes electronic. If there were no provisional measures that allowed for the immediate attachment of bank accounts this would mean that debtors could easily move their funds and try to hide them elsewhere.

However, electronic banking is also positive as it means payments to creditors can be processed much quicker. For countries that have advanced systems such as the Netherlands, they can process up to 4000 payments a day.[84] The Netherlands have been processing payments cheques free for 20 years and, it has been reported, therefore have advanced and efficient systems for processing payments. Norway also has a very advanced and effective system for recovering maintenance and processing cases.[85]

## B. Practice So Far

In the first year of operation of the Regulation very few applications made under the Regulation were enforced. Based on the information provided by the relevant States it was reported that 183 applications (4.4 per cent) had been fully processed within six months. Once the first maintenance payment had been discharged then an application would be fully processed because enforcement had begun. Alternatively an application is fully processed if maintenance is denied. It is unclear whether this was understood by all the Central Authorities that responded to the questionnaire. It is clear that this was understood by England and Wales, which queried what was meant by this

[82] Regulation (EC) No 1393/2007 of the European Parliament and of the Council of 13 November 2007 on the service in the Member States of judicial and extrajudicial documents in civil or commercial matters (service of documents), and repealing Council Regulation (EC) No 1348/2000 [2007] OJ L324/79 (Service Regulation).

[83] Study No JAI/A3/2002/02 General Report, 18, available at http://ec.europa.eu/civiljustice/publications/docs/enforcement_judicial_decisions_180204_en.pdf, accessed 9 June 2014.

[84] This was explained by Phillipe Lortie at the meeting of the partners of the Heidelberg project in The Hague in May 2012. Leo De Bakker from the Netherlands Central Authority, LBIO (National Office for the Collection of Maintenance Payments) gave a presentation on IT solutions at the Heidelberg Conference in March 2013. However, because the Netherlands Central Authority did not answer the questionnaire and only provided information on the total number of incoming cases (which included data on non EU States such as the USA and Brazil) judgment is reserved on how effective this system actually is.

[85] Norway operates under an administrative system which appears to be very efficient, although it did report that it has a relatively small population and therefore fewer cases to deal with. See J Saue et al, 'Administrative Establishment and Enforcement of Child Support in Norway' in P Beaumont et al (eds), *The Recovery of Maintenance in the EU and Worldwide* (Oxford, Hart Publishing, 2014) 161.

term a number of times. The requested States that reported that they had managed to fully process applications within six months are: Estonia (81), Finland (2), Greece (51), Latvia (4), Portugal (17), Slovenia (2), England and Wales (26).[86] The overall feedback suggests that it is possible to process applications relatively quickly under the new system, but this was not happening very often in the first year. It is hoped that the process speeds up once Central Authorities and States become used to the new system.

When looking at the number of cases that were fully processed in nine months not much progress was made on the numbers processed in six months. After nine months 226 (5.4 per cent) of the applications had been fully processed, only an increase of one per cent despite States having an extra three months to complete the applications.[87] One of the reasons for this could be that not many applications had actually been pending for nine months at the time the questionnaires were returned.[88] Therefore it would be very useful to repeat this study at a later date to determine how long applications are taking to process. Such a study could also ask how many applications were processed in a year and determine the amount of applications that it took over a year to process. When the Regulation is functioning effectively, and applications are being processed efficiently, then the majority of applications should be processed in under a year. This is especially true for child support applications which should usually be uncontested.

In addition to information on how long it takes to process applications, the questionnaire also sought to find out how much money had been recovered from requested States in respect of maintenance obligations. Not many Central Authorities answered this part of the questionnaire. The information provided under question 5 is listed below. This includes basic information on the amount of money recovered from the requested State as well as additional information where this was provided.

— Hungary recovered 409 Euros from Germany
— Latvia recovered 5480.18 LVL from Germany
— Latvia also recovers 360 LVL per month from Germany
— Latvia recovers 85 LVL per month from England and Wales
— Northern Ireland 45 Euro per week from Ireland (paid directly to applicant)
— Czech Republic 345,705 CZK from Germany (8.6 per cent of total amount)
— Czech Republic 80,879 CZK from Ireland (12.5 per cent of total amount)
— Czech Republic 12.606 CZK from Netherlands (21 per cent of total amount)
— Czech Republic 42,423 CZK from Slovakia (1.9 per cent of total amount)

[86] A full table containing all the results provided and percentages can be found in Annex VII. Unfortunately it is believed that the data provided by Estonia and Greece, might include data on requests for specific measures and not just full applications.

[87] Estonia processed one more case, Portugal three more and England and Wales 39 more (see table two in Annex VII for full results).

[88] For example the Irish Central Authority reported that it had received no applications for the first six months, therefore it would be very unlikely that the Central Authority had had any applications pending for nine months given the time period of the questionnaire.

— Czech Republic 20,000 CZK from Spain (2.3 per cent of total amount)
— Czech Republic 92,625 CZK from Sweden (18.7 per cent of total amount)
— Czech Republic 21,571 CZK from England and Wales (0.9 per cent of total amount)
— Portugal 50,000 Euros from Netherlands
— Sweden 3,484 SEK from Germany (55.2 per cent of total amount)
— Sweden 19,994 SEK from Poland (7.8 per cent of total amount).

Belgium reported that it cannot produce such data since the Belgian Central Authority does not centralise any payment.[89] Overall the limited data collected on enforcement shows that the new system is viable. However, it indicates that there is still a long way to go and it will take time before the Regulation is operating efficiently in each of the Member States.

## V. Case Law of the ECtHR on Enforcement

In the past the decisions of the European Court of Human Rights (ECtHR) have also been helpful in relation to the enforcement of cross border orders. Where State bodies have failed to take sufficient steps to ensure the enforcement of cross border orders, then the Court has held that the State has been in violation of the Convention. This can be seen in respect of maintenance orders as well as the non-enforcement of return orders under the Hague Convention of 25 October 1980 on the civil aspects of Child Abduction (Child Abduction Convention).

In *Romańczyk v France* the Court had to consider whether the French authorities had violated Article 6(1) of the European Convention on Human Rights (ECHR) by failing to execute a Polish maintenance decision under the 1956 New York Convention.[90] The order for maintenance (*pension alimentaire*) was awarded by the Polish courts when they granted divorce, in June 1999.[91] The award required the debtor to make monthly payments of 118 Euros,[92] which were payable as child support for the two children of the marriage. The debtor lived in France so the order had to be circulated under the 1956 New York Convention.[93] In December 1999 the Polish authorities contacted the French authorities, under the New York Convention, for the enforcement of the obligation in France. The French authorities responded in July 2000 with a letter that requested further information and documentation. In September 2003 the Polish authorities altered the award and increased the obligation to 127 Euros per month. This order

[89] Email correspondence 27 November 2012.
[90] *Romańczyk* (n 11).
[91] Ibid, para 7.
[92] Ibid.
[93] Poland did not join the EU until 2004, so the EU regime under the Brussels Convention was not applicable.

became effective in April 2004 and the French authorities were notified of this in May 2004.[94] The French authorities demanded the payment of the obligation in August 2004 and sought an execution of the order from the competent tribunal, but the debtor refused to pay.[95]

In September 2004 the French authorities indicated that the father had begun paying 108 Euros per month from 15 August 2004. The Polish authorities reviewed the situation in January 2005, and subsequently informed the French authorities that the maintenance had not been paid. The Polish authorities continued to contact the French authorities but received no response. In December 2008 the French authorities began to revive their attempts to recover the maintenance and demanded information on the situation of the debtor.[96] In April 2009 the debtor contended that he did not have sufficient means to pay the maintenance order. In June 2009 the French authorities informed the Polish authorities of the situation. The Polish authorities considered that the father had a duty to support his children and he had behaved in an irresponsible manner. Subsequently they demanded the enforcement of the order made in September 2003.[97] It was not until February 2010, that proceedings for the execution of the Polish judgment of 2003 began in the French courts.[98]

The European Court considered that the execution of a judgment by the authorities is an integral part of the process in the sense of Article 6 ECHR.[99] Therefore, where there is a requirement to obtain a definitive or final decision then the authorities should assist with this. In the case the French Court failed to assist with the recovery of maintenance and the execution of the decision.[100] The purpose of the New York Convention is to 'facilitate the recovery of maintenance'.[101] The Court noted that Article 6 of the New York Convention requires agencies to take the steps necessary to execute the judgment.[102] The 'agency shall take all "appropriate steps" for the recovery of maintenance and where *necessary* the institution and prosecution of an action for maintenance and the execution of any order or judicial act for the payment of maintenance.'[103] The Court noted that this obligation is not solely for the creditor or the Government in her State, but equally for the State bodies in the State of the debtor.[104] Therefore, each State was responsible for assisting the creditor to recover the maintenance by taking expedient appropriate measures.[105]

94 *Romańczyk* (n 11) paras 9–13.
95 Ibid, para 14.
96 Ibid, paras 16–30.
97 Ibid, paras 31–33.
98 Ibid, para 37.
99 Ibid, para 53.
100 Ibid, para 56.
101 Article 1 of the New York Convention.
102 *Romańczyk* (n 11) para 58.
103 Art 6 of the New York Convention, emphasis added.
104 *Romańczyk* (n 11) para 58.
105 Ibid, para 59.

The Court considered that in the circumstances the French authorities did not deploy sufficient effort to assist with the execution of the judgment and therefore there had been a violation of Article 6(1) of the Convention.[106]

In order for ECHR Contracting States to comply with the Convention they must take positive steps to assist applicants with both the execution of the decision and the final enforcement of the order. They do not have to take steps to block the enforcement, any lack of appropriate action will be sufficient for the State to be liable under the ECHR. In the present case the French authority's lack of action was enough to violate the applicants' rights under Article 6(1). The decision is welcome. Like the 1956 Convention the main objective of the Maintenance Convention is to 'ensure the effective international recovery of child support'.[107] Without the actual enforcement of the orders the objectives cannot be achieved and therefore the proper administration of justice cannot be ensured. There is little point having orders that can circulate freely and easily but never actually get enforced. Therefore, it is important that the ECtHR continues to be supportive of the efficient enforcement of cross border decisions and continues to hold States liable where they hinder enforcement whether this is because of their positive or negative actions.[108]

Similar dicta can be seen in the Court's case law on non-enforcement of orders made under the Abduction Convention. However, in this area the Court has found a violation of Article 8 respect for family life, rather than Article 6. The first case where the Court dealt with this is in *Ignaccolo Zenide v Romania*.[109] The Court considered that States have an obligation to take 'positive measures'[110] to ensure the enforcement of orders. In doing this States must take necessary adequate steps, and the adequacy of these steps will be judged by the swiftness of their implementation.[111] The Court concluded that the Romanian authorities had 'failed to make adequate and effective efforts to enforce'[112] the order and Romania was therefore liable under the Convention. This line of reasoning was followed

[106] Ibid, para 66. The same approach was taken by the Court in *K v Italy* (App no 38805/97) (2006) 43 EHRR 50, where the Italian authorities failed to enforce a maintenance order from Poland under the New York Convention.

[107] Art 1 of the 2007 Convention.

[108] See also, JK Škerl, 'European Public Policy (with an emphasis on *exequatur* proceedings) (2011) 7 *Journal of Private International Law* 461, 476. The ECtHR 'reiterated its conception of the enforcement being part of the judicial procedures and the obligation of contracting states to ensure the enforcement of judicial decisions, without regard to the country in which these decisions were issued.'

[109] *Ignaccolo Zenide v Romania* (App no 31679/96) ECHR 2000. For a full analysis of the case see A Schulz, 'The 1980 Hague Child Abduction Convention and the European Convention on Human Rights' (2002) 12 *Transnational Law and Contemporary Problems* 355, Beaumont (n 30) 28–31 and Walker (n 27) 651–52.

[110] *Ignaccolo Zenide v Romania* (App no 31679/96) (2001) 31 EHRR 7, para 94.

[111] Ibid, para 102.

[112] Ibid, para 113.

in subsequent cases.[113] The latest case on this issue is *Shaw v Hungary*.[114] In the case a return order was made in November 2008, but the order was not enforced. The Court held that the Hungarian authorities had violated the applicant's right to respect for family life under Article 8 of the Convention. In reaching its decision the Court considered that its case law on enforcement requires that 'the national authorities have taken all necessary steps to facilitate the execution as can reasonabl[y] be demanded in the special circumstances of each case'.[115]

The purpose of the new instruments is to secure the enforcement of cross border maintenance obligations. All of the Central Authorities' duties in the Maintenance Regulation and the Convention are ultimately designed to ensure the enforcement of maintenance decisions.[116] Each duty is a step in the process although not all will be necessary in each case. Therefore, following the dicta in *Romańczyk* (and the relevant case law on enforcement in the Abduction Convention) where State bodies are hindering the final enforcement of a maintenance obligation at any stage of the process, whether this is through positive or negative actions, then that State will potentially be liable for breaching its obligations under the ECHR.

## VI. Information Technology: iSupport

The importance of effective IT solutions cannot be emphasised enough, especially considering the expected high case loads under the new instruments. Information gained from the empirical study indicates some problems with the IT systems currently in place. It also highlighted that it would be preferable if all States used the same system to create coherence and common standards.[117] At present, each database holds different types of information, which was indicated by the fact that each Member State could answer different parts of the questionnaire. In this respect, the Spanish Central Authority reported in January 2013 that it still was not using an electronic database, despite the fact that the Regulation had been in force for a year and a half.[118]

[113] Examples are: *Sylvester v Austria* (App nos 36812/97 and 40104/98) (2003) 37 EHRR 17; *Morfis v France* (App no 10978/04) ECHR 12 April 2007; *Maire v Portugal* (App no 4826/99) (2006) 43 EHRR 13; *HN v Poland* (App no 77710/01) ECHR 13 September 2005; *Karadzic v Croatia* (App no 35030/04) (2005) 44 EHRR 896; *Bianchi v Switzerland* (App no 7548/04) ECHR 22 June 2006; and *PP v Poland* (App no 8677/03) ECHR 8 January 2008. See, Beaumont (n 30) 31–47 and Walker (n 27) 652–59.

[114] *Shaw v Hungary* (App no 6457/09) ECHR 26 July 2011.

[115] Ibid, para 65.

[116] See above at s III and ch 10 below.

[117] Data was also stored in different ways. So some databases store information on number of applications and others number of applicants (in particular Sweden). So in Sweden if you had two applications one involving one person and one involving three people, on that database it would be counted as four, but only counted as two applications on other databases.

[118] Email correspondence 29 January 2013. The delegates at this authority individually counted the applications in order to provide information on the total number of incoming cases. However, other

Even where databases did exist some errors were apparent. For example, in the questionnaire it would say that legal aid had been provided but there were no cases registered in the first column (number of applications) so it was unclear how legal aid could have been provided when there were no applications for that State. In one case one of these queries was followed up. It had been indicated by Sweden in the answer to question 5 that money had been recovered from Austria in respect of a maintenance obligation (2070SEK). However in question 4(b) no outgoing cases had been registered to Austria. The Central Authority was contacted in order to see where the problem lay. Three possible conclusions were considered.

1. The response to question 4 was wrong and the number of applications had been missed off by accident.
2. When the payment was made the database automatically deleted the file because the obligation had been discharged (this would not have been ideal and it would have been better if the file had just changed colour or moved to a different folder to indicate that it was no longer active).
3. The response to question 5 was wrong and there had been no applications sent to Austria.

The response received indicated the last option. There were in fact no applications sent to Austria so no money had been received. The Central Authority concluded that its 'system is definitely in need of a major checkup'.[119] Errors which suggest maintenance payments have been paid when they have not are a major cause for concern, even more so if they relate to a real application and the obligation has not actually been discharged. Therefore it would be preferable if all Central Authorities used one system that was designed specifically with the instruments in mind. Such a database would be able to store appropriate data and it could also be centrally managed so that any problems could be identified quickly and easily rectified in each State.[120]

delegates reported that even where they did have databases they did not store the information in the correct way so still every application had to be counted individually in order to answer some or all of the questionnaire (such as: Finland, Estonia, England and Wales and Ireland). It would be much easier if databases could generate statistics or highlight when the time period was up in respect of each application (see below at ch 10 s XV, B) to assist Central Authorities in monitoring applications, the progress they are making as a Central Authority and to help them to adequately and efficiently fulfil their duties.

[119] Email correspondence with the Swedish Central Authority, 5 December 2012.

[120] The partners of the Heidelberg project, in conclusion 3 of the Conclusions and Recommendations from the Conference, suggest that a 'coherent set of statistics, performance indicators, and analytic reports on the use of the Regulation in all Member States is essential to evaluate the implementation of the Regulation and to support improvements in its use. The use of a common IT system (see C and R 17 below) for keeping statistical data on the operation of Council Regulation 4/2009 (and the Hague Convention 2007) would be a great step forward in improving the enforcement of maintenance and the accountability of Central Authorities. A common IT system with the capability of analytical reporting could periodically assess future opportunities for programme improvement.' (Available at Annex VIII.)

The Hague Conference on Private International Law is working very hard to set up a system called iSupport which is designed to help with the effective application of the Convention when it is in force. At the moment there are insufficient funds to finalise the programme, and even when it is activated it will be up to Contracting States whether they choose to use this programme. However, if the objectives of the Convention are to be achieved Central Authorities should find it easier to operate efficiently if their State was using the iSupport programme. Key features of the iSupport system are that it can store all the necessary information in respect of each application, it can generate statistics and it can translate the necessary forms.[121]

This programme was developed because it was considered that the international recovery of maintenance requires

> the application of information technology for many reasons: the very large number of cases involved which is still increasing; maintenance cases often have a long life span (in some countries child support can last until the age of 25); maintenance cases are subject to a high number of transactions such as for example regular modifications (*i.e.* variations of the needs of the creditor and of the resources of the debtor) or regular transfer of funds; a high number of repetitive transactions take place which can be standardised; communications take place regardless of time zones; a vast amount of information has to be available in real time; and means of communications have to address language barriers.[122]

The need for an effective system is primarily in relation to child support cases, because Central Authorities need to assist with the ongoing enforcement of these obligations. As highlighted above child support cases last for many years (both instruments can cover obligations until the child is 21)[123] and they may need to be modified. Therefore an effective technical system and database will make it simpler, as changes to the payments can be updated and it will enable Central Authorities to keep track of payments and whether they are being discharged or not. This should make it easier for Central Authorities to ensure that the correct payments are being made on time, making the system more efficient. Any suitable system should be able to do this, however there are some benefits for all Contracting States making use of the iSupport system. Not only would it assist with the effective and efficient implementation of the Convention, but it would 'lead to greater consistency in practice in different States as it would follow the language of the Convention. The system would also help to significantly improve communications between Central Authorities'.[124] This would need to be a key

[121] So an authority in the UK can fill the form in in English and send it to Spain. When the form is opened in Spain it will be in Spanish. This is very clever and will help lower costs under the systems. Information gained at the Heidelberg Conference 2013.

[122] P Lortie, 'The Development of Medium and Technology Neutral International Treaties in Support of Post-Convention Information Technology Systems: The Example of the 2007 Hague Convention and Protocol' (2008), 10 *Yearbook of Private International Law* 359, 359–60.

[123] See ch 4 s II above.

[124] Lortie (n 122) 364 and P Lortie, 'Developing an Electronic Case Management and Communication System for the 2007 Hague Child Support Convention and 2009 EU Maintenance Regulation' in Beaumont et al (eds), (n 85) 275.

feature of any technical system as effective administrative cooperation will be imperative if the Convention is going to work efficiently.[125]

The iSupport programme has already been designed and contains several key features.[126] In respect of actual enforcement the design has a case specific function. This function includes 'a "Transfer of Funds" module that will assist the enforcement and monitoring of electronic transfer of funds.'[127] This will make it easier for Central Authorities to fulfill their duties in relation to enforcement as discussed above, help to transfer funds as quickly as possible, and has the additional benefit that all the information will be collated on one database. The programme that has been designed by the Hague Conference specifically for the Convention would fulfill this need and would be most effective if all Contracting States took advantage of it. The EU should make use of the iSupport system not only for external Convention cases but also for internal cases under the Regulation.[128]

## VII. Conclusion

It is acknowledged that traditionally enforcement has always been a matter for national law and procedure and, at this time, it would be impossible to gain consensus to allow national procedures for enforcement to be fully regulated by international instruments.[129] Therefore, the provisions on actual enforcement in the two new instruments are quite limited.

Both instruments try to regulate enforcement in an indirect way, by placing obligations on Central Authorities that relate to the enforcement of decisions. This is a step in the right direction, but it will only be effective if Central Authorities or enforcement bodies have effective enforcement mechanisms available to them under national law. Both instruments require that information is provided by national bodies on how Central Authorities will be able to discharge their duties under the instruments; however this information is not available at this point.

[125] See ch 10 below.

[126] See, information document no 1 of June 2006, 'Development of an international electronic case management and communication system in support of the future Hague Convention on the international recovery of child support and other forms of family maintenance', available at www.hcch.net/upload/maint_info1e2006.pdf, accessed 9 June 2014.

[127] Ibid, para 17.

[128] Once the system is ready, it should be simple to make any minor changes necessary so that the system could also work for the Regulation (Heidelberg Conference 2013). See Lortie (n 124) 279–283.

[129] However, this might be set to change in the EU given the procedures in the Brussels I recast (Regulation (EU) 1215/2012 of the European Parliament and of the Council of 12 December 2012 on jurisdiction and the recognition and enforcement of judgments in civil and commercial matters (recast) [2012] OJ L351/1). Because there is no longer a recognition and enforcement procedure as such, but safeguards, such as public policy, are retained, the Regulation begins to regulate the actual enforcement stage (Brussels I recast, Art 48 and see ch 7 s VIII above) It is unclear what will happen when the Regulation enters into force and how this will work in practice, but this could be the first step towards regulating the actual enforcement stage in EU instruments.

The Convention also regulates enforcement in a direct way by creating two legally binding principles: non-discrimination and effectiveness. This places an obligation on Contracting States to provide at least the same measures that are available in domestic enforcement cases. Contracting States are also required to ensure that the measures available are effective. The Convention has probably gone as far as it can in the aim to ensure effective enforcement. The Convention takes a robust approach by removing the requirement for creditors to have to make a separate application for enforcement, creates the principles of equivalence and effectiveness, and it lists possible methods of enforcement in order to try and guide Contracting States. The Hague Conference is also trying to get the iSupport system up and running, which is important because an efficient data programme will assist with the enforcement of decisions and the underlying objectives of the Convention.

The Regulation on the other hand fails to take positive steps in the area of actual enforcement, despite the fact that this was considered necessary in the original impact assessment. There was a great deal of effort put into tightening the provisions at the recognition and enforcement stage but this is likely to be insufficient for securing actual enforcement. It needs to be acknowledged that just because recognition and enforcement should now be virtually automatic, within the EU, this does not mean that actual enforcement will be. Further, even though there are other documents that may assist with enforcement, they are also not fully effective in dealing with enforcement. It would have been better if the Regulation dealt with actual enforcement in a more comprehensive way, or had taken the provisions directly from the Convention. It is clear that the provisions in the Regulation are supplemented by general concepts of EU law which already require equivalent and effective enforcement of EU law obligations. However it would have been preferable if the Regulation had also taken a more robust approach by indicating time periods in which orders should ideally be enforced.

No concrete conclusions can be made at this point, as not enough cases have been generated yet. The provisions in the Convention, which contains its own separate chapter on actual enforcement, are preferable to those in the EU Regulation. However, both the Regulation and the Convention are subject to the interpretation of the CJEU. This will extend to judicial review of Member States' application of the clear requirements contained in the texts, such as the duties of Central Authorities, in addition to States' compliance with the general principles of EU law when applying the instruments. The texts will also be subject to the interpretation of the ECtHR, which has previously taken a robust approach in this area.

# 10

# Administrative Cooperation

## I. Introduction

The instruments have a strong focus on administrative cooperation. This is created through a system of Central Authorities. Each State party is required to designate a Central Authority under each instrument. Then the Central Authorities are meant to coordinate with each other in order to resolve the application. The system of Central Authorities has been used in other Conventions and worked relatively well. The main problems with the system are the appropriate training of Central Authorities' personnel and whether or not these Authorities have sufficient powers to fulfil their duties. Therefore, although it is beneficial to have detailed provisions on the duties of Central Authorities, the work in this area for improving the system has to be done largely by the individual States.

Administrative cooperation has been an important aspect of the private international law of maintenance for many years. The New York Convention of 1956 focussed heavily on the concept of administrative cooperation.[1] In the Convention the bodies were known as agencies, and the text referred to 'Transmitting and Receiving agencies'.[2] However, the concept was the same. The agencies communicated directly with each other, and applicants were to make applications through the agencies. Similar systems are set up under the Child Abduction Convention,[3] the Hague Intercountry Adoption Convention[4] (which relies heavily on administrative cooperation) and the failed EU Convention on the Simplification of Procedures for the Recovery of Maintenance and other Payments.[5]

The previous Hague Conventions relating to maintenance did not provide for a system of Central Authorities. This is understandable in the applicable law Conventions, because they are solely to determine the law and do not provide for any particular procedure. However, the enforcement Conventions provided rules for recognition and enforcement but did not provide a system whereby the

[1] See ch 2 s III.

[2] UN Convention on the Recovery Abroad of Maintenance 1956 Art 1(1).

[3] Hague Convention of 25 October 1980 on the Civil Aspects of Child Abduction (Child Abduction Convention.

[4] Hague Convention of 29 May 1993 on Protection of Children and Co-operation in respect of Intercountry Adoption (Intercountry Adoption Convention).

[5] Rome Convention of 6 November 1990.

applicant could apply easily through Central Authorities. What was created was a system where if you were party to the New York Convention and one of the Hague Conventions, you had to use them all together. The system was rather incoherent.[6] It is unsurprising that the Hague Conventions did not contain provisions on Central Authorities, because the latest one was concluded in 1973. Even though the Evidence and Service Conventions predated this, the Abduction Convention, which was the first Hague Convention to include detailed provisions on Central Authorities, was not concluded until 1980. It was recognised at this stage that there was a need to 'draw up Conventions which respond to the international context of problems, rather than simply compromise between different domestic systems of private international law.'[7] One of the things that this involved was a 'shift of emphasis from the traditional "legislative co-operation" to conventions introducing more direct forms of transnational "judicial and administrative cooperation"'.[8]

Unlike the Abduction and Adoption Conventions, the Maintenance Convention deals with traditional private international law rules as well as judicial and administrative cooperation. The combination of these aspects is what should make the Convention workable and a success.[9] The traditional rules that were found in the Enforcement Convention are still necessary, but individuals trying to claim maintenance need a simple way of doing this. The Central Authority system allows individuals to make an initial application and then they do not have to worry since everything is dealt with through the Central Authorities, making an attempt to recover maintenance from abroad more attractive to individuals. This is important for individual States because if the system remained complicated and unworkable, individuals would find it much more attractive to claim money from national welfare systems.[10] Therefore, hopefully this combination

[6] See ch 2 s IV above.

[7] H van Loon, 'Unification and Cooperation in the Field of International Family Law: A Perspective From the Hague' in A Borrás, A Bucher, T Struycken and M Verwilghen (eds), *E Pluribus Unum Liber Amicorum Georges A.L. Droz on the Progressive Unification of Private International Law* (The Hague, Kluwer, 1996) 173, 175. This is evidence of the pragmatic approach taken by the Hague Conference when H van Loon was Secretary General. There was a strong emphasis on finding real solutions, rather than simply a best fit.

[8] Ibid, 175.

[9] (Hague Convention of 23 November 2007 on the International Recovery of Child Support and other Forms of Family Maintenance (Maintenance Convention.)) 'From the beginning of the preparation of the Convention there was a clear desire to establish strong cooperation between the authorities of the Member States, improving the system of the 1956 New York Convention. In this matter, the Hague Conference provides excellent examples of the 1980 Hague Child Abduction Convention and the 1993 Hague Intercountry Adoption Convention.' (A Borrás and J Degeling, 'Explanatory Report on the Convention on the International Recovery of Child Support and other Forms of Family Maintenance (HCCH, 2009) (Borrás and Degeling Report, para 19)).

[10] See for example Case C-363/08 *Romana Slanina* [2009] ECR I-11111, where the father was not paying maintenance so instead the mother was claiming money from the Austrian authorities. However data gathered suggests that the initial uptake of the Regulation has been slow and public awareness needs to be raised (see ch 2 s VI).

of both sets of rules will ensure the success of the Convention, making it simple yet effective.

The previous system in Europe was very different because it was under Brussels I.[11] This document had no provisions on administrative cooperation, because it was primarily a commercial document covering contract and tort. Brussels IIbis, the Regulation that deals with the other family matters (apart from matrimonial property), does have a system of Central Authorities. In the impact assessment the Commission identified this as an area where the Regulation should go further than the Convention.[12] Despite this, the two new maintenance documents have virtually identical provisions on administrative cooperation.

## II. Designation of Central Authorities

Each State must designate a Central Authority to discharge the duties which are imposed on it by the Convention and the Regulation.[13] The aim is that the

[11] Council Regulation (EC) 44/2001 of 22 December 2000 on jurisdiction and the recognition and enforcement of judgments in civil and commercial matters [2001] OJ L012/1 (Brussels I). See also ch 2 s V above.

[12] (Council Regulation (EC) 2201/2003 of 27 November 2003 on jurisdiction, recognition and enforcement of judgments in matrimonial matters and matters of parental responsibility, repealing Regulation (EC) No 1347/2000 [2003] OJ L 338/1 (Brussels IIbis).) See ch 2 n 106.

[13] Art 4 of the Maintenance Convention and Art 49 of the Maintenance Regulation (Council Regulation (EC) 4/2009 of 18 December 2008 on jurisdiction, applicable law, recognition and enforcement of decisions and cooperation in matters relating to maintenance obligations [2009] OJ L7/1). States can designate any body as the Central Authority however and therefore the structure and organisation is different in each State. Some Central Authorities are constituted of trained lawyers and other professionals and some are only made up of civil servants. Some Authorities deal specifically with maintenance and other Authorities, usually smaller ones, such as Luxembourg and Scotland deal with other issues; such as child abduction. Examples of different bodies posing as Central Authorities are: social insurance agencies, like in Sweden—*Försäkringskassan*; an independent enforcing organ, like in the Netherlands—LBIO; a ministerial department, like in Germany—*Bundesamt für Justiz*; and specially designated ministerial departments like in England and Wales and the Czech Republic. However the construction of these two Central Authorities is significantly different. There are five practitioners working at REMO (Reciprocal Enforcement of Maintenance Order) (Central Authority for England and Wales) and they are solely responsible for maintenance applications. None of these practitioners are legally trained and where they have a legal problem they should report to the Ministry of Justice, the ministerial department responsible for 'justice' matters. However, the body designated in the Czech Republic (Office for International Legal Protection of Children) is made up of 26 people: 15 lawyers, 3 psychologists and 8 administrative staff. This Authority also deals with child abduction and child protection, but it is clear that the office is extremely well staffed (particularly given the size of the State). There are also States like Finland that have two bodies which deal with different functions. There is the Ministry of Justice and the public body *Kansaneläkelaitos* (the Social Insurance Institution of Finland). This only begins to tell the story of the different structure and organisation of Central Authorities in each Member State and indicates the different backgrounds and experiences of the practitioners. (Information gained whilst carrying out the empirical study and at the Heidelberg Conference March 2013. See also I Curry Sumner, 'Administrative Co-operation and Free Legal Aid in International Child Maintenance Recovery: What is the Added Value of the Regulation? (2010) 3 *Nederlands Internationaal Privaatrecht* 611, s 3.2.)

Central Authorities liaise with each other in order to assist the applicant in getting a decision and then in helping with the ongoing enforcement of that decision. This takes into account one of the objectives of the Convention, which is to establish 'a comprehensive system of co-operation between the authorities of Contracting States'.[14] The Regulation simply states that in order to 'facilitate cross-border recovery of maintenance claims, provision should be made for a system of co-operation between Central Authorities designated by the Member States.'[15]

The instruments designate some of the duties that Central Authorities are expected to perform in broad terms (see below). However, in general the exact powers given to Central Authorities and the particular functions they are given can vary from State to State. This is because States have very different systems so 'the concept is left open, having regard to differences of capacity and administrative structures of each Contracting State, and taking account of the peculiarities of different legal systems.'[16] In relation to this both instruments recognise the problems with federal States, States that have more than one system of law, or States that have autonomous units. Where States are designed in one of these ways, they have the option to appoint more than one Central Authority, where this is necessary.[17] The United Kingdom has appointed four different Central Authorities under the Regulation. There is a Central Authority for England and Wales, Scotland, Northern Ireland and Gibraltar.[18] This is important firstly because they have different legal systems and secondly because of geographical location, as Gibraltar is nowhere near the UK and therefore it would be quite difficult to conduct operations from so far away. Where there is more than one Central Authority per State that State must designate a principal Central Authority where the communication can be sent initially.

Each State must inform either the Permanent Bureau or the Commission of the number of designated Central Authorities, and their contact details. They must also inform the bodies of the extent of the Central Authorities' duties where there is

[14] Maintenance Convention Art 1(a).

[15] Maintenance Regulation Recital 31.

[16] Borrás and Degeling Report (n 9) 28–29.

[17] Maintenance Convention Art 4(2) and Maintenance Regulation Art 49(2). 'The constitutional division of powers between federal, provincial or autonomous governments necessitates the flexibility to appoint multiple Central Authorities' (Borrás and Degeling Report (n 9) 29).

[18] Although in some cases it may be necessary to appoint more than one Central Authority, States should be careful not to designate too many because this defeats the purpose of having a centralised system. For example Poland has designated around 50 Central Authorities to work under the Maintenance Regulation. In Poland there are more than 2500 counties 'gmin' so they have indicated around 50 courts as forwarding authorities. 'The main task was to secure that the creditors have easy, direct access to the forwarding authorities.' (Email correspondence 16 January 2013.) Although this may be helpful for creditors residing in Poland, this will probably not be very helpful when the debtor is resident in Poland, and the requesting Central Authority is trying to discover the location of the debtor and correspond with the relevant authority in Poland. Even though the requesting Central Authority can contact the main Central Authority in Poland for assistance, it might still be difficult for them to pinpoint the relevant Polish authority.

more than one.[19] States should make sure that this information is kept up to date.[20] When and how States should inform these bodies is designated by each instrument.

## III. General Functions

The provisions on administrative cooperation are virtually identical in each document, and these are laid out as general functions and specific functions. The general functions are found in Article 50 of the Regulation and Article 5 of the Convention. These provisions require Central Authorities to 'co-operate with each other and to generate co-operation amongst the competent authorities in their States to achieve the purposes of the Convention' and to 'seek as far as possible solutions to difficulties which arise in the application of the Convention'. The text of the Regulation differs slightly from the Convention because it includes the phrase 'by exchanging information'.[21] However, this statement does not make any significant difference because the work of Central Authorities has to include an exchange of information at least to the extent of the transfer of applications between Central Authorities.[22] The functions are quite broad but it is clear that the focus is on cooperation, in order to achieve the aims of the Convention and the Regulation.

The broad terminology used in Articles 5 and 50, leaves flexibility to Contracting and Member States. It is argued in the Borrás and Degeling Report that the flexibility 'allows account to be taken of the limitations imposed by the resources and powers given to the Central Authority'.[23] However it is questioned whether this is ideal, especially as Central Authorities are entrusted with holding the instruments together, which is an enormous task. This is because they have a wide range of duties that range from locating the parties at the start of the process to assisting with the actual enforcement of the order at the other end. This includes not only enforcement of the first payment, but the ongoing enforcement of the maintenance obligation. Since Central Authorities play such a pivotal role in ensuring that the objectives of the instruments are discharged, there should

[19] Maintenance Convention Art 4(3) and Maintenance Regulation Art 49(3).

[20] At the latest Special Commission of the Abduction Convention the importance of this was emphasised. 'The Special Commission draws attention to the serious consequences for the operation of the 1980 Convention of failure to inform the Permanent Bureau promptly of changes in the contact details of Central Authorities. In addition, the Permanent Bureau should undertake to remind Central Authorities of their duties in this respect once a year.' Conclusions and Recommendations of the Sixth Meeting of the Special Commission, Part I—June 2011, p 1.

[21] Maintenance Regulation Art 50(1)(a).

[22] See L Walker, 'From Brussels I and the Maintenance Convention to the Maintenance Regulation: Is the Resulting Maintenance Regulation Consistent with the other EU PIL Instruments?' (2013) 6 *Nederlands Internationaal Privaatrecht* 167, s 2.1 and Curry Sumner (n 13) s 3.3.1.

[23] Borrás and Degeling Report (n 9) 30.

be minimum standards which they, or the State, are required to adhere to.[24] Too much flexibility in relation to the resources and powers governments give Central Authorities could have a direct correlation on what is considered an appropriate measure. This is significant as the specific functions have to be discharged by what is deemed an appropriate measure. Therefore, if too much flexibility is given this could result in a circular argument where lack of resources means that the definition of appropriate measures has a lower threshold in a particular State.[25]

The Borrás and Degeling Report goes on to state that: 'it envisages the possibility of a gradual improvement of services provided by the Central Authority.'[26] Improvement of any kind is always welcomed but how gradual is gradual and what level of improvement is being envisioned? Might this mean that in some countries improvement over 10 years takes a poorly functioning Central Authority to the level that might be considered as a minimum standard? This would be unacceptable and would not help with the major obstacle of actual enforcement, a step which Central Authorities should make sure happens. Any hope of improvement at the enforcement stage will not be reached if Central Authorities are not functioning effectively. Therefore, the European Commission and the Hague Conference should keep producing information on good practices for Central Authorities;[27] there should be regular training seminars at both a national and an international, or at least regional, level[28] and minimum standards should be established that State authorities should adhere to in terms of powers and resources.[29]

[24] See the discussion on minimum standards below, at s XVI.

[25] See above at ch 9 s III.

[26] Borrás and Degeling Report (n 9) 30.

[27] For example the Conference has published a Guide to Good Practice for Central Authorities operating under the Child Abduction Convention (Part I) and the first Guide to Good Practice on the Intercountry Adoption Convention has a chapter on Central Authorities (Ch 4). The Hague Conference has recently published a Practical Handbook for the Maintenance Convention. It would be very useful if there was also a Practice Guide on the Maintenance Regulation in due course. Informal discussions with practitioners working at Central Authorities suggest that they would find a practice guide on the Regulation very useful (there is a practice guide on Brussels IIbis).

[28] Where training is available it is important that the training in place is effective and clear. Most Central Authorities reported that they had not received any clear guidance or training at a national level. Within the European Union, there is the civil justice network where Central Authorities meet every six months for 'training' and can ask any questions. Practitioners have reported that these meetings are generally unhelpful, mainly because they are not given direct or clear answers to the questions they ask. (Informal discussions at the Heidelberg Conference, March 2013.) The questions were treated as an open discussion on the initial meaning of the Regulation which is useful for academics but not practitioners. They want clear simple answers to the specific problems that will help them carry out their duties. Therefore, it would be useful for the Commission to produce a practice guide, like the one for Brussels IIbis and then Central Authorities could receive training on specific areas that, would be based on and, build on the information contained in the practice guide.

[29] For example under Art 7a) of the Abduction Convention, Central Authorities are expected to help locate the child. In relation to this E Perez-Vera, 'Explanatory Report on the 1980 Hague Child Abduction Convention' (HCCH, 1982) (Perez-Vera Report) does little more than repeat the text, see para 91. At the latest Special Commission a standard was set. 'Contracting States that have not already done so are asked to provide their Central Authorities with sufficient powers to request, where needed for the purpose of locating the child, information from other governmental agencies and authorities,

The draft Convention of June 2007 also included a third general function. This was to: 'provide information to the Permanent Bureau as to the laws and procedures concerning maintenance obligations in their States'.[30] The final negotiations simply state that Article 5 was accepted as is.[31] However, the obligation to provide the information was transferred from the Central Authorities to the Contracting States and appears in Article 57(1)(a) of the Convention. This is more sensible as State bodies are better placed to provide this type of information and keep the information up to date. However, Central Authorities need to be aware of the laws and procedures in their State and should be notified by the relevant State bodies of any changes in the law. If Central Authorities know the law and procedures in their State it will be easier for them to carry out their work, advise individuals and transfer queries to the relevant body where necessary. If they have the correct information in advance this will also assist with the efficient and expeditious processing of applications.

## IV. Specific Functions

The specific functions in Article 51 of the Regulation and Article 6 of the Convention give a more detailed description of what may be expected of a Central Authority when processing a case. However, the list is not exhaustive and Central Authorities are generally expected to take whatever steps they can under their own law in order to facilitate the recovery of maintenance. State governments also have a part to play in this by ensuring that Central Authorities have appropriate powers in order to fulfil their duties. This Article was extensively debated during the negotiations to the Convention but,

> there seemed to be a consensus that the Convention should contain a broad range of administrative functions for Central Authorities in child support cases, but at the same time, Central Authorities should not be expected to act beyond their powers and resources, or be unreasonably burdened with too many functions.[32]

Specific measures are split into two sections. Firstly the measures contained under paragraph 1 are mandatory obligations that Central Authorities must perform. This is indicated by the word 'shall'.[33]

including the police and, subject to law, to communicate such information to the requesting Central Authority.' (Conclusions and Recommendations of the Sixth Meeting of the Special Commission, Part I—June 2011, p 1.) This highlights that there needs to be some minimum standards in terms of powers, because if a Central Authority cannot even request this information from its own authorities, how can it possibly discharge its duties? This must be a real problem or else it would not have been considered by the Special Commission.

30 Art (5b) of the Draft Convention of June 2007.

31 Procès verbal no 19, 2.

32 Ms Degeling, Procès Verbal no 7, 2.

33 Maintenance Convention Art 6 and Maintenance Regulation Art 51(1).

The minimum functions that Central Authorities are expected to perform are to:

— transmit and receive applications; and
— initiate or facilitate the institution of proceedings in respect of such applications.[34]

These are specific and primary functions of Central Authorities so they 'must be carried out comprehensively'.[35] It is extremely important that these functions are carried out because nothing could be done otherwise. However, is it really correct to put these in a different class from the other functions, thus deeming them more important? This is probably not the best approach because maintenance obligations will not necessarily be discharged unless all Central Authorities' duties are fulfilled.[36] The different class between the functions is indicated by the use of the term 'shall' in paragraph 1 in contrast to the term 'all appropriate measures' used in paragraph 2.

In order to fulfil the specific functions, in paragraph 2, Central Authorities are expected to take 'all appropriate measures'.[37] However, the terminology 'appropriate measures', is slightly ambiguous and it is unclear exactly how far the Central Authorities are required to go.[38] The ability of the Central Authority to effectively fulfil its duties in relation to the instruments is reliant on it having appropriate powers and resources to discharge its duties. As a result Central Authorities need to be given sufficient powers and resources by their States. The obligations in Article 6(2) which require all appropriate measures to be taken are

> less specific, and allowed Central Authorities or bodies more discretion as to how the functions would be performed—hence the term 'all appropriate measures'. Nevertheless, Ms Degeling explained that the obligation remained to do everything possible within the powers and resources of the Central Authority to provide the assistance requested.

[34] Maintenance Convention Art 6(1).

[35] Borrás and Degeling Report (n 9) para 113. In this respect Curry-Sumner notes that the mandatory obligations are non-exhaustive. He criticises this because 'the very essence of mandatory obligations is that one is aware of the nature of these obligations prior to discharging the duty. If a Central Authority is not aware that it is obliged to discharge a mandatory duty, can it later be held not to have satisfied this responsibility?' (Curry-Sumner (n 13) s 3.3.2.) Given the loose and ambiguous terms used such as 'initiate' 'facilitate' and 'appropriate' it is believed that the Commission would bring proceedings against a State only where the Regulation is not implemented appropriately or efficiently or a State body such as a Central Authority hinders or dilutes the effect of a Regulation through its lack of action. This is because the State would be in breach of the principle of 'effectiveness' (see ch 9 particularly nn 59–63). Similarly the European Court of Human Rights (ECtHR) would also take the same approach where there is a lack of action as demonstrated in *Romańczyk v France* (App no 7618/05) ECHR 18 November 2010, discussed above at ch 9 s V.

[36] Curry-Sumner suggests that the approach taken in relation to the functions in para 2 was because the functions needed to be flexible to cater for the diversity in the organisational structure of Central Authorities. However, he considers that there is not really any difference between the two categories of functions in practice, suggesting that the 'flexible approach is no more apparent than with respect to the specific, discretionary, delegable functions.' (Curry-Sumner (n 13) s 3.3.3.)

[37] Maintenance Convention Art 6(2).

[38] See above at ch 9 s III, particularly n 27.

> She emphasised, however, that the word 'shall' meant that there was a strong obligation to 'take all appropriate measures'. There was flexibility in how an obligation could be carried out, but not whether or not it would be carried out.[39]

Despite the fact that there is an obligation to take appropriate measures, this provides no clarification on what an 'appropriate measure' actually is nor indicates what an acceptable approach is.

Ultimately, the term 'all appropriate measures' may result in a broad variance between the functions and resources allocated to Central Authorities across Contracting and Member States. The phrase was included because it 'is expansive.'[40] It was considered that 'Central Authorities can be more proactive in finding appropriate ways to assist [and the term] lends itself more effectively to the principle of "progressive implementation" of the Convention.'[41] This seems to suggest that Central Authority personnel should seek to be as imaginative as possible. For example the use of the word 'proactive' would tend to imply that where the Central Authority does not have the powers or resources available to enforce the order in the most suitable and simple way, it should look for alternative solutions in order to fulfil the duty. This may be putting too much faith in Central Authorities. However, it is noted that the Convention includes a helpful provision in Article 57(1)(b), which requires that State authorities provide the Permanent Bureau with a description of measures it will take to meet the obligations in Article 6. Although the term may have been needed in The Hague to make the Convention more acceptable to Contracting States, it is questioned whether the Regulation goes far enough in this area by simply borrowing the terms from the Convention. This is particularly true when at the outset this was an area where it was identified that the Regulation should be capable of going further than the Convention.[42] Therefore, the creation of minimum standards and there acceptability will be discussed below.[43]

Central Authorities are expected to take all appropriate measures:

— To provide or facilitate the provision of legal aid.
— To help locate the debtor or the creditor.
— To help obtain relevant information concerning the income and other financial circumstances of the debtor or creditor, including the location of assets.
— To encourage amicable solutions with a view to obtaining the voluntary payment of maintenance.
— To facilitate the ongoing enforcement of maintenance decisions including any arrears.
— To facilitate the collection and expeditious transfer of maintenance payments.

[39] Procès Verbal no 7, 3.
[40] Borrás and Degeling Report (n 9) para 122.
[41] Ibid.
[42] See ch 2 n 106.
[43] See s XVI below.

— To facilitate the obtaining of documentary or other evidence.
— To provide assistance in establishing parentage where necessary.
— To initiate or facilitate the institution of proceedings to obtain any provisional measures which are territorial in nature and the purpose of which is to secure the outcome of a pending maintenance application.
— To facilitate the service of documents.

Therefore Central Authorities have a wide range of functions and should be involved in the process from the beginning until all payments have been made. This means that Central Authorities could be involved in a case for a number of years, because in relation to child support the Regulation covers children up to the age of 21 years. As such it would be sensible for all Central Authorities operating under the Regulation to have appropriate information stored on a suitable database in order to assist them with ensuring the ongoing enforcement of decisions.[44]

## V. Legal Assistance

Legal assistance covers a range of areas from legal aid to legal advice, and is defined in Article 3(c). It is defined as:

> the assistance necessary to enable applicants to know and assert their rights and to ensure that applications are fully and effectively dealt with in the requested State. The means of providing such assistance may include, as necessary, legal advice, assistance in bringing a case before an authority, legal representation and exemption from cost of proceedings.[45]

The exact body that fulfils these duties will vary from State to State, as the powers of Central Authorities may vary greatly. For example if there are no legally trained practitioners working for the Central Authority, then that authority is unlikely to be able to give legal advice.[46] This is why when performing this duty Central Authorities may 'provide or facilitate' legal assistance. Where Central Authority personnel have the relevant powers and the capability to discharge the duty themselves, then they should do that, if however they do not have adequate training to

[44] See ch 9 s VI above.

[45] Art 3(c) of the Convention. The Regulation does not contain a definition of the concept, see Art 2. In relation to how the Central Authorities should assist applicants under the Regulation, Recital 31 states: '[t]hese authorities should assist maintenance creditors and debtors in asserting their rights in another Member State by submitting applications for recognition, enforceability and enforcement of existing decisions, for the modification of such decisions or for the establishment of a decision.' This is helpful, in that it informs us of what the Central Authority should do but it doesn't give detail on how the Central Authority should go about this.

[46] None of the practitioners who work at REMO (the Central Authority for England and Wales) are legally trained. Any legal questions have to be transferred to the Ministry of Justice or private practitioners.

provide the particular assistance required then they should facilitate the provision of the assistance by contacting a competent authority.

In this context cooperation at the national as well as the international level is essential. In order for the instruments to function effectively it will be important for the competent bodies in each State to have a good working relationship.[47] In the process of the application of the Abduction Convention, in particular in relation to facilitating judicial communication, the Permanent Bureau has

> observed that the relationship between judges and Central Authorities was different in the various States. It was stressed that dialogue was important both on the international and domestic level and it was essential for all actors involved in the implementation and operation of the Convention, including Central Authorities and judges, *to understand their roles, functions and limitations*.[48]

It is imperative that Central Authorities understand exactly what their functions are and have good contacts with the bodies that applicants need to be directed to when the Central Authority cannot provide the necessary assistance. This is essential if applications are to be dealt with promptly and efficiently and also to ensure that applicants do not receive erroneous legal advice from unqualified staff.

The aim is that Central Authorities are the key bodies that function under the instruments. They are the main port of call for applicants and they should make sure that all stages of the application are dealt with correctly. Of course, they are not a super power that can do all this but this is why cooperation with the appropriate national bodies is essential, especially in regard to legal assistance. In the context of child abduction the Hague Conference has recommended to Contracting States of the Abduction Convention that:

> Efforts should be made to ensure that Central Authorities act as a focal point for the provision of services or the carrying out of functions contemplated under Article 7 of the 1980 Hague Convention. When the Central Authority does not provide a particular service or carry out a particular function, it should preferably itself engage with the body which provides that service or carry out that function.[49]

This concept should apply to Central Authorities working under each of the instruments. This is especially true under the maintenance instruments as administrative cooperation appears to be the cornerstone of the instruments, and is essential at every stage of the process.

[47] This will be particularly important, in the context of actual enforcement, where the enforcement has been stayed or suspended. Without sufficient dialogue the Central Authority will then be left unaware of what they need to do to discharge their enforcement duties.

[48] Report of the Fifth Meeting of the Special Commission to review the operation of the 1980 Hague Child Abduction Convention and the practical implementation of the 1996 Hague Protection of Children Convention, 2006, 28 (emphasis added).

[49] Conclusions and Recommendations of the Sixth Meeting of the Special Commission, Part I—June 2011, p 1.

## VI. Locate One of the Parties

The duty to help locate the debtor or the creditor is very broad. The standard of the requirements in the two instruments are slightly different, because the Regulation also includes provisions on access to information.[50] These Articles specify what information Central Authorities should be able to access and the conditions for this. These additional provisions should assist Central Authorities operating under the Regulation.[51] The duty to locate a party can apply to full applications but may also be used in a request for specific measures.[52] This is because one of the parties may know in what State the other party is living but not have an address. Alternatively, the applicant may have no idea where the debtor or creditor is living at that point.[53] The other possibility, which is in between the two, is where there is a federal State with more than one Central Authority, such as Canada, the applicant may only know that the debtor or creditor is in Canada but not which province they are in exactly. Central Authorities may be asked to locate one of the parties at the beginning of the proceedings. They also could be asked to go through a similar process in the future, if one of the parties seeks to modify the original order.

Firstly, there is the simple situation where the creditor knows in which State the debtor is residing. The creditor contacts the Central Authority in their State. That Central Authority can then make a direct application to the Central Authority in the receiving State. If the creditor knows the exact address of the debtor then the job of the Central Authority in the receiving State is simple as it can contact the debtor straight away. However, this will not always necessarily be the case, so the Central Authority in the receiving State will have to carry out some work in order to find the exact location of the debtor. It would be easier for the Central Authority to discharge this duty if it had access to relevant databases where it is simple to retrieve this information from.[54] This would be in harmony with the spirit of the instruments which call for expeditious procedures. However, the Borrás and Degeling Report makes it clear that where this is not the case, the Central Authority should not use this as an excuse not to fulfil this obligation.

[50] Maintenance Regulation Arts 61–63.

[51] This is also helpful where Central Authorities are seeking information on the income or the assets of a party (see below at s VII) See also Curry-Sumner (n 13) s 3.5.4.

[52] Art 7(1) of the Convention and Art 53(1) of the Regulation, see below at s XV, A.

[53] In this case the Central Authority does not have to waste time and resources on a full application. Instead it can make a request for a specific measure. Requests to locate a party accounted for the majority of the requests made (see below at s XV A).

[54] When writing on the interstate programme in the United States, Cavers recognises that the 'effectiveness of the program depends largely on the ability of the state agency to locate missing parents' (D Cavers, 'International Enforcement of Family Support' (1981) 81 *Columbia Law Review* 994, 1028). The Finnish Central Authority reported, in response to the questionnaire, that there had been three applications where recognition and enforceability had been refused because the debtor could not be located.

> [T]he requested Central Authority must do everything possible to locate the debtor or creditor. Whether or not the Central Authority has access to databases of information is irrelevant. The Central Authority knows, in its country, whether public records such as telephone lists or population registers with personal contact details can be searched, and if not, which public bodies store information about a person's address.[55]

This statement implies that a Central Authority could not use an argument that it took all appropriate measures based on the information that was available to it, and therefore a lack of access to suitable resources meant that it could not locate the debtor in this instance. Rather, the statement indicates that unless the Central Authority does everything it reasonably can to locate the debtor then 'all appropriate measures' will not have been taken. This is because Central Authorities should know who holds the information, and be able to retrieve this information from them. Contracting States should implement suitable legislation in this area where necessary, and Central Authorities should maintain a regular dialogue with all authorities and bodies in their State that can assist them with discharging this duty.

Although cooperation within a State is important, because there is a need for expeditious procedures it would be suitable if minimum standards were given in this area. In this situation a direct correlation is made between the fundamental importance of locating a child in an abduction case, and locating a debtor in a child support case.[56] It is clear that there is a different level of resources available in different countries, when trying to locate the child. These range from very sophisticated systems to virtually non-existent procedures where even the police are not willing to help.[57] Unsurprisingly, the lack of comparable standards in this area has been questioned. For example,

> [c]ertain experts asserted that it was important to know what Central Authorities of other States could do to assist in locating the child. Some experts expressed the desire to see other Central Authorities offering similar services to those offered by their own States.[58]

Therefore, although the Borrás and Degeling Report suggests that a Central Authority should be able to discharge this duty no matter what resources are available to them initially, evidence from the Abduction Convention shows a lack of comparable standards which suggests that minimum requirements are necessary.[59] In this area the additional provisions in the Regulation do at least set some

[55] Borrás and Degeling Report (n 9) p 37.

[56] Ibid, p 38.

[57] 'Some countries have very sophisticated locate services where abducting parents may be traced through information on government databases. In other countries, court orders may be sought to direct other bodies such as banks to disclose certain information. On the other hand, some countries are not able to obtain any police assistance if an address for the abducted child is not provided by the requesting country.' Borrás and Degeling Report (n 9) p 38.

[58] Report of the Fifth Meeting of the Special Commission (n 48) 26.

[59] See below at s XV A where the information provided on this area in relation to requests for specific measures suggests that locating parties is proving difficult within the EU.

minimum standards regarding the information that should be available to Central Authorities, whether this is through direct access or it is provided on request.[60]

There are not only problems with resources available and services offered, but Central Authorities may also come up against national privacy laws.[61] However, since most States will have an interest in obtaining the information, especially the location of the debtor in child support applications, because the right to privacy is in general subject to a public interest exception the information should be released.[62] This is because there is a public interest in upholding the moral obligation that parents should provide for their children, as well as an interest in saving public funds when the child's parents can and should pay instead.[63] The information is for the use of the authorities to protect the welfare of the child and therefore does not need to be released to the other party in the procedure. The rights of the child under the United Nations Convention on the Rights of the Child (UNCRC) are also relevant in this context. States should ensure that both parents are responsible for the upbringing of the child,[64] and should also provide social security taking into account the incomes of those having responsibility for the child.[65] In addition the child has the right to know both of his or her parents.[66] If it is unknown where one of the parents is located these rights and responsibilities cannot be complied with correctly.

Secondly, there is the more complicated situation of locating a debtor or creditor, when the applicant does not know which State they reside in. In this situation the requesting Central Authority may have a lot more work to do. They may have to do a lot of preliminary research in order to see if they can get any leads. In these

[60] Maintenance Regulation Arts 61 and 62.

[61] There is a guarantee under the Convention that the information obtained will be protected. (Arts 38, 39, 40 and see para 138 of Borrás and Degeling Report (n 9)).

[62] This can be seen in the European Convention on Human Rights Art 8.

[63] Under Art 27 of the UNCRC, the obligation to maintain children is primarily the responsibility of the parents.

[64] See Art 18 of the UNCRC.

[65] See Art 26 of the UNCRC. 'Article 26 acknowledges the link between children's citizenship and the distribution of material resources, including access to social security. Therefore, whilst the task of safeguarding a decent standard of living for children is considered a responsibility of the parents in the first place, ensuring the children's access to social security remains primarily a State obligation.' (European Union Agency for Fundamental Rights, 'Developing Indicators for the Protection, Respect and Promotion of the Rights of the Child in the European Union' (2010) 92.)

[66] See Art 7 and Art 9(3) of the UNCRC. However, although children have a right to know their parents and parents have a right to have access to their children (right to family life), these rights do not necessarily go hand in hand with the responsibility to pay maintenance. The English courts have held that where access has been denied by authorities this is not a sufficient ground on which to reduce maintenance payments (*Foot v Foot* [1987] 1 FLR 62). It has also been considered that where access is hindered by the children's other parent then this is also not sufficient to extinguish or vary a maintenance obligation (*R v Halifax Justices Ex p Woolverton* (1979) 123 SJ 80). Conversely the Canadian courts have held that where mothers are depriving the father of access rights, for example by moving away, maintenance could be suspended completely or until access orders were enforced (see, *Kett v Kett and Mitchell* (1976) 28 RFL 1 and *Shoot v Shoot* (1956) 6 DLR (2d) 366).

situations the Central Authorities' task may be virtually impossible and there may be little they can do in order to assist the applicant.[67]

When the applicant has an idea of where the debtor is, the process is made simpler for both the requesting and the requested Central Authority due to the possibility to make a request for a specific measure. This means that if there is a good chance that the debtor is residing in a particular State but this is not certain, a request can be made to simply confirm this matter or not before a full application is made. This saves the time and money of preparing a full application for no reason.[68] The requesting Authority simply sends the request, and the requested Authority just informs the first authority whether or not the debtor is residing there. No detailed information about the direct location of the debtor needs to be released at this point. If the request is successful a full application can be made.

However, information provided seems to suggest that the Latvian authorities are reluctant to make a request for a specific measure and would rather make a full application in this respect.[69] It is unclear what the reasoning behind this is. One possibility could be the fact that if the application is for child support, legal aid might not be provided for the request for a specific measure but it would for a full application. However, Central Authorities can only recover exceptional costs and the costs of locating a debtor are not included in this.[70] Therefore, this argument seems unlikely as the time and cost to make a request for a specific measure would be minimal compared to preparing a full application. Unlike the Convention where all requests are discretionary, 'in relation to locating the debtor or the debtor's assets, the Regulation converts the discretionary responsibility imposed on the requested Member State into a mandatory obligation'.[71] Although the requests under the Convention are discretionary, they are not completely discretionary, as the requested Central Authority is required to carry out the request if they are 'satisfied that they are necessary to assist a potential applicant'[72] in making a full application. Conversely, under the Regulation the requested Central Authority must carry out the request even if this appears unnecessary. This is an area where the Regulation did manage to go further than the Convention. However this might not be sensible as it may encourage States to go on fishing

[67] However, what realistically can be expected of a Central Authority in this situation, the Borrás and Degeling Report (n 9) does not seem to cover this situation. It is considered that this situation could easily crop up, although it is recognised that with the existence of social networking sites it is getting easier to locate people. A simple Google search can bring up the debtor as they appear on these sites. The person's full information is not always available because of privacy settings, but a simple search like this could easily throw up some leads.

[68] See the Borrás and Degeling Report (n 9) pp 37–38.

[69] Information gathered by P Beaumont when he attended a training session for the Latvian Central Authority. However, Latvia actually made 27 of these types of requests and received 4 of these types of requests. (See Annex V and s XV A below).

[70] Maintenance Regulation Art 54(2) and see s XV A below.

[71] Curry-Sumner (n 13) s 3.4.

[72] Art 7(1) of the Maintenance Convention.

expeditions and send out requests to a number of States at the same time,[73] which will waste resources.

## VII. Information on Income and other Financial Circumstances, Including the Location of Assets

The Central Authority needs to assist in obtaining information on the income and other financial circumstances of the parties for a number of reasons. The information obtained can be important for making the full application, but also for deciding whether or not to make an application. For example the Central Authority can make a request for a specific measure to determine what the debtor earns. If the debtor only earns a minimal amount there is no point going ahead with a full application as, even if an obligation was created, the order could not be enforced as you cannot make somebody pay something that they do not have.[74] Where the application is for child support, legal aid has to be provided, therefore it is in the interest of the State to ensure that their authorities are effectively using the request for specific measures in Article 7 of the Convention or Article 53 of the Regulation so that they are not wasting resources on laborious procedures when these are not necessary. The instruments were cleverly designed in order to balance the requirement to provide legal aid, with the option to make simple requests when there are some questions as to whether a full application is viable. States should make sure that authorities in their State are making use of all the provisions in the instruments in order to get the most cost effective result in each case.[75]

In cases where it is clear that the debtor has suitable funds to pay maintenance and or child support, the Central Authority could try to obtain information on the location of the debtor's assets. This can also be done through a request for a specific measure.[76] Once the assets are located, the Central Authority can also make a request for provisional measures for the assets to be frozen.[77] These requests can be made separately or together. Locating and then freezing the assets is important where the order is contested at the recognition and enforcement stage. Even if the procedure is drawn out the freezing of assets means that the debtor cannot take the chance to sell property, or move assets. This is more relevant in the context of the Convention, because in the Regulation the recognition

[73] See below under s XV A which shows there were a high number of these requests made under the Regulation.

[74] See ch 7 ss VI and VIII above.

[75] See s XV A below.

[76] Maintenance Convention Art 7(1) and Maintenance Regulation Art 53(1).

[77] Maintenance Convention Art 6(2)(i) and Maintenance Regulation Art 51(2)(i).

and enforcement procedure is virtually automatic.[78] However, the freezing of assets is important in the application of both instruments as there could also be delays at the actual enforcement stage and, because of electronic banking, assets can now be moved quickly.[79]

Gaining this type of information probably creates more data protection issues than simply discovering the location of the debtor. However, in relation to the first point, which is about 'relevant information concerning the income' of one of the parties the impact on the parties' privacy is not that great. This is because at this stage you do not need to know what the actual income is, this would only be relevant for determining the actual maintenance amount when the case went to court. All that is necessary is for the requested State to provide information about whether the applicant claims benefits or not. If they do, this would suggest they cannot afford to pay maintenance and therefore wasting time and money on a full application would not be beneficial. This would not require a major invasion of the debtor's privacy, it would just require a State body to consult its own databases to see if the individual was receiving money from the State. In this context the retrieval of this information could be imposed as a minimum standard, because if the debtor is completely supported by the State then that would be enough to end the application. However, more extensive information such as the exact amount the debtor gets paid is not something that a Central Authority necessarily needs to know.

On the other hand obtaining information on the debtor's assets, including the location of their bank accounts, might cause more problems. This is because there is an issue with banking laws as well as privacy laws. In this context it was stated that in some States 'such information could only be obtained by the judicial process.'[80] However, one State has 'resolved the issue by amending its legislation to exempt from its privacy and data protection laws any such requests if made in accordance with the Convention.'[81] At a first glance this may appear drastic, but on a closer analysis it should be an example that other States follow. There are two reasons for this. Firstly, all States that are party to the Convention must recognise that both parents should pay child support and recognise some form of spousal support where appropriate.[82] Secondly, the amount of maintenance payable can only be determined after there has been an analysis of the debtor's assets.[83] Therefore, at some

[78] See ch 7.

[79] See ch 9 s III above.

[80] Borrás and Degeling Report (n 9) p 39.

[81] Ibid.

[82] In the Regulation the scope is broader and other forms of family maintenance are also included. However, the forms of family maintenance that are covered should only be ones that are expected by that particular debtor under one of his own laws if the Hague Protocol is applied correctly (see chs 3 and 6).

[83] For example, see C-220/95 *Van den Boogaard v Laumen* [1997] ECR I-1147; *AB v CD* 2007 Fam LR 53, *Kremen v Agrest* [2012] EWHC 45 (Fam); *Miller v Miller* and *McFarlane v McFarlane* [2006] 2 AC 618 and the formula used in administrative systems such as Australia where child support is automatically calculated (www.heidelberg-conference2013.de/tl_files/downloads-abstracts/Presentation_Chapman.pdf, slide 6, accessed 9 June 2014). See also J Saue et al, 'Administrative Establishment and

point the debtor's assets have to become known to at least the judge, or an administrative authority. Due to the fact that the Central Authority would only be interested in the location of the debtor's assets for the purpose of possibly freezing them, in order to help with the actual enforcement of the order, in some ways a change in the law is sensible. However, this is not an area in which it would be appropriate for minimum standards to be imposed. Although at some point information on the debtor's assets needs to be exposed it is difficult to argue that this is something the Central Authority needs to know. If certain States want to retain this information only for the purpose of court proceedings then this has to be respected.

## VIII. Encourage Amicable Solutions

Where possible amicable solutions should be reached. This is because if both parties discuss the matter and agree to the terms then it is much more likely that the payment will be made, and the order will be enforced.[84] Therefore due to problems with the enforcement of obligations amicable solutions are the desired outcome where appropriate. It also saves money compared to lengthy judicial proceedings.

Central Authorities should aim to promote or encourage amicable solutions where this is suitable. One issue with mediation is consolidating the need for expeditious procedures and the preference for gaining amicable solutions. Therefore, bodies need to know that while amicable solutions are beneficial there is no point carrying on with mediation, or other similar processes, if it appears unlikely that an agreement will be reached. For instance in the context of the Abduction Convention, different States have very different ideas of how mediation should fit into the structure of the Convention. This covers when it should commence, whether it should be done prior to judicial proceedings or at the same time as them, and whether there should be time limits.[85] Dingwall argues that mediation 'introduces delays, uncertainty, stress and postponed resolutions that are serious negative outcomes for some families.'[86] So although the promotion of amicable solutions to encourage compliance can be beneficial, the use of mediation has to be balanced with the aim of guaranteeing prompt and efficient procedures,[87] and protecting the parties.

Enforcement of Child Support in Norway' in Beaumont et al (eds), *The Recovery of Maintenance in the EU and Worldwide* (Oxford, Hart Publishing, 2014) 161.

[84] See, W Duncan, 'Transfrontier Access/Contact and the Hague Convention of 25 October 1980 on the Civil Aspects of Child Abduction (2002) Preliminary Document no 5, para 89.

[85] See, the Report on the 5th Meeting of the Special Commission to review the operation of the 1980 Convention and the practical implementation of the 1996 Convention, 2006, pp 30–31. See also S Vigers, *Mediating International Child Abduction Cases* (Oxford, Hart Publishing, 2011).

[86] R Dingwall, 'Divorce Mediation: Should We Change Our Mind?' (2010) 32 *Journal of Social Welfare and Family* Law 107, 113.

[87] See the Preamble to the Maintenance Convention.

Within the EU the text of the Regulation is supplemented by the Mediation Directive.[88] However it has been questioned whether this additional text achieves anything in the context of family proceedings, as the Maintenance Regulation (and Brussels IIbis) refer specifically to amicable solutions.[89] Key aspects of the Directive are that; it recognises that access to justice is fundamental,[90] mediation should be a voluntary process[91] and that Member States should encourage the training of mediators.[92] The Directive does not attempt to regulate jurisdiction, however Article 5 suggests that parties should be invited to mediate by an appropriate court. This means that jurisdiction would first have to be established by the Regulation, then the parties could be invited to mediate by the court seised. It is important that mediation remains voluntary, as emphasised by the Directive, for a number of reasons—primarily the fact that mediation is supposed to be a voluntary procedure because there has to be a certain level of understanding and respect between the parties or at least a willingness to try, if mediation will have any chance of being successful.[93]

In addition to the concern of ensuring that mediation retains its voluntary nature, there are other concerns prevalent in the area of cross-border mediation. Firstly, the parties have to meet for a sufficient period of time, possibly over a number of weeks, in order to reach an agreement that is suitable. This is difficult in cross border situations where the parties may live far away from each other. In these cases, 'it is not uncommon for face-to-face mediation to be conducted over a single weekend, often placing intense pressure on all concerned and militating against an exhaustive and thoughtful agreement.'[94] This will be even more problematic if a judge has suggested mediation where there is animosity between the parties, as it is unlikely they will even be able to cooperate with each other over a short space of time, never mind reach an agreement that they are both happy to cooperate with. The second major problem is accommodating cultural diversity.[95] In order for mediation to operate effectively and ensure 'access to justice' the parties must be considered as equal by all those involved. As such Stalford argues that mediation is based on 'a series of presumptions and preconditions that are,

[88] Directive 2008/52/EC of the European Parliament and of the Council of 21 May 2008 on certain aspects of mediation in civil and commercial matters [2008] OJ L136/3 (Mediation Directive).

[89] H Stalford, *Children and the European Union: Rights, Welfare and Accountability* (Oxford, Hart Publishing, 2012) 137–38.

[90] Mediation Directive Recital 2.

[91] Ibid, Recital 13 and Art 3(a).

[92] Ibid, Recital 16.

[93] See, J Nolan-Haley, 'Is Europe Headed Down the Primrose Path with Mandatory Mediation?' (2012) 37 *North Carolina Journal of International Law and Commercial Regulation* 981 and J Marcil and N Thornton, 'Avoiding Pitfalls: Common Reasons for Mediation Failure and Solutions for Success' (2009) 3 *American Journal of Mediation* 25, 30–31.

[94] H Stalford, 'Crossing Boundaries: Reconciling Law, Culture and Values in International Family Mediation' (2010) 32 *Journal of Social Welfare and Family Law* 155, 159.

[95] Ibid, 160–61. See also Dennison who recognises that even within the UK culture diversity is a major issue. (G Dennison, 'Is Mediation Compatible with Children's Rights?' (2010) 32 *Journal of Social Welfare and Family Law* 169, 175.)

in themselves, culturally specific. They are predicated on a resolutely Western ideal that presumes open and balanced communication between the parties, as well as equality of status and outcome.'[96] It is clear that mediation is premised on autonomy and power. Therefore judges and Central Authorities should be wary of placing too much emphasis on amicable solutions as forced mediations are unlikely to promote access to justice,[97] and will most likely delay proceedings.

## IX. Ongoing Enforcement

The provisions on enforcement are new, and even Central Authorities that have worked under other Conventions in the past may not be used to the idea that they will have some duties in relation to actual enforcement of the case. As such they may need training and support in this area.[98]

One potential problem in the area of enforcement is the Central Authority having suitable powers and resources to ensure the enforcement of the order. The need for Central Authorities to have suitable resources in order to fulfil their duties regarding enforcement is discussed in detail above.[99] The benefit of suitable databases in order to support the ongoing enforcement of maintenance obligations was also discussed.[100] The prime example being the Hague Conference's own database iSupport which was designed specifically for the Convention. The database is not yet up and running as the Conference is still waiting on funding, however when it is operating it would be reasonable to ask all Contracting States to use the database. This would create a common standard that all States had to adhere to, and may assist with cooperation if all Central Authorities were using the same system. For example if they were having problems, they could contact other Central Authorities to ask for their advice. To expect States to implement a system that should in the end save them time and money, is perfectly reasonable. Therefore, the requirement to use the database could be acceptable as a common standard.

In relation to the cooperation side in general, a major obstacle to enforcement could be that the Central Authority is not actually aware that there is a maintenance obligation to be enforced. It just appears to be taken as accepted that the Central Authority would be made aware of the matter. Neither of the instruments cover this point; they just jump from recognition and enforcement to actual

[96] Stalford (n 94) 160.

[97] 'Triage, which has been introduced in Arizona, Connecticut and British Colombia, increases efficiency by eliminating referrals to mediation where success is unlikely. It also reduces the burden on families by acknowledging the demanding nature of participation in mediation, both in psychological and economic terms.' (Dingwall (n 86) 113.)

[98] See above at ch 9 s III A.

[99] See ch 9.

[100] See ch 9 s VI above.

enforcement. It would seem logical for the court order just to be passed to the Central Authority, but it appears that common sense seems to be lacking. This is probably due to the fact that the duty of Central Authorities to enforce the order is new. Therefore, not enough thought has been given to the implications of how this will work under national law; some implementing measures may be required in this respect.

Problems in this area are already becoming apparent under the Regulation. A first response to the questionnaire from the Central Authority for England and Wales stated that there were a number of questions that they could not answer and the information would have to be obtained from the court.[101] These were: Question 1, part III the number of applications where modification of a decision was obtained; and any questions relating to whether a declaration of enforceability was refused or enforcement was not given. This is very unfortunate because in order to assist with the enforcement of the decision the Central Authority needs to know if there is an order to enforce. The Central Authority also needs to be aware of any modification to the order so that they know exactly what they have to enforce and from what date. However, following the first response to the questionnaire the Central Authority altered the information they were going to keep and the amount of time they were going to keep files open for. Now, instead of files being closed when a decision was given, or the obligation was created, the file will remain open until the first payment is made. The file will then remain dormant.[102] It is understood this means that the file will not be touched unless any problems are raised either by the applicant or another Central Authority.

As a first step this is positive because it means that the Central Authority is considering its duty as regards actual enforcement because it is continuing to monitor the progress of the case until the first payment is made. However, will a file remaining dormant be enough to 'facilitate the ongoing enforcement of maintenance decisions'? It might be as long as the Central Authority acts quickly if notified of any problems. For example this position might be justified, if following the first payment the Central Authority makes the creditor aware that the case will now be closed. The Central Authority should inform the creditor that if the debtor defaults on any payments in the future they should notify the Central Authority straight away, so that the Authority can take steps to rectify this. This would have to be the very minimum standard in order for the Central Authority to effectively discharge this duty. It would be preferable for case information to be kept on a centralised database, so that the Authority was immediately aware if a payment was being made on time, or if the debtor had defaulted.[103]

[101] Email of 7 February 2012.

[102] Information obtained at 'A Year On—Taking Stock of the EU Maintenance Regulation'—event hosted by Dawson Cornwell on 26 June 2012.

[103] See ch 9 s VI above. This happens in administrative systems such as those operating in Australia and Norway. (See www.heidelberg-conference2013.de/tl_files/downloads-abstracts/Presentation_Chapman.pdf, http://www.heidelberg-conference2013.de/tl_files/downloads-abstracts/abstracts-ab-3-3-2013/Presentation_Saettem_Saue_final.pdf, accessed 9 June 2014 and Saue et al (n 83) 179–80).

The Latvian Central Authority also highlighted a similar problem at a conference for practitioners in Latvia.[104] Article 19, which applies to decisions that originated from States that are party to the Protocol on applicable law, allows the defendant the right to apply for a review in the country of origin, if he did not appear at the original proceedings and meets the specified requirements.[105] It was mentioned at the conference that, where a party has contested the order under Article 19 in the country of origin, the Central Authority knew that enforcement had to be, or could be, stayed.[106] However, following this the Central Authority was then not necessarily made aware of the outcome of the decision. It was suggested that there may need to be implementing legislation in this respect. All the Regulation says on this matter is that if 'the court rejects the application for a review referred to in paragraph 1 on the basis that none of the grounds for a review set out in that paragraph apply, the decision shall remain in force.'[107] Therefore although it is clear that the decision remains in force there is absolutely no consideration of how all the interested parties will be notified or how to proceed.[108] This does not assist with the proper administration of justice and in fact impedes access to justice for both creditors and debtors. This highlights a further problem with the abolition of *exequatur* and the two tracks in the Regulation. The shift of emphasis from the enforcing court to the court of origin in Article 19 only creates further difficulties and will result in delays in procedures, if there is not appropriate implementing legislation (which should not be necessary) instead of creating more expeditious procedures which was the aim.[109] Ultimately if the new procedures and the emphasis put on Central Authorities is going to work, then this is an area where cooperation between all practitioners working in Member States is going to be imperative.[110]

[104] June 2012, feedback from Professor Beaumont who attended and spoke at the conference.

[105] See Maintenance Regulation Art 19.

[106] However, in this situation enforcement does not even need to be stayed. The enforcing State 'may' suspend enforcement but this is not a requirement (see ch 7 s VI, B). This suggests that very complicated situations might arise. There is no case law in this area as yet so it is impossible to predict what the outcomes might be. However, there is an indication that there will be potential problems in this area which could affect enforcement of applications processed under the Protocol route.

[107] Art 19(3) of the Regulation.

[108] Curry-Sumner notes that once a decision has been sent for recognition and enforcement or enforcement there are no provisions included on further communication requirements between the Central Authorities. This could mean that 'at this stage the Central Authority in the requested State is more-or-less removed from the equation. The lack of clarity of the procedure is, although understandable, disappointing.' Curry-Sumner (n 13) s 3.5.2. At first sight 'disappointing' seems a suitable terminology, but given the context of Art 19 and the difference in the review procedures from other instruments, lack of descriptive duties and legal mechanisms at this stage is a failure of the Regulation. This is in stark contrast to Brussels IIbis where the procedure and the issuing of the certificate in Art 42 is clearly laid out.

[109] See ch 7 ss IV–VI above.

[110] See the section on legal assistance above. Cooperation and dialogue is not only important at the first stage between judges and Central Authorities, but also then between judges, Central Authorities and enforcement agencies.

In order to fulfil the purpose of the instruments which is a simple and expeditious procedure for the transfer of such payments, it is essential that where an order is contested the Central Authority is informed of the outcome as soon as possible. If for some reason this is incompatible with national enforcement law, then implementing legislation will need to be created to ensure that Central Authorities are aware of what is happening so that they can discharge their duties. This is a small practical problem, but if it is not dealt with efficiently then it is an area that could cause serious problems as enforcement has always been a major obstacle.[111]

## X. Collection and Expeditious Transfer

This duty is directly related to the duty on enforcement, emphasising that the Central Authorities' duties in relation to enforcement extend to helping with the collection of the money. This would again require dialogue with enforcement officers where necessary and possibly even banks. Effective discharge of this duty requires effective banking systems which facilitate the expeditious transfer of funds. A database of information would be helpful in order to keep details of what payments have gone through all on one system, and this should be acceptable as a common standard for the reasons highlighted above.[112]

## XI. Obtaining of Documentary or Other Evidence

This duty comes from the New York Convention. The provision allowed competent tribunals to submit letters of request for documentary or other evidence to other Contracting Parties.[113] The provision in the current instruments is 'intended to supplement sub-paragraph c) on obtaining information on the income, financial circumstances and assets of the parties.'[114] This provision could also be useful when providing assistance to establish parentage.

The provision is essentially there to assist with obtaining the information listed in the other sections of Article 6(2). It is just there in order to supplement the other provisions. However, it is understood that States that are parties to the Taking of Evidence Convention will probably choose to circulate the necessary

[111] See above at ch 8.
[112] See above at ch 9 ss III and VI.
[113] Art 7 of the New York Convention.
[114] See the Borrás and Degeling Report (n 9) p 41.

evidence through the procedures under this Convention.[115] The provisions in the maintenance instruments are simply there to add clarity but have no effect on the other conventions or any bilateral agreements.[116] Where the State is not party to other agreements the provision in the Maintenance Convention 'could be used on its own to seek evidence abroad in accordance with the applicable internal laws.'[117]

## XII. Parentage

In cases where it is unclear who the parent is, or the presumed father is contesting parentage, the Central Authority should assist the creditor in establishing parentage. In this respect the Central Authority again has the option of making a request for a specific measure rather than making a full application.[118] This was included in the Convention because in many States

> the establishment of parentage has become so inextricably linked to the establishment of child support that it was felt that its omission from the new Convention would be a failure to live up to the objective of developing a forward looking instrument.[119]

It is hoped that in most cases parentage will already be established, but where it is not this is a useful addition to the documents. However, with medical developments and new forms of reproductive technology, biological parentage will not always be sufficient to establish whether or not there is a maintenance obligation.[120]

[115] Hague Convention of 18 March 1970 on the Taking of Evidence Abroad in Civil or Commercial Matters (Evidence Convention) which applies in 58 States, see www.hcch.net/index_en.php?act=conventions.status&cid=82, accessed 9 June 2014. In intra-EU cases the Evidence Regulation will be used.

[116] The Chair stated that; 'it was the common understanding of delegates that Central Authorities were not obliged to serve documents or provide evidence themselves, but that they were obliged to do all that was necessary to assist in the procurement thereof. Accordingly, if a Contracting State to another Convention required the taking of evidence or the service of documents abroad, it could address another State through the Central Authority contemplated in another Convention. She added that this would be clarified through the information made available per Article 51 of the preliminary draft Convention' (Procès Verbal no 7, 8).

[117] Borrás and Degeling Report (n 9) para 167.

[118] Very few of these types of request were made (see below at s XV A and Annex V).

[119] Borrás and Degeling Report (n 9) p 42.

[120] For example, in these situations (usually surrogacy) it would be the intended parents that had obligations towards the child and not the biological parents (see ch 1 s V above).

## XIII. Provisional Measures that have the Purpose of Securing the Outcome of a Pending Maintenance Application

The decision to include this provision in the final draft of the Convention was not made until late on in the proceedings. In the draft from June 2007, this provision was still in square brackets but the other provisions relating to Central Authorities had already been agreed upon.[121] The inclusion of this provision in the final text of the Convention is very beneficial, because it is very simple for a debtor to conceal their assets or move them around due to electronic banking. This provision can be used in a full application, or as a request for a specific measure.[122] The provisional measures can only be sought in respect of a pending maintenance application, and should be designed to assist with the outcome of that application. It is envisioned that provisional measures will include 'measures to prevent the dissipation of assets, or measures to prevent the debtor leaving the jurisdiction to avoid legal proceedings.'[123] Where court proceedings are necessary, a request to freeze the debtor's assets will probably be the most frequently used measure in this respect.[124]

This provision should assist with the overall enforcement of maintenance claims.[125] However, it is difficult to see how this provision could effectively be used as a request for a specific measure. This is because a requirement of the provision is that the requested measure is to 'secure the outcome of a pending maintenance application.'[126] It is understood that a request for a specific measure should be made before a full application to discover necessary information, ie the location of the debtor, whether the debtor has sufficient means to pay maintenance or to make a request to establish parentage. Once all these things are known then the response would be to make a full maintenance application, which it would appear that you would need to make anyway in order to obtain a provisional measure since the measure has to have the objective of securing a maintenance application. Therefore, this would seem to suggest that you would need to make a full application in order to ask for a provisional measure so it seems odd to then do this outside the full application. As a result it is believed that this provision will rarely be used as a request for a specific measure and instead be used as part of a full application.[127]

[121] Available at www.hcch.net/index_en.php?act=publications.details&pid=4136&dtid=35, accessed 9 June 2014.

[122] See Art 7 of the Maintenance Convention and Art 53 of the Maintenance Regulation.

[123] Borrás and Degeling Report (n 9) para 176.

[124] Ibid.

[125] See ch 9 above.

[126] Art 6(2)(i) of the Maintenance Convention and see para 179 of the Borrás and Degeling Report (n 9).

[127] However, there were some of these requests made, but only 19. These were all received by Estonia (see Annex V and s XV A below).

# XIV. Service

This provision is similar to the one on transferring evidence, in the sense that the current documents that cover service still apply and service should be made under these instruments in States that are party to them.[128] The provision is included to ensure that defendants are duly served documents, for example when the creditor is applying for a modification of the maintenance order or applying for a new order. Again the provision in the Maintenance Convention is generally only relevant where other instruments on service do not apply.[129] Under this provision Central Authorities will either have to ensure the service of documents in their jurisdiction or ensure they are sent to another jurisdiction so they can be served there.[130] In either case it is not the job of the Central Authority to serve the documents on the person. They must simply facilitate this by, for example, sending 'the documents to a private process server, the Public Prosecutor or any other authority or person competent to effect service, or to have service effected, in that jurisdiction.'[131] The documents will be served in accordance with the law in the State they are to be served in.

# XV. Practical Application of Selected Provisions

This section will discuss what has been learnt from data collected on the first year of operation of the Regulation by looking at selected provisions.

## A. Requests for Specific Measures

In addition to the ability to make full applications, the new instruments introduce the possibility to make requests for specific measures.[132] This allows Central Authorities to make a request rather than wasting money on a full application when an answer to a specific question is unclear. This could be for example to locate the debtor if it is unclear to the applicant where he or she actually lives, so rather than make a full application it is better to check that the debtor lives in that State first. A request can also be made to determine if the debtor has sufficient funds to pay

[128] The Hague Convention of 15 November 1965 on the Service Abroad of Judicial and Extrajudicial Documents in Civil or Commercial Matters (Service Convention) applies in 68 States; see www.hcch.net/index_en.php?act=conventions.status&cid=17, accessed 9 June 2014. In intra-EU cases the Service Regulation will be applied.

[129] Borrás and Degeling Report (n 9) para 185.

[130] Ibid, paras 182–83.

[131] Ibid, para 182.

[132] See Maintenance Regulation Art 53.

a maintenance obligation. This is important, because where the debtor's means are very limited the cost of the international transfer could be higher than the obligation and in such cases it would be pointless to proceed with an application. Requests can also be made to:

— facilitate the obtaining of documentary or other evidence;
— provide assistance in establishing parentage where necessary;
— initiate or facilitate the institution of proceedings to obtain any necessary provisional measures which are territorial in nature and the purpose of which is to secure the outcome of a pending maintenance application; and
— facilitate the service of documents.

All the requests available relate to one of the specific functions that Central Authorities are expected to carry out.[133] There were at least 1463 requests made in the first year of operation of the Regulation.[134] The vast majority of these requests were made in order to locate one of the parties, presumably the debtor (see the chart below).[135]

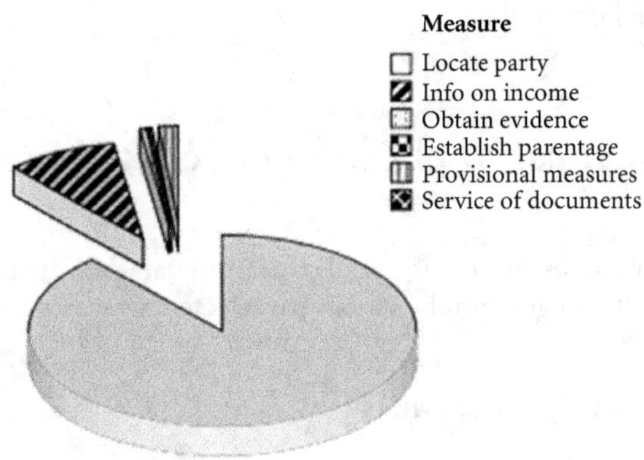


**Figure 10.1: Requests for specific measures**

Where Authorities provided information on what the request was for, requests to locate a party were by far the most important, suggesting that many creditors do not know where their ex-spouse, ex-partner or the father of their child is

[133] These are discussed above in the relevant sections. See Arts 53 and 51 of the Regulation.

[134] This number is the total number of incoming requests received by the Central Authorities that filled in the relevant part of the questionnaire. See Annex IV for a full table.

[135] Not all Central Authorities provided information on what the request was for. If these requests are excluded (as in the graph above), requests to locate a party account for 88% of all requests. If the unknown requests are included these account for 20%, so requests to locate a party account for 70% of all requests.

living. The next most popular request was to receive information on the income or assets of a party (nine per cent). All other requests were minimal. In terms of requests received by specific States, the spread was more or less even (see the graph below).[136]

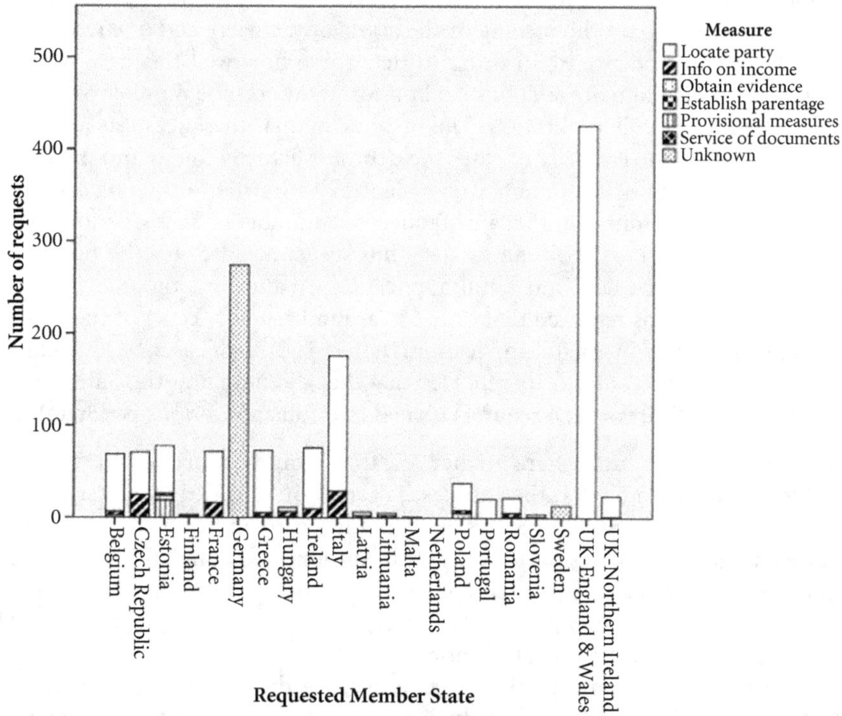


**Figure 10.2: Requests received by Member State**

It is unfortunate that the nature of the requests sent to Germany are unknown, since the German Authority received the second highest number of requests (274). All requests sent to England and Wales and Northern Ireland (as well as the majority of requests received by the Republic of Ireland) were to locate a party. This could be because of the structure of the UK system, so the creditor is aware that the debtor is residing somewhere in the UK or Ireland but they are not sure where, so that is why the request is needed. Most other States received requests for both the location of a party or for information on the income or assets of a party. The most interesting is Estonia which also received a number of requests for provisional measures (24 per cent). The other interesting point is that there were only

[136] A breakdown of the information in this graph can be found in Annex V.

three requests for establishment of parentage, Belgium received two and Romania one, suggesting that establishment of parentage is not in reality a problem in the majority of cross border maintenance cases.[137]

The majority of the requests received by these States were sent by Poland, 749.[138] Of these requests 531 (70 per cent) were to locate a party, 28 (four per cent) were to gain information on the income or the assets of the party and one request was made to obtain evidence.[139] In order to determine how well this new system is working the questionnaire sought to gain information on the number of requests that turned into a full application. The hope being that these requests are meaningful, so that in the majority of cases the debtor is actually found and therefore a full application can be made rather than Central Authorities just going on fishing expeditions and sending out the same request to a number of States. Unfortunately it was very difficult, at the time of the study, to gather data on the number of requests that had turned into a full application. At the time the questionnaires were returned it was reported that only 55 (around four per cent) of the requests received had turned into a full application. In the majority of cases, 942 (around 65 per cent), the Central Authority reported that they did not know the outcome (the graph below indicates which requests turned into full applications per State).[140]

This is definitely an area where further research should be carried out. The main problem here could be that the study was carried out too early to determine the outcome.[141] However, some States have managed to indicate the outcome in at least some of the cases and the Central Authority for England and Wales in every case. Given that the majority of requests have been sent in order to locate the debtors there are two potential problems that could arise in this area. The first conclusion is that Central Authorities are going on fishing expeditions and sending requests to more than one State because they have no idea where the debtor actually is. The second conclusion is that the outcome of these requests is delayed because Central Authorities are finding it very difficult to locate debtors and fulfill their function in Article 51(2)(b). As such it is imperative that further research is carried out at a later date to discover what is happening here. In relation to the latter, it is very important that Central Authorities are provided with sufficient powers and resources to enable them to be able to locate the necessary parties as quickly and easily as possible.[142] In the case of the former,

137 There was a lengthy discussion on this during the negotiations of the Convention when deciding whether legal aid should be provided for establishing paternity (see Procès verbal no 15).

138 See Annex IV for a full breakdown by State.

139 In respect of the other 189 requests (20%), it was not reported what the request was for.

140 A breakdown of this information can be found in Annex VI.

141 This was indicated by both the Swedish and Belgian Central Authorities in their responses (email correspondence 30 November 2012 and 27 November 2012).

142 See above at s VI.

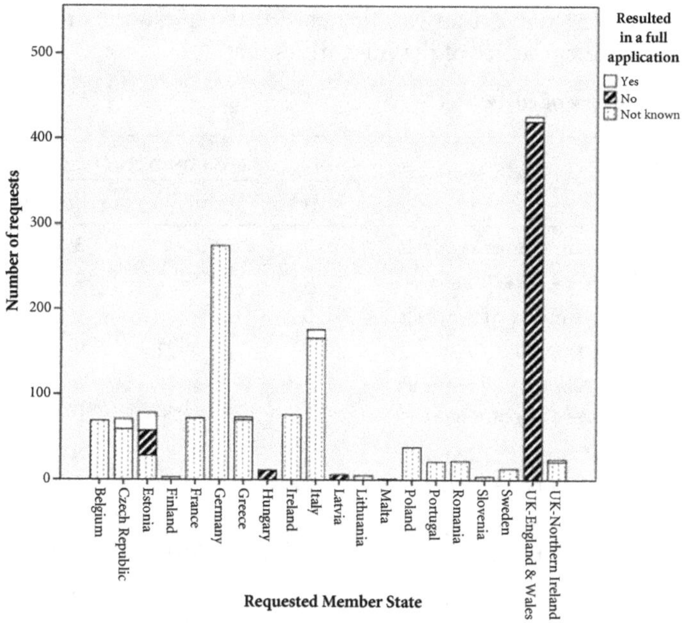


**Figure 10.3: Requests that resulted in a full application**

Central Authority personnel should not be wasting their time and resources, or the requested Central Authorities sending pointless requests. They should at least try to gain some indication of where the debtor might be before proceeding with requests.[143]

Unlike the rest of the Regulation, where Central Authorities must cover their own costs, they are allowed to recover the costs arising from a request for a specific measure.[144] However, they are only supposed to recover 'exceptional costs'.[145] It is also stated that costs related to 'locating the debtor shall not be regarded as exceptional'.[146] A Central Authority is only allowed to recover 'exceptional costs' where they have the prior consent of the applicant.[147] As such, given that the majority of requests were related to locating the debtor, Central Authorities should have rarely recovered their costs under Article 54(2). The majority of

[143] Ibid.
[144] See Maintenance Regulation Art 54.
[145] Ibid, Art 54(2).
[146] Ibid.
[147] Maintenance Regulation Art 54(3).

Central Authorities did not answer this part of the questionnaire, but the table below indicates the practice of the Authorities that did.

**Table 10.1: Recovery of costs**

| **Requested State** | | **Costs recovered?** | | | **Total** |
|---|---|---|---|---|---|
| | | **yes** | **no** | **not known** | |
| Estonia | Number of requests | 0 | 75 | 3 | 78 |
| | As a percentage | 0.0% | 96.2% | 3.8% | |
| Finland | Number of requests | 0 | 3 | 0 | 3 |
| | As a percentage | 0.0% | 100.0% | 0.0% | |
| Hungary | Number of requests | 2 | 9 | 0 | 11 |
| | As a percentage | 18.2% | 81.8% | 0.0% | |
| Ireland | Number of requests | 0 | 76 | 0 | 76 |
| | As a percentage | 0.0% | 100.0% | 0.0% | |
| Italy | Number of requests | 176 | 0 | 0 | 176 |
| | As a percentage | 100.0% | 0.0% | 0.0% | |
| Latvia | Number of requests | 0 | 6 | 0 | 6 |
| | As a percentage | 0.0% | 100.0% | 0.0% | |
| Sweden | Number of requests | 13 | 0 | 0 | 13 |
| | As a percentage | 100.0% | 0.0% | 0.0% | |
| UK-England & Wales | Number of requests | 0 | 426 | 0 | 426 |
| | As a percentage | 0.0% | 100.0% | 0.0% | |
| Total | | 191 | 595 | 3 | 789 |

This indicates that the majority of these Authorities: Estonia, Finland, Ireland, Latvia and England and Wales did not recover their costs. Hungary recovered their costs in two out of 11 requests. Only five of the requests received by Hungary were for the location of the debtor,[148] so the recovery of costs in two requests could in this case be justified as exceptional costs. Both Sweden and Italy recovered their costs for every request. A possible explanation for this could be that these States misunderstood the question or inserted the numbers in the wrong column by accident. However, if it is presumed that the questionnaire was filled in correctly then this could suggest that the Italian, and probably the Swedish Central Authority are misinterpreting this provision in the Regulation.

[148] See Annex V.

In relation to Sweden it is not clear what the requests were for so this may have been justified. However, given the high number of requests for the location of a party, it seems highly unlikely that none of the requests made to Sweden were for this. Further, it seems unlikely that the Central Authority would incur 'exceptional costs' in relation to every request. Italy cannot be justified in recovering costs in all 176 requests. They could not legitimately argue that they incurred 'exceptional costs' in so many requests. In addition 147 of these requests were for the location of a party.[149] Although requests can be made to locate either party and Central Authorities are only barred from recovering costs in relation to locating debtors, it is expected that the majority of requests will be made in order to locate debtors, rather than the other way around. Therefore, provided the questionnaire was completed correctly, it has to be concluded that the Italian Central Authority is in violation of Article 54 of the Regulation for recovering costs in respect of every request.

## B. Meeting the Time Requirements

When carrying out their work under the Regulation, Central Authorities are expected to meet certain time requirements. In particular they have to meet the time requirements in Articles 58(3) and (4). Firstly, Central Authorities are meant to acknowledge receipt of the application, inform the requesting State what steps have been taken or will be taken to deal with the application, and they may also request additional information from the requesting State.[150] They should do this within 30 days of receiving the application. During this time they should also provide the requesting Authority with 'the name and contact details of the person or unit responsible for responding to inquiries regarding the progress of the application.'[151] Secondly, they must inform the requesting Central Authority of the status of the application within 60 days of acknowledging receipt.[152]

At the outset, these requirements appear fair. In the first case the requested Central Authority has a month to decide how it should proceed with the application and inform the requesting Central Authority of this. It then has up to two

[149] See Annex V.

[150] Maintenance Regulation Art 58(3).

[151] Ibid, Art 58(3). It is noted that under the Convention the Central Authority has six weeks to do this (Art 12(3)).

[152] Maintenance Regulation Art 58(4). The equivalent provision in the Convention requires that this is done in 3 months (Art 12(4)). This is probably more sensible as it is unlikely much progress will have been made between the two time periods given in the Regulation.

months to provide the requesting Central Authority with an update on the progress. However, the second time requirement may be too close to the first, because little progress may have been made in 60 days. It would appear that meeting these requirements is proving harder than expected in practice. This might be because of the high volume of applications, compared to a lack of personnel, although it is expected that applications will in fact increase as time goes on.[153] It might also be because the current databases are inefficient and therefore Central Authorities are finding it difficult to keep track of applications and what stage they are at. Finally, Central Authorities might be prevented from meeting the requirements due to national procedural laws.

According to the information provided by the Central Authorities that completed the relevant part of the questionnaire, the 30 day requirement in Article 58(3) was met in around 76 per cent of applications.[154] However, the overall figure is not a true representation of the practice across the States (as highlighted in the table below). It should also be noted that this figure could even be slightly optimistic as Central Authorities were responding in relation to their own practice.[155]

**Table 10.2: Meeting the 30 day requirement**

| Requested State | | Art 58 (3) met | | Total |
|---|---|---|---|---|
| | | Yes | No | |
| Belgium | Number of Applications | 38 | 100 | 138 |
| | As a percentage | 27.5% | 72.5% | |
| Czech Republic | Number of Applications | 122 | 5 | 127 |
| | As a percentage | 96.1% | 3.9% | |
| Estonia | Number of Applications | 80 | 53 | 133 |
| | As a percentage | 60.2% | 39.8% | |
| Finland | Number of Applications | 51 | 0 | 51 |
| | As a percentage | 100.0% | 0.0% | |
| Greece | Number of Applications | 125 | 1 | 126 |
| | As a percentage | 99.2% | 0.8% | |

(*Continued*)

[153] See above at ch 2 s VI.

[154] This is based on data provided in respect of incoming applications to that Central Authority. So the data is reliant on the Central Authority being honest in relation to how often it met the requirements.

[155] Where data was provided on outgoing cases, the requesting Central Authorities indicated that requested Central Authorities only managed to meet the 30 day requirement in around 54% of applications. However, because only some Central Authorities provided this data, it does not necessarily correspond with the data on incoming cases. For example data in respect of Bulgaria, France, Austria, Luxembourg, Spain and Scotland is also included (but this only covers applications received by those States that were sent by the States that completed the questionnaire and not all the applications they received). Because not all States answered the full questionnaire, the data on incoming cases is more reliable as we get to see the full picture in the State that answered the relevant questions.

| Requested State | | Art 58 (3) met | | Total |
|---|---|---|---|---|
| | | Yes | No | |
| Hungary | Number of Applications | 14 | 2 | 16 |
| | As a percentage | 87.5% | 12.5% | |
| Italy | Number of Applications | 120 | 1 | 121 |
| | As a percentage | 99.2% | 0.8% | |
| Latvia | Number of Applications | 11 | 0 | 11 |
| | As a percentage | 100.0% | 0.0% | |
| Portugal | Number of Applications | 60 | 2 | 62 |
| | As a percentage | 96.8% | 3.2% | |
| Slovenia | Number of Applications | 1 | 6 | 7 |
| | As a percentage | 14.3% | 85.7% | |
| Sweden | Number of Applications | 127 | 3 | 130 |
| | As a percentage | 97.7% | 2.3% | |
| UK-England & Wales | Number of Applications | 611 | 251 | 862 |
| | As a percentage | 70.9% | 29.1% | |
| UK-Northern Ireland | Number of Applications | 26 | 2 | 28 |
| | As a percentage | 92.9% | 7.1% | |
| Total | Applications | 1,386 | 426 | 1,812 |
| | percentage | 76.5% | 23.5% | |

According to data provided there is quite a disparity between the Central Authorities in this respect. Both Finland and Latvia met the requirement in all cases. Latvia had a very small number of incoming applications, only 11, and initially there were two people working at the Central Authority but there have been three since March 2012.[156] Finland had more applications, but 51 is still relatively low. There were two practitioners working on maintenance applications in the Finnish Central Authority at the time the questionnaire was completed.[157] The majority of Central Authorities reported that they met the time requirement in around 90 per cent of applications. This seems viable and these Central Authorities should be considered to be functioning effectively. England and Wales and Estonia should seek to meet the requirement more often in order to function

[156] Email correspondence with Linda Strazdina, 3 December 2012. It should also be noted that these practitioners only work on maintenance; they are not in charge of other instruments such as Brussels IIbis.

[157] At the moment they feel like they can cope with the case load, however they are concerned that if applications increase this would be difficult. In this case they think that if they were provided with a more efficient database that could provide quick access to information on time requirements for example, then two practitioners would be enough to cope with an increase in applications. In relation to databases, they reported that in order to complete the questionnaire they had to go through each paper application and count everything separately even though they do have a working database. (Informal discussion with the practitioners at the Heidelberg Conference, March 2013.)

more efficiently. However, it is recognised that incoming applications to these States are high. England and Wales received 862 applications in a nine month period.[158] It has been suggested that they have to deal with around 180 new applications a month, the majority of which are incoming, and there were five practitioners working at that Central Authority, at the relevant time.[159] Estonia received 133 incoming applications, but there was only one practitioner working there at the relevant time.[160] This Central Authority could be more efficient if the current practitioner had some assistance.

The major causes for concern are the Slovenian and Belgian Central Authorities. The Slovenian Central Authority only had seven incoming applications, and only managed to meet the requirement in one of these applications. There is no further information on the structure of this Central Authority, or the national law, but this is clearly not good enough. The Belgian Central Authority only met the requirement in around 27 per cent of applications but it had many more incoming applications, 138. The poor performance by the Belgian Central Authority, in meeting the time requirements, appears to be related to national laws of procedure rather than the efficient or inefficient practice of the Central Authority. This is because, when completing the questionnaire, it only included applications 'for which a royal decree was effectively sent within the allotted time.'[161] It would be very difficult to meet the requirement if a royal decree had to be sent in each case. This could mean that Belgium's practice breaches the EU principle of effectiveness, because this national administrative practice makes this provision of the Regulation 'excessively difficult' to meet.[162] Therefore, States should refrain from imposing cumbersome national laws of procedure where possible, in order to ensure that the process under the Regulation operates as efficiently and expeditiously as possible.

The feedback in respect of the 60 day requirement in Article 58(4) was even worse. The requirement was only met in 29 per cent of applications.[163] Again the figures were very different in each State that completed this part of the questionnaire. However, poor performance under Article 58(3) does not necessarily indicate poor performance under Article 58(4) and vice versa (see table below). Finland and Latvia maintained their 100 per cent record. Estonia met the requirement in the vast majority of cases, and the worst performers were: Portugal,[164] Italy, England and Wales and Belgium.

[158] See ch 2 s VI above.

[159] Informal discussion with one of the practitioners at 'A Year On—Taking Stock of the EU Maintenance Regulation' (n 102).

[160] Email correspondence and informal discussion at the Heidelberg Conference 2013.

[161] Email correspondence, 27 November 2012.

[162] See C-147/01 *Weber's Wine World Handels-GmbH and Others v Abgabenberufungskommission Wien* [2003] ECR I-11365, 11418, see ch 9 s IV, A above.

[163] In this case, there was not much difference between the data provided by requested Central Authorities and requesting Central Authorities. Where information was given on outgoing cases requesting Central Authorities reported that the requirement was met by the requested Central Authority in around 27% of applications.

[164] There were five practitioners working at the Portuguese Central Authority at the relevant time, email correspondence, 6 November 2012.

**Table 10.3: Meeting the 60 day requirement**

| Requested State | | Art 58 (4) | | Total |
|---|---|---|---|---|
| | | Yes | No | |
| Belgium | Number of Applications | 13 | 125 | 138 |
| | As a percentage | 9.4% | 90.6% | |
| Czech Republic | Number of Applications | 124 | 3 | 127 |
| | As a percentage | 97.6% | 2.4% | |
| Estonia | Number of Applications | 126 | 7 | 133 |
| | As a percentage | 94.7% | 5.3% | |
| Finland | Number of Applications | 51 | 0 | 51 |
| | As a percentage | 100.0% | 0.0% | |
| Greece | Number of Applications | 53 | 73 | 126 |
| | As a percentage | 42.1% | 57.9% | |
| Hungary | Number of Applications | 9 | 7 | 16 |
| | As a percentage | 56.2% | 43.8% | |
| Italy | Number of Applications | 0 | 121 | 121 |
| | As a percentage | 0.0% | 100.0% | |
| Latvia | Number of Applications | 11 | 0 | 11 |
| | As a percentage | 100.0% | 0.0% | |
| Portugal | Number of Applications | 0 | 62 | 62 |
| | As a percentage | 0.0% | 100.0% | |
| Slovenia | Number of Applications | 3 | 4 | 7 |
| | As a percentage | 42.9% | 57.1% | |
| Sweden | Number of Applications | 80 | 50 | 130 |
| | As a percentage | 61.5% | 38.5% | |
| UK-England & Wales | Number of Applications | 45 | 817 | 862 |
| | As a percentage | 5.2% | 94.8% | |
| UK-Northern Ireland | Number of Applications | 12 | 16 | 28 |
| | As a percentage | 42.9% | 57.1% | |
| Total | Applications | 527 | 1,285 | 1,812 |
| | percentage | 29.1% | 70.9% | |

Although 'no sanctions are imposed on the requested Central Authority for failure to deliver speedy. and timely responses to applications',[165] within the text of the Regulation, this should not stop the Commission from bringing an action against a State for failure to meet these targets because they are a 'requirement' under the Regulation. Therefore, States must ensure that the requirements are

[165] Curry-Sumner (n 13) s 3.5.2.

met, in order to comply with the principle of 'effectiveness'.[166] It is clear from the feedback that the majority of Central Authorities are not functioning efficiently when it comes to fulfilling the requirements in Articles 58(3) and (4). These tasks are fairly minimal, all that is required is receipt of the application, some contact details and an update of the application. If Central Authorities are not achieving these menial tasks it is questionable how effectively they are carrying out their specific functions (discussed above) since these functions will generally be much more difficult to carry out. Although some difficulties have been identified, the overall picture is incomplete. State bodies should ensure that Central Authorities are suitably staffed and that the personnel are given appropriate equipment to carry out their tasks and keep track of applications.

## XVI. Potential Future Developments: Designing Suitable Minimum Standards

As the term appropriate measures is used when describing the action Central Authorities should take in regards to their duties, common minimum standards should be set. These could be different in the EU than at the international level, as a higher standard may be more appropriate at the EU level. There are particular areas where common minimum standards could be developed and some of these have been identified in the relevant sections above.

Efficient practice guides and relevant training would be very useful given the differing backgrounds and expertise of those working at Central Authorities.[167] This is particularly important; firstly given the vast duties of Central Authorities and secondly because they are now required to work under more than one maintenance instrument and the procedures vary under each instrument. Curry-Sumner points out that even though the new system is meant to simplify things, when it comes to Central Authorities it is more complicated because now they are expected to operate under three instruments rather than just one (the New York Convention).[168] Therefore, they should be given appropriate advice and training on the relevant procedures in each instrument. This is particularly true where the procedures are not the same within an instrument such as those on recognition and enforcement. This highlights potential problems with designating four different routes for recognition and enforcement under the two instruments.[169]

[166] See ch 9 s IV A, above.

[167] See in particular n 13. The Hague Conference has recently published their Practice Guide, to accompany the Convention. 'The European Union would do well to follow the lead of the HMC and create a similar *Practical Guide* for the EMR' (Curry-Sumner (n 13) s 6.5).

[168] Curry-Sumner (n 13) s 6.2 and see ch 2 above.

[169] See chs 7 and 8 above.

This problem is exacerbated where the role of Central Authorities in the process is not particularly clear, such as where the defence in Article 19 is raised.[170] In these situations, a practice guide on cooperation as well as information on suitable implementing legislation would be very useful.

Although guidelines are non-binding and do not have the same legal effect as the instruments, 'there is ample evidence that they do make a difference and that they have contributed substantially to the better functioning of the 1980 Convention.'[171] Examples which are also relevant to the instruments on maintenance are: the interpretation of the Convention and the safe and prompt return of the child (equivalent to the prompt enforcement of an order).[172] Practice guides have contained a section on aids to interpretation, States have taken into account other State practices and courts have also drawn from the conclusions of Special Commissions.[173] Similar practice under the maintenance instruments would be very useful. The development of relevant practice guides should be the first step in the process, followed by training and the holding of relevant meetings and discussions. The recent Conference held in Heidelberg was the first major meeting of those interested in maintenance since the Regulation entered into force and it was an excellent arena to open a discussion because participants came from a wide range of fields.[174] These discussions and the empirical research carried out highlighted the need for practice guides and training in this area.[175] The Hague Conference has just published its Handbook for Caseworkers. This is a practical handbook that is designed to assist caseworkers with the actual management of cases under the Convention. It is not a legal guide for lawyers, judges and decision makers.[176] The Handbook provides detailed information on how Central Authorities should respond to each type of request and provides step by step guidance. However, because it is designed specifically for Central Authorities, there is no guidance on what resources should be available to those working there.

In addition to further information and coherent training on the provisions and the procedures, the Commission could also give guidance on the structure of

[170] See above at s IX.

[171] W Duncan, 'The Maintenance of a Hague Convention. Adapting to Change. A Discussion of Techniques to Ensure that a Convention Remains "Fit for Purpose"' in G Venturini and S Bariatti (eds), *Liber Fausto Pocar: Vol. II, Nuovi instrumenti del diritto internazionale private-New Instruments of Private International Law* (Milan, Giuffrè, 2009) 291, 299.

[172] Ibid, 300–03.

[173] Ibid, 301.

[174] See www.heidelberg-conference2013.de/Presentations.html, accessed 9 June 2014.

[175] See, www.heidelberg-conference2013.de/tl_files/downloads-abstracts/abstracts-ab-3-3-2013/Presentation_Walker_final.pdf, accessed 9 June 2014. 'A **guide to good practice**, prepared under the auspices of the EU Commission, would be of great assistance to ensure the coherent and effective implementation and operation of Council Regulation 4/2009. Training programmes for all relevant stakeholders should ensure **continuing capacity** building.' (Conclusion 9 of the Heidelberg Conference, available at Annex VIII.)

[176] HCCH, 'Practical Handbook for Caseworkers under the 2007 Hague Child Support Convention' (The Hague, HCCH, 2013) para 4.

Central Authorities and requirements for those who work there.[177] Although this is a slight imposition on national law, because EU law is based on the principle of 'effectiveness' the Commission should be able to suggest standards that should be applied to ensure that Regulations are 'effective'. They could require that one member of each Central Authority was legally trained; because as shown in the preceding discussion the Regulation contains some very technical elements that would be better dealt with by a lawyer. These standards could also identify a minimum number of personnel that have to be employed per Y number of cases.

In the future it could be possible to create some kind of basic formula based on the number of employees required per application flow. However, at this stage this is difficult for a number of reasons, which have been identified above. Practitioners are still familiarising themselves with the new instruments so they are not necessarily working effectively yet. The Regulation is still in a transitional stage, so the old system still applies to a number of applications. Central Authorities have generally not received appropriate training on the new system, and the current databases are not necessarily practical and some contain errors. Therefore, until these problems are resolved it is difficult to suggest minimum standards in terms of structure as the Central Authorities are not necessarily functioning efficiently at this time due to these difficulties they face.[178] However a first attempt will be made.

In relation to meeting the time requirements in Article 58, Finland and Latvia were identified as Central Authorities that functioned effectively.[179] However, both these authorities received a relatively low number of applications in the period for which data was collected.[180] Finland received a higher number of applications and have less staff members than Latvia,[181] so Finland will be used as an example.

X (number of cases) : 51 + 3 = 54[◆]
Number of personnel: 2
Therefore: X/2 = Y
54/2 = 27

So if an extremely well-functioning authority like Finland is used,[182] that always meets the time requirements but has a relatively low number of applications then Y = 27, indicating that you need one staff member per every 27 applications.

[177] This will probably not be possible at the international level because each State ratifies individual Conventions at its own discretion. Therefore, in order to ensure that the Convention is as widely ratified as possible it would not be suitable to prescribe such strict standards at this level.

[178] See ch 9 ss IV and VI and s XV above in particular.

[179] See s XV, B.

[180] See Table 10.2 and Annex II.

[181] See s XV, B above.

[◆] This is the number of incoming applications plus the number of requests for specific measures (see Annexes II and IV).

[182] See n 157.

This is slightly unrealistic though, especially if the figure is applied to England and Wales.

X = 1288
1288/27 = 47

It would not be possible or realistic for England and Wales to employ so many case workers so therefore a different Member State has to be selected in the first instance.[183] This could be the Czech Republic which received over 100 applications but still managed to reach the time requirements in Art 58(3) and (4) in over 95 per cent of applications.[184] However, as mentioned previously the Czech Central Authority is extremely well staffed with 26 practitioners working there.[185] The case load was 198 so X = 198.[186]

198/26
Y = 7

This is even more unrealistic than the previous value for Y that was generated by using the Finnish Central Authority as an example. The final example that will be tested is Greece. Greece performed well under Article 58(3), meeting the requirement in almost 100 per cent of cases, but did not perform so well in relation to Article 58(4). This Central Authority is set up differently. There are two practitioners. One deals with full applications and the other with requests for specific measures.[187] It seems quite sensible to separate the case load in this way. It received 126 full applications and there is one person dealing with this. So in relation to the performance in Greece, Y=126. If this was applied to the UK it would need at least 10 practitioners (based on a case load of 1288 where each practitioner should deal with no more than 126 applications). This is much more achievable and realistic than the earlier figures produced, but it should be recognised that although the Greek Central Authority is functioning relatively well it could do better so this would be the minimum standard.

It would also be useful for the European Commission and the Hague Conference to determine minimum standards in terms of other resources available. This is because it is unclear what is meant by 'appropriate measure', so it would be useful to establish suitable standards. This is especially so when the term appropriate measure is often linked to available resources. States and/or authorities should not be able to argue that they cannot perform their duties, because what is an

[183] Currently the practitioners at this Central Authority are dealing with 257 applications each.
[184] See s XV B.
[185] See n 11.
[186] See Annexes II and IV.
[187] Email correspondence, 22 May 2013.

appropriate measure is a lower standard due to resources.[188] Minimum standards and best practices should be acceptable to States because all these things work as a direct correlation. For example, cost of work force would be cheaper in countries that may argue they have less money, and so would the cost of some resources.[189]

A system of cooperation has generally been seen as attractive for the reason that: Conventions that use this system 'are essentially channels for international co-operation between courts and administrations and do not require modifications of domestic rules of private international law. This makes them easier to absorb by countries.'[190] Therefore, a system of minimum standards although workable may not be particularly attractive to individual States. In the past the Hague Conference has tried to enforce best practices rather than minimum standards.[191] However, as the Maintenance Convention is slightly different in the sense that it contains traditional private international law rules as well as rules on administrative cooperation, minimum standards in relation to Central Authorities' duties may be easier to absorb under this Convention as Contracting States will already have accepted other necessary rules (indirect rules of jurisdiction and recognition and enforcement). Another reason that States may be willing to accept minimum standards in this area is the fact that, at least in the context of child support, they will have to provide legal aid in every case. So where the State has invested money in individual cases, it would appear to be in the State's best interests to ensure that Central Authorities have sufficient resources to efficiently fulfil their duties which include the ultimate enforcement of the order. Otherwise, States will have to pay legal aid but this may not be beneficial, because if the order is not enforced the State will most likely have to continue paying for the child through some form of family support.[192]

Minimum standards in Europe for the Regulation may be more easily absorbed in the first instance, than trying to establish minimum standards worldwide. Another option is that the Commission or the Court of Justice of the European Union (CJEU) sets some kind of minimum standards in the future.[193] This could be in Judicial Network meetings, through preliminary references to the CJEU to

[188] See above at s VI where States have been unimpressed with other States' efforts to locate children under the Child Abduction Convention.

[189] Norway, which is seen as an efficient authority, reported that it only spends one Euro per 33 Euros collected, see J Saue et al (n 83) 175.

[190] Van Loon (n 7) 183.

[191] See the Special Commission and practice guides on Child Abduction and Intercountry adoption.

[192] See ch 9 n 51.

[193] When discussing earlier instruments Beaumont and Moir recognise that one reason that EU private international law regulations are successful is because the CJEU is in a position to adjudicate on the provisions where necessary. 'The conferral of this jurisdiction has allowed the Convention to blossom and overcome interpretative difficulties which would have rent assunder other instruments aimed at the harmonisation or unification of laws' (G Moir and P Beaumont, 'Brussels Convention II: A New Private International Law Instrument in Family Matters for the European Union or the European Community' (1995) 20 *European Law Review* 268, 279).

determine the meaning of the term 'all appropriate measures',[194] or the Commission may raise enforcement proceedings against a Member State if it feels that State is not performing its duties effectively under the Regulation.[195] This may be of particular relevance in the context of maintenance as the duties of Central Authorities include actual enforcement.[196] A further thought that is rather far reaching at this stage, but in no way impossible, is that if Central Authorities are not given minimum resources which allow them to fulfil their duties, including the enforcement of the order, the State may be liable in damages for failure to fulfil Union law.[197]

A mechanism to assist Central Authorities with their work and encourage collaboration between them is the European Judicial Network. Under the Regulation, Central Authorities are required to meet regularly.[198] The meetings must be carried out in compliance with the provisions in the Decision establishing the Judicial Network.[199] The purposes of these meetings are to: enable practitioners to get to know each other and exchange experiences, provide a platform for discussion of practical and legal problems encountered by them, identify best practices in cooperation and exchange data and views,[200] and to deal with any specific questions.[201] These meetings provide an excellent platform for practitioners to get to know each other and to help them to find solutions to problems based on the experience of other practitioners and the advice of the Commission and the Council.[202]

However, information gathered suggests that these meetings have not been as helpful as they could be. This is because practitioners often find that when they raise points they are given an overview of what was initially intended by the provision, rather than a direct answer.[203] Practitioners would prefer a direct answer to

[194] Maintenance Regulation Art 51(2). However, it is recognised that the term 'all appropriate steps' is used in the Brussels IIbis Regulation (Art 55), and no reference has been made in respect of this at this date. It is considered that the duties considered in Brussels IIbis are much narrower than those contained in the Maintenance Regulation. Since the duties in the Maintenance Regulation are more extensive, particularly because they encompass actual enforcement, the exact meaning of this term may be more important in the context of maintenance.

[195] Art 258 of the Treaty on the Functioning of the European Union (TFEU), formerly Art 226 EC. This applies when a State fails to fulfil an obligation under the Treaty. This could include 'actions as well as omissions on the part of States, failure to implement directives, breaches of specific Treaty provisions or of other secondary legislation, or of any rule or standard which is an effective part of Community law.' P Craig and G de Burca, *EU Law: Text, Cases and Materials*, 5th edn (Oxford, Oxford University Press, 2011) 423 and see 415–32.

[196] See above at n 194 and see ch 9 nn 38–39.

[197] See C-479/93 *Francovich v Italy* [1995] ECR I-03843 and Craig and de Burca (n 195) 241–53.

[198] Maintenance Regulation Art 60(1).

[199] Council Decision (2001/470/EC) of 28 May 2001 establishing a European Judicial Network in civil and commercial matters [2001] OJ L 174/25 (Decision 2001/470/EC) and Art 60(2) of the Maintenance Regulation.

[200] Decision 2001/470/EC (n 199) Art 10(1).

[201] Ibid, Art 11.

[202] Ibid, Art 12(1). The Commission convenes the meetings, chairs them and provides a secretarial role.

[203] Information gathered at the Heidelberg Conference, where practitioners suggested that the European Network meetings were difficult to follow.

their questions so they know exactly what to do when applying the Regulation.[204] Hence the conclusion that a practice guide with clear guidelines that could serve as a basis for future training of Central Authorities would be a more effective way forward. Another issue is that the meetings are supposed to provide a platform for exchanging data. However, many Central Authorities do not currently have a method of collating data so this is not happening.[205] It was clear from the Heidelberg Conference that practitioners are interested in this data, and therefore it would be useful if they could gather their own data and discuss and exchange this information at the Judicial Network meetings. Finally, although these meetings can aid practitioners with the application of the Regulation and suggest what measures they should take, they will not necessarily solve the problem of lack of powers and resources for Central Authorities which are distributed at State level.

In the absence of a practical guide or other guidance on what is an 'appropriate measure' it might be possible to get an interpretation of what is intended by the term, and possibly therefore setting minimum standards in this area, through the preliminary reference system.[206] However, in order for a reference of this type to reach the CJEU, a number of things need to happen. Firstly, an individual who had made an application under the Regulation would have to raise a claim before the courts in a Member State, presumably against the Central Authority. This could be in relation to non-enforcement of an order for example. Secondly, the court hearing the case must consider that a reference to the CJEU would be necessary, on the particular question, for example, 'what is an appropriate measure' in order for it to determine the outcome of the case.[207] It is at the discretion of the national court whether it decides to make a reference or not. However, in such a case a reference would be important to secure the 'effectiveness' of EU law.[208] If the national court decides that it is not necessary to make a reference to the CJEU to decide the outcome of the case then it is up to the individual applicant to decide whether to proceed further with the case. They might accept the judgment of the court, or they may not have sufficient means to proceed further.

If the applicant does decide to proceed further, they would have to appeal to the court where there would be no further judicial remedy in that case, under the national system, before they are guaranteed that the question will be referred to the CJEU.[209] At this point in time this issue has not been raised before the CJEU so technically this court must refer the question.[210] Unfortunately this is not decisive as this court still has some discretion because of the 'acte clair' doctrine. If the

[204] Ibid. Discussions highlighted that practitioners would prefer more specific training and that they would find a practice guide useful.

[205] See ch 9 s VI above.

[206] Art 267 TFEU.

[207] Ibid, Art 267(2).

[208] See ch 9 s IV, A, and Craig and de Búrca (n 195) 478.

[209] Art 276 (3) TFEU. See C-99/00 *Criminal Proceedings against Lyckeskog* [2002] ECR I-4839 and C-210/06 *Cartesio Okató és Szolgáltató bt* [2008] ECR I-9641.

[210] C-28-30/62 *Da Costa en Shaake NV, Jacob Meijer NV and Hoechst-Holland NV v Nederlands Belastingadministratie* [1963] ECR 31.

national court considers that the term 'appropriate measures' is clear to them, then no reference is required.[211] However, this is only possible where certain conditions are met.[212] It is difficult to predict what the outcome will be in these particular types of situations as the conditions in *CILFIT* refer to the unique character of European Union law. However, although the term is incorporated into EU law, it is actually a Hague term that has been borrowed and instilled into EU law, therefore it is difficult to apply the *CILFIT* terminology in this situation. Despite this, because there is no guidance on what this term means, apart from the case law of the European Court of Human Rights (ECtHR),[213] it would be difficult to argue that the correct application or interpretation of the term is 'so obvious as to leave no scope for any reasonable doubt'[214] and that it is 'equally obvious to the courts of other Member States and the Court of Justice'.[215] Therefore the preliminary reference procedure could be useful for getting a definition of the term all appropriate measures but, depending on how the reference is worded and the CJEU answers the question, the solution given might only be appropriate for one or two duties. There are also a number of steps that have to be taken before a reference is made. However only one State needs to make a reference and now that there are 28 Member States it is possible that a reference could be made in this area.

The Treaty on the Functioning of the European Union also provides for enforcement mechanisms involving judicial proceedings against the Member States, which are brought either by the Commission or by a Member State. Article 258 establishes the general enforcement procedure, giving the Commission broad powers to bring enforcement proceedings against Member States which it considers to be in breach of Union law.[216] Commission enforcement proceedings are intended to ensure the general and uniform observance of Union law.[217] Therefore, if a State's Central Authority is working at a much lower standard than the others, this may suggest that this State is not complying with the 'uniform' observance of Union Law.

The procedure begins with the Commission notifying the State by way of a reasoned opinion. The State then has time to respond and try to comply with the requests sent by the Commission. If this does not happen then the Commission can bring proceedings before the CJEU. It is then up to the CJEU to decide if the State is in breach of its obligations under EU law. In this case it would be the inadequate implementation of EU law, specifically the Maintenance Regulation. If the Central Authority is not doing its job to a high enough standard, according to the

[211] C-283/81 *Srl CILFIT and Lanificio di Garvardo SpA v Ministry of Health* [1982] ECR 3415 para 16.

[212] Ibid, 16–21.

[213] See ch 9 n 27.

[214] *CILFIT* (n 211) para 16.

[215] Ibid. However, if a court does not refer when they should they could be liable to pay damages (C-224/01 *Köbler v Austria* [2003] ECR I-10239).

[216] See for example Communication (2002) 725.

[217] See Case-28/67 *Molkerei Zentrale Westfalen-Lippe v Hauptzollamt Paderborn* [1986] ECR 00211, 153.

Commission, this would suggest that the Regulation is inadequately implemented as the Central Authority plays an integral role in the application of the Regulation. If such a case went to the CJEU, the CJEU may have to determine what 'all appropriate measures' actually means, in the context of the Regulation, in order for the case to stand. In contrast, unless the Central Authority is virtually achieving nothing it may be difficult for the Commission to argue its case before the CJEU under the 'all appropriate measures' clause because there are no minimum standards set. If there were minimum standards set, then the Commission's job would be simpler as it would be easier to determine when the standards were not being met.[218]

Therefore, this creates another circular argument whereby a case before the CJEU may assist as this may allow us to determine what 'all appropriate measures are'. However, it may be difficult for the Commission to argue its case when no minimum standards are set. This highlights a major issue with the term 'all appropriate measures': it can be directly linked to available resources. Therefore, the term 'all appropriate measures' is insufficient by itself, and a set of minimum or common standards needs to be established and adhered to.

## XVII. Conclusion

Central Authorities are given a great deal of responsibility under the two new instruments. They are effectively accountable for the success of the instruments as a result of the wide range of duties they are given. Consequently, it is essential that Central Authorities' personnel are given appropriate training and provided with adequate resources in order to fulfil their duties under the instruments.

The resources and training put into the individual Central Authorities will be a key factor in determining how successful the Convention or Regulation will be in the Contracting or Member States. When discharging their duties Central Authorities are expected to take 'all appropriate measures'. Since what is appropriate can be directly correlated with resources, minimum standards should be set in order to make the instruments viable. This is because the responsibility given to Central Authorities is so extensive that their role is central to the success of the instruments. As such their role needs to be adequately fulfilled and cannot be diminished due to the fact that the term 'appropriate measure' is limited by resources.

It is unfortunate that the term 'appropriate measure' was taken directly from the Convention and placed in the Regulation. This is especially true when this was an area where originally the Regulation sought to achieve more than the

[218] It is noted that this could also happen under the Maintenance Convention and the Hague Protocol because the EU has ratified them as an organisation, it is a matter of Union law that can be interpreted by the CJEU in the same way as the Regulation.

Convention.[219] Therefore, it would be beneficial if minimum standards were set that Central Authorities had to adhere to, especially within Europe. In some areas the Regulation did go further than the Convention. It incorporates the term 'exchanging information' although it has been argued that this term does not make any significant difference in reality. The provisions concerning the location of parties also go further. Although no minimum standards have been set in terms of steps that should be taken in order to locate missing parties, minimum standards have been set in relation to information that Central Authorities should have access to. This additional provision should be beneficial and puts the Regulation a significant step ahead of the Convention. However, the final step taken by the Regulation may be unhelpful. This requirement removes the 'discretionary' nature of carrying out a request for a specific measure to locate the debtor. This could encourage spurious requests in this area, which will waste time and resources.

Data collected are incomplete but they do give some indication of how the Regulation is being implemented. Data suggests that there have been many requests relating to the location of debtors. At this point not many of these requests have resulted in full applications, so it is difficult to tell whether this means there were a number of spurious requests sent. There is also an indication that there may be a misunderstanding of when Central Authorities are allowed to recover their costs. Further, the study implies that some Central Authorities are finding it very difficult to meet the time requirements in Article 58. This is likely to be the result of a variety of factors such as: insufficient staffing, ineffective databases and over burdensome national laws of procedure. State bodies should try to appropriately staff Central Authorities and remove procedural obstacles where possible.

It is imperative that appropriate training seminars and programmes are provided and a Guide to Good Practice for the Regulation is produced. These elements should assist Central Authorities in carrying out their tasks under the Regulation in the future. This is because practitioners will understand the Regulation better and be clearer on what is expected of them. Practitioners would also be assisted if they had efficient databases that could help them monitor applications, and their progress, in order to assist them with fulfilling the time requirements and facilitating the ongoing enforcement of maintenance obligations.

[219] See ch 2 n 106.

# 11

# Conclusion

This book describes the previous maintenance regimes in the European Union and worldwide, before going on to analyse selected provisions in the new regime. This has been done to determine what the objectives were, indicate what has been achieved by the new regime and to highlight areas where problems still exist and further developments are required. The developments indicated relate to: amendments to the text of the Maintenance Regulation,[1] drawing up of practice guides, interpretation of the current instruments, appropriate training for Central Authorities personnel and the creation of minimum standards for Central Authorities in terms of both structure and the procedures available to them. The improvements identified aim to correspond with the pragmatic approach which seeks to find solutions which ensure the proper administration of justice, whilst respecting the rights and legitimate expectations of the parties.

When analysing the instruments the initial aims of the Regulation and the Hague Convention[2] are taken into account in order to determine to what extent these have been met. This can be seen particularly in the analysis of the Regulation where four of the five areas identified by the Commission are selected and then discussed in detail. Areas that were not identified by the Commission were also selected and analysed in order to highlight why the Regulation should have tried to address these specific areas. Finally, the book incorporates data collected from an empirical study on the first year of operation of the Regulation. The incorporation of these data is important because they are the first data collected on the circulation of maintenance applications within the EU, both under the Regulation and previously. Therefore even data on the number of applications and the number of requests for specific measures is invaluable.[3] The European Commission and the Hague Conference require this information in order to monitor how the instruments are working. State Governments can use the information to monitor how many applications were received and whether they are effectively resourcing the bodies that work in the area (the UK Government used these data for its

[1] Council Regulation (EC) 4/2009 of 18 December 2008 on jurisdiction, applicable law, recognition and enforcement of decisions and cooperation in matters relating to maintenance obligations [2009] OJ L7/1.

[2] Hague Convention of 23 November 2007 on the International Recovery of Child Support and other forms of Family Maintenance.

[3] See Annexes II and IV.

civil justice impact assessment). Practitioners are interested in the information in order to analyse the spread of applications and see how other authorities are performing. Practitioners should be able to produce and access this information through simplified electronic systems in order to keep track of applications and monitor their progress.

First observations of data collected indicated that there were a relatively modest number of applications. This would suggest that State bodies are not doing enough to promote the new instruments and there is a lack of public awareness in this area. This argument is strengthened by the fact that there were only a small number of applications to obtain a new decision, and Ireland reported that it received no applications at all in the first six months. This indicates that despite the fact the new systems make it simpler for applicants to claim child support, and possibly other forms of maintenance from abroad, a lack of public awareness means that the Regulation is not being well utilised. This is problematic for States because in the context of child support it will generally mean that the State has to pay out in benefits to support the child, where the absent parent does not. If the instruments were properly advertised then there would probably be a higher number of applications. This could be done by producing an information handbook for potential applicants in order to raise awareness and understanding of the instruments.

It is also shown that some States received many more applications than others. It is concluded that the number of applications received is not directly linked to population. Instead it is linked to two types of migration trends. Firstly, migration trends that have been prevalent for many years due to: geographical location, language and better quality of life. This is seen between Finland ↔ Estonia, Poland → Germany and UK ↔ Ireland. Secondly, there are migration trends which are linked directly to membership of the EU combined with the opening of the labour market. For example, Poland → UK, Poland → Ireland, Poland → Sweden, Poland → Netherlands. These trends are also prevalent for other States that joined the EU in 2004 such as Latvia. However, since the economic downturn these trends are changing again, with Ireland become a leading State for emigration. This book only begins to explore these trends but it is clear that data collected on maintenance applications supports earlier information on migration. Ultimately, as migration trends continue to change more families will become displaced which will result in more need for recovery of child support from abroad. Therefore, it is important that public awareness of the Regulation is increased in order to save public funds as far as possible.

## I. Scope and Characterisation

There is a gap in the instruments in that they give no definition of 'maintenance'. This is problematic because 'maintenance' is often characterised in a variety of ways in different States, however, this results in a discrepancy in the instruments in the sense that the scope is unclear. This is important when considering the distinction between maintenance and matrimonial property on divorce, since each aspect will be dealt with by different instruments and therefore possibly different courts. It is concluded that it would be impossible to give a clear definition of maintenance in the instruments and EU Member States will have to try and provide an 'autonomous interpretation' as envisaged in the Regulation by giving respect to the principles in *Van den Boogaard*.[4] However, the interpretation of this is far from clear cut and this could result in irreconcilable judgments. This will mean decisions may not be enforced, which will interfere with the proper administration of justice. This affects both Protocol and non-Protocol track cases in the same way.

## II. EU Solutions

Problems in relation to the characterisation of maintenance, which result from the fact that 'maintenance' remains undefined, should be dealt with in the EU under the direct grounds of jurisdiction. At some point in the future there should be one instrument that coordinates jurisdiction for divorce, maintenance and matrimonial property. However, it is recognised that this cannot be achieved at this stage. A first step towards this would be to coordinate the grounds of jurisdiction in each of the instruments. This would mean that the Maintenance Regulation should be amended to contain a hierarchy of jurisdictional grounds. The court determining status would be placed first on the list to ensure that where maintenance was linked to divorce, the divorce court would also hear the maintenance aspects. The court which had jurisdiction under Brussels IIbis would also have jurisdiction for adult maintenance, no matter what ground was selected under Brussels IIbis.[5] Although the grounds in Brussels IIbis could be revised and narrowed themselves, this would be a first step towards coherence in this area. To complete the picture the same hierarchy could be included in the future instrument on matrimonial property so that the divorce court had jurisdiction to rule on the divorce as well as the financial aspects of divorce.

Coherence in this area will increase certainty for parties, prevent conflicting and exorbitant proceedings in different courts (which will dissipate assets), reduce irreconcilable judgments and make a step towards reducing the practice

[4] C-220/95 *Van den Boogaard v Laumen* [1997] ECR I-1147.

[5] Council Regulation (EC) 2201/2003 of 27 November 2003 on jurisdiction, recognition and enforcement of judgments in matrimonial matters and matters of parental responsibility, repealing Regulation (EC) No 1347/2000 [2003] OJ L 338/1 (Brussels IIbis). It is noted that the current grounds contained in Brussels IIbis are far from perfect but a full analysis of these grounds is beyond the scope of this book.

of a 'rush to court'. An amendment in this area is extremely important because the practice of a 'rush to court' is exacerbated by the *lis pendens* provisions. Under the Regulation the court first seised must hear the case and there is no option to transfer to a court more closely connected. Further, the rules on *lis pendens* and related actions will not necessarily resolve problems in this area. This is because the English language *lis pendens* provision requires that the two proceedings have the same cause of action. The other language versions also refer to the same objective but they require that both the objective and the cause of action is the same. It would be preferable if they referred to the same cause of action 'or' the same objective, and the English language version matched the other official texts. The current *lis pendens* provision therefore cannot solve the current problems and neither can the related action provision because this does not require that proceedings will be stayed.

A further problem with the provisions on *lis pendens* and related actions is that they only apply to proceedings in other Member States and do not apply to proceedings in third States, whereas the provisions on irreconcilable judgments do. Therefore this means that under the current system there are many contexts in which irreconcilable judgments can arise. It has been argued previously by Weller,[6] that it is preferable to resolve irreconcilable judgments at the jurisdiction stage rather than the recognition and enforcement stage. Therefore, a coherent approach between the relevant EU private international law instruments in this area would be preferable. Lessons can be learned from the Brussels I recast which has discretionary *lis pendens* and related actions provisions in relation to third States.

Recognition and enforcement, primarily the abolition of *exequatur*, was an area identified by the Commission in its impact assessment and is one of the key features of the Regulation. However, regardless of what route is applied, the irreconcilable judgments defence is retained. It is shown in the conclusions above that irreconcilable judgments could arise for a variety of reasons and thereby impede the free movement of judgments. It is argued that many of these problems could be dealt with at the jurisdiction stage. However, it is also suggested that there are problems with the decision in *Hoffmann* and it has been wrongly followed in subsequent judgments. Where judges are unsure of the impact of a divorce on an earlier maintenance decision, and consider that the obligation to pay maintenance still stands, they should consider referring the question to the Court of Justice of the European Union (CJEU) in order to solve this problem rather than automatically following *Hoffmann*.[7]

The Regulation goes too far by abolishing the *exequatur* process without retaining safeguards such as the public policy defence, particularly given that

[6] Weller in B Hess, T Pfeiffer and P Schlosser, *The Brussels I Regulation 44/2001. The Heidelberg Report on the Application of Regulation Brussels I in 25 Member States* (Study JLS/C4/2005/03) (Munich, Verlag CH Beck, 2008) (Heidelberg Report) 71.

[7] C-145/86 *Hoffmann v Krieg* [1988] ECR 645.

this premise is based on the harmonisation of applicable law. This step was not necessary and was definitely not proportionate to the aim. This is highlighted by the fact that all the relevant documents and studies carried out suggest that the *exequatur* process rarely causes delays and does not contribute to the delay at the actual enforcement stage. Although the public policy defence will rarely be necessary in maintenance cases it is still useful to retain this as a safety valve in exceptional cases, and it is shown that there will be situations where this is necessary. This is because the limited safeguards in the Protocol will not assist in some exceptional situations. Further it is demonstrated that in nearly every child support application, and in many other applications the likely outcome will be the application of the *lex fori*. Therefore it is questioned how it is justifiable to put decisions originating in the UK and Denmark in a different category to those originating elsewhere in the EU when in many cases the same law will be applied (the *lex fori*) whether the Protocol is applied or not.

In certain situations it may be possible for States to refuse to enforce orders under national rules of enforcement. A case in point could be where parentage cannot be established. Because parentage is not covered by the instruments, an assessment of the claim based on a review of parentage is not a review of the substance of the maintenance claim. If parentage is not established the maintenance obligation should not usually exist because the two aspects, although severed in the instrument, are mutually exclusive. Where parentage does not exist there is usually no moral obligation to pay maintenance. It is believed it would be possible for a State to refuse to enforce a child support obligation on this basis. However, at this point this is merely speculative and it is hard to establish whether this would pass the scrutiny of the CJEU.

In respect of fundamental human rights, which are covered by the public policy defence, the European Court of Human Rights (ECtHR) has suggested that the enforcing court should review the human rights points when the State of origin is party to the European Convention on Human Rights (ECHR) (which includes all EU Member States), but this requirement is currently subject to the Bosphorus presumption.[8] However, an order or obligation that was made in violation of human rights will also violate the human rights of an individual at the point at which it is enforced. Therefore, ultimately if a Member State enforces a decision which violates an individual's fundamental rights then it will be in breach of its obligations under the ECHR regardless of which State the decision originated in. Therefore the retention of the public policy exception as a safety valve will also prevent the State of enforcement from possibly being liable for breach of its human rights duties in exceptional cases. This is because its human rights obligations withstand, despite the fact there is limited scope for review under the Maintenance Regulation. Overall, because the whole system is biased towards

[8] However this presumption should no longer be viable post accession. See ch 7 s V and P Craig and G de Búrca, *EU Law Text Cases and Materials*, 5th edn (Oxford, Oxford University Press, 2011) 404 (*Bosphorus Hava Yollari Turizm v Ireland* (2006) 42 EHRR 1).

creditors, then it would be better to retain the public policy safeguard to protect debtors where necessary in order to ensure that the legitimate expectations of parties are upheld.

It is not sensible to have two different procedures (a Protocol and non-Protocol track) operating within the EU. Data collected suggests that these procedures are not necessarily clear in practice and it is also shown that the available applications for recognition and enforcement and actual enforcement could be improved. Therefore, it would be sensible to amend the Regulation in this area. Another problem with the Protocol track is that it contains a limited right for review where the debtor was not heard in the initial proceedings, if this was not his fault.[9] The provision requires that the debtor seeks a review in the State of origin rather than the State of enforcement. There are two problems with this. Firstly, the enforcing court can continue with enforcement proceedings whilst the review is ongoing. Secondly, where the enforcing court has stayed proceedings there is no mechanism in the Regulation to inform that court of the outcome of the review in the State of origin. If the proceedings remain in limbo this does not assist with the proper administration of justice and does not necessarily uphold the legitimate expectations of either party. Therefore this gap in the Regulation may mean that enforcement proceedings are delayed further under the Protocol track, than when *exequatur* proceedings are retained, despite the fact that the abolition of *exequatur* was meant to prevent unnecessary delays.

Finally, where the public policy defence is retained the rights of the defence exception is unnecessary. This is because the right to a fair trial, under Article 6 ECHR and Article 47 of the Charter of Fundamental Rights of the European Union,[10] falls under a European notion of public policy. Although some maintain that it is better to keep the defences separate for clarity, it is shown that the rights of the defence exception is in fact not capable of doing what it sets out to do.[11] This is because it does not adequately protect the right to a fair trial, unlike the relevant provisions in the human rights documents. Further, in other ways it is broader than the human rights protection which means recognition of decisions could be denied when in fact there is no true violation of the rights of the defence. Therefore, it would be preferable to eliminate the rights of the defence exception because this would mean that all decisions would be recognised and enforced unless there is a true breach of public policy which would include a violation of one of the parties' human rights.

The overall conclusion in this area is that the process would be simpler and clearer if there was one track for recognition and enforcement. This would either be the same procedure that is contained in the non-Protocol track of the Regulation and the original Brussels I, or the process that will be contained in

[9] See Hague Protocol Art 19.

[10] [2000] OJ C364/01.

[11] For example see C-7/98 *Krombach v Bamberski* [2000] ECR I-1395.

the Brussels I recast.[12] Both procedures retain necessary safeguards that should ensure that parties are protected in exceptional circumstances. However, the proposed amendment to the Maintenance Regulation differs from both these as the only safeguards available will be the public policy defence and irreconcilable judgments. The rights of the defence exception will be eliminated. The public policy defence should be interpreted strictly and only be used in exceptional cases in order to uphold the rights and the legitimate expectations of the parties. The irreconcilable judgments defence is problematic and it has been suggested the earlier decision in *Hoffmann*[13] is difficult to follow and could be wrong. National courts should make use of their ability to make a preliminary reference to the CJEU if they need clarity in this area so that decisions are enforced as far as possible. Any review of the Regulation should try to provide more coherence at the jurisdiction stage in order to reduce the occurrence of irreconcilable judgments, so that refusal of enforcement on this ground is kept to a minimum.

The Regulation does little in the area of actual enforcement, despite the fact that the initial proposal sought to eliminate delays in this area and also included a directive on the enforcement of decisions.[14] The directive failed, however. This is because enforcement has always been a matter for national law, but it is regulated indirectly by the principles of 'equivalence' and 'effectiveness' as interpreted by the CJEU. Even though actual enforcement is not regulated directly by the Regulation (apart from the provisions on irreconcilable judgments and prescription and limitation in Article 21 of the Regulation) the processes available at this stage are still subject to the scrutiny of the CJEU and the Commission because the Maintenance Regulation is still a matter of EU law. Enforcement proceedings are also subject to the scrutiny of the ECtHR. The ECtHR has in the past taken a robust approach in relation to enforcement proceedings and held States liable for failure to enforce cross border decisions. Despite the fact that there are delays before the Strasbourg Court, it is important that the ECtHR continues to do this in order to strengthen the application of international documents.

Practice in the first year of the operation of the Regulation indicated that it is possible to get an order enforced quickly, within six months of the initial application, but this did not happen on a regular basis. It is anticipated that the number of applications enforced expeditiously should increase as practitioners become more familiar with the system under the Regulation. However, it is expected that the number of applications circulated under the Regulation will also increase as

[12] Council Regulation (EC) 44/2001 of 22 December 2000 on jurisdiction and the recognition and enforcement of judgments in civil and commercial matters [2001] OJ L012/1 (Brussels I); Regulation (EU) 1215/2012 of the European Parliament and of the Council of 12 December 2012 on jurisdiction and the recognition and enforcement of judgments in civil and commercial matters (recast) [2012] OJ L351/1(Brussels I recast).

[13] *Hoffmann* (n 7).

[14] Staff Working Document, Annex to the Proposal for a Council Regulation on jurisdiction, applicable law, recognition and enforcement of decisions and cooperation in matters relating to maintenance obligations—Impact assessment, SEC/2005/1629, ss 1.4 and 3(iii).

public knowledge and awareness increases. Therefore, it is again important that practitioners working on these instruments have sufficient resources, such as appropriate IT systems, to assist them with securing the enforcement of orders whether they do this themselves or they have a monitoring role to ensure that the relevant enforcing body does this. The EU could have taken a more robust approach in this area. The Regulation could have included minimum standards for enforcement such as time requirements in order to prevent excessive delays, and given a list of enforcement mechanisms. This is again related to the conclusions on administrative cooperation. Setting minimum standards, such as time requirements, would not impede drastically on national enforcement laws or insist that a specific designated body deal with the enforcement. It would just require that the national enforcement procedures already in place were applied efficiently to ensure that the order was enforced within a suitable time period.

Administrative cooperation is an area where the Regulation initially intended to go further than the Convention, but this was not really achieved. The provisions on administrative cooperation are virtually identical, with a few small differences. The only additional provision that makes a significant positive development is the requirement that Central Authorities have access to relevant databases, or the information stored on them, so that they can assist applicants to locate the other party.[15] However, apart from this the Regulation does not go far enough and the direct implementation of the term 'appropriate measures' from the Convention was insufficient.

Additional minimum standards should have been set in Europe in order to help ensure that the Regulation is applied appropriately and effectively. Although the Commission and the CJEU can monitor the performance of Central Authorities it would have been better if the instrument had set clearer standards that Member States had to adhere to. The standards set should have been in relation to the resources available. This would include access to suitable information and databases. The collection of data indicated that Central Authorities were having difficulty effectively monitoring applications with the information available and also indicated errors with the systems. Follow up dialogue with Central Authority staff via email and at the Heidelberg Conference indicated that they were not happy with the resources available to them and also that they were unaware of the true extent of their duties such as those on actual enforcement. In fact, first correspondence with the Reciprocal Enforcement of Maintenance Orders Unit (REMO) indicated that they were basically a postal system that stamped documents but were unaware of what was happening in individual applications. Therefore the Heidelberg project raised awareness of the requirements under the Regulation, resulting in increased engagement with individual applications.

Minimum standards could also cover minimum staffing requirements. Based on data collected and follow up information on the structure of Central

[15] Maintenance Regulation Arts 61 and 62.

Authorities, it is clear that some Central Authorities operate more efficiently than others. The information gathered has been analysed in order to create a simple formula which suggests how many applications a staff member can deal with in a year in order for the applications to be processed efficiently. This is something that should be worked on as Central Authorities become more aware of how to apply the Regulation and applications increase. Ideally the collection of follow up data which would give a complete picture of the operation of the Regulation, including the length of time taken for orders to be enforced, would be used to finalise the formula. This would then be presented as a suitable minimum standard to be added to the text when the Regulation is reviewed. There should also be a requirement that there is one qualified lawyer working at each Central Authority.

The European Commission should develop a Practice Guide for the Maintenance Regulation. The provisions of the new instrument are quite complicated and it is believed that practitioners would find the instrument easier to apply if they had clear guidance and were given effective training. Dialogue with Central Authorities and information collected indicated that they would welcome a Practice Guide which would explain how to apply the Regulation. They also specified that they would like clear, concise and coherent training on the Regulation. It was pointed out that the civil justice meetings are ineffective because they are not provided with direct answers. This feedback supports the argument that Central Authorities need at least one legally trained lawyer who can begin to assist the other practitioners with their questions relating to the detailed legal rules in the Regulation. It is the job of international institutions and national governments to ensure that all staff working at Central Authorities are appropriately trained and have sufficient knowledge of the relevant laws and procedures. This will assist with the effective implementation of the instruments. Simple guides for the general public should also be produced to increase knowledge and awareness of the Regulation, and to assist maintenance creditors with making a claim and enforcing their rights.

Although data collected gives some indication of how the Regulation is operating, further research is required when the Regulation has been in force for longer. Future data collection should be followed up by interviews with practitioners in order to check any disparities in the information provided. These data should provide more definitive answers in areas such as: how many requests for specific measures are turning into full applications, how long it is taking for applications to be enforced and how well the provisions on the restriction of jurisdiction of debtors in modification proceedings are working. It is also hoped that more information will be provided on legal aid. Data collected this time in this area was so minimal that it could not be analysed fully. More comprehensive data collected at a later date would supplement the initial findings and mean conclusions could be reached in the areas where current data does not provide definitive answers.

So overall does the Regulation really 'eliminate all obstacles to the cross border recovery of maintenance'? The conclusions reached in each chapter would suggest not. In regard to the initial aims not enough has been achieved in the area of actual enforcement or administrative cooperation. There is no way that all obstacles could be removed unless the Union regulated every matter fully including 'actual enforcement'.[16] It is also difficult to achieve without setting suitable standards and requirements on the structure and organisation of Central Authorities including requirements on the qualifications and training of staff.[17] This will get more difficult as the Union continues to grow.[18] Finally, because there is no definition of maintenance it is likely that problems with the recognition of decisions will arise in the context of spousal maintenance due to questions surrounding the characterisation of maintenance which is exacerbated by the numerous grounds of jurisdiction available.[19]

## III. International Solutions

The provisions in the Convention on recognition and enforcement differ greatly from the provisions in the Regulation. This is because the Convention contains indirect rules of jurisdiction as well as additional grounds for the refusal of enforcement. Because the Convention will not be amended for some time, if at all, the suggestions in this area relate solely to the interpretation of the Convention and any reservations or declarations that are made in a particular State. Judges should try to enforce decisions by accepting the indirect ground of jurisdiction adopted by the court of origin, as far as possible, and interpreting the exceptions to recognition and enforceability as restrictively as possible. This is an area where judicial cooperation is essential and judges should work together to establish on what basis the indirect grounds of jurisdiction will be accepted.

In this respect the Hague Conference holds regular Special Review Commissions on the operation of its Conventions. It should ensure that Commissions are also held on the Maintenance Convention and that these are well advertised in order to encourage wide attendance. This opens the forum for discussions and gives practitioners, judges and officials from all over the world a chance to meet and discuss problems and issues. Recommendations and Conclusions are also produced at the end of each Commission which could be used as an aid to interpretation. The Hague Conference should provide regular training seminars, correspond with practitioners and produce follow up Practical Guides and Handbooks as necessary. They should also consider setting up a database like INCADAT (for the

[16] See ch 9.

[17] See ch 10.

[18] For example, the Bulgarian Central Authority had still not provided the European Commission with an email address, almost two years after the Regulation entered into force.

[19] See chs 3, 5 and 7. The Regulation did nothing to address any of these issues, even the abolition of *exequatur* does not achieve much in this area because refusal of enforcement on the basis of irreconcilable judgments still exists (see ch 7).

Abduction Convention) in order for cases under the Maintenance Convention to be made available to those interested, in the official languages of the Hague Conference. This would be another way for judges and practitioners to be kept up to date with practice in other Contracting States.

The Convention makes a major development in the area of actual enforcement. It is the first Hague Convention to include a separate chapter on actual enforcement. This chapter provides comparable provisions to the EU law principles of equivalence and effectiveness in the body of the Convention, through adopting a non-discrimination principle and by requiring that Contracting States make 'effective' enforcement mechanisms available. The Convention also gives an illustrative list of enforcement mechanisms that Contracting States should think about making available.

## IV. Overall Comments

Both instruments require Central Authorities to take steps to facilitate and assist with the enforcement of decisions. It is a positive development that the instruments list three requirements for Central Authorities in the context of actual enforcement. However, because Central Authorities are only required to take 'appropriate measures' in this regard, they may not take all the steps necessary to ensure enforcement is secured. However, the effort made by State bodies, including Central Authorities, is subject to the review of the CJEU, the European Commission and the ECtHR. This applies not only to the Regulation, but also to the Convention where the application involves a European State. The use of an efficient database, such as iSupport, should assist with the ongoing enforcement of obligations under the instruments and also the collection of further data. The empirical research suggests that the databases in place are ineffective and also flagged up the fact that not every State is using a database. In this regard lessons can be learnt from the operation of the Regulation for the implementation of the Convention. Suitable databases that work correctly and produce statistics should be utilised from the outset. Follow up data should be collected on the Regulation and the Hague Conference should collect data on the operation of the Convention when it applies in more States.

## V. Final Remarks

Overall, the current system for the cross border recovery of child support and maintenance is much more comprehensive than the previous system. The Regulation and the Hague 2007 Convention are supplemented by the Hague

Protocol for States which also wish applicable law to be regulated, creating a flexible system. However, it is clear that further developments are still required. In the context of the Regulation it is argued that the instrument should be changed in the areas of jurisdiction and recognition and enforcement. This is to create a more coherent approach, which should increase certainty for individuals and in turn secure the enforcement of more maintenance obligations whilst still protecting the rights and expectations of the parties. It is also considered that the provisions on actual enforcement and administrative cooperation could be tightened in the future by setting official minimum standards. However, if this is not possible then the Commission, the CJEU, the ECtHR and national bodies should ensure that the provisions are interpreted appropriately to achieve the aims of the Regulation. Central Authorities should also be given appropriate training and the Commission should produce a Guide to Good Practice. In the context of the Convention all the arguments insist on its proper interpretation in addition to training programmes and the development of other documents that can work as an aid to interpretation. It is imperative that the Convention and Regulation are implemented properly and appropriate training and guidance is given in order to ensure that they operate as effectively as possible.

UNIVERSITY OF ABERDEEN

Institut für ausländisches und internationales Privat- und Wirtschaftsrecht
der Ruprecht-Karls-Universität Heidelberg

DIJuF
Forum für Fachfragen

# STATISTICAL QUESTIONNAIRE ON THE MAINTENANCE APPLICATIONS RECEIVED FROM 1 October 2011 TO 30 September 2012 FROM THE EUROPEAN UNION MEMBER STATES

## EMPIRICAL RESEARCH ON THE APPLICATION OF THE NEW MAINTENANCE REGULATION

**(Council Regulation No 4/2009 of 18 December 2008 on jurisdiction, applicable law, recognition and enforcement of decisions and cooperation in matters relating to maintenance obligations)**

# Question 1: Applications to obtain a new decision or the modification of a decision (Articles 56(1)(c)–(f) and 56(2)(b)–(c) Annex VII)*

## a) Incoming

*Part I: Applications to obtain a decision (Articles 56(1)(c) and (d))*

**Please type in as appropriate for each Member State**

| Member States | Number of incoming applications per Member State | Number of applications where a positive decision was obtained | Number of applications falling under Article 46 | Number of applications, if any, that were found manifestly unfounded under Article 46 (2) |
|---|---|---|---|---|
| Austria | | | | |
| Belgium | | | | |
| Bulgaria | | | | |
| Cyprus | | | | |
| Czech Republic | | | | |
| Denmark | | | | |
| Estonia | | | | |
| Finland | | | | |
| France | | | | |
| Germany | | | | |
| Greece | | | | |
| Hungary | | | | |
| Ireland | | | | |
| Italy | | | | |
| Latvia | | | | |
| Lithuania | | | | |
| Luxembourg | | | | |
| Malta | | | | |

*(Continued)*

* When answering the questions please only include applications submitted between 1st October 2011 and 30th September 2012.

| Member States | Number of incoming applications per Member State | Number of applications where a positive decision was obtained | Number of applications falling under Article 46 | Number of applications, if any, that were found manifestly unfounded under Article 46 (2) |
|---|---|---|---|---|
| Netherlands | | | | |
| Poland | | | | |
| Portugal | | | | |
| Romania | | | | |
| Slovakia | | | | |
| Slovenia | | | | |
| Spain | | | | |
| Sweden | | | | |
| United Kingdom | | | | |
| a) England and Wales | | | | |
| b) Scotland | | | | |
| c) Northern Ireland | | | | |
| d) Gibraltar | | | | |

### *Part II: Applications for modification of a decision by a creditor (Articles 56 (1)(e) and (f))*

**Please type in as appropriate for each Member State**

| Member States | Number of incoming applications per Member State | Number of applications where modification was obtained | Number of applications falling under Article 46 | Number of applications, if any, that were found manifestly unfounded under Article 46 (2) |
|---|---|---|---|---|
| Austria | | | | |
| Belgium | | | | |
| Bulgaria | | | | |
| Cyprus | | | | |
| Czech Republic | | | | |

*(Continued)*

| Member States | Number of incoming applications per Member State | Number of applications where modification was obtained | Number of applications falling under Article 46 | Number of applications, if any, that were found manifestly unfounded under Article 46 (2) |
|---|---|---|---|---|
| Denmark | | | | |
| Estonia | | | | |
| Finland | | | | |
| France | | | | |
| Germany | | | | |
| Greece | | | | |
| Hungary | | | | |
| Ireland | | | | |
| Italy | | | | |
| Latvia | | | | |
| Lithuania | | | | |
| Luxembourg | | | | |
| Malta | | | | |
| Netherlands | | | | |
| Poland | | | | |
| Portugal | | | | |
| Romania | | | | |
| Slovakia | | | | |
| Slovenia | | | | |
| Spain | | | | |
| Sweden | | | | |
| United Kingdom | | | | |
| a) England and Wales | | | | |
| b) Scotland | | | | |
| c) Northern Ireland | | | | |
| d) Gibraltar | | | | |

## *Part III: Applications for modification of a decision by a debtor (Articles 56(2)(b) and (c))*

**Please type in as appropriate for each Member State**

| Member States | Number of incoming applications per Member State | Number of applications where modification was obtained |
|---|---|---|
| Austria | | |
| Belgium | | |
| Bulgaria | | |
| Cyprus | | |
| Czech Republic | | |
| Denmark | | |
| Estonia | | |
| Finland | | |
| France | | |
| Germany | | |
| Greece | | |
| Hungary | | |
| Ireland | | |
| Italy | | |
| Latvia | | |
| Lithuania | | |
| Luxembourg | | |
| Malta | | |
| Netherlands | | |
| Poland | | |
| Portugal | | |
| Romania | | |
| Slovakia | | |
| Slovenia | | |
| Spain | | |
| Sweden | | |
| United Kingdom | | |
| a) England and Wales | | |
| b) Scotland | | |
| c) Northern Ireland | | |
| d) Gibraltar | | |

## b) Outgoing

*Part I: Applications to obtain a decision (Articles 56(1)(c) and (d))*

**Please type in as appropriate for each Member State**

| Member States | Number of outgoing applications per Member State | Number of applications where a positive decision was obtained | Number of applications falling under Article 46 | Number of applications, if any, that were found manifestly unfounded under Article 46 (2) |
|---|---|---|---|---|
| Austria | | | | |
| Belgium | | | | |
| Bulgaria | | | | |
| Cyprus | | | | |
| Czech Republic | | | | |
| Denmark | | | | |
| Estonia | | | | |
| Finland | | | | |
| France | | | | |
| Germany | | | | |
| Greece | | | | |
| Hungary | | | | |
| Ireland | | | | |
| Italy | | | | |
| Latvia | | | | |
| Lithuania | | | | |
| Luxembourg | | | | |
| Malta | | | | |
| Netherlands | | | | |
| Poland | | | | |
| Portugal | | | | |
| Romania | | | | |
| Slovakia | | | | |
| Slovenia | | | | |

*(Continued)*

| Member States | Number of outgoing applications per Member State | Number of applications where a positive decision was obtained | Number of applications falling under Article 46 | Number of applications, if any, that were found manifestly unfounded under Article 46 (2) |
|---|---|---|---|---|
| Spain | | | | |
| Sweden | | | | |
| United Kingdom | | | | |
| a) England and Wales | | | | |
| b) Scotland | | | | |
| c) Northern Ireland | | | | |
| d) Gibraltar | | | | |

*Part II: Applications for modification of a decision by a creditor (Articles 56(1)(e) and (f))*

**Please type in as appropriate for each Member State**

| Member States | Number of outgoing applications per Member State | Number of applications where modification was obtained | Number of applications falling under Article 46 | Number of applications, if any, that were found manifestly unfounded under Article 46 (2) |
|---|---|---|---|---|
| Austria | | | | |
| Belgium | | | | |
| Bulgaria | | | | |
| Cyprus | | | | |
| Czech Republic | | | | |
| Denmark | | | | |
| Estonia | | | | |
| Finland | | | | |
| France | | | | |
| Germany | | | | |
| Greece | | | | |

*(Continued)*

| Member States | Number of outgoing applications per Member State | Number of applications where modification was obtained | Number of applications falling under Article 46 | Number of applications, if any, that were found manifestly unfounded under Article 46 (2) |
|---|---|---|---|---|
| Hungary | | | | |
| Ireland | | | | |
| Italy | | | | |
| Latvia | | | | |
| Lithuania | | | | |
| Luxembourg | | | | |
| Malta | | | | |
| Netherlands | | | | |
| Poland | | | | |
| Portugal | | | | |
| Romania | | | | |
| Slovakia | | | | |
| Slovenia | | | | |
| Spain | | | | |
| Sweden | | | | |
| United Kingdom | | | | |
| a) England and Wales | | | | |
| b) Scotland | | | | |
| c) Northern Ireland | | | | |
| d) Gibraltar | | | | |

## *Part III: Applications for modification of a decision by a debtor (Articles 56(2)(b) and (c))*

**Please type in as appropriate for each Member State**

| Member States | Number of outgoing applications per Member State | Number of applications where modification was obtained |
|---|---|---|
| Austria | | |
| Belgium | | |
| Bulgaria | | |
| Cyprus | | |
| Czech Republic | | |
| Denmark | | |
| Estonia | | |
| Finland | | |
| France | | |
| Germany | | |
| Greece | | |
| Hungary | | |
| Ireland | | |
| Italy | | |
| Latvia | | |
| Lithuania | | |
| Luxembourg | | |
| Malta | | |
| Netherlands | | |
| Poland | | |
| Portugal | | |
| Romania | | |
| Slovakia | | |
| Slovenia | | |
| Spain | | |
| Sweden | | |
| United Kingdom | | |
| a) England and Wales | | |
| b) Scotland | | |
| c) Northern Ireland | | |
| d) Gibraltar | | |

## Question 2: Number of requests for specific measures (Art 53 and Annex V)

### a) Incoming (part I)

| Member States | Total number of incoming requests for specific measures per Member State under Article 53 | Number of requests to take appropriate specific measures under Article 51(2)(b)[i] | Number of requests to take appropriate specific measures under Article 51(2)(c)[ii] | Number of requests to take appropriate specific measures under Article 51(2)(g)[iii] | Number of requests to take appropriate specific measures under Article 51(2)(h)[iv] | Number of requests to take appropriate specific measures under Article 51(2)(i)[v] | Number of requests to take appropriate specific measures under Article 51(2)(j)[vi] |
|---|---|---|---|---|---|---|---|
| Austria | | | | | | | |
| Belgium | | | | | | | |
| Bulgaria | | | | | | | |
| Cyprus | | | | | | | |
| Czech Republic | | | | | | | |
| Denmark | | | | | | | |
| Estonia | | | | | | | |
| Finland | | | | | | | |
| France | | | | | | | |
| Germany | | | | | | | |
| Greece | | | | | | | |
| Hungary | | | | | | | |

(Continued)

| Member States | Total number of incoming requests for specific measures per Member State under Article 53 | Number of requests to take appropriate specific measures under Article 51(2)(b)[i] | Number of requests to take appropriate specific measures under Article 51(2)(c)[ii] | Number of requests to take appropriate specific measures under Article 51(2)(g)[iii] | Number of requests to take appropriate specific measures under Article 51(2)(h)[iv] | Number of requests to take appropriate specific measures under Article 51(2)(i)[v] | Number of requests to take appropriate specific measures under Article 51(2)(j)[vi] |
|---|---|---|---|---|---|---|---|
| Ireland | | | | | | | |
| Italy | | | | | | | |
| Latvia | | | | | | | |
| Lithuania | | | | | | | |
| Luxembourg | | | | | | | |
| Malta | | | | | | | |
| Netherlands | | | | | | | |
| Poland | | | | | | | |
| Portugal | | | | | | | |
| Romania | | | | | | | |
| Slovakia | | | | | | | |
| Slovenia | | | | | | | |
| Spain | | | | | | | |
| Sweden | | | | | | | |

*(Continued)*

| Member States | Total number of incoming requests for specific measures per Member State under Article 53 | Number of requests to take appropriate specific measures under Article 51(2)(b)[i] | Number of requests to take appropriate specific measures under Article 51(2)(c)[ii] | Number of requests to take appropriate specific measures under Article 51(2)(g)[iii] | Number of requests to take appropriate specific measures under Article 51(2)(h)[iv] | Number of requests to take appropriate specific measures under Article 51(2)(i)[v] | Number of requests to take appropriate specific measures under Article 51(2)(j)[vi] |
|---|---|---|---|---|---|---|---|
| United Kingdom | | | | | | | |
| a) England and Wales | | | | | | | |
| b) Scotland | | | | | | | |
| c) Northern Ireland | | | | | | | |
| d) Gibraltar | | | | | | | |

[i] To help locate the debtor or the creditor.
[ii] To facilitate the search for information on the income or assets of the debtor or the creditor.
[iii] To facilitate the obtaining of documentary or other evidence.
[iv] To obtain assistance in establishing parentage.
[v] Initiate or facilitate the institution of proceedings to obtain a necessary provisional measure which is territorial in nature.
[vi] Facilitate service of a document.

## Incoming (part II)

**Please type in as appropriate for each Member State**

| Member States | Number of incoming requests in which legal aid was provided | Number of incoming requests where the Central Authority recovered its costs under Article 54(2) | Number of requests under Annex V which resulted in a full application |
|---|---|---|---|
| Austria | | | |
| Belgium | | | |
| Bulgaria | | | |
| Cyprus | | | |
| Czech Republic | | | |
| Denmark | | | |
| Estonia | | | |
| Finland | | | |
| France | | | |
| Germany | | | |
| Greece | | | |
| Hungary | | | |
| Ireland | | | |
| Italy | | | |
| Latvia | | | |
| Lithuania | | | |
| Luxembourg | | | |
| Malta | | | |
| Netherlands | | | |
| Poland | | | |
| Portugal | | | |
| Romania | | | |
| Slovakia | | | |
| Slovenia | | | |
| Spain | | | |
| Sweden | | | |
| United Kingdom | | | |
| a) England and Wales | | | |
| b) Scotland | | | |
| c) Northern Ireland | | | |
| d) Gibraltar | | | |

## b) Outgoing (part I)

| Member States | Total number of outgoing requests for specific measures per Member State under Article 53 | Number of requests to take appropriate specific measures under Article 51(2)(b)[i] | Number of requests to take appropriate specific measures under Article 51(2)(c)[ii] | Number of requests to take appropriate specific measures under Article 51(2)(g)[iii] | Number of requests to take appropriate specific measures under Article 51(2)(h)[iv] | Number of requests to take appropriate specific measures under Article 51(2)(i)[v] | Number of requests to take appropriate specific measures under Article 51(2)(j)[vi] |
|---|---|---|---|---|---|---|---|
| Austria | | | | | | | |
| Belgium | | | | | | | |
| Bulgaria | | | | | | | |
| Cyprus | | | | | | | |
| Czech Republic | | | | | | | |
| Denmark | | | | | | | |
| Estonia | | | | | | | |
| Finland | | | | | | | |
| France | | | | | | | |
| Germany | | | | | | | |
| Greece | | | | | | | |
| Hungary | | | | | | | |
| Ireland | | | | | | | |
| Italy | | | | | | | |
| Latvia | | | | | | | |
| Lithuania | | | | | | | |
| Luxembourg | | | | | | | |

(Continued)

| Member States | Total number of outgoing requests for specific measures per Member State under Article 53 | Number of requests to take appropriate specific measures under Article 51(2)(b)[i] | Number of requests to take appropriate specific measures under Article 51(2)(c)[ii] | Number of requests to take appropriate specific measures under Article 51(2)(g)[iii] | Number of requests to take appropriate specific measures under Article 51(2)(h)[iv] | Number of requests to take appropriate specific measures under Article 51(2)(i)[v] | Number of requests to take appropriate specific measures under Article 51(2)(j)[vi] |
|---|---|---|---|---|---|---|---|
| Malta | | | | | | | |
| Netherlands | | | | | | | |
| Poland | | | | | | | |
| Portugal | | | | | | | |
| Romania | | | | | | | |
| Slovakia | | | | | | | |
| Slovenia | | | | | | | |
| Spain | | | | | | | |
| Sweden | | | | | | | |
| United Kingdom | | | | | | | |
| a) England and Wales | | | | | | | |
| b) Scotland | | | | | | | |
| c) Northern Ireland | | | | | | | |
| d) Gibraltar | | | | | | | |

[i] To help locate the debtor or the creditor.
[ii] To facilitate the search for information on the income or assets of the debtor or the creditor.
[iii] To facilitate the obtaining of documentary or other evidence.
[iv] To obtain assistance in establishing parentage.
[v] Initiate or facilitate the institution of proceedings to obtain a necessary provisional measure which is territorial in nature.
[vi] Facilitate service of a document.

## Outgoing (part II)

**Please type in as appropriate for each Member State**

| Member States | Number of outgoing requests in which legal aid was provided | Number of requests under Annex V which resulted in a full application |
|---|---|---|
| Austria | | |
| Belgium | | |
| Bulgaria | | |
| Cyprus | | |
| Czech Republic | | |
| Denmark | | |
| Estonia | | |
| Finland | | |
| France | | |
| Germany | | |
| Greece | | |
| Hungary | | |
| Ireland | | |
| Italy | | |
| Latvia | | |
| Lithuania | | |
| Luxembourg | | |
| Malta | | |
| Netherlands | | |
| Poland | | |
| Portugal | | |
| Romania | | |
| Slovakia | | |
| Slovenia | | |
| Spain | | |
| Sweden | | |
| United Kingdom | | |
| a) England and Wales | | |
| b) Scotland | | |
| c) Northern Ireland | | |
| d) Gibraltar | | |

## Question 3: Number of applications for recognition, declaration of enforceability or enforcement of a decision (Annex VI)

### a) Incoming

*Part I: Applications by a creditor for recognition or for recognition and declaration of enforceability of a decision, under Article 56(1)(a)*

**Please type in as appropriate for each Member State**

| Member States | Number of incoming applications per Member State | Number of applications falling under Article 46 | Number of applications based on a decision of a court or administrative authority | Number of applications based on a court settlement | Number of applications based on an authentic instrument | Number of applications where recognition or declaration of enforceability was refused |
|---|---|---|---|---|---|---|
| Austria | | | | | | |
| Belgium | | | | | | |
| Bulgaria | | | | | | |
| Cyprus | | | | | | |
| Czech Republic | | | | | | |
| Denmark | | | | | | |
| Estonia | | | | | | |
| Finland | | | | | | |
| France | | | | | | |

*(Continued)*

| Member States | Number of incoming applications per Member State | Number of applications falling under Article 46 | Number of applications based on a decision of a court or administrative authority | Number of applications based on a court settlement | Number of applications based on an authentic instrument | Number of applications where recognition or declaration of enforceability was refused |
|---|---|---|---|---|---|---|
| Germany | | | | | | |
| Greece | | | | | | |
| Hungary | | | | | | |
| Ireland | | | | | | |
| Italy | | | | | | |
| Latvia | | | | | | |
| Lithuania | | | | | | |
| Luxembourg | | | | | | |
| Malta | | | | | | |
| Netherlands | | | | | | |
| Poland | | | | | | |
| Portugal | | | | | | |
| Romania | | | | | | |
| Slovakia | | | | | | |
| Slovenia | | | | | | |
| Spain | | | | | | |

(Continued)

| Member States | Number of incoming applications per Member State | Number of applications falling under Article 46 | Number of applications based on a decision of a court or administrative authority | Number of applications based on a court settlement | Number of applications based on an authentic instrument | Number of applications where recognition or declaration of enforceability was refused |
|---|---|---|---|---|---|---|
| Sweden | | | | | | |
| United Kingdom | | | | | | |
| a) England and Wales | | | | | | |
| b) Scotland | | | | | | |
| c) Northern Ireland | | | | | | |
| d) Gibraltar | | | | | | |

*Part II: Applications by a debtor for recognition of a decision, under Article 56(2)(a)*

**Please type in as appropriate for each Member State**

| Member States | Number of incoming applications per Member State | Number of applications based on a decision of a court or administrative authority | Number of applications based on a court settlement | Number of applications based on an authentic instrument | Number of applications where recognition was refused |
|---|---|---|---|---|---|
| Austria | | | | | |
| Belgium | | | | | |
| Bulgaria | | | | | |
| Cyprus | | | | | |
| Czech Republic | | | | | |
| Denmark | | | | | |
| Estonia | | | | | |
| Finland | | | | | |
| France | | | | | |
| Germany | | | | | |
| Greece | | | | | |
| Hungary | | | | | |
| Ireland | | | | | |
| Italy | | | | | |
| Latvia | | | | | |

*(Continued)*

| Member States | Number of incoming applications per Member State | Number of applications based on a decision of a court or administrative authority | Number of applications based on a court settlement | Number of applications based on an authentic instrument | Number of applications where recognition was refused |
|---|---|---|---|---|---|
| Lithuania | | | | | |
| Luxembourg | | | | | |
| Malta | | | | | |
| Netherlands | | | | | |
| Poland | | | | | |
| Portugal | | | | | |
| Romania | | | | | |
| Slovakia | | | | | |
| Slovenia | | | | | |
| Scotland | | | | | |
| Spain | | | | | |
| Sweden | | | | | |
| United Kingdom | | | | | |
| a) England and Wales | | | | | |
| b) Scotland | | | | | |
| c) Northern Ireland | | | | | |
| d) Gibraltar | | | | | |

*Part III: Applications by a creditor for enforcement of a decision given or recognised in the requested Member State, under Article 56(1)(b)*

**Please type in as appropriate for each Member State**

| Member States | Number of incoming applications per Member State | Number of applications falling under Article 46 | Number of applications based on a decision of a court or administrative authority | Number of applications based on a court settlement | Number of applications based on an authentic instrument | Number of applications where the decision was not enforced |
|---|---|---|---|---|---|---|
| Austria | | | | | | |
| Belgium | | | | | | |
| Bulgaria | | | | | | |
| Cyprus | | | | | | |
| Czech Republic | | | | | | |
| Denmark | | | | | | |
| Estonia | | | | | | |
| Finland | | | | | | |
| France | | | | | | |
| Germany | | | | | | |
| Greece | | | | | | |
| Hungary | | | | | | |
| Ireland | | | | | | |

(Continued)

| Member States | Number of incoming applications per Member State | Number of applications falling under Article 46 | Number of applications based on a decision of a court or administrative authority | Number of applications based on a court settlement | Number of applications based on an authentic instrument | Number of applications where the decision was not enforced |
|---|---|---|---|---|---|---|
| Italy | | | | | | |
| Latvia | | | | | | |
| Lithuania | | | | | | |
| Luxembourg | | | | | | |
| Malta | | | | | | |
| Netherlands | | | | | | |
| Poland | | | | | | |
| Portugal | | | | | | |
| Romania | | | | | | |
| Slovakia | | | | | | |
| Slovenia | | | | | | |
| Spain | | | | | | |
| Sweden | | | | | | |
| United Kingdom | | | | | | |
| a) England and Wales | | | | | | |
| b) Scotland | | | | | | |
| c) Northern Ireland | | | | | | |
| d) Gibraltar | | | | | | |

## Question 3 (b) Outgoing

*Part I: Applications by a creditor for recognition or for recognition and declaration of enforceability of a decision, under Article 56(1)(a)*

**Please type in as appropriate for each Member State**

| Member States | Number of outgoing applications per Member State | Number of applications falling under Article 46 | Number of applications based on a decision of a court or administrative authority | Number of applications based on a court settlement | Number of applications based on an authentic instrument | Number of applications where recognition or declaration of enforceability was refused |
|---|---|---|---|---|---|---|
| Austria | | | | | | |
| Belgium | | | | | | |
| Bulgaria | | | | | | |
| Cyprus | | | | | | |
| Czech Republic | | | | | | |
| Denmark | | | | | | |
| Estonia | | | | | | |
| Finland | | | | | | |
| France | | | | | | |
| Germany | | | | | | |
| Greece | | | | | | |
| Hungary | | | | | | |

(Continued)

| Member States | Number of outgoing applications per Member State | Number of applications falling under Article 46 | Number of applications based on a decision of a court or administrative authority | Number of applications based on a court settlement | Number of applications based on an authentic instrument | Number of applications where recognition or declaration of enforceability was refused |
|---|---|---|---|---|---|---|
| Ireland | | | | | | |
| Italy | | | | | | |
| Latvia | | | | | | |
| Lithuania | | | | | | |
| Luxembourg | | | | | | |
| Malta | | | | | | |
| Netherlands | | | | | | |
| Poland | | | | | | |
| Portugal | | | | | | |
| Romania | | | | | | |
| Slovakia | | | | | | |
| Slovenia | | | | | | |
| Spain | | | | | | |
| Sweden | | | | | | |
| United Kingdom | | | | | | |
| a) England and Wales | | | | | | |
| b) Scotland | | | | | | |
| c) Northern Ireland | | | | | | |
| d) Gibraltar | | | | | | |

*Part II: Applications by a debtor for recognition of a decision, under Article 56(2)(a)*

**Please type in as appropriate for each Member State**

| Member States | Number of outgoing applications per Member State | Number of applications based on a decision of a court or administrative authority | Number of applications based on a court settlement | Number of applications based on an authentic instrument | Number of applications where recognition was refused |
|---|---|---|---|---|---|
| Austria | | | | | |
| Belgium | | | | | |
| Bulgaria | | | | | |
| Cyprus | | | | | |
| Czech Republic | | | | | |
| Denmark | | | | | |
| Estonia | | | | | |
| Finland | | | | | |
| France | | | | | |
| Germany | | | | | |
| Greece | | | | | |
| Hungary | | | | | |
| Ireland | | | | | |
| Italy | | | | | |

*(Continued)*

| Member States | Number of outgoing applications per Member State | Number of applications based on a decision of a court or administrative authority | Number of applications based on a court settlement | Number of applications based on an authentic instrument | Number of applications where recognition was refused |
|---|---|---|---|---|---|
| Latvia | | | | | |
| Lithuania | | | | | |
| Luxembourg | | | | | |
| Malta | | | | | |
| Netherlands | | | | | |
| Poland | | | | | |
| Portugal | | | | | |
| Romania | | | | | |
| Slovakia | | | | | |
| Slovenia | | | | | |
| Spain | | | | | |
| Sweden | | | | | |
| United Kingdom | | | | | |
| a) England and Wales | | | | | |
| b) Scotland | | | | | |
| c) Northern Ireland | | | | | |
| d) Gibraltar | | | | | |

*Part III: Applications by a creditor for enforcement of a decision given or recognised in the requested Member State, under Article 56(1)(b)*

**Please type in as appropriate for each Member State**

| Member States | Number of outgoing applications per Member State | Number of applications falling under Article 46 | Number of applications based on a decision of a court or administrative authority | Number of applications based on a court settlement | Number of applications based on an authentic instrument | Number of applications where the decision was not enforced |
|---|---|---|---|---|---|---|
| Austria | | | | | | |
| Belgium | | | | | | |
| Bulgaria | | | | | | |
| Cyprus | | | | | | |
| Czech Republic | | | | | | |
| Denmark | | | | | | |
| Estonia | | | | | | |
| Finland | | | | | | |
| France | | | | | | |
| Germany | | | | | | |
| Greece | | | | | | |
| Hungary | | | | | | |
| Ireland | | | | | | |

*(Continued)*

| Member States | Number of outgoing applications per Member State | Number of applications falling under Article 46 | Number of applications based on a decision of a court or administrative authority | Number of applications based on a court settlement | Number of applications based on an authentic instrument | Number of applications where the decision was not enforced |
|---|---|---|---|---|---|---|
| Italy | | | | | | |
| Latvia | | | | | | |
| Lithuania | | | | | | |
| Luxembourg | | | | | | |
| Malta | | | | | | |
| Netherlands | | | | | | |
| Poland | | | | | | |
| Portugal | | | | | | |
| Romania | | | | | | |
| Slovakia | | | | | | |
| Slovenia | | | | | | |
| Spain | | | | | | |
| Sweden | | | | | | |
| United Kingdom | | | | | | |
| a) England and Wales | | | | | | |
| b) Scotland | | | | | | |
| c) Northern Ireland | | | | | | |
| d) Gibraltar | | | | | | |

## Question 4: Meeting the specified time requirements

### a) Incoming

**Please type in as appropriate for each Member State**

| Member States | Total number of all incoming applications per Member State | Number of applications where this Central Authority met the target in Article 58(3)[i] | Number of applications where this Central Authority met the target in Article 58(4)[ii] | Number of applications that were not fully processed as a result of the failure of the requesting authority under Article 58(9)[iii] | Number of applications that were fully processed within 6 months | Number of applications that were fully processed within 9 months |
|---|---|---|---|---|---|---|
| Austria | | | | | | |
| Belgium | | | | | | |
| Bulgaria | | | | | | |
| Cyprus | | | | | | |
| Czech Republic | | | | | | |
| Denmark | | | | | | |
| Estonia | | | | | | |
| Finland | | | | | | |
| France | | | | | | |
| Germany | | | | | | |
| Greece | | | | | | |

(Continued)

| Member States | Total number of all incoming applications per Member State | Number of applications where this Central Authority met the target in Article 58(3)[i] | Number of applications where this Central Authority met the target in Article 58(4)[ii] | Number of applications that were not fully processed as a result of the failure of the requesting authority under Article 58(9)[iii] | Number of applications that were fully processed within 6 months | Number of applications that were fully processed within 9 months |
|---|---|---|---|---|---|---|
| Hungary | | | | | | |
| Ireland | | | | | | |
| Italy | | | | | | |
| Latvia | | | | | | |
| Lithuania | | | | | | |
| Luxembourg | | | | | | |
| Malta | | | | | | |
| Netherlands | | | | | | |
| Poland | | | | | | |
| Portugal | | | | | | |
| Romania | | | | | | |
| Slovakia | | | | | | |
| Slovenia | | | | | | |
| Spain | | | | | | |
| Sweden | | | | | | |

*(Continued)*

| Member States | Total number of all incoming applications per Member State | Number of applications where this Central Authority met the target in Article 58(3)[i] | Number of applications where this Central Authority met the target in Article 58(4)[ii] | Number of applications that were not fully processed as a result of the failure of the requesting authority under Article 58(9)[iii] | Number of applications that were fully processed within 6 months | Number of applications that were fully processed within 9 months |
|---|---|---|---|---|---|---|
| United Kingdom | | | | | | |
| a) England and Wales | | | | | | |
| b) Scotland | | | | | | |
| c) Northern Ireland | | | | | | |
| d) Gibraltar | | | | | | |

[i] Receipt of the application and appropriate contact details were provided within 30 days.
[ii] Inform requesting Central Authority of the status of the application within 60 days of sending the receipt of the application.
[iii] The requesting Central Authority does not provide additional documents requested within 90 days, or a longer specified period.

## b) Outgoing

Please type in as appropriate for each Member State

| Member States | Total number of all outgoing applications per Member State | Number of applications where the requested Central Authority met the target in Article 58(3)[i] | Number of applications where the requested Central Authority met the target in Article 58(4)[ii] | Number of applications where this Central Authority did not meet the requirement in Article 58(9)[iii] | Number of applications that were fully processed within 6 months | Number of applications that were fully processed within 9 months |
|---|---|---|---|---|---|---|
| Austria | | | | | | |
| Belgium | | | | | | |
| Bulgaria | | | | | | |
| Cyprus | | | | | | |
| Czech Republic | | | | | | |
| Denmark | | | | | | |
| Estonia | | | | | | |
| Finland | | | | | | |
| France | | | | | | |
| Germany | | | | | | |
| Greece | | | | | | |
| Hungary | | | | | | |
| Ireland | | | | | | |
| Italy | | | | | | |
| Latvia | | | | | | |

*(Continued)*

| Member States | Total number of all outgoing applications per Member State | Number of applications where the requested Central Authority met the target in Article 58(3)[i] | Number of applications where the requested Central Authority met the target in Article 58(4)[ii] | Number of applications where this Central Authority did not meet the requirement in Article 58(9)[iii] | Number of applications that were fully processed within 6 months | Number of applications that were fully processed within 9 months |
|---|---|---|---|---|---|---|
| Lithuania | | | | | | |
| Luxembourg | | | | | | |
| Malta | | | | | | |
| Netherlands | | | | | | |
| Poland | | | | | | |
| Portugal | | | | | | |
| Romania | | | | | | |
| Slovakia | | | | | | |
| Slovenia | | | | | | |
| Spain | | | | | | |
| Sweden | | | | | | |
| United Kingdom | | | | | | |
| a) England and Wales | | | | | | |
| b) Scotland | | | | | | |
| c) Northern Ireland | | | | | | |
| d) Gibraltar | | | | | | |

[i] Receipt of the application and appropriate contact details were provided within 30 days.
[ii] Inform requesting Central Authority of the status of the application within 60 days of sending the receipt of the application.
[iii] The requesting Central Authority does not provide additional documents requested within 90 days, or a longer specified period.

## Question 5: The amount paid and recovery rate of maintenance in outgoing cases?

**Please answer at least the top part of this question which just asks the total amount recovered. If you can answer this in respect of each State individually then this data would be helpful.**

| Member States | Total amount paid | Recovery rate of total amount (as a percentage) | Total reductions obtained by debtors |
|---|---|---|---|
| **All States** | | | |
| Austria | | | |
| Belgium | | | |
| Bulgaria | | | |
| Cyprus | | | |
| Czech Republic | | | |
| Denmark | | | |
| Estonia | | | |
| Finland | | | |
| France | | | |
| Germany | | | |
| Greece | | | |
| Hungary | | | |
| Ireland | | | |
| Italy | | | |
| Latvia | | | |
| Lithuania | | | |
| Luxembourg | | | |
| Malta | | | |
| Netherlands | | | |
| Poland | | | |
| Portugal | | | |
| Romania | | | |
| Slovakia | | | |
| Slovenia | | | |
| Spain | | | |
| Sweden | | | |
| United Kingdom | | | |
| a) England and Wales | | | |
| b) Scotland | | | |
| c) Northern Ireland | | | |
| d) Gibraltar | | | |

# ANNEX II

| | | ***Sending Member State*** (according to information provided by the requested State on incoming applications) | | | | | | | | | | | | | | | | | | | | | | | | | | | |
|---|---|---|---|---|---|---|---|---|---|---|---|---|---|---|---|---|---|---|---|---|---|---|---|---|---|---|---|---|---|
| | | AT | BE | CY | CZ | EE | FI | FR | DE | GR | HU | IE | IT | LV | LT | LU | MT | NL | PL | PT | RO | SK | SI | ES | SW | GBEW | GBS | GBNI | Unknown | **Total** |
| ***Requested*** | Austria (AT) | | 0 | 0 | 0 | 0 | 0 | 0 | 0 | 0 | 0 | 0 | 0 | 0 | 0 | 0 | 0 | 0 | 0 | 0 | 0 | 0 | 0 | 0 | 0 | 0 | 0 | 0 | 113 | **113** |
| ***Member*** | Belgium (BE) | 2 | | 0 | 3 | 0 | 8 | 4 | 3 | 0 | 1 | 1 | 0 | 1 | 0 | 2 | 0 | 60 | 50 | 2 | 0 | 1 | 0 | 0 | 0 | 0 | 0 | 0 | 0 | **138** |
| ***State*** | Cyprus (CY) | 1 | 0 | | 0 | 1 | 4 | 0 | 0 | 4 | 0 | 0 | 0 | 1 | 0 | 0 | 0 | 0 | 11 | 0 | 0 | 4 | 0 | 0 | 1 | 5 | 0 | 0 | 0 | **32** |
| | Czech Republic (CZ) | 2 | 0 | 0 | | 0 | 0 | 0 | 0 | 0 | 0 | 1 | 0 | 1 | 0 | 0 | 0 | 2 | 23 | 0 | 0 | 96 | 0 | 0 | 1 | 1 | 0 | 0 | 0 | **127** |
| | Estonia (EE) | 0 | 0 | 0 | 0 | | 128 | 0 | 1 | 0 | 0 | 0 | 0 | 3 | 0 | 0 | 0 | 0 | 1 | 0 | 0 | 0 | 0 | 0 | 0 | 0 | 0 | 0 | 0 | **133** |
| | Finland (FI) | 0 | 0 | 0 | 0 | 40 | | 0 | 0 | 0 | 0 | 0 | 0 | 2 | 0 | 0 | 0 | 1 | 1 | 0 | 0 | 1 | 0 | 0 | 5 | 1 | 0 | 0 | 0 | **51** |
| | France (FR) | 0 | 0 | 0 | 0 | 0 | 0 | | 0 | 0 | 0 | 0 | 0 | 0 | 0 | 0 | 0 | 0 | 0 | 0 | 0 | 0 | 0 | 0 | 0 | 0 | 0 | 0 | 178 | **178** |
| | Germany (DE) | 144 | 6 | 0 | 36 | 0 | 18 | 3 | | 0 | 17 | 5 | 0 | 17 | 3 | 0 | 1 | 60 | 466 | 7 | 3 | 16 | 2 | 1 | 10 | 9 | 0 | 0 | 0 | **824** |
| | Greece (GR) | 6 | 2 | 2 | 3 | 0 | 26 | 0 | 9 | | 0 | 0 | 1 | 0 | 0 | 0 | 0 | 1 | 72 | 0 | 2 | 2 | 0 | 0 | 0 | 0 | 0 | 0 | 0 | **126** |
| | Hungary (HU) | 2 | 0 | 0 | 1 | 0 | 0 | 0 | 0 | 0 | | 1 | 0 | 0 | 0 | 0 | 0 | 0 | 2 | 0 | 2 | 7 | 0 | 1 | 0 | 0 | 0 | 0 | 0 | **16** |
| | Ireland (IE) | 2 | 0 | 0 | 6 | 2 | 22 | 2 | 4 | 0 | 0 | | 0 | 28 | 6 | 0 | 0 | 4 | 165 | 3 | 0 | 13 | 0 | 0 | 2 | 16 | 4 | 14 | 0 | **293** |
| | Italy (IT) | 17 | 0 | 0 | 5 | 0 | 14 | 1 | 5 | 0 | 3 | 0 | | 0 | 2 | 0 | 0 | 1 | 55 | 2 | 3 | 9 | 3 | 0 | 0 | 1 | 0 | 0 | 0 | **121** |
| | Latvia (LV) | 0 | 0 | 0 | 0 | 0 | 3 | 0 | 0 | 0 | 0 | 5 | 0 | | 1 | 0 | 0 | 0 | 1 | 0 | 0 | 0 | 0 | 0 | 0 | 1 | 0 | 0 | 0 | **11** |
| | Lithuania (LT) | 0 | 0 | 0 | 0 | 0 | 4 | 0 | 0 | 0 | 0 | 4 | 0 | 8 | | 0 | 0 | 0 | 5 | 0 | 0 | 0 | 0 | 0 | 0 | 0 | 0 | 0 | 0 | **21** |
| | Luxembourg (LU) | 0 | 3 | 0 | 0 | 1 | 1 | 3 | 12 | 0 | 0 | 0 | 0 | 0 | 1 | | 0 | 2 | 1 | 17 | 0 | 0 | 0 | 0 | 0 | 1 | 0 | 0 | 0 | **42** |
| | Malta (MT) | 0 | 0 | 0 | 0 | 0 | 0 | 0 | 0 | 0 | 0 | 0 | 0 | 0 | 0 | 0 | | 0 | 0 | 0 | 0 | 0 | 0 | 0 | 0 | 0 | 0 | 0 | 0 | **0** |
| | Netherlands (NL) | 4 | 22 | 0 | 0 | 0 | 12 | 1 | 23 | 0 | 3 | 0 | 1 | 1 | 1 | 0 | 0 | | 158 | 4 | 0 | 0 | 0 | 1 | 6 | 7 | 0 | 0 | 0 | **244** |
| | Poland (PL) | 13 | 3 | 0 | 2 | 0 | 4 | 4 | 17 | 0 | 0 | 5 | 0 | 0 | 0 | 0 | 0 | 4 | | 0 | 1 | 4 | 0 | 0 | 80 | 35 | 0 | 0 | 0 | **172** |
| | Portugal (PT) | 2 | 4 | 0 | 0 | 0 | 14 | 4 | 13 | 0 | 0 | 0 | 0 | 0 | 0 | 1 | 0 | 3 | 6 | | 0 | 0 | 0 | 0 | 8 | 7 | 0 | 0 | 0 | **62** |
| | Romania (RO) | 9 | 1 | 0 | 1 | 0 | 1 | 0 | 6 | 0 | 6 | 2 | 0 | 1 | 0 | 0 | 0 | 1 | 10 | 0 | | 1 | 0 | 0 | 0 | 2 | 0 | 0 | 0 | **41** |
| | Slovakia (SK) | 6 | 0 | 0 | 20 | 0 | 0 | 0 | 0 | 5 | 1 | 0 | 0 | 0 | 0 | 0 | 0 | 0 | 9 | 0 | 0 | | 0 | 1 | 1 | 0 | 0 | 0 | 0 | **43** |
| | Slovenia (SI) | 1 | 0 | 0 | 1 | 0 | 0 | 0 | 0 | 0 | 0 | 0 | 0 | 0 | 0 | 0 | 0 | 1 | 2 | 0 | 0 | 1 | | 0 | 1 | 0 | 0 | 0 | 0 | **7** |
| | Spain (ES) | 0 | 0 | 0 | 0 | 0 | 0 | 0 | 0 | 0 | 0 | 0 | 0 | 0 | 0 | 0 | 0 | 0 | 0 | 0 | 0 | 0 | 0 | | 0 | 0 | 0 | 0 | 267 | **267** |
| | Sweden (SW) | 5 | 0 | 0 | 3 | 0 | 0 | 0 | 1 | 0 | 4 | 1 | 0 | 2 | 1 | 0 | 0 | 3 | 94 | 0 | 2 | 0 | 0 | 0 | | 14 | 0 | 0 | 0 | **130** |
| | England & Wales (GBEW) | 15 | 5 | 0 | 14 | 1 | 59 | 9 | 22 | 1 | 6 | 45 | 0 | 45 | 6 | 0 | 0 | 15 | 551 | 16 | 0 | 18 | 0 | 4 | 30 | | | | 0 | **862** |
| | Scotland (GBS) | 0 | 0 | 0 | 1 | 1 | 5 | 1 | 0 | 0 | 4 | 5 | 0 | 11 | 0 | 0 | 0 | 1 | 49 | 0 | 0 | 0 | 0 | 0 | 2 | | | | 0 | **80** |
| | Northern Ireland (GBNI) | 0 | 0 | 0 | 0 | 0 | 1 | 0 | 0 | 0 | 0 | 5 | 0 | 0 | 0 | 0 | 0 | 1 | 20 | 0 | 0 | 1 | 0 | 0 | 0 | | | | 0 | **28** |
| **Total** | | 231 | 46 | 2 | 96 | 46 | 324 | 32 | 116 | 10 | 45 | 80 | 2 | 121 | 21 | 3 | 1 | 160 | 1752 | 51 | 13 | 174 | 5 | 7 | 147 | 100 | 4 | 14 | 558 | 4,162 |

# ANNEX III

**Applications for enforceability and enforcement by sending country**

| **Requesting State** | | **Art 56(1)(a)** | **Art 56(1)(b)** | **Total** |
|---|---|---|---|---|
| | | **Enforceability** | **Enforcement** | |
| Austria | Number of applications | 54 | 5 | 59 |
| | As a percentage | 91.5% | 8.5% | |
| Belgium | Number of applications | 7 | 1 | 8 |
| | As a percentage | 87.5% | 12.5% | |
| Cyprus | Number of applications | 2 | 0 | 2 |
| | As a percentage | 100.0% | 0.0% | |
| Czech Republic | Number of applications | 33 | 1 | 34 |
| | As a percentage | 97.1% | 2.9% | |
| Estonia | Number of applications | 40 | 3 | 43 |
| | As a percentage | 93.0% | 7.0% | |
| Finland | Number of applications | 142 | 60 | 202 |
| | As a percentage | 70.3% | 29.7% | |
| France | Number of applications | 15 | 5 | 20 |
| | As a percentage | 75.0% | 25.0% | |
| Germany | Number of applications | 36 | 4 | 40 |
| | As a percentage | 90.0% | 10.0% | |
| Greece | Number of applications | 1 | 0 | 1 |
| | As a percentage | 100.0% | 0.0% | |
| Hungary | Number of applications | 17 | 0 | 17 |
| | As a percentage | 100.0% | 0.0% | |
| Ireland | Number of applications | 31 | 3 | 34 |
| | As a percentage | 91.2% | 8.8% | |
| Italy | Number of applications | 0 | 1 | 1 |
| | As a percentage | 0.0% | 100.0% | |
| Latvia | Number of applications | 56 | 14 | 70 |
| | As a percentage | 80.0% | 20.0% | 100.0% |

(*continued*)

**Applications for enforceability and enforcement by sending country**

| **Requesting State** | | **Art 56(1)(a)** | **Art 56(1)(b)** | **Total** |
|---|---|---|---|---|
| | | **Enforceability** | **Enforcement** | |
| Lithuania | Number of applications | 14 | 4 | 18 |
| | As a percentage | 77.8% | 22.2% | |
| Luxembourg | Number of applications | 0 | 2 | 2 |
| | As a percentage | 0.0% | 100.0% | |
| Netherlands | Number of applications | 83 | 10 | 93 |
| | As a percentage | 89.2% | 10.8% | |
| Poland | Number of applications | 926 | 54 | 980 |
| | As a percentage | 94.5% | 5.5% | |
| Portugal | Number of applications | 21 | 1 | 22 |
| | As a percentage | 95.5% | 4.5% | |
| Romania | Number of applications | 6 | 0 | 6 |
| | As a percentage | 100.0% | 0.0% | |
| Slovakia | Number of applications | 133 | 15 | 148 |
| | As a percentage | 89.9% | 10.1% | |
| Slovenia | Number of applications | 3 | 0 | 3 |
| | As a percentage | 100.0% | 0.0% | |
| Spain | Number of applications | 5 | 0 | 5 |
| | As a percentage | 100.0% | 0.0% | |
| Sweden | Number of applications | 6 | 2 | 8 |
| | As a percentage | 75.0% | 25.0% | |
| UK-England & Wales | Number of applications | 13 | 0 | 13 |
| | As a percentage | 100.0% | 0.0% | |
| UK-Scotland | Number of applications | 0 | 1 | 1 |
| | As a percentage | 0.0% | 100.0% | |
| UK-Northern Ireland | Number of applications | 5 | 0 | 5 |
| | As a percentage | 100.0% | 0.0% | |
| **Total** | Applications | **1,649** | **186** | **1,835** |
| | Percentage | 89.9% | 10.1% | |

# ANNEX IV

| | | Sending Member State (according to information provided by the requested State on incoming requests for specific measures) | | | | | | | | | | | | | | | | | | | | | | | | | | | |
|---|---|---|---|---|---|---|---|---|---|---|---|---|---|---|---|---|---|---|---|---|---|---|---|---|---|---|---|---|---|
| | | AT | BE | CY | CZ | EE | FI | FR | DE | GR | HU | IE | IT | LV | LT | LU | MT | NL | PL | PT | RO | SK | SI | ES | SW | GBEW | GBS | GBNI | Unknown | **Total** |
| ***Requested*** | Belgium (BE) | 0 | | 0 | 0 | 0 | 3 | 0 | 9 | 0 | 2 | 0 | 0 | 1 | 0 | 0 | 0 | 3 | 39 | 0 | 1 | 1 | 0 | 0 | 10 | 0 | 0 | 0 | 0 | **69** |
| ***Member*** | Czech Republic (CZ) | 0 | 0 | 0 | | 0 | 0 | 0 | 0 | 0 | 0 | 0 | 0 | 0 | 0 | 0 | 0 | 1 | 11 | 0 | 0 | 59 | 0 | 0 | 0 | 0 | 0 | 0 | 0 | **71** |
| ***State*** | Estonia (EE) | 0 | 0 | 0 | 0 | | 75 | 0 | 1 | 0 | 0 | 0 | 0 | 2 | 0 | 0 | 0 | 0 | 0 | 0 | 0 | 0 | 0 | 0 | 0 | 0 | 0 | 0 | 0 | **78** |
| | Finland (FI) | 0 | 0 | 0 | 0 | 2 | | 0 | 0 | 0 | 0 | 1 | 0 | 0 | 0 | 0 | 0 | 0 | 0 | 0 | 0 | 0 | 0 | 0 | 0 | 0 | 0 | 0 | 0 | **3** |
| | France (FR) | 0 | 0 | 0 | 0 | 0 | 0 | | 0 | 0 | 0 | 0 | 0 | 0 | 0 | 0 | 0 | 0 | 0 | 0 | 0 | 0 | 0 | 0 | 0 | 0 | 0 | 0 | 72 | **72** |
| | Germany (DE) | 25 | 1 | 0 | 10 | 1 | 7 | 0 | | 0 | 5 | 2 | 2 | 7 | 0 | 0 | 0 | 6 | 183 | 1 | 3 | 4 | 0 | 0 | 16 | 1 | 0 | 0 | 0 | **274** |
| | Greece (GR) | 1 | 2 | 0 | 0 | 0 | 3 | 0 | 7 | | 0 | 0 | 0 | 0 | 0 | 0 | 0 | 0 | 57 | 0 | 2 | 1 | 0 | 0 | 0 | 0 | 0 | 0 | 0 | **73** |
| | Hungary (HU) | 6 | 0 | 0 | 0 | 0 | 0 | 0 | 0 | 0 | | 0 | 0 | 0 | 0 | 0 | 0 | 2 | 0 | 0 | 0 | 3 | 0 | 0 | 0 | 0 | 0 | 0 | 0 | **11** |
| | Ireland (IE) | 0 | 2 | 0 | 0 | 0 | 0 | 0 | 5 | 0 | 1 | | 0 | 2 | 0 | 0 | 0 | 0 | 55 | 0 | 0 | 2 | 0 | 1 | 1 | 2 | 0 | 5 | 0 | **76** |
| | Italy (IT) | 9 | 1 | 0 | 3 | 1 | 5 | 0 | 11 | 0 | 3 | 0 | | 0 | 0 | 0 | 0 | 0 | 130 | 0 | 4 | 6 | 0 | 0 | 3 | 0 | 0 | 0 | 0 | **176** |
| | Latvia (LV) | 0 | 0 | 0 | 0 | 0 | 1 | 0 | 3 | 0 | 0 | 0 | 0 | | 0 | 0 | 0 | 0 | 2 | 0 | 0 | 0 | 0 | 0 | 0 | 0 | 0 | 0 | 0 | **6** |
| | Lithuania (LT) | 0 | 0 | 0 | 0 | 0 | 0 | 0 | 0 | 0 | 0 | 0 | 0 | 1 | | 0 | 0 | 0 | 4 | 0 | 0 | 0 | 0 | 0 | 0 | 0 | 0 | 0 | 0 | **5** |
| | Malta (MT) | 0 | 0 | 0 | 0 | 0 | 0 | 0 | 0 | 0 | 0 | 0 | 0 | 0 | 0 | 0 | | 0 | 0 | 0 | 0 | 0 | 0 | 0 | 0 | 1 | 0 | 0 | 0 | **1** |
| | Poland (PL) | 0 | 0 | 0 | 2 | 0 | 1 | 1 | 5 | 0 | 0 | 0 | 0 | 0 | 0 | 0 | 0 | 0 | | 0 | 2 | 0 | 0 | 0 | 25 | 2 | 0 | 0 | 0 | **38** |
| | Portugal (PT) | 1 | 2 | 0 | 0 | 0 | 3 | 0 | 9 | 0 | 0 | 0 | 0 | 0 | 0 | 0 | 0 | 0 | 3 | | 0 | 0 | 0 | 0 | 2 | 1 | 0 | 0 | 0 | **21** |
| | Romania (RO) | 3 | 1 | 0 | 0 | 0 | 0 | 0 | 8 | 0 | 2 | 0 | 0 | 0 | 0 | 0 | 0 | 0 | 5 | 0 | | 2 | 0 | 0 | 0 | 1 | 0 | 0 | 0 | **22** |
| | Slovenia (SI) | 0 | 0 | 0 | 0 | 0 | 0 | 0 | 0 | 0 | 0 | 0 | 0 | 0 | 0 | 0 | 0 | 0 | 1 | 0 | 0 | 2 | | 0 | 1 | 0 | 0 | 0 | 0 | **4** |
| | Sweden (SW) | 1 | 0 | 0 | 2 | 0 | 0 | 0 | 0 | 1 | 0 | 0 | 0 | 1 | 0 | 0 | 0 | 0 | 6 | 0 | 0 | 0 | 0 | 1 | | 1 | 0 | 0 | 0 | **13** |
| | England & Wales (GBEW) | 2 | 3 | 0 | 6 | 0 | 10 | 1 | 26 | 0 | 7 | 5 | 0 | 4 | 0 | 0 | 0 | 7 | 234 | 2 | 1 | 31 | 0 | 0 | 87 | | | | 0 | **426** |
| | Northern Ireland (GBNI) | 0 | 0 | 0 | 0 | 0 | 0 | 0 | 0 | 0 | 0 | 1 | 0 | 1 | 0 | 0 | 0 | 0 | 19 | 0 | 0 | 1 | 0 | 0 | 2 | | | | 0 | **24** |
| **Total** | | 48 | 12 | 0 | 23 | 4 | 108 | 2 | 84 | 1 | 20 | 9 | 2 | 19 | 0 | 0 | 0 | 19 | 749 | 3 | 13 | 112 | 0 | 2 | 147 | 9 | 0 | 5 | 72 | 1,463 |

# ANNEX V

| Requested State | | Requests received under Art 53 | | | | | | Total |
|---|---|---|---|---|---|---|---|---|
| | | Locate party | Info on income | Obtain evidence | Establish parentage | Provisional measures | Unknown | |
| Belgium | Number of requests | 63 | 4 | 0 | 2 | 0 | 0 | 69 |
| | As a percentage | 91.3% | 5.8% | 0.0% | 2.9% | 0.0% | 0.0% | |
| Czech Republic | Number of requests | 46 | 25 | 0 | 0 | 0 | 0 | 71 |
| | As a percentage | 64.8% | 35.2% | 0.0% | 0.0% | 0.0% | 0.0% | |
| Estonia | Number of requests | 52 | 2 | 5 | 0 | 19 | 0 | 78 |
| | As a percentage | 66.7% | 2.6% | 6.4% | 0.0% | 24.4% | 0.0% | |
| Finland | Number of requests | 2 | 1 | 0 | 0 | 0 | 0 | 3 |
| | As a percentage | 66.7% | 33.3% | 0.0% | 0.0% | 0.0% | 0.0% | |
| France | Number of requests | 56 | 16 | 0 | 0 | 0 | 0 | 72 |
| | As a percentage | 77.8% | 22.2% | 0.0% | 0.0% | 0.0% | 0.0% | |
| Germany | Number of requests | 0 | 0 | 0 | 0 | 0 | 274 | 274 |
| | As a percentage | 0.0% | 0.0% | 0.0% | 0.0% | 0.0% | 100.0% | |
| Greece | Number of requests | 68 | 4 | 1 | 0 | 0 | 0 | 73 |
| | As a percentage | 93.2% | 5.5% | 1.4% | 0.0% | 0.0% | 0.0% | |
| Hungary | Number of requests | 5 | 5 | 0 | 0 | 0 | 1 | 11 |
| | As a percentage | 45.5% | 45.5% | 0.0% | 0.0% | 0.0% | 9.1% | |
| Ireland | Number of requests | 67 | 9 | 0 | 0 | 0 | 0 | 76 |
| | As a percentage | 88.2% | 11.8% | 0.0% | 0.0% | 0.0% | 0.0% | |
| Italy | Number of requests | 147 | 29 | 0 | 0 | 0 | 0 | 176 |
| | As a percentage | 83.5% | 16.5% | 0.0% | 0.0% | 0.0% | 0.0% | |

*(Continued)*

| Requested State | | Requests received under Art 53 | | | | | | Total |
|---|---|---|---|---|---|---|---|---|
| | | Locate party | Info on income | Obtain evidence | Establish parentage | Provisional measures | Unknown | |
| Latvia | Number of requests | 4 | 2 | 0 | 0 | 0 | 0 | 6 |
| | As a percentage | 66.7% | 33.3% | 0.0% | 0.0% | 0.0% | 0.0% | |
| Lithuania | Number of requests | 3 | 2 | 0 | 0 | 0 | 0 | 5 |
| | As a percentage | 60.0% | 40.0% | 0.0% | 0.0% | 0.0% | 0.0% | |
| Malta | Number of requests | 0 | 0 | 0 | 0 | 0 | 1 | 1 |
| | As a percentage | 0.0% | 0.0% | 0.0% | 0.0% | 0.0% | 100.0% | |
| Poland | Number of requests | 30 | 3 | 0 | 0 | 0 | 5 | 38 |
| | As a percentage | 78.9% | 7.9% | 0.0% | 0.0% | 0.0% | 13.2% | |
| Portugal | Number of requests | 21 | 0 | 0 | 0 | 0 | 0 | 21 |
| | As a percentage | 100.0% | 0.0% | 0.0% | 0.0% | 0.0% | 0.0% | |
| Romania | Number of requests | 17 | 4 | 0 | 1 | 0 | 0 | 22 |
| | As a percentage | 77.3% | 18.2% | 0.0% | 4.5% | 0.0% | 0.0% | |
| Slovenia | Number of request | 3 | 1 | 0 | 0 | 0 | 0 | 4 |
| | As a percentage | 75.0% | 25.0% | 0.0% | 0.0% | 0.0% | 0.0% | |
| Sweden | Number of requests | 0 | 0 | 0 | 0 | 0 | 13 | 13 |
| | As a percentage | 0.0% | 0.0% | 0.0% | 0.0% | 0.0% | 100.0% | |
| UK-England & Wales | Number of requests | 426 | 0 | 0 | 0 | 0 | 0 | 426 |
| | As a percentage | 100.0% | 0.0% | 0.0% | 0.0% | 0.0% | 0.0% | |
| UK-Northern Ireland | Number of requests | 23 | 1 | 0 | 0 | 0 | 0 | 24 |
| | As a percentage | 95.8% | 4.2% | 0.0% | 0.0% | 0.0% | 0.0% | |
| **Total** | Requests | **1,033** | **108** | **6** | **3** | **19** | **294** | **1,463** |
| | Percentage | 70.6% | 7.4% | 0.4% | 0.2% | 1.3% | 20.1% | |

# ANNEX VI

**Requests that resulted in a full Application**

| Requested State | | Resulted in full application? | | | Total |
|---|---|---|---|---|---|
| | | Yes | No | Not known | |
| Belgium | Number of requests | 0 | 0 | 69 | 69 |
| | As a percentage | 0.0% | 0.0% | 100.0% | |
| Czech Republic | Number of requests | 12 | 0 | 59 | 71 |
| | As a percentage | 16.9% | 0.0% | 83.1% | |
| Estonia | Number of requests | 21 | 29 | 28 | 78 |
| | As a percentage | 26.9% | 37.2% | 35.9% | |
| Finland | Number of Requests | 0 | 0 | 3 | 3 |
| | As a percentage | 0.0% | 0.0% | 100.0% | |
| France | Number of Requests | 0 | 0 | 72 | 72 |
| | As a percentage | 0.0% | 0.0% | 100.0% | |
| Germany | Number of Requests | 0 | 0 | 274 | 274 |
| | As a percentage | 0.0% | 0.0% | 100.0% | |
| Greece | Number of Requests | 3 | 0 | 70 | 73 |
| | As a percentage | 4.1% | 0.0% | 95.9% | |
| Hungary | Number of Requests | 0 | 11 | 0 | 11 |
| | As a percentage | 0.0% | 100.0% | 0.0% | |
| Ireland | Number of Requests | 0 | 0 | 76 | 76 |
| | As a percentage | 0.0% | 0.0% | 100.0% | |
| Italy | Number of Requests | 10 | 0 | 166 | 176 |
| | As a percentage | 5.7% | 0.0% | 94.3% | |
| Latvia | Number of Requests | 0 | 6 | 0 | 6 |
| | As a percentage | 0.0% | 100.0% | 0.0% | |
| Lithuania | Number of Requests | 0 | 0 | 5 | 5 |
| | As a percentage | 0.0% | 0.0% | 100.0% | |
| Malta | Number of Requests | 0 | 0 | 1 | 1 |
| | As a percentage | 0.0% | 0.0% | 100.0% | |

(*continued*)

**Requests that resulted in a full Application**

| Requested State | | Resulted in full application? | | | Total |
|---|---|---|---|---|---|
| | | Yes | No | Not known | |
| Poland | Number of Requests | 0 | 0 | 38 | 38 |
| | As a percentage | 0.0% | 0.0% | 100.0% | |
| Portugal | Number of Requests | 0 | 0 | 21 | 21 |
| | As a percentage | 0.0% | 0.0% | 100.0% | |
| Romania | Number of Requests | 0 | 0 | 22 | 22 |
| | As a percentage | 0.0% | 0.0% | 100.0% | |
| Slovenia | Number of Requests | 0 | 0 | 4 | 4 |
| | As a percentage | 0.0% | 0.0% | 100.0% | |
| Sweden | Number of Requests | 0 | 0 | 13 | 13 |
| | As a percentage | 0.0% | 0.0% | 100.0% | |
| UK-England & Wales | Number of Requests | 6 | 420 | 0 | 426 |
| | As a percentage | 1.4% | 98.6% | 0.0% | |
| UK-Northern Ireland | Number of Requests | 3 | 0 | 21 | 24 |
| | As a percentage | 12.5% | 0.0% | 87.5% | |
| **Total** | Total requests | **55** | **466** | **942** | **1,463** |
| | percentage | 3.8% | 31.9% | 64.4% | |

# ANNEX VII

**Table 1: Fully processed within 6 months**

| Requested State | | 6 months | | | | Total |
|---|---|---|---|---|---|---|
| | | **Fully processed** | **Pending** | **Not applicable** | **Unclear** | |
| Austria | Number of applications | 0 | 0 | 0 | 113 | 113 |
| | As a percentage | 0.0% | 0.0% | 0.0% | 100.0% | |
| Belgium | Number of applications | 0 | 138 | 0 | 0 | 138 |
| | As a percentage | 0.0% | 100.0% | 0.0% | 0.0% | |
| Cyprus | Number of applications | 0 | 0 | 0 | 32 | 32 |
| | As a percentage | 0.0% | 0.0% | 0.0% | 100.0% | |
| Czech Republic | Number of Applications | 0 | 127 | 0 | 0 | 127 |
| | As a percentage | 0.0% | 100.0% | 0.0% | 0.0% | |
| Estonia | Number of applications | 81 | 48 | 4 | 0 | 133 |
| | As a percentage | 60.9% | 36.1% | 3.0% | 0.0% | |
| Finland | Number of applications | 2 | 49 | 0 | 0 | 51 |
| | As a percentage | 3.9% | 96.1% | 0.0% | 0.0% | |
| France | Number of applications | 0 | 0 | 0 | 178 | 178 |
| | As a percentage | 0.0% | 0.0% | 0.0% | 100.0% | |
| Germany | Number of applications | 0 | 0 | 0 | 824 | 824 |
| | As a percentage | 0.0% | 0.0% | 0.0% | 100.0% | |
| Greece | Number of applications | 51 | 75 | 0 | 0 | 126 |
| | As a percentage | 40.5% | 59.5% | 0.0% | 0.0% | |
| Hungary | Number of applications | 0 | 15 | 1 | 0 | 16 |
| | As a percentage | 0.0% | 93.8% | 6.2% | 0.0% | |

(*continued*)

**Table 1: Continued**

| Requested State | | 6 months | | | | Total |
|---|---|---|---|---|---|---|
| | | Fully processed | Pending | Not applicable | Unclear | |
| Ireland | Number of applications | 0 | 0 | 0 | 293 | 293 |
| | As a percentage | 0.0% | 0.0% | 0.0% | 100.0% | |
| Italy | Number of applications | 0 | 115 | 6 | 0 | 121 |
| | As a percentage | 0.0% | 95.0% | 5.0% | 0.0% | |
| Latvia | Number of applications | 4 | 7 | 0 | 0 | 11 |
| | As a percentage | 36.4% | 63.6% | 0.0% | 0.0% | |
| Lithuania | Number of applications | 0 | 0 | 0 | 21 | 21 |
| | As a percentage | 0.0% | 0.0% | 0.0% | 100.0% | |
| Luxembourg | Number of applications | 0 | 0 | 0 | 42 | 42 |
| | As a percentage | 0.0% | 0.0% | 0.0% | 100.0% | |
| Netherlands | Number of applications | 0 | 0 | 0 | 244 | 244 |
| | As a percentage | 0.0% | 0.0% | 0.0% | 100.0% | |
| Poland | Number of applications | 0 | 0 | 0 | 172 | 172 |
| | As a percentage | 0.0% | 0.0% | 0.0% | 100.0% | |
| Portugal | Number of applications | 17 | 45 | 0 | 0 | 62 |
| | As a percentage | 27.4% | 72.6% | 0.0% | 0.0% | |
| Romania | Number of applications | 0 | 0 | 0 | 41 | 41 |
| | As a percentage | 0.0% | 0.0% | 0.0% | 100.0% | |
| Slovakia | Number of applications | 0 | 0 | 0 | 43 | 43 |
| | As a percentage | 0.0% | 0.0% | 0.0% | 100.0% | |
| Slovenia | Number of applications | 2 | 5 | 0 | 0 | 7 |
| | As a percentage | 28.6% | 71.4% | 0.0% | 0.0% | |
| Spain | Number of applications | 0 | 0 | 0 | 267 | 267 |
| | As a percentage | 0.0% | 0.0% | 0.0% | 100.0% | |

*(continued)*

**Table 1: Continued**

| **Requested State** | | **6 months** | | | | **Total** |
|---|---|---|---|---|---|---|
| | | **Fully processed** | **Pending** | **Not applicable** | **Unclear** | |
| Sweden | Number of applications | 0 | 130 | 0 | 0 | 130 |
| | As a percentage | 0.0% | 100.0% | 0.0% | 0.0% | |
| UK-England & Wales | Number of applications | 26 | 613 | 223 | 0 | 862 |
| | As a percentage | 3.0% | 71.1% | 25.9% | 0.0% | |
| UK-Scotland | Number of applications | 0 | 0 | 0 | 80 | 80 |
| | As a percentage | 0.0% | 0.0% | 0.0% | 100.0% | |
| UK-Northern Ireland | Number of applications | 0 | 28 | 0 | 0 | 28 |
| | As a percentage | 0.0% | 100.0% | 0.0% | 0.0% | |
| **Total** | Applications | **183** | **1,395** | **234** | **2,350** | **4,162** |
| | Percentage | 4.4% | 33.5% | 5.6% | 56.5% | |

**Table 2: Fully processed within 9 months**

| Requested State | | 9 months | | | | Total |
|---|---|---|---|---|---|---|
| | | Fully processed | Pending | Not applicable | Unclear | |
| Austria | Number of applications | 0 | 0 | 0 | 113 | 113 |
| | As a percentage | 0.0% | 0.0% | 0.0% | 100.0% | |
| Belgium | Number of applications | 0 | 138 | 0 | 0 | 138 |
| | As a percentage | 0.0% | 100.0% | 0.0% | 0.0% | |
| Cyprus | Number of applications | 0 | 0 | 0 | 32 | 32 |
| | As a percentage | 0.0% | 0.0% | 0.0% | 100.0% | |
| Czech Republic | Number of applications | 0 | 127 | 0 | 0 | 127 |
| | As a percentage | 0.0% | 100.0% | 0.0% | 0.0% | |
| Estonia | Number of applications | 82 | 47 | 4 | 0 | 133 |
| | As a percentage | 61.7% | 35.3% | 3.0% | 0.0% | |
| Finland | Number of applications | 2 | 49 | 0 | 0 | 51 |
| | As a percentage | 3.9% | 96.1% | 0.0% | 0.0% | |
| France | Number of applications | 0 | 0 | 0 | 178 | 178 |
| | As a percentage | 0.0% | 0.0% | 0.0% | 100.0% | |
| Germany | Number of applications | 0 | 0 | 0 | 824 | 824 |
| | As a percentage | 0.0% | 0.0% | 0.0% | 100.0% | |
| Greece | Number of applications | 51 | 75 | 0 | 0 | 126 |
| | As a percentage | 40.5% | 59.5% | 0.0% | 0.0% | |
| Hungary | Number of applications | 0 | 15 | 1 | 0 | 16 |
| | As a percentage | 0.0% | 93.8% | 6.2% | 0.0% | |
| Ireland | Number of applications | 0 | 0 | 0 | 293 | 293 |
| | As a percentage | 0.0% | 0.0% | 0.0% | 100.0% | |

(*continued*)

**Table 2: Continued**

| Requested State | | 9 months | | | | Total |
|---|---|---|---|---|---|---|
| | | Fully processed | Pending | Not applicable | Unclear | |
| Italy | Number of applications | 0 | 115 | 6 | 0 | 121 |
| | As a percentage | 0.0% | 95.0% | 5.0% | 0.0% | |
| Latvia | Number of applications | 4 | 7 | 0 | 0 | 11 |
| | As a percentage | 36.4% | 63.6% | 0.0% | 0.0% | |
| Lithuania | Number of applications | 0 | 0 | 0 | 21 | 21 |
| | As a percentage | 0.0% | 0.0% | 0.0% | 100.0% | |
| Luxembourg | Number of applications | 0 | 0 | 0 | 42 | 42 |
| | As a percentage | 0.0% | 0.0% | 0.0% | 100.0% | |
| Netherlands | Number of applications | 0 | 0 | 0 | 244 | 244 |
| | As a percentage | 0.0% | 0.0% | 0.0% | 100.0% | |
| Poland | Number of applications | 0 | 0 | 0 | 172 | 172 |
| | As a percentage | 0.0% | 0.0% | 0.0% | 100.0% | |
| Portugal | Number of applications | 20 | 42 | 0 | 0 | 62 |
| | As a percentage | 32.3% | 67.7% | 0.0% | 0.0% | |
| Romania | Number of applications | 0 | 0 | 0 | 41 | 41 |
| | As a percentage | 0.0% | 0.0% | 0.0% | 100.0% | |
| Slovakia | Number of applications | 0 | 0 | 0 | 43 | 43 |
| | As a percentage | 0.0% | 0.0% | 0.0% | 100.0% | |
| Slovenia | Number of applications | 2 | 5 | 0 | 0 | 7 |
| | As a percentage | 28.6% | 71.4% | 0.0% | 0.0% | |
| Spain | Number of applications | 0 | 0 | 0 | 267 | 267 |
| | As a percentage | 0.0% | 0.0% | 0.0% | 100.0% | |
| Sweden | Number of applications | 0 | 130 | 0 | 0 | 130 |
| | As a percentage | 0.0% | 100.0% | 0.0% | 0.0% | |

(*continued*)

**Table 2: Continued**

| **Requested State** | | **9 months** | | | | **Total** |
|---|---|---|---|---|---|---|
| | | **Fully processed** | **Pending** | **Not applicable** | **Unclear** | |
| UK-England & Wales | Number of applications | 65 | 574 | 223 | 0 | 862 |
| | As a percentage | 7.5% | 66.6% | 25.9% | 0.0% | |
| UK-Scotland | Number of applications | 0 | 0 | 0 | 80 | 80 |
| | As a percentage | 0.0% | 0.0% | 0.0% | 100.0% | |
| UK-Northern Ireland | Number of applications | 0 | 28 | 0 | 0 | 28 |
| | As a percentage | 0.0% | 100.0% | 0.0% | 0.0% | |
| **Total** | Applications | **226** | **1,352** | **234** | **2,350** | **4,162** |
| | Percentage | 5.4% | 32.5% | 5.6% | 56.5% | |

Recovery of Maintenance in the European Union and Worldwide

# Conclusions and Next Steps

of the Heidelberg Conference from 5 to 8 March 2013

DIJuF
FORUM FÜR FACHFRAGEN

1 4 9 5
UNIVERSITY OF ABERDEEN

Universität Heidelberg

HccH
HAGUE CONFERENCE ON PRIVATE INTERNATIONAL LAW
CONFÉRENCE DE LA HAYE DE DROIT INTERNATIONAL PRIVÉ

NCSEA

Bundesministerium der Justiz

IDCEL
INSTITUT DE DROIT COMPARÉ EDOUARD LAMBERT

MAX-PLANCK-GESELLSCHAFT

Funded by the European Commission

# HEIDELBERG CONFERENCE 2013

## "Recovery of Maintenance in the European Union and Worldwide"

From 5 to 8 March 2013, **more than 230 experts** representing **key relevant fields**, including politicians and government officials, members of Central Authorities, academics, lawyers, judges, child support administrators, the private sector, and others from **States of every continent**—***Africa:*** Namibia, Nigeria, Tunisia; ***Asia:*** Azerbaijan, Indonesia, Kazakhstan, China (including Hong Kong SAR), Israel, Japan; ***Europe:*** Austria, Belgium, Bulgaria, Croatia, Czech Republic, Denmark, Estonia, Finland, France, Germany, Greece, Hungary, Ireland, Italy, Latvia, Lithuania, Luxembourg, Republic of Macedonia, the Netherlands, Norway, Poland, Portugal, Romania, Russian Federation, Slovakia, Spain, Sweden, Switzerland, Turkey, United Kingdom; ***Australia & Oceania:*** Australia, New Zealand; ***North America:*** Canada, Cuba, United States of America; and, ***South America:*** Argentina, Brazil, Chile, Colombia met in Heidelberg, Germany, to discuss the "Recovery of Maintenance in the European Union and Worldwide".

*Recalling* that the Heidelberg Conference was the centre piece of a project funded by the European Commission and organised by the German Institute for Youth Human Services and Family Law (DIJuF). **Partners** in the project are the University of Aberdeen (Professor Paul Beaumont) and the University of Heidelberg/Max Planck Institute Luxembourg for International, European and Regulatory Procedural Law (Professor Dr. Burkhard Hess) as well as the National Child Support Enforcement Association (NCSEA), the Hague Conference on Private International Law, the Federal Ministry of Justice of Germany, and the University of Lyon (Professor Frédérique Ferrand).

*Recognising* that **the project** aims to improve the implementation and application of the new global and regional maintenance instruments[1] and to strengthen cross-border co-operation in Europe and worldwide by establishing a platform for multi-professional international contact and collaboration. The goal of the

[1] The Hague *Convention of 23 November 2007 on the International Recovery of Child Support and Other Forms of Family Maintenance* (the "Hague Convention 2007"), the Hague *Protocol of 23 November 2007 on the Law Applicable to Maintenance Obligations* (the "Hague Protocol 2007") and the *EC Regulation No 4/2009 of 18 December 2008 on jurisdiction, applicable law, recognition and enforcement of decisions and co-operation in matters relating to maintenance obligations* (the "Council Regulation 4/2009").

Heidelberg Conference was to provide an opportunity for participants to share their experience and expertise, increase their mutual knowledge about child support, family maintenance law, procedures and enforcement in their respective countries or organisations, to discuss unresolved issues and to develop models for good practice.

*Underlining* that in the course of the project **qualitative and quantitative research** was carried out by the Universities of Aberdeen and Heidelberg. All Member States of the European Union were asked via a questionnaire to give feedback as to how the Council Regulation 4/2009 has been implemented and how it has operated in its first year in force. The research identified problems in practice and in jurisprudence, and highlighted the need for further education and training.

The participants of the conference reached the following conclusions and made the following recommendations for next steps:

## Implementation of the Hague Convention 2007

1. We look forward to the **speedy implementation** of the Convention in as many States as possible in the near future as a means for States to implement their obligations under Article 27(4) of the 1989 *United Nations Convention on the Rights of the Child*.
2. We are committed to **engaging with the international community** in order to provide support, assistance and information on best practices to States implementing the Convention.

## Implementation of Council Regulation 4/2009

3. A coherent set of **statistics, performance indicators, and analytic reports** on the use of the Regulation in all Member States is essential to evaluate the implementation of the Regulation and to support improvements in its use. The use of a common IT system (see C&R 17 below) for keeping statistical data on the operation of Council Regulation 4/2009 (and the Hague Convention 2007) would be a great step forward in improving the enforcement of maintenance and the accountability of Central Authorities. A common IT system with the capability of analytical reporting could periodically assess future opportunities for programme improvement.
4. The right to apply for a review (Article 19 of Council Regulation 4/2009) raises questions regarding the legal situation in Member States and should be more thoroughly analysed, in particular with regard to the procedure to follow and remedies primary to the right to apply for a review. This thorough analysis will permit a determination as to whether the minimum procedural protection of the debtor is sufficiently guaranteed by Council Regulation 4/2009.

5. The initial experience with the implementation and practical operation of the Regulation has exposed certain **problems** that should be addressed including:
   a. There are indications that the provisions on **data protection** may hinder the sharing of relevant information in situations where confidentiality has been adequately taken into account. If further examination confirms this evaluation, **amendments to Article 62** of Council Regulation 4/2009 should be made at the next possible opportunity.
   b. In relation to **public bodies** a clarification is needed to provide that jurisdiction under Chapter II lies with the court of the venue where the public body has its administrative centre.
   c. **Direct applications** under Council Regulation 4/2009 to competent authorities in the requested Member State are allowed. Chapter VII of Council Regulation 4/2009 contains the framework for applications made with the assistance of the Central Authorities in the requested and requesting Member States. This does not exclude direct applications without the assistance of Central Authorities under the substantive scope of Council Regulation 4/2009. This has caused confusion in certain countries and should be made clearer in a way similar to Article 37 of the Hague Convention 2007.
   d. **Amicable solutions** are mentioned but not facilitated by the procedures set out in Council Regulation 4/2009; incentives to employ amicable solutions are needed in order to receive appropriate support for them from Central Authorities.
   e. Consideration should be given to **amending Article 56(1)(b) and Annex VI** of Council Regulation 4/2009 to reduce the current risk of confusion by **separating applications** for actual enforcement of decisions given in the requested Member State (which apply to all Member States) from: a) applications for actual enforcement of decisions given in other Member States bound by the Hague Protocol 2007 which are automatically recognised in the requested State without a declaration of enforceability; and, b) applications for actual enforcement of decisions given in other Member States not bound by the Hague Protocol which have already been the subject of a declaration of enforceability in the requested State.
   f. **Regular examination of the Annexes** of Council Regulation 4/2009 for any needed updates should be undertaken (e.g., inclusion of Denmark and the United Kingdom in Annexes I to VI).
6. Council Regulation 4/2009 is an essential instrument to enable cross-border recovery of child support and other forms of family maintenance. **Flexible and additional mutual administrative assistance by Central Authorities** is allowed and should be encouraged within national legal frameworks where it is helpful to the families we serve.
7. Consideration should be given to measures **facilitating the location of debtors** throughout the European Union.

8. We look forward to a schedule for the **drafting of a list of difficulties** and obstacles with respect to the implementation of Council Regulation 4/2009, set by the EU Commission, and to participating in the development of such a list.
9. A **guide to good practice**, prepared under the auspices of the EU Commission, would be of great assistance to ensure the coherent and effective implementation and operation of Council Regulation 4/2009. Training programmes for all relevant stakeholders should ensure **continuing capacity building**.

**Creation of a Global Network**

10. We look forward to and will assist in **establishing a global community** of international child support and family maintenance professionals, including practitioners, academics, legislators, judicial officers, members of the bar and government professionals responsible for maintenance and child support matters.
11. We will encourage the development of a series of **regional networks** in different parts of the world and their merger into a larger **global network** to address the global implications and challenges associated with the implementation and operation of Council Regulation 4/2009, the Hague Convention 2007 and the Hague Protocol 2007.
12. The networks will form the foundation of a **trust- and competence-building forum** to facilitate cross-border cooperation in the recovery of maintenance and child support. As such, they will be open to all interested professionals and organisations involved with maintenance and child support.
13. We believe it is important to encourage and support the networks to
    a. provide a **forum** for dialogue, research, and sharing of expertise within the maintenance and child support community to assist in the implementation and operation of the Hague Convention 2007, Council Regulation 4/2009, and the Hague Protocol 2007;
    b. **connect experts** from different States within and between stakeholder groups and to be the primary facilitator of the exchange of best practices, legal and other expertise and relevant information;
    c. involve and **encourage stakeholders** to use the network, to improve their communications and to challenge their thinking;
    d. **share expertise** between stakeholders of all relevant fields in States across the world.
14. The networks will foster a **global understanding** of the importance of family maintenance, will support the diversity of families and communities and will respect the legal processes that exist in various jurisdictions.
15. **Contributions to the Heidelberg Conference** will be made publically available and will be part of a platform for information sharing. We will plan follow-up events and find opportunities for further dialogue, in person or through other modes of direct communication.

16. The facilitation of **easy access to relevant information and to training programmes** is a core goal for the networks.

**Improved cooperation through the use of IT**

17. The future of cross border cooperation under Council Regulation 4/2009 and the Hague Convention 2007 lies in the **electronic processing of cases, information and data sharing, and transfer of funds.** The inclusive and transparent development of a common user-friendly application and practical solution, as modelled in the iSupport project of the Hague Conference, cannot be underestimated and is crucial to ensuring accessible, prompt, efficient, cost effective, responsive and consistent recovery of child support and other forms of maintenance worldwide. Such a development deserves broad and strong support.
18. To ensure that fundamental rights and ethical aspects for sharing personal information are sufficiently taken into account in the course of the development of IT-based information sharing solutions, we strongly promote the establishment of a **working group on data protection issues.**

**Next steps**

19. A book of selected papers from the Conference will be **published** by Hart Publishing in 2014 under the title "Recovery of Maintenance in the European Union and Worldwide".
20. A **space** where materials can be publically accessed and available by way of the Internet will be created.
21. We will plan **follow-up events** and develop opportunities for further dialogue. Another worldwide conference should be held subsequent to the further application of Council Regulation 4/2009 and experiences gained after broader ratification of the Hague Convention 2007.
22. We encourage any and all **implementing strategies** that ensure that the public knows of the existence of Council Regulation 4/2009, the Hague Convention 2007 and the Hague Protocol 2007, so that families in need will receive assistance in recovering child support and other forms of family maintenance in cross-border circumstances.
23. The focus of all of these actions should be to ensure that both governments and the public understand the **importance of child support** and other forms of family maintenance to families around the world, and the positive impact that maintenance has upon the lives of children and their emotional, physical, spiritual and moral well-being.

# BIBLIOGRAPHY

## Explanatory Reports Accompanying Selected Hague Conventions


Bonomi A, 'Explanatory Report on the Protocol of 23 November 2007 on the Law Applicable to Maintenance Obligations' (HCCH, 2009) (Bonomi Report)

Borrás A and Degeling J, 'Explanatory Report on the Convention on the International Recovery of Child Support and other Forms of Family Maintenance (HCCH, 2009) (Borrás and Degeling Report)

Hartley T and Dogauchi M, 'Explanatory Report on the 2005 Hague Choice of Court Agreements Convention' (HCCH, 2007) (Hartley and Dogauchi Report)

Perez-Vera E, 'Explanatory Report on the 1980 Hague Child Abduction Convention' (HCCH, 1982) (Perez-Vera Report)

Verwilghen M, 'Explanatory Report on the 1973 Hague Maintenance Conventions' (HCCH, 1975) (Verwilghen Report)


## Hague Documents


Accreditation and Adoption Accredited Bodies, Guide to Good Practice no 2 (2012)

Conclusions of the Special Commission of May 2000 on General Affairs and Policy of the Hague Conference

General Conclusions of the Special Commission of November 1995 on the Operation of the Hague Conventions Relating to Maintenance Obligations and of the New York Convention of 20 June 1956 on the Recovery Abroad of Maintenance

Kessidijian C, 'Synthesis of the Work of the Special Commission of March 1998 on International Jurisdiction and the Effects of Foreign Judgments in Civil and Commercial Matters'

Nygh and Pocar Report, Preliminary Document no 11 of August 2000

Practical Handbook for Caseworkers under the Hague Child Support Convention (HCCH, 2014)

Preliminary Document no 1, M Pelichet, 'Note on the Operation of the Hague Conventions Relating to Maintenance Obligations and of the New York Convention on the Recovery Abroad of Maintenance'

Preliminary Document no 10 of June 2000

Preliminary Document no 13 of January 2005—Working Draft of a Convention on the International Recovery of Child Support and other Forms of Family Maintenance

Preliminary Document no 16 of September 2005—Tentative Draft on the International Recovery of Child Support and other Forms of Family Maintenance

Proceedings of the 21st Session (November 2007): Including Procès Verbal and Working Documents

Report on and the Conclusions of the Special Commission on Maintenance Obligations of April 1999 (December 2009)

## Reports, Proposals and Agreements of the EU Institutions

Agreement between the European Community and the Kingdom of Denmark on jurisdiction and the recognition and enforcement of judgments in civil and commercial matters [2009] OJ L149/80, 12 June 2009

Council Decision of 30 November 2009 on the conclusion by the European Community of the Hague Protocol of 23 November 2007 on the Law Applicable to Maintenance Obligations [2009] OJ L331/17

Council Decision of 31 March 2011 on the signing, on the behalf of the European Union, of the Hague Convention of 23 November 2007 on the International Recovery of Child Support and other forms of Family Maintenance [2011] OJ L93/9

Council Decision of 9 June 2011 on the approval, on the behalf of the European Union, of the Hague Convention of 23 November 2007 on the International Recovery of Child Support and other forms of Family Maintenance [2011] OJ L192/39

Draft programme of measures for the implementation of the principle of mutual recognition of decisions in civil and commercial matters (the Action Programme) adopted by the JHA Council on 30 November 2000, OJ C12, 15 January 2001

Green Paper on Maintenance Obligations (presented by the Commission) COM (2004) 245 final

Jenard P, Report on the Convention on jurisdiction and the enforcement of judgments in civil and commercial matters signed at Brussels, 27 September 1968 [1979] OJ C59 (Jenard Report)

November 1997, the Commission published a communication on free movement of judgments COM (97) 609 final, OJE

Proposal for a Council Decision amending Annexes II and III of Council Decision of 9 June 2011 on the approval, on behalf of the European Union, of The Hague Convention of 23 November 2007, on the International Recovery of Child Support and Other Forms of Family Maintenance' Brussels, 29 January 2013 COM (2013) 35

Report from the Commission to the European Parliament, the Council and the European Economic and Social Committee on the Application of Council Regulation (EC) No 44/2001 on jurisdiction and the recognition and enforcement of judgments in civil and commercial matters, COM (2009) 174 final

Schlosser Report on the Brussels Convention [1998] OJ C59/71 (Schlosser Report)

Staff Working Document, Annex to the Proposal for a Council Regulation on jurisdiction, applicable law, recognition and enforcement of decisions and cooperation in matters relating to maintenance obligations—Impact Assessment, SEC/2005/1629

## Studies and Reports Commissioned by the EU

EPEC, Study to Inform a Subsequent Impact Assessment on the Commission Proposal on Jurisdiction and Applicable Law in Divorce Matters (EPEC Study)

Hess B, Pfeiffer T and Schlosser P, The Brussels I Regulation 44/2001. The Heidelberg Report on the Application of Regulation Brussels I in 25 Member States (Study JLS/C4/2005/03) Munich: Verlag CH Beck 2008 (Heidelberg Report)

Professor A Nuyts, Study on Residual Jurisdiction, JLS/C4/2005/07-30-CE)0040309/00-37 (2007)

Study No JAI/A3/2002/02 General Report

Study No JAI/A3/2002/02 on making more efficient the enforcement of judicial decisions within the European Union: Transparency of a Debtor's Assets, Attachment of Bank Accounts and Provisional Enforcement and Protective Measures, Version of 18/2/2004 (Efficiency of Enforcement Study)

## Books

Beaumont P, Hess B, Walker L and Spancken S (eds), *The Recovery of Maintenance in the EU and Worldwide* (Oxford, Hart Publishing, 2014)

—— and McEleavy P, *Private International Law, Anton* 3rd edn (Edinburgh, SULI/W Green, 2011)

Boele-Woelki K, Braat B and Sumner I (eds), *European Family Law in Action, Volume II* (Antwerp, Intersentia 2003)

—— Ferrand F, González Beilfuss C, Jänterä-Jareborg M, Lowe N, Martiny D and Pintens W, *Principles of European Family Law Regarding Divorce and Maintenance Between Former Spouses* (Oxford, Intersentia, 2004)

Council of Europe, *Legal Problems Relating to Parentage: Proceedings XXVIIth Colloquy on European Law Foundation for International Studies* (Valletta (Malta) 15–17 September 1997)

Craig P and de Búrca G, *EU Law: Text, Cases and Materials*, 5th edn (Oxford, Oxford University Press, 2011)

Fawcett J and Carruthers J, *Cheshire, North and Fawcett: Private International Law*, 14th edn (Oxford, Oxford University Press 2008)

Gragl P, *The Accession of the European Union to the European Convention on Human Rights* (Oxford, Hart Publishing, 2013)

Hodgkin R and Newell P, *Implementation Handbook for the Convention on the Rights of the Child*, 3rd edn (Geneva, UNICEF, 2007)

Kegel G, 'Fundamental Approaches' in *International Encyclopaedia of Comparative Law Volume III, Private International Law* (Tübingen, Mohr Siebeck,1986)

Magnus U, Mankowski P and Fentiman R, *Brussels I Regulation*, 2nd edn (Munich, Sellier, 2012)

Stalford H, *Children and the European Union: Rights, Welfare and Accountability* (Oxford, Hart Publishing, 2012)

Vigers S, *Mediating International Child Abduction Cases* (Oxford, Hart Publishing, 2011)

## Chapters in Books

Beaumont P, 'The European Court of Justice Prioritises the Abolition of Exequatur Over Fundamental Rights in Zarraga' in J Diez-Hochleitner, C Martinez Capdevila, I Blazquez

Navarro and J Frutos Miranda (eds), *Recent Trends in the Case Law of the Court of Justice of the European Union (2008-2011)* (Madrid, Wolters Kluwer Espana, 2012) 621

—— and Walker L, 'Administrative and Judicial Cooperation in the Hague 2007 Maintenance Convention' in J Forner Delaygua, C González Beilfuss, R Viñas Farré (eds), *Entre Bruselas y la Haya. Estudios sobre la unificación internacional y regional del Derecho internacional privado Liber Amicorum Alegría Borrás* (Madrid, Marcial Pons, 2013) 185

Biagioni G, 'The Aguirre Zarraga Case: Freedom of Circulation of Judgments Goes One Step Further' in J Diez-Hochleitner, C Martinez Capdevila, I Blazquez Navarro and J Frutos Miranda (eds), *Recent Trends in the Case Law of the Court of Justice of the European Union (2008-2011)* (Madrid, Wolters Kluwer Espana, 2012) 605

Boele Woelki K, '(Cross-Border) Surrogate Motherhood: We Need to Take Action Now!' in Permanent Bureau (eds), *A Commitment to Private International Law* (The Hague, Intersentia 2013) 47

Borrás A, 'The Necessary Flexibility in Applying the New Instruments on Maintenance' in K Boele-Woelki, T Einhorn, D Girsberger, S Symeonides (eds), *Convergence and Divergence in Private International Law, Liber Amicorum Kurt Siehr* (Eleven International Publishing & Schulthess, 2010) 173

—— 'Reservations, Declarations and Specifications: Their Function in the Hague Convention on the International Recovery of Child Support and other Forms of Family Maintenance' in G Venturini and S Bariatti (eds), *Liber Fausto Pocar: Vol. II, Nuovi instrumenti del diritto internazionale private—New Instruments of Private International Law* (Milan, Giuffrè, 2009) 127

Diduck A, 'Autonomy and Vulnerability in Family Law: The Missing Link' in J Wallbank and J Herring (eds), *Vulnerabilities, Care and Family Law* (Oxon, Routledge, 2014) 95

Duncan W, 'The Maintenance of a Hague Convention. Adapting to Change. A Discussion of Techniques to Ensure that a Convention Remains "Fit for Purpose"' in G Venturini and S Bariatti (eds), *Liber Fausto Pocar: Vol. II, Nuovi instrumenti del diritto internazionale private-New Instruments of Private International Law* (Milan, Giuffrè, 2009) 291

——, 'Jurisdiction to Make and Modify Maintenance Decisions—The Quest for Uniformity' in T Einhorn and K Siehr (eds), *Intercontinental Cooperation through Private International Law Essays in Memory of Peter E. Nygh* (TCM Asser Press, 2004) 89

Groff M, 'The Potential of the 2007 Child Support Convention: Addressing Global Poverty and Supporting Economic Rights' in Beaumont et al (eds), *The Recovery of Maintenance in the EU and Worldwide* (Oxford, Hart Publishing, 2014)

Hellner M, 'The Maintenance Regulation: A Critical Assessment of the Commission's Proposal' in K Boele-Woelki and T Sverdrup (eds), *European Challenges in Contemporary Family Law* (Antwerp, Intersentia 2009) 343

Laquer Estin A, 'Migration, Remittances and Child Support' in Beaumont et al (eds), *The Recovery of Maintenance in the EU and Worldwide* (Oxford, Hart Publishing, 2014)

Martiny D, 'Objectives and Values of (Private) International Law in Family Law' in J Meeusen et al (eds), *International Family Law for the European Union* (Antwerp, Intersentia, 2007)

Miles J, 'Financial Relief between Cohabitants on Separation: Options for European Jurisdictions' in K Boele-Woelki and T Sverdrup (eds), *European Challenges in Contemporary Family Law* (Antwerp, Intersentia, 2008)

Nagy C, 'Love and Money: Problems of Characterisation in Matrimonial Property and Maintenance Matters in the European Union' in Beaumont et al (eds), *The Recovery of Maintenance in the EU and Worldwide* (Oxford, Hart Publishing, 2014)

Pertegás M, 'Beyond Nationality and Habitual Residence: Other Connecting Factors in European Private International Law in Family Matters' in J Meeusen et al (eds), *International Family Law for the European Union* (Antwerp, Intersentia, 2007) 319

Saue J et al, 'Administrative Establishment and Enforcement of Child Support in Norway' in Beaumont et al (eds), *The Recovery of Maintenance in the EU and Worldwide* (Oxford, Hart Publishing, 2014)

Schulz A, 'The Abolition of Exequatur and State Liability for Human Rights Violations through the Enforcement of Judgments in European Family Law' in *A Commitment to Private International Law—Essays in Honour of Hans van Loon* (The Hague, Intersentia, 2013) 515

Seihr K, 'The EU Maintenance Regulation and the Hague Maintenance Protocol of 2007' in Permanent Bureau (eds), *A Commitment to Private International Law* (The Hague, Intersentia, 2013) 529

Tebbens H, 'Divorce—A Fundamental Right?' in Permanent Bureau (eds), *A Commitment to Private International Law* (The Hague, Intersentia 2013) 123

Torga M, 'Drawing a Demarcating Line between Spousal Maintenance Obligations and Matrimonial Property in the Context of the New Instruments of European Union Private International Law' in Beaumont et al (eds), *The Recovery of Maintenance in the EU and Worldwide* (Oxford, Hart Publishing, 2014)

Trimmings K and Beaumont P, 'General Report on Surrogacy' in K Trimmings and P Beaumont (eds), *International Surrogacy Arrangements: Legal Regulation at the International Level* (Oxford, Hart Publishing, 2013) 439

Van Loon H, 'Unification and Cooperation in the Field of International Family Law: A Perspective From the Hague' in A Borrás, A Bucher, T Struycken and M Verwilghen (eds), *E Pluribus Unum Liber Amicorum Georges A.L. Droz on the Progressive Unification of Private International Law* (The Hague, Kluwer, 1996) 173

Viarengo I, 'The Enforcement of Maintenance Decisions in the EU: Requiem for Public Policy? Family Relationships and the (Partial) Abolition of Exequatur' in Beaumont et al (eds), *The Recovery of Maintenance in the EU and Worldwide* (Oxford, Hart Publishing, 2014)

Vlas P, 'Public Policy in Private International Law and its Continuing Importance' in Permanent Bureau (eds), *A Commitment to Private International Law* (The Hague, Intersentia, 2013) 621

Walker L and Beaumont P, 'Empirical Study on the Early Operation of the EU Maintenance Regulation' in Beaumont et al (eds), *The Recovery of Maintenance in the EU and Worldwide* (Oxford, Hart Publishing, 2014)

Zupan M, 'Novelties of the 2007 Hague Maintenance Protocol' in Beaumont et al (eds), *The Recovery of Maintenance in the EU and Worldwide* (Oxford, Hart Publishing, 2014)

# Journal Articles

Abdul-Kareem M and Killian A (eds), 'Assisted Reproductive Technologies' (2010) 11 *Georgetown Journal of Gender and the Law* 411

Bartlett L, 'Full Faith and Credit Comes to the Common Market an Analysis of the Convention on Jurisdiction and Enforcement of Judgments in Civil and Commercial Matters' (1975) 24 *International and Comparative Law Quarterly* 44

Beaumont P, 'International Family Law in Europe—the Maintenance Project, the Hague Conference and the EC: A Triumph of Reverse Subsidiarity' (2009) 73 *Rabels Zeitschrift* 509

—— 'The Jurisprudence of the European Court of Human Rights and the European Court of Justice on the Hague Convention on International Child Abduction' (2008) 335 *Recueil des Cours* 9

—— and Johnston E, 'Can *Exequatur* be Abolished in Brussels I whilst Retaining a Public Policy Defence' (2010) 6 *Journal of Private International Law* 249

Bonomi A, 'The Interaction Among the Future EU Instruments on Matrimonial Property, Registered Partnerships and Successions' (2011) 13 *Yearbook of Private International Law* 217

—— 'The Hague Protocol of 23 November 2007 on the Law Applicable to Maintenance Obligations' (2008) 10 *Yearbook of Private International Law* 333

Borm-Reid M, 'Recognition and Enforcement of Foreign Judgments' (1954) 3 *International and Comparative Law Quarterly* 49

Bremner P, 'The EU Maintenance Regulation: A Qualified Success for European Family Law' (2010) *Kings Student Law Review* 5

Bulterman MK and Kranenborg HR, 'What if the Rules on Free Movement and Human Rights Collide? About Laser Games and Human Dignity: The Omega Case' (2006) *European Law Review* 93

Callus T, 'A New Parenthood Paradigm for Twenty-First Century Family Law in England and Wales?' (2012) 32 *Legal Studies* 347

Campuzano Diaz B, 'The Coordination of the EU Regulations on Divorce and Legal Separation with the Proposal on Matrimonial Property Regimes' (2011) 13 *Yearbook of Private International Law* 233

Carruthers J, 'Party Autonomy in the Legal Regulation of Adult Relationships: What Place for Party Choice in Private International Law?' (2012) 61 *International and Comparative Law Quarterly* 881

—— 'De Facto Cohabitation: The International Private Law Dimension' (2008) 12 *Edinburgh Law Review* 51

Cavers D, 'International Enforcement of Family Support' (1981) 81 *Columbia Law Review*, 994

Costello C, 'The *Bosphorus* Ruling of the European Court of Human Rights: Fundamental Rights and Blurred Boundaries in Europe' (2006) 6 *Human Rights Law Review* 87

Cuniberti G, 'Recognition of Foreign Judgments Lacking Reasons in Europe' (2008) 57 *International and Comparative Law Quarterly* 25

—— and Reuda I, 'Abolition of Exequatur—Addressing the Commission's Concerns' (2011) 75 *Rabels Zeitschrift* 286

Curry-Sumner I, 'Administrative Co-operation and Free Legal Aid in International Child Maintenance Recovery: What is the Added Value of the Regulation?' (2010) 3 *Nederlands Internationaal Privaatrecht* 611

Dennison G, 'Is Mediation Compatible with Children's Rights? (2010) 32 *Journal of Social Welfare and Family Law* 169

De Winter LI, 'Excessive Jurisdiction in Private International Law' (1968) 17 *International and Comparative Law Quarterly* 706

Dingwall R, 'Divorce Mediation: Should We Change Our Mind?' (2010) 32 *Journal of Social Welfare and Family* Law 107

Duncan W, 'The New Hague Child Support Convention: Goals and Outcomes of the Negotiations' (2009) 43 *Family Law Quarterly* 1

—— 'The New Hague Maintenance Convention and Protocol' (2008) 10 *Yearbook of Private International Law,* 313

Fawcett JJ, 'The Impact of Article 6(1) of the ECHR on Private International Law' (2007) 56 *International and Comparative Law Quarterly* 1

Fitchen J, 'Authentic Instruments and European Private International Law in Civil and Commercial Matters: Is Now the Time to Break New Ground?' (2011) 7 *Journal of Private International Law* 33

Forde M, 'The "Ordre Public" Exception and Adjudicative Jurisdiction Conventions' (1980) 29 *International and Comparative Law Quarterly* 259

Gillies L, 'Creation of Subsidiary Jurisdiction Rules in the Recast of Brussels I: Back to the Drawing Board?' (2012) 8 *Journal of Private International Law* 489

Goessl S, 'Preliminary Questions in EU Private International Law' (2012) 8 *Journal of Private International Law* 63

Gotlieb AE, 'The Incidental Question Revisited—Theory and Practice in the Conflict of Laws' (1977) 26 *International and Comparative Law Quarterly* 734

Harding M, 'The Harmonisation of Private International Law in Europe: Taking the Character Out of Family Law? (2011) 7 *Journal of Private International Law* 203

Hartley T, 'Review: Private International Law by AE Anton' (2012) 8 *Journal of Private International Law* 407

—— 'The Modern Approach to Private International Law International Litigation and Transactions from a Common Law Perspective' (2006) 319 *Recueil des Cours* 9

—— 'Case Comment: Interim Measures under the Brussels Jurisdiction and Judgments Convention' (1999) 24 *European Law Review* 674

—— 'Case Comment, Maintenance Orders—Irreconcilable Judgments' (1991) 16 *European Law Review* 64

Hess B, 'The Brussels I Regulation: Recent Case Law of the Court of Justice and the Commission's Proposed Recast' (2012) 49 *Common Market Law Review* 1075

Hodson D, 'Quo Vadis? The Family Lawyer Goes Forum Shopping' (2012) *Private Client Business* 158

Jacobs FG, 'Human Rights in the European Union: The Role of the Court of Justice' (2001) *European Law Review* 331

Jacqué JP, 'The Accession of the EU to the ECHR' (2011) 48 *Common Market Law Review* 995

Jayme E, 'Party Autonomy in International Family and Succession Law: New Tendencies' (2009) *Yearbook of Private International Law* 1

Kramer X, 'Abolition of Exequatur under the Brussels I Regulation: Effecting and Protecting the Rights in the European Judicial Area' (2011) 4 *Nederlands Internationaal Privaatrecht* 633

Kuipers JJ, 'The (Non) Application of the Charter of Fundamental Rights to a Certificate for the Return of the Child' (2012) *European Human Rights Law Review* 397

Lipstein K, 'The Hague Conventions on Private International Law, Public Law and Public Policy' (1959) 8 *International and Comparative Law Quarterly* 18

—— 'A Draft Convention on the Recovery Abroad of Claims for Maintenance' (1954) 3 *International and Comparative Law Quarterly* 125

Lock T, 'Walking on a Tightrope: The Draft ECHR Agreement and the Autonomy of the EU Legal Order' (2011) 48 *Common Market Law Review* 1025

Lortie P, 'The Development of Medium and Technology Neutral International Treaties in Support of Post-Convention Information Technology Systems: The Example of the 2007 Hague Convention and Protocol' (2008) 10 *Yearbook of Private International Law* 359

Ma W, 'Recommendations on Public Policy in the Enforcement of Arbitrarial Awards' (2009) *Arbitration* 14

Maclean M and Eekelaar J, 'The Obligations and Expectations of Couples within Families: Three Modes of Interaction' (2004) 26 *Journal of Social Welfare and Family Law* 117

Marcil J and Thornton N, 'Avoiding Pitfalls: Common Reasons for Mediation Failure and Solutions for Success' (2009) 3 *American Journal of Mediation* 25

Marinai S, 'Matrimonial Matters and the Harmonization of Conflict of Laws: A Way to Reduce the Role of Public Policy as a Ground for Non-Recognition of Judgments' (2011) 13 *Yearbook of Private International Law* 255

Martiny D, 'Maintenance Obligations in the Conflict of Laws' (1994) 247 *Recueil des Cours* 131

Mathews P, 'Provisional and Protective Measures in England and Ireland at Common Law and under the Conventions: A Comparative Survey' (1995) *Civil Justice Quarterly* 190

Megens P and Finch D, 'Setting Aside an Award on Public Policy Grounds: *AJT* v *AJU*' (2011) *Arbitration* 155

Meidanis HP, 'Public Policy and *ordre public* in Private International Law of the EU: Traditional Positions and Modern Trends' (2005) 30 *European Law Review* 95

Mills A, 'The Dimensions of Public Policy in Private International Law' (2008) 4 *Journal of Private International Law* 201

Moir G and Beaumont P, 'Brussels Convention II: A New Private International Law Instrument in Family Matters for the European Union or the European Community' (1995) 20 *European Law Review* 268

Ni Shuilleabhain M, 'Ten Years of European Family Law: Retrospective Reflections from a Common Law Perspective' (2010) 59 *International and Comparative Law Quarterly* 1021

Nic Shuibhne N, 'Margins of Appreciation: National Values, Fundamental Rights and EC Free Movement Law' (2009) *European Law Review* 230

Nolan-Haley J, 'Is Europe Headed Down the Primrose Path with Mandatory Mediation?' (2012) 37 *North Carolina Journal of International Law and Commercial Regulation* 981

Philip A, 'General Course on Private International Law' 1978 (II) *Recueil des cours* 9

Rabel E, 'An Interim Account on Comparative Conflicts Law' (1947–1948) 46 *Michigan Law Review* 625

Rodger B and Maher G, 'Provisional and Protective Remedies: The British Experience of the Brussels Convention' (1999) 48 *International and Comparative Law Quarterly* 302

Sampson JJ, 'Introductory Note to the New Hague Maintenance Convention' (2008) 47 *International Legal Materials* 255

—— and Brooks BJ, 'Uniform Interstate Family Support Act (2001) With Prefatory Note and Comments (With Still More Unofficial Notations)' (2002–2003) 36 *Family Law Quarterly* 36

Sarmiento D, 'Who's Afraid of the Charter? The Court of Justice, National Courts and the New Framework of Fundamental Rights Protection in Europe' (2013) 50 *Common Market Law Review* 1267

Schmidt T, 'The Incidental Question in Private International Law' (1992) 233 *Hague Academy Collected Courses* 315

Schulz A, 'The 1980 Hague Child Abduction Convention and the European Convention on Human Rights' (2002) 12 *Transnational Law and Contemporary Problems* 355

Škerl JK, 'European Public Policy (With an Emphasis on *Exequatur* Proceedings)' (2011) 7 *Journal of Private International Law* 461

Spector RG, 'Toward an Accommodation of Divergent Jurisdictional Standards for the Determination of Maintenance Obligations in Private International Law' (2002) 36 *Family Law Quarterly* 273

Stalford H, 'Crossing Boundaries: Reconciling Law, Culture and Values in International Family Mediation' (2010) 32 *Journal of Social Welfare and Family Law* 155

Timmer L, 'Abolition of *Exequatur* under the Brussels I Regulation: Ill Conceived and Premature? (2013) 9 *Journal of Private International Law* 129

Von Mehren AT, 'Theory and Practice of Adjudicatory Authority in Private International Law: A Comparative Study of the Doctrine, Policies and Practices of Common and Civil Law Systems' (2002) 295 *Receuil des Cours* 9

Walker L, 'From Brussels I and the Maintenance Convention to the Maintenance Regulation: Is the Resulting Maintenance Regulation Consistent with the Other EU PIL Instruments?' (2013) 6 *Nederlands Internationaal Privaatrecht* 167

—— 'The Impact of the Hague Abduction Convention on the Rights of the Family in the Case-Law of the European Court of Human Rights and the UN Human Rights Committee: The Danger of *Neulinger*' (2010) 6 *Journal of Private International Law* 649

—— and Beaumont P, 'Shifting the Balance Achieved by the Abduction Convention: The Contrasting Approaches of the European Court of Human Rights and the European Court of Justice' (2011) 7 *Journal of Private International Law* 239

# Hansard

HC Deb 27 June 1927 vol 208 cc15–6

HC Deb 19 December 1945 vol 417 cc1448–64

HC Deb 02 February 1948 vol 446 cc229–31W

HC Deb 8 December 1967 vol 755 cc1837–95

# Miscellaneous

'A Year On—Taking Stock of the EU Maintenance Regulation' 26 June 2012, event hosted by Dawson Cornwell

CIA World Factbook at www.cia.gov/library/publications/the-world-factbook/wfbExt/region_eur.html

Cuniberti G, 'French Supreme Court Rules on European Enforcement Order' at http://conflictoflaws.net/2012/french-supreme-court-rules-on-european-enforcement-order/#more-10874

European Union Agency for Fundamental Rights, 'Developing Indicators for the Protection, Respect and Promotion of the Rights of the Child in the European Union' (2010)

Eurostat, 'Migrants in Europe A Statistical Portrait of the First and Second Generation' (2011)

Heidelberg Conference (March 2013)

Lowe N, 'A Statistical Analysis of Applications Made in 2008 under the Hague Convention of 25 October 1980 on the Civil Aspects of International Child Abduction'

Muir Watt H on Abolition of Exequatur and Human Rights, particularly section III, at http://conflictoflaws.net/2013/muir-watt-on-povse/

Recovery of Maintenance in the European Union and Worldwide, Conclusions and Next Steps of the Heidelberg Conference (see Annex VII)

Templeton S, 'Consent to Create 3-Parent Embryos', *The Sunday Times*, 17 March 2013, p 9

http://epp.eurostat.ec.europa.eu/statistics_explained/index.php/Migration_and_migrant_population_statistics

http://migrationinformation.org/Profiles/display.cfm?ID=800

http://treaties.un.org/Pages/ViewDetails.aspx?src=TREATY&mtdsg_no=IV-11&chapter=4&lang=en

http://migrationinformation.org/Profiles/display.cfm?ID=800

www.euractiv.com/socialeurope/free-movement-labour-eu-27-linksdossier-188290

www.heidelberg-conference2013.de/tl_files/downloads-abstracts/Presentation_Chapman.pdf

www.heidelberg-conference2013.de/tl_files/downloads-abstracts/abstracts-ab-3-3-2013/Presentation_Reynolds_Paikin_Parentage.pdf

www.heidelberg-conference2013.de/tl_files/downloads-abstracts/abstracts-ab-3-3-2013/Presentation_Saettem_Saue_final.pdf

www.heidelberg-conference2013.de/tl_files/downloads-abstracts/abstracts-ab-3-3-2013/Presentation_Walker_final.pdf

www.migrationinformation.org/Feature/display.cfm?ID=825

www.ohchr.org/EN/HRBodies/Pages/TreatyBodies.aspx

www.un.org/esa/population/migration/hld/Text/Migration_factsheet.pdf

www.un.org/migration/presskit/pressrelease12sept.pdf

# INDEX

www.ingramcontent.com/pod-product-compliance
Lightning Source LLC
LaVergne TN
LVHW052243200926
848481LV00002B/260